Diversity at Work

What effects do racism, sexism, and other forms of discrimination have on the functioning of organizations? Is there a way of managing organizations so that we can benefit both the members of traditionally disadvantaged groups and the organizations in which they work?

Discrimination on the basis of race or gender, whether implicit or explicit, is still commonplace in many organizations. Organizational scholars have long been aware that diversity leads to dysfunctional individual, group, and organizational outcomes. What is not well understood is precisely when and why such negative outcomes occur. In *Diversity at Work*, leading scholars in psychology, sociology, and management address these issues by presenting innovative theoretical ways of thinking about diversity in organizations. With each contribution challenging existing approaches to the study of organizational diversity, the book sets a demanding agenda for those seeking to create equality in the workplace.

ARTHUR P. BRIEF is the George Eccles Chair in Business Ethics and Presidential Professor at the University of Utah. He was formerly a Fulbright Fellow in Lisbon, a Batten Fellow at the Darden Graduate School of Business at the University of Virginia, and the Thomas S. Murphy Distinguished Research Professor at Harvard Business School. Professor Brief has published widely on the moral dimensions of organizational life including *Attitudes in and around Organizations* (1998).

D1023927

Cambridge Companions to Management

Cambridge Companions to Management is an essential new resource for academics, graduate students and reflective business practitioners seeking cutting-edge perspectives on managing people in organizations. Each *Companion* integrates the latest academic thinking with contemporary business practice, dealing with real-world issues facing organizations and individuals in the workplace, and demonstrating how and why practice has changed over time. World-class editors and contributors write with unrivalled depth on managing people and organizations in today's global business environment, making the series a truly international resource.

FORTHCOMING IN THIS SERIES

Cappelli   *Employment Relations: New Models of White Collar Work*
Sitkin, Cardinal and Bijlsema-Frankema   *Organizational Control*
Smith, Battacharya, Vogel and Levine   *Global Challenges in Responsible Business*
Tjosvold and van Knippenberg   *Power and Interdependence in Organizations*

Diversity at Work

Edited by

ARTHUR P. BRIEF
University of Utah

CAMBRIDGE
UNIVERSITY PRESS

CAMBRIDGE UNIVERSITY PRESS
Cambridge, New York, Melbourne, Madrid, Cape Town, Singapore, São Paulo, Delhi

Cambridge University Press
The Edinburgh Building, Cambridge CB2 8RU, UK

Published in the United States of America by Cambridge University Press, New York

www.cambridge.org
Information on this title: www.cambridge.org/9780521677639

First published 2008

Printed in the United Kingdom at the University Press, Cambridge

A catalogue record for this publication is available from the British Library

Library of Congress Cataloguing in Publication data
Diversity at work / edited by Arthur P. Brief.
p.   cm. – (Cambridge companions to management)
ISBN 978-0-521-86030-7
1. Diversity in the workplace.   I. Brief, Arthur P., 1946–   II. Title.   III. Series.
HF5549.5.M5D553   2008
658.3008–dc22
2007050028

ISBN 978-0-521-86030-7 hardback
ISBN 978-0-521-67763-9 paperback

To the people that count the most,
the ones that truly make my life worth living –
Kay, Laura, and now, Noah Jacob Fernandez.

Contents

Part III Moving ahead: Agendas for practice and research

Figures

Tables

Contributors

MANUELA BARRETO obtained her PhD in social psychology from the Free University, Amsterdam, the Netherlands, and is currently an associate professor in social and organizational psychology at Leiden University, Leiden, the Netherlands. She has been awarded several prizes and prestigious grants, and has published in prestigious peer-reviewed journals and edited books. Her research interests are on the psychology of the disadvantage, exemplified by her work on identity respect, reactions to prejudice, and the psychology of concealed identities.

WILLIAM T. BIELBY is Professor of Sociology at the University of Illinois at Chicago. He was on the Sociology faculty at UC Santa Barbara for over twenty-five years, and he served as President of the American Sociological Association in 2003. In the spring of 2003 he was Visiting Distinguished John D. Macarthur Professor of Sociology at Northwestern University. He teaches graduate and undergraduate courses on organizational behavior, research methods for the social sciences, labor markets, quantitative methods, social inequality, media, and popular culture. Over the past twenty years, much of his research has more generally focused on issues of workplace discrimination, and on organizational policies and practices. Currently, he is researching the use of statistical evidence in class action employment discrimination litigation, on how the use of managerial discretion affects EEO outcomes, and on the emergence of "home grown" rock and roll bands in the late 1950s. In addition to his academic work, Bill has served as an expert witness on matters relating to organizational practice and discrimination in class action employment litigation.

ARTHUR PAUL BRIEF is the George Eccles Chair in Business Ethics and Presidential Professor at the University of Utah. His research focuses on the moral dimensions of organizational life (e.g., ethical decision making, race relations, and worker well-being). In addition to having published dozens of journal articles, Art is author of several books including *Attitudes in and around Organizations* (1998). Art is a past editor of the *Academy of Management Review*. He now co-edits *Research in Organizational Behavior* and the new *Academy of Management Annals*. He is a Fellow of the Academy of Management, American Psychological Society, and the American Psychological Association. He has been a Fulbright Fellow, a Batten Fellow at the Darden Graduate School of Business at the University of Virginia, and the Thomas S. Murphy Distinguished Research Professor at Harvard Business School.

HEATHER MAIIRHE CARUSO is in her fourth year of the PhD program in organizational behavior and social psychology, a joint program at Harvard Business School and the Psychology department at Harvard University. She came to the program inspired by early managerial experience in a multinational startup, where she became fascinated by the identity-relevant issues people from different cultures encounter when attempting to collaborate. In both independent and joint research she now explores the expression, perception, and negotiation of diverse identities, as well as the critical roles they play in the success of collaborative learning, creativity, and decision making. Her current research focuses on identity-relevant territorial behavior and self-satisfaction as barriers to effective collaboration in diverse contexts, especially where emergent information sharing and coordination are desired.

DOLLY CHUGH is an assistant professor in the Management and Organizations department at New York University Stern School of Business. Professor Chugh's research focuses on the psychological constraints on the quality of decision making with ethical import, a phenomenon known as "bounded ethicality". She is particularly interested in unintentional forms of race and gender bias, and the influence these biases have on behaviors in the workplace. Professor Chugh received a BA from Cornell University where she earned a double major in psychology and economics (1990), an MBA from Harvard Business School (1994), and a PhD in organizational behavior/social psychology from Harvard University (2006).

NAOMI ELLEMERS received her PhD (cum laude) from the University of Groningen in 1991. She worked as an assistant professor and associate professor at the Free University in Amsterdam from 1991 to 1999, when she was appointed as a full professor in social and organizational psychology at Leiden University. Her research, for which she has received various grants, focuses on group processes and intergroup relations, and their effects on social behavior in organizations. She has published extensively on this topic in national and international journals, and has (co-)edited a number of books on social identity and stereotyping. She has been an active member of the international scientific community, for instance as Associate Editor of the *Journal of Personality and Social Psychology*, and as President of the European Association of Experimental Social Psychology.

ROBIN J. ELY is Professor of Organizational Behavior at Harvard Business School. She investigates how organizations can better manage their race and gender relations while at the same time increasing their effectiveness. Her research in this area focuses on organizational change, group dynamics, learning, conflict, power, and identity. Robin has published numerous articles on these topics in books and journals and lectures both in the US and abroad to academics and practitioners alike. For the past ten years, she has maintained an active faculty affiliation at the Center for Gender in Organizations, Simmons Graduate School of Management, in Boston. Prior to joining the faculty at Harvard Business School, she was at the School of International and Public Affairs, Columbia University, and at Harvard's John F. Kennedy School of Government. She received her PhD in organizational behavior from Yale University and her bachelor's degree from Smith College.

SUSAN T. FISKE is Professor of Psychology, Princeton University (PhD, Harvard University; honorary doctorate, Université Catholique de Louvain-la-Neuve, Belgium). She investigates emotional prejudices at cultural, interpersonal, and neural levels. Her expert testimony was cited by the US Supreme Court in a 1989 landmark decision on gender bias. In 1998, she testified before President Clinton's Race Initiative Advisory Board, and from 2001 to 2003, she co-authored the National Academy of Science's *Methods for Measuring Discrimination*. She edits the *Annual Review of Psychology* (with Schacter and Kazdin) and the *Handbook of Social Psychology* (with Gilbert and Lindzey). She wrote *Social Beings: A Core Motives Approach to Social Psychology* (2004) and *Social Cognition* (1984, 1991, 2007, with Taylor). She won the American Psychological Association's Early Career Award for Distinguished Contributions to Psychology in the Public Interest, the Society for the Psychological Study of Social Issues' Allport Intergroup Relations Award for ambivalent sexism theory (with Glick), and Harvard's Graduate Centennial Medal. She was elected President of the American Psychological Society and member of the American Academy of Arts and Sciences.

LINDRED L. GREER is a doctoral student in organizational psychology at Leiden University. She received a BS from the Wharton School at the University of Pennsylvania. She is currently conducting research on group composition and conflict in organizations. Specific topics she has looked at include differences between perceived and actual group composition and conflict, the consequences for both individuals and teams of different sorts of faultline placement, and the roles of status and power in defining group composition and its effects on group outcomes. She has conducted research and training in the telecommunications and financial sectors.

KAREN A. JEHN is a professor of social and organizational psychology at Leiden University in the Netherlands. Her research focuses on intragroup conflict, group composition and performance, and lying in organizations. Professor Jehn has authored numerous scholarly publications in these areas, including articles in the *Academy of Management Journal, Administrative Science Quarterly, Journal of Personality and Social Psychology, International Journal of Conflict Management, Research in Organization Behavior, Journal of Business Ethics, Business Ethics Quarterly*, and *Group Decision and Negotiation*. She has served on the editorial boards of *Administrative Science Quarterly, Academy of Management Review*, the *Journal of Organizational Behavior*, and the *International Journal of Conflict Management* where she was an associate editor. She was also an associate director of the Solomon Asch Center for the Study of Ethnopolitical Conflict, the Research Director of the Alfred P. Sloan

Foundation's Diversity Research Network, and the Chair of the Conflict Management Division of the Academy of Management.

CAROL T. KULIK is a research professor of human resource management at the University of South Australia. She received her BSc (1981) and PhD (1987) from the University of Illinois at Urbana-Champaign. Carol's interests encompass cognitive processes, demographic diversity, and procedural fairness in organizations, and her research focuses on explaining how human resource management interventions influence the fair treatment of people in organizations. Recent research projects have examined the effectiveness of organizational diversity training, the role of demographic characteristics in mentoring relationships, and the ways organizational insiders and outsiders discuss organizational justice on the Internet. Carol recently finished a term as Senior Associate Editor at the *Journal of Management*, and is currently serving on the Executive Committee for the Organizational Behavior Division of the Academy of Management.

TIANE L. LEE is a PhD candidate in social psychology at Princeton University. She received a BA in psychology and political science, and an MA in social psychology, from Stanford University, where she worked on cultural psychology. Her research centers on culture and relationships, as well as diversity and intergroup perceptions. With Dr. Susan Fiske, she studies how culture and ambivalent gender ideologies affect close relationship preferences; how cultural understandings affect experiences of friendship; and how immigrants are perceived in the US. With Dr. Virginia Kwan, she studies the impact of identity framing on people's reactions to diversity. In the future, she hopes to pursue a research career in culture and diversity.

JEFFREY T. POLZER is a professor of organizational behavior at Harvard Business School. His research explores how group affiliations affect people's decisions, perceptions, and social interactions, especially in diverse work teams. Jeff has worked with a variety of co-authors to publish research in several top management and psychology journals. He serves on the editorial boards of *Administrative Science Quarterly*, *Academy of Management Journal*, and *Organizational Behavior and*

Human Decision Processes. He received his PhD in organizational behavior from the Kellogg Graduate School of Management at Northwestern University in 1994. Before coming to Harvard Business School, he was an assistant professor at the University of Texas at Austin for four years and a visiting scholar in the program on negotiation at Harvard University for one year.

LORIANN ROBERSON is a professor of psychology and education in the social-organizational psychology program at Teachers College, Columbia University. She received her PhD from the University of Minnesota. Her current research interests focus on workforce diversity, including the study of situational and individual influences on racioethnic group differences in important outcomes such as turnover and job performance, and the examination of diversity interventions in organizations. Recent research projects have examined organizational diversity training, the role of stereotype threat in work settings, and differences in voluntary turnover rates among members of different racioethnic and gender groups. Loriann is currently an associate editor for the *Academy of Management Review*, and serves on the editorial boards for the *Journal of Applied Psychology* and *Equal Opportunities International*.

LAURA MORGAN ROBERTS, PhD, is an educator, researcher, and organizational consultant. She has been an assistant professor of organizational behavior at the Harvard Business School since 2002 and has served on the faculties of the Wharton School at the University of Pennsylvania, Simmons School of Management, and the University of Michigan's Ross School of Business.

She earned her BA in psychology from the University of Virginia and received her MA and PhD in organizational psychology from the University of Michigan. Her research, teaching, and consulting interests center on personal practices and organizational systems which promote authentic engagement and powerful connections in diverse workplaces. Laura explores these dynamics in various contexts, including medicine, financial services, higher education, faith-based institutions, and journalism. She has published her work in top-tier research journals and practice-oriented journals such as the *Academy of Management Review* and *Harvard Business Review*.

JOYCE RUPERT is a PhD student in social and organizational psychology at Leiden University in the Netherlands. Her research interests include group composition, diversity faultlines, group processes, and team learning, with a special emphasis on different aspects of team learning such as social learning, task learning, and process learning.

Foreword

We are pleased to introduce Art Brief's *Diversity at Work*, as part of the Cambridge Companions to Management series. The series is intended to advance knowledge in the fields of management by presenting the latest scholarship and research on topics of growing importance. Bridging the gap between journal articles and student textbooks, the volumes offer in-depth treatment of selected management topics, exploring the current knowledge base and identifying future opportunities for research. Each topic covered in the series is one with great future promise, and one that also has developed a sufficient body of research to allow informed reviews and debate.

Management scholarship is increasingly international in scope. No longer can scholars read only the work conducted in their own countries, or talk only to their near neighbors. Creative and innovative work in management is now being conducted throughout the world. Each volume is organized by one of our most prominent scholars who brings researchers from several countries together to provide cross-national perspectives and debate. Through this series we hope to introduce readers to scholarship in their field they may not yet know, and open scholarship debate to a wider set of perspectives.

We feel fortunate to be working with Cambridge University Press. Their rigorous independent scholarly reviews and board approval process helps ensure that only the highest-quality scholarship is published. We feel confident that scholars will find these books useful to their own research programs, as well as in their doctoral courses.

In this volume, Art Brief and his chapter authors explore the growing field of diversity at work. The editor highlights the fact that, since 2000, 19% and 14% of the work published in peer-reviewed psychology and sociology journals (respectively) dealt with race or gender or diversity. On the other hand, only 5% of articles on these topics have appeared in the Academy of Management journals since that date. There is evidence, however, that, throughout the management literature, the topics of ethnicity, gender, and religion are becoming fertile areas for research.

Diversity at Work draws on leading researchers in the field from countries such as the Netherlands, Australia, and the USA. They examine issues surrounding the study of diversity in organizations, which leads into an assessment of the metaphors of gateways and pathways toward diversity. Chapters include an exploration of workplace discrimination derived from a mostly individual, cognitive orientation towards stereotypes and prejudice, together with a study highlighting how members of disadvantaged groups perpetuate or exacerbate their disadvantage. Three further chapters assess the pathway from a dyadic or group orientation, with a study of team-diversity research, diversity and conflict, and identity negotiation. And finally, the volume concludes with two chapters looking at what organizations can do to encourage greater diversity by promoting racial diversity at work and by the establishment of diversity initiatives through recruitment, training, and formal mentoring programs.

We know that you will find this up-to-date and innovative volume a useful resource, both in doing further research and in the practice of improving diversity effectiveness.

Cary Cooper, Lancaster University, England
Jone L. Pearce, University of California, Irvine
Series Editors

Preface

At its heart, this is a book about social inequalities. I have been an academic long enough not to set terribly high expectations for my work. But with this book, more than any other project in which I have been involved, I will not expect, but do hope and pray it matters, matters to scholars and, through their efforts, to those who have been treated unjustly because of their race and/or sex.

Editing this book, relatively speaking, has been a breeze. This is so largely due to the immensely talented and highly reliable contributors. To all of you, a big, big thanks for crafting thoughtful, insightful, and provocative chapters in a timely fashion. I am especially grateful to my co-author of two of the chapters, Dolly Chugh and to Max Bazerman for introducing us. Dolly has been a joy to work with and learn from. Administratively, the book would not have happened without the terrific support of Ethel Matshiya at Tulane University and Amanda Bailey at the University of Utah. Finally, the folks at Cambridge University Press were simply wonderful to work with.

1 | Introduction: *Where the sweet spot is: Studying diversity in organizations*

DOLLY CHUGH AND ARTHUR P. BRIEF

Since 2000, 19% and 14% of the work published in peer-reviewed psychology and sociology journals (respectively) dealt with race or gender or diversity.[1] Much of this work is based on a deep theoretical foundation and demonstrates innovative social science methods. It is rigorous, empirical, and exciting.

Having established that these topics were receiving significant research attention in the social sciences, we did a similar search in the *Academy of Management* journals. Since 2000, only 5% of organizational research tackled these topics. What does this small percentage imply about the other 95% of organizational scholarship? What assumptions rest in most organizational work about the composition of the workforce, particularly the racial composition?

In fact, most of organizational scholarship looks as if no people of color work in organizations, else we would see more attention paid to research topics such as race and racism, as well as those often entwined with race – social class, immigration status, and coping with discrimination. As of now, all of these topics remain neglected in the management literature. In this chapter, we introduce this volume about diversity at work with a focused look at the topic we see most lacking in organizational research: race. We believe this narrow focus is required, given the infrequent attention the topic is receiving in our top journals and the serious racial inequalities that exist in organizations. In the United States, the group most persistently affected by issues of race has been African-Americans, so much of our discussion will focus on this group. Based on the underrepresentation of race as a research topic, we fear that much of organizational scholarship unwittingly assumes a workplace characterized by whiteness, homogeneity, and equality.

---

[1] Based on a keyword search in CSA Illumina on-line search databases conducted in December 2006.

We believe these assumptions of whiteness, homogeneity, and equality are (a) inaccurate, (b) shortsighted, and/or (c) immoral. Consider these projections, based on census data trends. In 2000, 19% of the US resident population was non-white; in 2020, 22.4% is expected to be non-white; by 2050, 27.9% of the population is expected to be non-white. Additionally, by 2050, non-Hispanic whites are expected to make up 50.1% of the US populations, thus making the term "minority" short-lived and shortsighted (US Bureau of the Census, 2004).

Within this rapidly changing workforce, there is little evidence that equality is the norm. White workers have an unemployment rate of 4.1% versus 9.4% for black workers (US Bureau of Labor Statistics, 2006a). Blacks earn an average of $0.79 on every dollar earned by white employees (US Bureau of Labor Statistics, 2006a). Blacks make up only 11% of management and executive positions, but 16% of service occupations (US Bureau of Labor Statistics, 2006b). Similar statistics could be cited for Hispanics versus non-Hispanics. Many scholars have analyzed these gaps, searched for explanatory variables, and controlled for potential confounds, but the gaps still persist in the data. In light of statistics like these, any assumption of equality in our research needs to be seriously examined, and justified, in order for the research to be truly meaningful.

With these inequalities in mind, it is awkward to recall that the United States was founded with a declaration that "all men are created equal," and furthermore, like other nations, the United States enacted laws to help ensure equal opportunity for people of all colors (188 years after its founding). And, of course, not dependent on such legalities is the idea that equal opportunity is a moral imperative. Rawls (1971), for example, argued that "fair equality of opportunity" is a principle of justice, indeed, he defined injustice in terms of "inequalities that are not to the benefit of all" (p. 62). If there is almost no dimension along which blacks and whites, or Hispanics and non-Hispanics, are on an equal footing, then assumptions of whiteness, homogeneity, and equality in our work beg for moral re-examination.

This extraordinary speed of change on an issue of such moral import requires a parallel response from our field, and yet, it seems like what we are producing is an extraordinarily slow response. The need for a speedy response becomes particularly urgent in light of what we know so far about the potentially negative effects of diversity in the workplace. Williams and O'Reilly's (1998) excellent and systematic review of eighty studies on organizational demography and diversity notes that a number of field studies find that heterogeneity in race and gender lead to negative group process and performance outcomes, while laboratory studies tend to produce positive outcomes. Milliken and Martins (1996) review the literature and find that "diversity appears to be a double-edged sword, increasing the opportunity for creativity as well as the likelihood that group members will be dissatisfied and fail to identify with the group." Mannix and Neale (2005) explore the "diversity-process-performance linkage" in trying to understand the lack of a consistent main effect in the literature and conclude that surface-level differences (race/ethnicity, gender, age) are more likely to lead to negative group functioning than underlying differences (education, personality).

In other words, change is coming, and coming fast, and we are not ready. What should be a positive trend, consistent with the value of equality and the promise of performance benefits is, in fact, on track to be a social and economic debacle. The issue is no longer one of business necessity (or not), or of moral imperatives (or not). And, we assert, the debate is no longer whether (or not) diversity's benefits outweigh its costs (a rather unseemly debate we are happy to abandon). We are a diverse nation, by design, and the issue that faces us is how to draw the most from the benefits of diversity and how to use organizations as a tool for enacting justice, despite a national history of mixed results on both fronts.

Ten years ago, Brief and Hayes (1997) wrote that "workplace race relations are an enduring problem" and that "organizational scientists have not adequately fulfilled their responsibility for informing discussions of how this problem might be resolved." Recently, significant progress has been made in the social sciences which has contributed greatly to our understanding of the issues. We have tools and theories that help us distinguish intentional forms of racism and sexism from unintentional forms. We are aware of many of the practices (e.g., relying on current employees' social networks for recruiting) that maintain occupational segregation. And, organizational researchers, whose focus is on the workplace and the management of it, are uniquely positioned to contribute knowledge on this issue, using the work of social scientists as a base.

The organization is not only the breeding ground for many of these problems, but also a potential instrument of change. Pfeffer (1998)

observed that more than 90 percent of Americans will earn their liveli-
hoods working for an organization. Almost thirty years ago, Baron and
Bielby (1980)) encouraged us to "bring the firm back in," because
"firms ... link the 'macro' and 'micro' dimensions of work organization and inequality" (p. 738). Similarly, Henry Mintzberg (1975)
expressed a parallel thought about managers: "No job is more vital to
our society than that of the manager. It is the manager who determines
whether our social institutions serve us well or whether they squander
our talents and resources" (p. 61). Organizations and managers can
either facilitate social inequality, or facilitate social equality. As
researchers, we can help shape which outcome emerges.

Recently, Brief, Colella, and Smith (unpublished) drafted an appeal
to social psychologists to "think organizationally" because the organization is "where the action is." Here, we launch a mirror image of that
campaign, appealing to organizational researchers to think about
diversity, particularly race, because that is where the *impact* is. In
fact, we see diversity research as falling into a unique "sweet spot."
Imagine a graph with one axis representing the degree to which
research is theoretically motivated and rich, and the other axis representing the degree to which research is relevant and important for
practitioners. Diversity research is, or at least should be, in the top
right quadrant: theoretically deep and deeply relevant. It is a privileged
place for an academic to situate his or her research. So, why, we
wonder, isn't more being done by all of us?

We offer four possible explanations for our collective failure to
produce meaningful amounts of diversity research, particularly regarding race. First, we acknowledge the extreme sensitivity of the topic; it is
a *touchy* topic. Second, we describe the unique challenges of doing this
research; it is *difficult*. Third, we consider the role of personal values in
shaping our research agendas; to some, it is *less important*. And fourth,
we argue strongly that the lack of underrepresented minorities in our
own workplaces is not only morally appalling, but also sabotaging our
capacity to view the organizational realities of today's workplace as
concrete; it is *abstract*. All of these factors contribute to what we
believe is an explainable, but inexcusable, dearth of organizational
research on diversity.

Touchy: We all know that race is a charged topic. In the United States,
very few people feel comfortable in public discussions about diversity,
particularly in terms of race. The topic is difficult and complex. When

the conversations go sour, people's feelings get hurt. People are often misheard, misunderstood, and misread. There is usually a group that finds the conversation unnecessary while at the same time, another group that finds the conversation insufficient. And, somehow, everyone involved ends up feeling falsely accused of something.

For researchers, the touchiness of the topic is a challenge. Some findings are uncomfortable to present and unpopular to defend. Presenting and defending socially controversial research requires unusual oratory and social skills, coupled with deep reserves of personal resilience, beyond what is usually required for most research topics. So, just as most Americans play it safe, treating conversations about race like land mines, best buried and remote, where no one will get hurt, our field does the same.

Difficult: Other reasons may be related to the difficulty of this kind of research. The data can be difficult to obtain. Organizational researchers often are inclined towards field-based research, but field-based diversity research is particularly challenging. Organizations are extremely wary of any measurement related to race, gender, or any other bias-related topic, fearful of creating evidence for a lawsuit against them, as well as evidence that they were aware of cultural deficits that they did not, or did not know how to, address.

Even among those who study race for a living, the topic borders on the overwhelming. The literatures on stereotyping, prejudice, and discrimination are numerous, deep, and complex, and no one is a master of it all. Differences in terminology and assumption challenge those who attempt to wade into related literatures. These challenges leave researchers struggling for a shared vocabulary to discuss an already sensitive topic.

Another factor might be that organizational researchers are more inclined towards prescription than description (Bazerman, 2003), yet diversity research is still very shallow in the prescriptive end of the pool. Regrettably, we know very little about how to learn from diversity in ways that enhance how organizations function. Consistent with simple-minded (and we believe wrong-headed) notions that race matching customers/clients and sales/service personnel will boost revenues, most advice to managers appears to rest more on untested, intuitively appealing, relatively low-effort strategies and tactics, rather than scientific evidence. It seems we have failed the managers we seek to service as well as those striving for their rightly organizational place.

Less important: This avoidance is unlike, for instance, our peers in social psychology and sociology, where the study of such topics as prejudice and inequality are more bread-and-butter issues. Moreover, it may be that organizational researchers suffer from a managerial bias (Brief *et al.*, 2000) that contributes to their relative silence on the subject of race. That is, we previously noted that managers shy away from confronting the possibility of racism within their organizations and it may be the case that organizational researchers have adopted this same aversion in the zeal to attend to what managers deem important.

We also wonder about the role of personal values as a determinant of one's occupation, and for those who choose academia, of one's research program. The Rokeach Value Survey (Rokeach, 1973) surveyed academics in five different fields (business, biological science, physical science, social science, arts), as well as non-academic adult Americans, and found that social scientists ranked "equality" as their third most important value (out of eighteen values), while business academics ranked equality as seventh. Similarly, adult Americans ranked equality as seventh.

Abstract: Our fourth explanation for the scarcity of diversity research requires an examination of our own workplace. We propose that we, as individuals working in organizations, are not experiencing the realities of the changing American workforce in our daily work lives. Business schools have an embarrassingly small number of African-American and Hispanic faculty. We found the statistics to be shocking. Out of approximately 22,000 faculty in AACSB-accredited business schools,[2] 834 are African-American, Hispanic, or Native American, or less than 4% (PhD Project, 2006). We did our own review of the faculty of *Business Week*'s top thirty business schools ("2006 Full-Time MBA Program Rankings," 2006); only 56, or 1.76%, of the tenure-track faculty are African-American.[3]

Furthermore, we are both embarrassed and puzzled to report that at the business schools in which we work (University of Utah and New York University), we have a total of (based on our own personal,

---

[2] The appropriate denominator is not obvious for this statistic as the AACSB only reports the number of faculty at schools that respond to their survey. The actual denominator is probably higher than 22,000, and thus, the 4% is likely overstated.

[3] We recognize the imperfection of making an external assessment of how an individual self-identifies his or her race, so present this data as estimated rather

unofficial counts, at the time of this writing) approximately two African-American and three Hispanic-American tenure-track collea-gues (out of a combined total of approximately 260 tenure-track colleagues).

Some might rightfully respond that our faculties are not homogenous at all. We tend to have good representation from foreign-born academics, and also, growing representation from US-born Asian-Americans. Still, this response is not convincing. The positive stereotype – smart and hard-working – that accompany members of most of these groups is supportive of a career path in academia. African-Americans and Hispanic Americans do not enjoy the luxury of such positive stereotypes, but rather, must contend with the burden of implicit and explicit negative stereotypes (e.g., dumb, lazy). So, the issues of a diverse workforce composed of individuals whose stereo-typed qualities are positive is not the same as when the diverse work-force is characterized by negatively stereotyped qualities.

We think that this current portrait of our own workplaces is criti-cally important. Let us be very, very clear about our point here. We are *not* arguing that we need more black and Hispanic business school colleagues so that they will go study diversity; quite the contrary, in fact. It is not our goal to add to the challenges that underrepresented group members already face, nor is studying diversity any more the responsibility of minority academics than it is of anyone else. Rather, we believe that part of our unusually slow pace at recognizing a critical trend in the workforce stems in part from a lack of personal experience with the issue. Bring diversity into the scholarly workplace, and sud-denly, the benefits and challenges will emerge, in our own lives, and subsequently, in our own research programs. In the absence of the firsthand experience of a diverse workplace, the topic remains an abstraction.

This "firsthand experience effect" is unlikely to lead to a wholesale change in research programs, but it is likely to provoke empirically-testable questions that might otherwise not occur to the researcher. As examples, an innovation researcher might consider how in-group bias contributes or detracts from idea generation, or a leadership researcher might examine how ambiguous leadership signals about diversity

than precise. Many thanks to Modupe Akinola and Amanda Lee Willis for their assistance in conducting this quick study.

contribute to unchanging workforce demographics. Organizational researchers would, of course, maintain their primary research focus, but with a mind open to the range of issues, including issues related to diversity, that intersect with that focus. They would also check and test the underlying assumptions of whiteness or homogeneity in the workforce. The sweet spot of theoretical richness and practical relevance would become accessible to a wide range of organizational researchers.

Akinola and Thomas (2006) note the importance of senior leadership in ensuring that diversity remains on the "radar screen" of corporations. While the same claim might be made for academic institutions, particularly when it comes to hiring, there is one important difference when it comes to the setting of research agendas. The agenda of managers in corporations is typically set from above. However, the research agenda of academics in universities is typically set from within; autonomy rules. So, if we are to see diversity on the research radar screen, it will likely emerge "bottom-up," rather than "top-down," thus increasing the importance of the firsthand experience effect we noted earlier.

We are optimistic that the burden of our homogenous workplaces can be relieved, and that the firsthand experience effect can be unleashed, thus freeing our research programs to become richer and more relevant. While the number of minority business school faculty today is 834, amazingly, eleven years ago, this number was only 294 (personal correspondence with Tara Perino, December 2006). In that year, an organization called the PhD Project (www.phdproject.org) was created with the far-sighted and innovative purpose of increasing the number of minorities in corporate America ... by increasing the number of minority MBA students ... by increasing the number of minority faculty at business schools ... by increasing the number of minority doctoral students in business school PhD programs. Through the facilitation of social networks and connectedness, the dissemination of accurate information about academic careers, and the recruiting of potential doctoral students, the PhD Project has contributed to a growing pipeline of talent in a remarkably short amount of time. Furthermore, the PhD Project reports that their students have a lower doctoral program dropout rate (7%) than the national norm (35%), and are more likely to take academic positions (98%) than the national norm (60–70%) (personal correspondence with Tara Perino, December 2006). We hear a fairly clear message in this story: the talent is there and can be cultivated, so it is time for business schools to seize the opportunity to do so.

Similarly, we are optimistic that diversity will not be an underrepresented research topic for long. We are behind, but we can recover, and in doing so, have meaningful impact on a critical issue in society and organizations today. For all of these reasons, this book is about diversity at work. Generally, this volume focuses on the dimensions of diversity that are highly salient and highly stable – race and gender. While diversity can exist along many dimensions – "any attribute that another person may use to detect individual differences" (Williams and O'Reilly, 1998) – our focus here is deliberately narrow because these are the dimensions: (1) where the benefits seem most difficult to attain, (2) undergoing rapid change in the workforce, (3) which put bedrock American values ("American Dream") most in conflict with the reality, (4) most confounded by historical, societal, and local events, all occurring outside of organizational boundaries.

Readers will find a fascinating assortment of research from psychologists, sociologists, and organizational scholars. May you feel as inspired as we are by the excellent work in this volume. These scholars are converging on that sweet spot of research – theoretically deep and deeply relevant – and their passion shows in the rigor of their thinking and the innovation of their models. We hope you will feel encouraged to join this privileged group of scholars.

References

2006 Full-Time MBA Program Rankings. (2006). *Business Week*.

Akinola, M., and Thomas, D. A. (2006). Racial diversity initiatives in professional services firms: What factors differentiate successful from unsuccessful initiatives? *HBS Working Paper*.

Baron, J. N., and Bielby, W. T. (1980). Bringing the firm back in: Stratification, segmentation, and the organization of work. *American Sociological Review*, 45, 737–765.

Bazerman, M. H. (2003). Psychology in business schools. *American Psychological Society*, 16(5).

Brief, A. P., Colella, A., and Smith, A. N. (unpublished). Where the action is: Studying unfair discrimination and its causes in and around organizations.

Brief, A. P., Dietz, J., Cohen, R. R., Pugh, S., and Vaslow, J. B. (2000). Just doing business: Modern racism and obedience to authority as explanations for employment discrimination. *Organizational Behavior and Human Decision Processes*, 81(1), 72–97.

Brief, A. P., and Hayes, E. L. (1997). The Continuing "American Dilemma": Studying Racism in Organizations. In C. L. Cooper and D. M. Rousseau (eds.), *Trends in Organizational Behavior* (Vol. 4). New York: John Wiley & Sons.

Mannix, E., and Neale, M. A. (2005). What differences make a difference? The promise and reality of diverse teams in organizations. *Psychological Science in the Public Interest*, 6(2), 31–55.

Milliken, F. J., and Martins, L. L. (1996). Searching for common threads: Understanding the multiple effects of diversity in organizational groups. *Academy of Management Review*, 21(2), 402–433.

Mintzberg, H. (1975). The manager's job: Folklore and fact. *Harvard Business Review*, 53(4), 49–61.

Pfeffer, J. (1998). *The Human Equation: Building Profits by Putting People First*. Boston: Harvard Business School Press.

Rawls, J. (1971). *A Theory of Justice*. Cambridge: Harvard University Press.

Rokeach, M. (1973). *The Nature of Human Values*. New York: Free Press.

US Bureau of the Census (2004). *US Interim Projections by Age, Sex, Race, and Hispanic Origin*. Retrieved on January 3, 2007 from www.census.gov/ipc/www/usinterimproj/.

US Bureau of Labor Statistics (2006a). *Characteristics of the Unemployed: Unemployed Persons by Marital Status, Race, Hispanic, or Latino Ethnicity, Age, and Sex*. Retrieved May 15, 2006 from ftp.bls.gov/pub/special. requests/lf/aat24.txt.

US Bureau of Labor Statistics (2006b). *Employed Persons by Detailed Occupation, Sex, Race, and Hispanic or Latino Ethnicity*. Retrieved May 15, 2006 from ftp.bls.gov/pub/special.requests/lf/aat11.txt.

Williams, K. Y., and O'Reilly, C. A. (1998). Demography and diversity in organizations. In B. M. Staw and L. L. Cummings (eds.), *Research in Organizational Behavior* (Vol. 20, pp. 77–140). Greenwich: JAI Press.

PART I

Conceptual foundations

2 | *Stereotypes and prejudice create workplace discrimination*

SUSAN T. FISKE AND TIANE L. LEE

John Williams is a black American. On his first day of work at a new job at a mid-size print advertising firm, he arrived early to set up his office, only to find that his "office" was not with the other two new recruits but in the basement, in what was previously a janitor's closet. Displayed prominently on his computer was a noose.

Kevin Nakamoto is a Japanese-American, entry-level market analyst who recently transferred to another office. In deciding where to eat for lunch, one of his new co-workers asked if Kevin would mind if they did not have Chinese food. Later that day, another co-worker came by to introduce herself. As they chatted, she assumed that Kevin would be helpful in computer consulting and she volunteered that no one would mind if he was a social loner.

Mary Carpenter is a white, 22-year-old interested in construction. For the past six months, she has been unsuccessfully searching for a job. Though she has submitted applications to all jobs for which she felt qualified, she has had no luck. In the same time period, she saw her male friends receive offers in the same field, so she knows the demand is definitely there.

McKenzie Wilkes is a married, mother-of-two, successful attorney at a large firm. She is one of the most feared litigators in the courtroom and one of the most referred among her clients. Despite her impressive resumé, she was turned down as a partner at the firm. Her co-workers' and supervisors' confidential evaluations revealed that she was more than competent to be partner, but was lacking in "social skills," that her demeanor wasn't personable, or feminine enough.

All four scenarios describe discrimination at the workplace. The first two reflect negative affect – one blatant, the other more subtle, but both prejudicial – which discriminates against racial minorities in the workplace and subsequently hinder diversity. The second two implicate gender stereotypes that limit women, through descriptive stereotypes which declare them unfit for certain roles, and prescriptive stereotypes

13

that punish those who dare to violate them. In common, these key psychological mechanisms disadvantage underrepresented groups in their careers, among other contexts. We will revisit each of these scenarios later as we discuss the social psychology of racial and gender discrimination.

Roadmap

Several objectives inspire this chapter. First, we identify intergroup stereotypes and prejudice as key forces that hinder minority groups' attainment of career goals and, of more global impact, hinder workplace diversity. Second, we detail relevant theoretical perspectives, focusing on specific mechanisms that illustrate *how* stereotypes and prejudice undermine diversity. Third, we discuss differing models of diversity that complicate matters. Finally, we recommend ways that organizations can prevent stereotypes and prejudice from hindering diversity.

Background on intergroup perception

Stereotypes, prejudice, and discrimination make up the tripartite foundation of intergroup relations. Stereotypes are the categorical associations – including traits, behaviors, and roles – perceivers make to group members based on their membership. Prejudice generally refers to the affect resulting from intergroup perception. Discrimination refers to perceiver behaviors that advantage one group over another. The three intergroup phenomena interlock: The effects of stereotyping increase concomitantly with prejudice, so prejudiced perceivers are much more likely to discriminate against negatively stereotyped groups (Dovidio *et al.*, 1996; Talaska, Fiske, and Chaiken, 2008).

How do stereotypes form?

Intergroup phenomena stem from categorization processes. In social identity theory, people conceptualize the self at different levels of abstraction that range from the subordinate to the superordinate, and within which the corresponding identity (personal, social, or collective) is salient, dictated by context (Tajfel and Turner, 2004). Through social identity, the person views the self as a member of an ingroup that is distinctive and usually more subjectively positive than out-groups. According to self-categorization theory, depersonalization creates group phenomena, including stereotyping and prejudice (Turner and Oakes, 1989).

Two principles of self-categorization theory guide intergroup perception. *Comparative fit*, also known as the meta-contrast ratio, refers to the ratio of the perceived average difference between target group members and outgroup members over the average difference among target group members (Turner *et al.*, 1987). The smaller the ratio, the more the target group embodies a coherent unit; therefore, categorized groups minimize within-group differences and maximize between-group differences. Further, *normative fit* requires that these differences, both within and between, align with the perceiver's beliefs about the group in that context, that the group fits expectations, or socially shared meanings of those groups (Turner and Oakes, 1989). An interplay between comparative fit and normative fit processes guides stereotype construction. Under the first principle, within-group variability decreases, increasing perceived homogeneity among group members; under the second, perceived group categories reflect a perceiver's expectations about that group, or the content of normative beliefs, and therefore, shape their interactions with others. Comparative fit guides the degree of group differentiation while normative fit influences the content of a group's meaning.

This account of categorization processes brings us to the stereotype contents that result. Person and group perception utilizes two recurring dimensions that are variations of morality/warmth, and ability/competence (Alexander, Brewer, and Herrmann, 1999; Peeters, 2002; Phalet and Poppe, 1997; Rosenberg, Nelson, and Vivekananthan, 1968; Wojciszke, 1994; see Fiske, Cuddy and Glick, 2007 for a review). In the stereotype content model, perception immediately answers two key questions for the perceiver: Do outgroup members intend good or ill toward me and my group? and Are they able to act on these intentions? (Fiske *et al.*, 2002). The answers to these questions produce stereotypes in three quadrants: ambivalent (or cross-dimensional) stereotypes (e.g., elderly people are stereotypically nice but incompetent, Asian people are stereotypically competent but not nice); stereotypically neither warm nor competent (e.g., poor people); and stereotypically both warm and competent (e.g., middle class).

Because stereotypes differentiate "us" from "them," stereotyped targets usually fall outside the cultural default: (in the US) not young, not white, not male, not heterosexual, not middle class, not Christian, etc. Groups whose members are the least representative (visibly) of the default receive the most stereotypes (Fiske, 1998). The high prevalence of age, racial or ethnic, and gender stereotypes results in part from the speed of categorizing people on these dimensions. As such, racial or ethnic and gender biases are two of the most ubiquitous and salient contexts in the workplace, and we will attend to each later in the chapter.[1]

Stereotypes are not exclusive to the visibly different. Stereotypes also form when a person perceives an illusory correlation between a group and a particular characteristic (Hamilton and Gifford, 1976); in actuality, group membership and the characteristic might covary by chance or because of historical context, or not even covary at all. But perceiving a fundamental connection strengthens the stereotype for that group. For example, people spuriously associate rare people (e.g., minorities) and rare events (e.g., violent crime), so they misperceive or exaggerate their cooccurrence.

A stereotype often reflects the perceiver's knowledge of power relations in society. National stereotypes exemplify such contextual influences on stereotype formation, with perceivers relying on features of a nation – political, economic, religious, geographic, and status vis-à-vis one's own nation, among others – to characterize its residents. Because they are shaped by the social context, stereotypes reflect cultural beliefs but shift over time – when social conditions change, societies update their stereotypes of groups because the social relations of those groups transform. As an example, many ethnic groups in the US now receive more favorable stereotypes than they did 70 years ago, including originally mistrusted immigrants (e.g., Irish, Italian, Jewish) who now

---

[1] Of course, other physically salient characteristics also disadvantage employees. Certainly, older adults (Cleveland and Landy, 1983; Cuddy, Norton, and Fiske, 2005; Finkelstein, Burke, and Raju, 1995), people with disabilities (Younes, 2001), and those with physical deformities (West, *et al.*, 2005) receive differential treatment. Furthermore, physical saliency is not the only eliciting factor for workplace discrimination; people with nontraditional lifestyles (e.g., sexual orientation; Clausell and Fiske, 2005; Horvath and Ryan, 2003) or from other cultures (Evans and Kelley, 1991; Matsouka and Ryujin, 1991) are other examples.

join the mainstream (Lee and Fiske, 2006; Leslie, Constantine, and Fiske, 2006).

Where does intergroup prejudice originate?

Researchers identify group threats as a primary source of intergroup prejudice. Fiske and Ruscher (1993) implicate negative interdependence in which the perceiver sees outgroups as potentially inhibiting one's own goals, thereby forcing their outcomes to become negatively correlated. This anticipation of the other person's interrupting one's goals produces anxious emotions (anxiety, fear, frustration, and anger) that breed prejudice toward the outgroup. This threat translates into intergroup prejudice. Likewise, emotions play a central role in Smith's (1993) analysis, when perceivers appraise perceived threats to the group as if they were threats to the self. Specific situations evoke particular emotions (e.g., perceptions of an outgroup's unjustifiable harm produces anger).

Both of the negative interdependence and appraisal theories address interpersonal perception and emotions extended to intergroup situations. When people conceive of themselves in terms of group delineations, their actions reflect their social identity concerns, especially if the situation makes that identity more salient. Groups of people are perceived to be more competitive than individuals (Schopler and Insko, 1992) and especially more so as they increase in homogeneity and power (Dépret and Fiske, 1999). People may feel prejudice as a result of perceived economic threat to their group or as a result of perceived value threat to their group (Altemeyer, 1988; Duckitt, 2001; Sidanius and Pratto, 1999).

Stereotypes *are* convenient, at times . . .

So far it might seem that intergroup cognitions are just random emanations from our brains; however, they can serve cognitive and social purposes. We briefly review two models of impression formation that clarify how people use stereotypes sometimes but not at other times, depending on information and motivation.

Person perception models

Fiske and Neuberg's (1990) Continuum Model (CM) describes impression-formation processes as composing a continuum from category-based perception to attribute-based perception, and which include particular steps: automatic categorization, category reconfirmation, and transformation of the initial category into just another attribute. These processes are mediated by both the configuration of available information and motivational circumstances. Notably, the default is category-based perception.

Brewer (1998) proposes a Dual Process Model of Impression Formation that also identifies two routes to impression formation. Controlled processing refers to bottom-up processing which concludes with a holistic or integrated understanding of the target person. Controlled processing is volitional, therefore effortful, and goal-directed. However, automatic processing is considered to be the default mode, in which existing knowledge systems are immediately activated and the target is represented as a conceptual whole and in terms of its associations. This process is overridden only by conscious effort.

Both models emphasize two processing modes – stereotype-based and attribute-based – and assume primacy of the first. Stereotype-based processing emphasizes the need to make quick decisions through categorical information, while the second underscores the need to be accurate through effortful use of individuating information. In the CM, attention and motivation dictate which route a perceiver follows. The perceiver who prioritizes among interaction goals is the motivated tactician (Fiske and Taylor, 1991). People's motivations can and do overcome initial stereotyped-based processing, as long as they have enough cognitive resources.

Stereotype utility

Stereotypes can be beneficial because they save mental effort, in the cognitive miser view (Fiske and Taylor, 2008). For reasons of cognitive economy, perceivers more readily keep preconceptions than seek stereotype-inconsistent information; this leads people to rely on stereotypes to increase available on-line resources when they face cognitively overwhelming tasks with limited attention and effort. People rely more on stereotypes when under cognitive load (Biernat, Kobrynowicz, and Weber, 2003; Corneille, Vescio, and Judd, 2000; Dijksterhuis, Spears, and Lepinasse, 2001; Van Knippenberg, Dijksterhuis, and Vermeulen, 1999).

Another purpose of stereotyping may be to maintain the status quo (Jost and Banaji, 1994; Jost, Banaji, and Nosek, 2004). Under this system justification view, people are motivated to perceive their world as fair and legitimate, and stereotypes serve that purpose. Stereotypes justify the current state: Both positively and negatively stereotyped groups are that way because they deserved it (my group deserves to be rich because we work hard; poor people are too lazy to succeed). Researchers also suggest that complementary stereotypes (e.g., poor but happy, rich but miserable) support the status quo because they satisfy people's desire to perceive their world as fair (Jost and Kay, 2005; Kay and Jost, 2003).

In addition to system-justifying motivations, people's social interaction priorities also influence stereotyping. People may go along with others' expectations of them, whether or not they are accurate (Snyder, 1984). This is especially pertinent to power differentials in the workplace. Employees on lower rungs may not necessarily want to correct their supervisor even if that supervisor prejudges them on certain attributes. Using stereotypes can smooth interactions if both people agree on the stereotype or if the interaction is brief and inconsequential for the holder of the stereotype (Copeland, 1994; Leyens, Dardenne, and Fiske, 1998).

Stereotypes come in handy when we meet a new person, and we do not have adequate situational cues about whether that person is friend or foe. In this situation, stereotypes tell us whether to approach or avoid the other person. They are our first impressions of others about whom we know little else.

Problems with stereotyping and prejudice

Accuracy

Stereotypes: how accurate are they? Judd and Park (1993) identify inaccuracies of three types. *Stereotypic inaccuracy* over-estimates the target group's stereotypicality or under-estimates its stereotype-inconsistent qualities. *Valence inaccuracy* exaggerates the negativity or positivity of the group's stereotypes. *Dispersion inaccuracy* over- or under-generalizes the variability between group members. Nonetheless, some other researchers argue for studying the accuracies contained within stereotypes because under this view they reflect reality (Madon *et al.*, 1998).

However, other scholars argue that it is premature to study content accuracy. Instead, research on stereotype application may better deserve scholarly attention since stereotypes for groups are not only well differentiated but most of them also involve personality traits which are difficult to interpret (Stangor, 1995).

Processing biases

The issue of content accuracy aside, processing biases plague intergroup perception. Among the many intergroup perception phenomena that limit diversity in organizations are attentional, memory, and attributional biases that favor the ingroup and reinforce the perception of outgroup homogeneity.

First, at an immediate perceptual level, and consistent with the cognitive miser view, people prefer to confirm their stereotypes, detecting stereotype-consistent information more easily (Fiske, 1998). Sometimes confirmation occurs even in the face of disconfirming information. One striking example is the tenacity of the "stigma of incompetence" that afflicts people who are perceived to have benefited from equal opportunity programs (Heilman, Block, and Stathatos, 1997).

Two specific mechanisms through which people continue to confirm stereotypes are to ignore subgroups and to create subtypes. Subgroups describe clusters of targets that differ from the overall stereotype; perceiving multiple subgroups increases the perceived variability of the category and undermines its stereotypicality. If people ignore subgroups, then they maintain their stereotypes. Sometimes actively creating subtypes is the preferred method to maintain an overall stereotype. Subtyping allows the perceiver to isolate cognitively a few people who are stereotype-inconsistent by explaining that while they belong to the stereotyped group, they do not entirely represent it (Richards and Hewstone, 2001).

People also display memory biases, both recall and recognition, that favor stereotype-consistent information over stereotype-inconsistent information, especially if they are busy dealing with their complex environments (Stangor and McMillan, 1992). Other memory biases favor the ingroup: people remember their ingroups better than outgroups (Greenwald and Banaji, 1989).

People also are biased in their use of situational or dispositional explanations for ingroup and outgroup behaviors, depending on whether the target behavior is a success or failure, and stereotype-consistent or stereotype-inconsistent. First, biases attribute situational causes for ingroup failures (e.g., not our fault; it was due to circumstance) and outgroup successes (e.g., they were lucky; it was a fluke) and dispositional causes for ingroup successes (e.g., this reflects who we really are) and outgroup failures (e.g., they are incapable of this task). In addition, a similar bias explains stereotype-consistent and stereotype-inconsistent behaviors: An outgroup's stereotype-consistent behavior elicits internal attributions to the group's enduring dispositions ("just as we thought!"), while stereotype-inconsistent behavior elicits external attributions to chance or temporary circumstances ("this doesn't mean anything"), and the opposite for ingroup behaviors. If a particular negative stereotype afflicts a target group, that group's failures could be attributed to the supposed negative trait. If an outgroup member does behave negatively and stereotypically (e.g., criminal activity with black people), situational factors will likely be disregarded in explaining that person's behavior.

The reviewed biases are best characterized as biases favoring the ingroup more than biases against the outgroup. In a study measuring associative strengths between race and valenced (positive and negative) characteristics, white undergraduates showed faster response times to positive attributes (e.g., smart, ambitious) paired with white stimuli (compared to black stimuli), but showed no differences for negative attributes (Gaertner and McLaughlin, 1983). Thus, it is more acceptable for people to discriminate between their ingroup and outgroup in a positive dimension than in a negative dimension (Mucchi-Faina, Costarelli, and Romoli, 2002; Wenzel and Mummendey, 1996). This is not discrimination as outgroup derogation but via ingroup favoritism, which precipitates the former (Brewer and Brown, 1998; Mummendey and Wenzel, 1999). What this implies is that outgroup discrimination does not have to be caused by conscious and uniform antipathy or active exclusion. Outgroups do not necessarily have to be hated to be targets of discrimination in hiring and promotion; more often, they are consistently passed over for others in the ingroup, so they are in fact, excluded.

Now we turn to how these ingroup-favoring biases in perception, memory, and interpretation restrict workplace diversity, by looking at two specific examples: racial and gender stereotypes, prejudice, and discrimination.

Racial stereotypes, prejudice, and discrimination

Blatant prejudice and discrimination definitely persist. John Williams at the beginning of the chapter is a target of such obvious gestures.

There is no doubt that he was physically segregated as well as receiving blatant threats. If he continues to stay at the job, he will most likely continue to be taunted and isolated. Other blatant forms of discrimination include highly prejudiced employers who are unwilling to hire immigrants and minorities even if it compromises their business profits (Evans and Kelley, 1991). However, the same researchers found that this is rare; indeed, it took a very high level of *explicit* prejudice to discriminate in hiring. Other psychologists agree that intergroup prejudice is not all about hatred and active discrimination toward the outgroup. In fact, many theories, some of which follow, indicate that it is the cooler (indirect, cognitive), calmer (subtler, unconscious), and collected (seemingly rational, unemotional) evaluations that distinguish one's ingroup from the outgroup. The following, therefore, focuses on some theories of contemporary racism that help explain racial disparities in the workplace.[2]

Ambivalent racism refers to white Americans' anti-black sentiments coexisting with sympathy for blacks (Katz, 1981; Katz, Wackenhut, and Hass, 1986). On the one hand, a white person might think of black people as inherently deviant because they are stereotypically lazy or incompetent, but simultaneously perceive them to be disadvantaged in society and therefore feel sympathy. Ambivalent attitudes reflect a distinction people make between responsibility for a problem and responsibility for finding a solution for that problem (Brickman *et al.*, 1982) and imply that an ambivalent racist might concede that blacks were targets of discrimination, but blame them for not doing enough to improve their situation. Furthermore, these ambivalent attitudes arise from two fundamentally conflicting core American values: humanitarianism-egalitarianism and the Protestant work ethic (Katz and Hass, 1988). Americans endorse democratic ideals such as equality and justice for all, which results in sympathy for low-status, societally disadvantaged groups. But Americans also champion independence, hard work, and achievement, characteristics associated with the self-reliant rags-to-riches archetypal citizen. Thus, whoever falls behind must not have worked enough, or did not have the necessary traits to "make it." Ambivalence thus rests on internally conflicting views.

---

[2] One example of a theory not covered here is *laissez-faire* racism, which is a theory rooted in sociology, and emphasizes the broader historical and economic developments of a "kinder, gentler" racism today.

Aversive racists also experience intrapsychic conflict, but in this case between interracial antipathy and concerns for egalitarian principles (Gaertner and Dovidio, 1986). While they might consciously consider themselves to be fair and non-prejudiced people – and even sympathize with and support minorities' equal rights movements – they harbor negative attitudes toward minority groups, producing layered attitudes and consequently avoidant behaviors. They are averse to the idea of their own racism, as well as their attempts at avoiding interracial interactions, and behave in possibly accountable ways when they cannot be avoided. The theory of aversive racism predicts when discrimination is most likely to occur, namely when "normative structure is weak, when the guidelines for appropriate behavior are vague, or when the basis for social judgment is ambiguous" (Gaertner and Dovidio, 2005, p. 620) as well as when it is easy to justify discrimination on the basis of something other than race. The latter condition allows aversive racists to protect their self-image while discriminating, especially in reducing help (Dovidio and Gaertner, 1981; Gaertner and Dovidio, 1977). A more general form of aversive prejudice explains similar results for gender discrimination in helping behaviors (Dovidio and Gaertner, 1983; for additional evidence on subtle bias, see Dovidio and Gaertner, 2004).

Symbolic racism, modern racism, and racial resentment are three related sociocultural theories that have been conceived by a lineage of researchers. For convenience, we will refer to the general concept (a mix of both prejudiced emotions and conservative values) as contemporary racism. Symbolic racism (Kinder and Sears, 1981; Sears and Kinder, 1971) refers to a "blend" of anti-black sentiments and conservative values. These attitudes are abstract and moralistic because they did not form from direct contact with the target but instead, constitute part of the perceiver's value system. The most current conceptualization of symbolic racism emphasizes four components: blacks' failures are allegedly due to a lack of work ethic, blacks make excessive demands, blacks no longer endure discrimination, and blacks now receive an undeserved advantage (Henry and Sears, 2002). Modern racism (McConahay, Hardee, and Batts, 1981; McConahay and Hough, 1976) acknowledged contemporary racism's connection to old-fashioned racism by recognizing that it also was rooted in socialization and in moralistic beliefs. However, racial resentment (Kinder and Sanders, 1996) emphasizes the role of values in contemporary racism.

Because of its roots in a moral belief system, contemporary racism persists despite the absence of realistic competition (e.g., limited jobs). However, research has repeatedly shown that the Modern Racism Scale is correlated with hiring and work policy decisions (Brief *et al.*, 2000; James *et al.*, 2001; McConahay, 1983). It therefore has its critics: both symbolic and modern racism sometimes confound political conservatism (Fazio *et al.*, 1995; Sniderman and Piazza, 1993). Whether it is related to political ideology or not, the take-away message stands: Modern racism predicts job discrimination, and for that alone it is a useful instrument. In addition, symbolic racism actually increases with respondent education level, contradicting what one would predict if symbolic racism is confounded with political conservatism; it also predicts racial policy attitudes more than political ideology (Sears *et al.*, 1997).

Blatant and subtle prejudice are distinct but related constructs, the latter being far more common and problematic on a day-to-day basis for most minorities (Pettigrew and Meertens, 1995). Subtle racism comprises three themes: The perceiver believes the target group violates traditional values, the perceiver believes the target group endorses extremely divergent cultural values from the ingroup, and the perceiver withholds positive emotions toward the target group (as opposed to applying negative emotions). Subtle racism manifests not so much to hide prejudice from others but rather to protect oneself from the realization that one harbors prejudiced attitudes (as is true for aversive racism). Subtle racists have partially internalized egalitarian norms but not deeply enough that their biases are entirely suppressed from indirect expression. Subtle racism extends racism research to European societies and broadens target groups from race to ethnicity and nationality (immigrants).

We discussed several forms of racism in which people who think they are nonprejudiced, or want to be nonprejudiced, still discriminate in perception and in manner (Gaertner and Dovidio, 1986; McConahay, Hardee, and Batts, 1981; Pettigrew and Meertens, 1995). This shows the dissociation between one's thoughts and behaviors (Dissociation Model; Devine, 1989). To the extent that stereotypes reflect a cultural belief, activation of a stereotype does not necessarily mean the perceiver with that knowledge endorses it (Devine, 1989; Lepore and Brown, 1997) or will apply it (Gilbert and Hixon, 1991). The Dissociation Model of stereotypes argues that regardless of a person's explicit prejudice level, a person may be primed to think of groups stereotypically. For example, the presentation of a group label facilitates the activation of subsequent stereotype-consistent associations, for both low- and high-prejudiced people. The Dissociation Model argues that perceivers are often unaware of their own cognitive associations. In addition, egalitarian cultural norms discourage unfavorable prejudgments of others, so perceivers have a self-interest to refrain from expressing prejudice, either to protect their public image or their self-concept as fair.

Dissociation between personal endorsement and cultural knowledge appears in incongruent results from explicit and implicit stereotype measures. Implicit stereotypes can persist, even when explicit stereotypes do not. Thus, implicit measures reveal these automatic stereotypic associations (Fazio and Olson, 2003). Some involve subliminally priming category-relevant stimuli. Study participants then perform various tasks – including word searches, lexical decision tasks, fluency-manipulated tasks, interpretation of ambiguous behaviors – in which they might produce responses that indicate stereotypic associations to the primes. Reaction speed, performance quality, and stereotypicality of responses indicate levels of stereotype activation. Compared to this preconscious (subliminal) presentation of stimuli, other priming manipulations explicitly present stimuli; thus the activated associations are post-consciously produced by the perceiver (Bargh, 1989). The implicit association test consciously primes two categories and then measures differential reaction times to concepts that are stereotype-consistent to one of the primes but not the other (Greenwald and Banaji, 1995; 2002). People often react more quickly to negative words following outgroup primes and to positive words following ingroup primes. Also using post-conscious priming, neuroimaging studies show increased amygdala activation to images of outgroups (Hart *et al.*, 2000; Phelps *et al.*, 2000; Wheeler and Fiske, 2005). Automatic associations escape our conscious awareness, and only implicit measures capture them.

Our opening example of Kevin Nakamoto has well-meaning and friendly co-workers, who all exemplify many co-workers' ideals. However, in their attempts to include Kevin, they make stereotypic assumptions about his preferences and social identities. If this continues, rather than feeling accepted, Kevin will ironically become alienated. And this holds even when the stereotype has model-minority-type positive components (Lin *et al.*, 2005).

Common to the reviewed racism theories is that racism is expressed not just in hostility but automatically, indirectly, unemotionally, and ambivalently – so subtly that the perceiver remains unaware, and even the target may not be too sure. Moreover, racism does not reside only in poor, uneducated people, but actually prevails even among college-educated and otherwise liberal Americans and Europeans (Pettigrew and Meertens, 1995). Contemporary racism manifests through ingroup promotion more than active outgroup exclusion, and through isolation more than active harm. Overt displays of hostility toward outgroups violate social and legal norms. Racism today bypasses these legal checkpoints, when it takes any of the more subtle, unexamined forms. These forms of racism may first impact hiring, keeping out competent potential minorities, but being hired is only the first step for minorities. If hired, they may receive unfavorable performance attributions (dispositional for failure, luck for success), thus limiting opportunities for advancement. And memory for their performance may be biased – even when interviewers hire black and white applicants in equal proportion, they recall the black employees as less intelligent (Frazer and Wiersma, 2001).

Furthermore, theories of disparate evaluation standards help explain who advances among those hired and who does not. Using expectation states and attribution research, Foschi (1989; 2000)[3] argue that perceivers often use a performer's status characteristic (e.g., race, ethnicity, gender) to infer competence, and they consequently use different standards to judge similar performances by people from different status groups. In other words, a person's group membership doubles as an attribute that implies a certain level of competence, such that for different status levels (e.g., whites versus blacks), the perceiver will use different standards for scrutinizing those performances. Under double standards, the perceiver will hold a lower standard for the low-status person, meaning that performance on par with that of the high-status person (because it was unexpected) will be scrutinized more intensely. However, the perceiver requires a lower or more lenient standard before acknowledging that a similar performance by the high-status person reflects the actual competence level. A high-status performer's display of competence confirms ability, more than for a low-status person who produces the same output. Conversely, failure

---

[3] For a related concept, see Foddy and Smithson (1989).

results in an attribution of incompetence more strongly for the low-status performer than for the high-status performer. In summary, group status implies stereotypes about competence (for review of racial and ethnic stereotypes in the US, see Devine and Elliott, 1995; Fiske, 1998; Gilbert, 1951; Karlins, Coffman, and Walters, 1969; Katz and Braly, 1933; Leslie, Constantine, and Fiske, 2006); these levels of status evoke different judgment standards, which lead to ability inferences that reinforce the status differentials that caused this cycle in the first place.

The shifting standards model argues that perceivers evaluate people on stereotyped dimensions by comparing them within-group (Biernat and Manis, 1994; Biernat, Manis, and Nelson, 1991). For example, to evaluate a black applicant's verbal skills, the perceiver uses stereotypes of other blacks as a comparison – and for a white applicant, stereotypes of other whites. What might stereotypically seem "good, for a black person" might not stereotypically seem "good, for a white person." The implication here is that a "good verbal skills" judgment may not reflect similar actual skills. As with the double standards idea, the shifting standards model argues that a performer's group membership determines the leniency or strictness of judgment standards; unlike double standards, shifting standards imply that the relevant comparison is the target's group, not across groups, and that judgment standards can be more lenient or harsh for either status group, depending on the judgment's stereotype relevance. In short, perceivers set lower expectation standards but higher evaluation standards; thus low-status groups easily make the first cut for employment but do not get hired (Biernat and Kobrynowicz, 1997). Though the result might seem at first favorable, a perceiver's lower minimum-competency standards are only subjectively positive, but not good enough for the minority to be hired. We think of this as the "short-list problem": Minorities make the feel-good short list but do not get hired. Similarly, gender ideologies emphasizing subjectively positive attitudes limit women's chances, as we shall see in the next section.

Gender stereotypes, prejudice, and discrimination

Until recently, sexism researchers primarily identified hostile attitudes toward women. As old-fashioned prejudice, sexism entails male dominance and antipathy toward women, especially those who stray outside traditional roles (Spence, Helmreich, and Stapp, 1973). The Attitudes Toward Women scale captured resentment of women who violated social conventions (e.g., swearing, proposing marriage). However, more recent work, including neosexism (Tougas *et al.*, 1995) and modern sexism (Swim *et al.*, 1995), considers more modern, nuanced hostility. The neosexism scale employs subtle-enough questions that a respondent can express sexist attitudes without admitting socially undesirable beliefs (e.g., women are inferior to men). In this sense, neosexism resembles subtle prejudice (Pettigrew and Meertens, 1995). In both, knowledge of egalitarian norms discourages expressed hostility toward the target group, but the norms are not internalized enough that the neosexist or the subtle racist can successfully guard against leaking animosity. Modern sexism, similar to modern racism, expresses doubts about the current prevalence of sexism (e.g., "Discrimination against women is no longer a problem in the United States") and disapproves of those who disagree.

Viewing sexism as just another type of prejudice, with unequal power and gender stereotypic roles, focuses on antipathy. But considering sexism in the context of close relationships, attitudes toward women include a benevolent aspect complementary to the long-recognized hostility; the result is ambivalence (Glick and Fiske, 1996; 1999; 2001). Men who hold these benevolent attitudes toward women want their mates to fulfill roles that emphasize tradition. However, benevolence extends beyond its obvious application to romance (pure, virtuous) and domesticity (barefoot, pregnant). Benevolent sexism also explains women's work-related outcomes: In a survey of Polish adults, the two most common reasons given for why women could deal better than men with unemployment were that women are more adapting and flexible, and that they are emotionally stronger (Reszke, 1995). What's more, benevolent as well as hostile sexism predicts national-level empowerment of women (leadership roles) across nations (Glick *et al.*, 2000). Subjectively positive stereotypes reinforce subordination. Ambivalent gender ideologies explain why subgroups of women (e.g. housewives, career women) receive different stereotypes and mixed evaluations (Cikara and Fiske, 2006; Cuddy, Fiske, and Glick, 2004; Eckes, 2002; Glick *et al.*, 1997).

Note that viewing woman as adapting and emotionally resilient would count as generally positive, desirable traits. But as descriptive stereotypes, they limit women's career advancement. Descriptive stereotypes portray what people of a gender stereotypically are like and how they act, think, and feel; in contrast, prescriptive gender stereotypes communicate expectations of what people of a gender *should* be like and how they *should* act, think, and feel. Both matter (Burgess and Borgida, 1999).

Descriptive stereotypes have disparate impact on women's career advancement (Burgess and Borgida, 1999), limiting women by depicting them as unsuitable for certain jobs that require stereotypically masculine traits and attributes. Disparate impact assimilates women into their stereotypes, many of which are positive but do not match, or are incompatible with, characteristics required to succeed in a career. Descriptive stereotypes disadvantage women because they imply "lack of fit" (Heilman, 1983). Stereotyping may implicitly be the strategy of employers who actively recruit some groups over others, so for jobs that require stereotypically masculine traits (which the most valued ones do), women's perceived lack of fit disadvantages them.

Mary Carpenter, though she was as qualified to be a construction worker as her male friends, was repeatedly denied access. The process is subtle in the sense that she cannot prove that it was her gender, she was deemed unfit for a job that is stereotypically dominated by men.

Moreover, descriptive stereotypes encourage perceivers to use shifting standards to evaluate women employees. Shifting standards for gender occur in, for example, verbal ability, writing competence, aggression, leadership, and job-related competence (Biernat and Kobrynowciz, 1997). Similar to comparing blacks and whites, minimum standards for women were lower, but ability standards were higher (Biernat and Kobrynowicz, 1997); consequently, women were more likely than men to make the initial cut for a job but less likely to be hired (Biernat and Fuegen, 2001). The initial survival was due to low minimal-competence standards given comparison to other women, but hiring decisions were based more on inferred ability, whose standard was higher for women.

Descriptive stereotypes disadvantage women by influencing reward allocation and performance evaluations, once they have been hired. As for race, gender is a status characteristic with women holding a lower status, and perceivers expecting less competence, so being skeptical and requiring higher performance for demonstrating competence (Foschi, Lai, and Sigerson, 1994; Foschi, Sigerson, and Lembesis, 1995), even when the woman is evaluating herself (Foschi, 1996). The research shows that women employees are not given credit for their successes, and to overcome discrimination, must show abnormally good performance. Whether caused by shifting standards, double standards, or some other mechanism, evaluations of female employees are less positive than for men (see reviews: Olian, Schwab, and Haberfeld, 1988; Swim *et al.*, 1989; Swim and Sanna, 1996). We would expect to find different evaluation standards along stereotypic dimensions: Men are better leaders than women, but only as leadership has been traditionally viewed (Eagly and Johannesen-Schmidt, 2001); men are allegedly more competent, more ambitious, and more qualified than women (Fiske and Stevens, 1993); men are stereotypically more agentic than women (Jost and Kay, 2005).

More recently, researchers have extended their investigation into the *prescriptive* component of stereotypes. Prescriptive stereotypes discriminate against women through disparate treatment, whereby they are punished when they violate expectations of how women *should* behave (Burgess and Borgida, 1999).

When searching for jobs, women who self-promote during interviews may succeed in establishing perceived competence, but forfeit perceived likability and therefore, hirability. Self-promoting women were less liked and less likely to be hired than similarly self-promoting men (Rudman, 1998). Further, self-effacing men were seen as less competent and therefore less hirable. People who violate gender prescriptions (modest for women, ambitious or self-promoting for men) suffer both socially and professionally. Women who work are punished through hostile reactions because they violate prescriptive stereotypes of women as homemakers (Glick *et al.*, 1997). However, those who fulfill the traditional role receive favorable responses, predicted by benevolent gender attitudes.

Responses to women authority figures, those in the most masculine positions, assume they violate gender-role prescriptions. Responses are most negative to women leaders who work in traditionally male-dominated fields and who are directive (i.e., masculine) in demeanor (Eagly, Makhijani, and Klonsky, 1992). Both conditions defy gender prescriptions for women and therefore, these women most acutely violate societal expectations for women; correspondingly, they receive the most backlash.

In our opening examples, McKenzie Wilkes did not obtain a partnership at her firm because she lacked the stereotypically feminine traits, but she was in a predicament because she also had to demonstrate stereotypically job-required masculine traits.[4] Hence, she is punished for violating prescriptive social stereotypes of women, though they may be pragmatically irrelevant to her career aptitude, and of course, unfeminine men become partners.

Prescriptive stereotypes moreover include gender-intensified and gender-relaxed prescriptions (Prentice and Carranza, 2002). Gender-intensified refers to prescriptions for people in general, but which are especially required of members of one gender, while gender-relaxed refers to prescriptions that pertain to only one gender, which the other may safely ignore. When we apply this distinction to the reviewed literature, it may be that women who assertively self-promote would be received better if they simultaneously fulfill gender-intensified prescriptions of modesty and sensitivity. In fact, people do like competent, effective, and strong women who are also caring and well-groomed (Rudman and Glick, 1999). In another example, women are more influential if they are *both* self-oriented and cooperative rather than only the first (Ridgeway, 1982). Of course, cooperation does not add to men's influence beyond self-orientation. In the case of women leaders, they are more effective if they fulfill the gender-intensified stereotype for women by being democratic in relational style (Eagly, Karau, and Makhijani, 1995).

In short, descriptive gender stereotypes might deem women unfit for jobs but prescriptive stereotypes could be more pernicious because they encourage punishing violators.[5] Women have to walk a delicate balance in order to succeed and be liked.

The target's perspective

So far, we have discussed stereotype and prejudice as originating within the high-status person, influenced by the power dynamics. This accurately reflects an important effect of stereotypes and prejudices: If the decision-maker is biased, the low-status (potential) employee usually

---

[4] This essentially was the Ann Hopkins situation at Price Waterhouse (Fiske *et al.*, 2002).

[5] Though we discuss several psychological constructs and mechanisms (ambivalent ideologies, double or shifting standards) in direct relevance to race and gender, these processes do not operate only in these contexts. We recognize that they can certainly explain how other minority groups may be disadvantaged.

suffers and may not be able to do much. However, the low-status member can influence these processes and can experience impact beyond limitations in professional advancement.

One issue for all targets is stereotype threat, awareness of their groups' negative stereotypes in a particular and consequential performance domain; they can ironically perform worse than those who do not care about that domain. Stereotype threat creates an added performance burden because failure injures not only self, but one's group as well, by confirming the stereotype. This added burden leads to the targets under-performing, paradoxically fulfilling the stereotype that haunted them in the first place (Steele and Aronson, 1995). Some examples are black students in an academic setting and women in mathematical tasks, but only when performance is labeled as diagnostic of ability. The effects of stereotype threat differ from self-fulfilling prophecies because it affects people without their encountering a prejudiced person. In self-fulfilling prophecy, targets may conform behaviorally to others' expectations, conveyed nonverbally (Word, Zanna, and Cooper, 1974).

Going along with stereotypes may also be useful for targets who want to avoid conflict or focus on an aspect of the interaction they deem more important (Leyens, Dardenne, and Fiske, 1998). Alternatively, targets may compensate for the other person's prejudice, and they may do so effectively, but at a temporary cognitive and emotional cost (Shelton and Richeson, 2006).

Targets also incur health-related effects, for example, on physical health, emotional well-being, and job satisfaction (Jackson, Potter, and Dale, 1998). Minority group members are more likely to leave an organization, presumably because they are less satisfied and committed (for review, see Williams and O'Reilly, 1998). In short, without going in depth here, we note that it matters to look at both sides of the story.

Understanding attitudes toward diversity

So far, we have discussed individual psychological processes that result in consequences at the group level. In this mostly cognitive vein, people automatically act on unexamined processes and emotions: They fall prey to categorization effects, favor the ingroup, guard against the outgroup, and painfully, yet ineffectively, try to block their biases. However, humans are willful and agentic in another sense. They are cognizant of their preferences and experiences in diversity. As we will see, some situations make people uncomfortable because they are too diverse, not diverse enough, factional, or superficially sugar-coated. People's experiences of diversity, conceptions of diversity management, and ideals of diversity, matter. A chapter on psychological processes impacting diversity is incomplete without an accompanying recognition of people's lived experiences in and models of diversity.

Managing diversity

Diversity attitudes matter because they address not only recruitment but what happens after the recruitment. Even when people generally respond positively to the idea of diversity and are receptive of promoting it, how to operate in a diverse context generates disagreement. Using a very coarse classification, we first review two major varieties of attitudes on how to manage diversity. One variety of models or interpretation of diversity is a type of pluralism, and the other stresses a color-blind commonality between people. We briefly review the work of two researchers here.

Two main sociocultural models of diversity, the "systems of widely distributed, often tacit meanings, understandings, and practices that provide frameworks for daily life" (Plaut, 2003, p. 21), are the awareness and inclusion of differences (multicultural) and color-blindness models. The premise of the first is that differences between people are real, substantial, and consequential and therefore, important for how we should treat each other; differences should be acknowledged and valued in daily interactions (Plaut, 2002). Under this mosaic framework are value-added (differences add value) and mutual-accommodation models (Plaut, 2002). Similar conceptions in diversity research are cultural pluralism (Frederickson, 1999), the integration-and-learning perspective (Ely and Thomas, 2001), and in the acculturation literature, integration (Berry, 1980).

In contrast, the color-blind model of diversity proposes that differences between people are merely superficial and therefore, irrelevant to how people should treat each other (Plaut, 2002). In this view, ignoring differences in daily interactions helps avoid conflict. The basic metaphor is the classic melting pot: Newcomers assimilate into the basic, existing identity by dissolving their old memberships and value systems. Other conceptualizations that endorse a melting pot ideology include one-way assimilation models (Frederickson, 1999; Gordon, 1971) and assimilation (Berry, 1980).

The awareness-and-inclusion and color-blind models resemble two classifications for organizational culture (Martin, 1992): the differentiation and integration perspectives. The *differentiation* perspective recognizes subgroup differences and reveals power struggles within an organization. It understands culture as a shared meaning system at the subgroup level; thus multiple cultures within an organization might conflict. To argue that culture is organizational is, in this view, merely a dominant group's exercise of its control over others. In contrast, the *integration* perspective emphasizes organization-wide consensus, consistency, and clarity in culture. It relegates subgroup differences into a second-tier status, in favor of shared values, beliefs, and expectations that promote the survival of the organization. It treats culture as a means of reducing uncertainty by clarifying ambiguity; thus in this view, culture exists at the organizational (not subgroup) level. "Culture" at the subgroup level creates disharmonious components that threaten the integrity and survival of the organization.

The argument for color-blindness

Given that stereotypes and prejudices reduce diversity, one obvious solution might seem color-blindness in official company policy and less formally, in interpersonal encounters. An institutional stance theoretically could take the form of a blind application process as well as solely quantitative evaluations using objective measures. To bypass group stereotypes, an organization theoretically could resort to blind applications. To bypass multiple or shifting standards in evaluation, it theoretically could refrain from using imprecise terminology (e.g., "good"). It could insist that new employees immediately trade in their subgroup allegiances for loyalty to the organization as a whole.

To recognize and consider people in terms of their group memberships risks cornering them into immutable groups and exaggerating group differences to the point of essentializing those differences, as in cultural divides (Miller and Prentice, 1999). To the extent that minority members' subgroup identities prevent their forming an overall identity with the organization as a whole (Sidanius *et al.*, 1997), it might seem necessary to cast away those inconvenient identities in a caldron to form a more generic identity.

But is the color-blind policy realistic in practice? No organization would be willing to hire without an interview, social science to the contrary. Even supposing it would, an organization that hires solely by blind application eventually will meet the hired employee. The socialization process itself would not overcome stereotypes and prejudice. Quantitative measures do not eliminate biases, including expectancy-fulfilling biases. Nor could *any* group members (minority or majority) really refute their own identities and all their manifestations (interpretations, beliefs, and values). Despite its intuitive appeal in some quarters, the color-blind vision overlooks the automaticity, ambiguity, and ambivalence of bias, as reviewed earlier. It also ignores minority perspectives.

The color-blind perspective lacks wide support

People's social identities and group memberships undeniably and profoundly influence their way of being, including cognition (Markus and Kitayama, 1991), in all its specific aspects (e.g., thinking, Nisbett *et al.*, 2001, and learning, Li, 2005). To insist that people are all really the same and that one should discard the so-understood peripheral values that detract from the functioning of the bigger group is to deny subgroup and minority perspectives. Consistent with this concern, minority and majority group members differentially evaluate diversity models. Minority members are more exposed to diversity, *and* more often believe that diversity offers value, in contrast to white respondents who emphasize people's similarities and advocate people concentrating on their commonality (Plaut, 2003). High-status people (whites and men), more so than minorities and women, show an inverse relationship between work-group heterogeneity, attachment to, and intent to stay with the organization (Tsui, Egan, and O'Reilly, 1992). For women and minorities, identity-conscious policies, as opposed to identity-blind, result in more positive employment status (Konrad and Linnehan, 1995).

Relational dimensions of diversity (Chattopadhyay, 1999; Tsui and O'Reilly, 1989) highlight diversity as not a single dimension (no diversity to completely diverse) but rather a multidimensional variable. In relational demography, analysis focuses on the individual-level difference in demographics between team members rather than on the group or organizational level. For example, white and male employees care more about fairness and equal treatment in formal processes such as mentoring programs, evaluation procedures, and job assignments

(Mor Barak, Cherin, and Berkman, 1998); they care about structure in the hiring process, asking only job-related, pre-determined questions (Seijts and Jackson, 2001). By contrast, low-status or minority members value relational and informal processes over structural ones, including personal comfort in relating to different others (Mor Barak, Cherin, and Berkman, 1998), perceived procedural justice (Wesolowski and Mossholder, 1997), and diversity in relationships (Plaut, 2003). A possible response to these priorities may be what Chen and Eastman (1997) termed a civic culture, in which organizations emphasize relational values (e.g., respect for differences and equality) as well as substantive values (e.g., product quality and timeliness).

People are often unaware that they immediately process others categorically

In addition to the mixed evaluations and impact of color-blindness as a practice, it also does not realistically portray interpersonal perception. Earlier we discussed immediate category-based processing as the default mode in perception (Brewer, 1998; Fiske and Neuberg, 1990). The Dissociation Model (Devine, 1989) corroborates that despite one's values, people perceive others stereotypically. It is also unrealistic to assume that people can prevent their immediate perceptual processes from occurring. Not only is thought suppression counteractive – people instructed not to think of white bears ironically thought more about them than people who were actively trying to think about them (Wegner *et al.*, 1987) – but color-blind policy in practice also backfires (Schofield, 1986).

What do we do now?

As social psychologists, what do we recommend to combat stereotyping and prejudice? To answer this question, examine what is available. First, recall the two routes to perception, automatic/categorical and controlled/attribute-based. We know that motivated tacticians are willing to take the second route if it fits with their goal (they are motivated to do so) and if they have enough cognitive resources in that moment (they have the attention to do so). This being so, organizations can take advantage of the conditions under which people are motivated to form accuracy-oriented impressions of others. When people are motivated and informed, they make more complex assess-ments (Hilton and Darley, 1991) by attending more to stereotype-inconsistent information (Fiske and Neuberg, 1990).

What's more, organizations need to acknowledge the role of power. Powerful people – defined as those who have asymmetrical control over another person's outcomes (Dépret and Fiske, 1999) – are more vulnerable to stereotype because they are more cognitively loaded, have fewer incentives to do so (their welfare is less dependent on the powerless than vice versa), and they may be power-oriented so that they lack motivation to want to perceive others individually (Fiske, 1993). This being so, organizations must focus attention on the actions of those in power. These include people in authority positions, people who make up the dominant group, and people who make decisions on behalf of their organization, sets that presumably overlap significantly.

How might one intervene? People's personal values and self-concepts matter. People are motivated to see themselves in a positive light, and one can use this to encourage individuating assessments. Emphasizing one or the other self-concept influences people to treat others either individually or categorically (Fiske and Von Hendy, 1992). To empha-size individuation, the protocol provides feedback that they are fair people who treat others justly and judge them on their own character-istics. Similarly, one can also remind people that the goal is to be accurate (Neuberg, 1989). These appeals to people's better natures can, at least in the short term, alter how people make decisions. Their utility in the long term, and in organizational settings, remains to be tested.

A second type of approach involves manipulating the perceiver's relationship with the target, creating interdependence. An interdepen-dent relationship makes the perceiver pay more attention to the target because outcomes depend on that person. As social scientists, one of our main goals should be to understand the power differentials between groups both outside and within an organization (Tsui, Egan and O'Reilly, 1992; Zimmer, 1988): If high-status group members also occupy authority positions within the organization, that structure reinforces the existing power differentials in society (Alderfer, 1987). However, organizations can increase interdependence between high-status and low-status people that will motivate the powerful to form accurate impressions of the less powerful, if for no other reason than to retain a sense of prediction and control. This approach takes advantage of the fact that people's perceptions of others are more individuated when they work together (Neuberg and Fiske, 1987; Pendry and Macrae, 1994) and when their outcome depends on the other person (Dépret and Fiske, 1999). Relatedly, creating shared goals that depend on the low-status person probably makes the higher status person attend to their joint interactions (Pettigrew and Martin, 1995). Interdependence is also one of the main components of the common ingroup identity model, which reduces intergroup bias (Gaertner, Dovidio, and Bachman, 1996; Gaertner et al. 1994).

Instituting local egalitarian norms, and with them, accountability to third parties matters, so that authorities and the organization as a whole endorse and monitor egalitarian outcomes. Part of such programs might include workshops as an endorsement of the sanctioned norms (Kawakami et al., 2000; Rudman, Ashmore, and Gary, 2001). Because social context cues behavior, situations with egalitarian norms discourage intergroup bias (Kawakami, Spears, and Dovidio, 2002).

And lastly, organizational diversity research itself can emphasize the dynamics underlying intergroup relations in real-world settings. Promising areas for focusing research include at least four topics: relational diversity, diversity attitudes, target perspectives, and employee retention. As discussed briefly earlier, relational diversity captures diversity as more than a variable indicating an amount. People's models of diversity will add richness to the current research on lay evaluations of diversity because they help explain people's outcomes (besides giving insight into their expectations).

Most of the literature reviewed in this chapter takes the perspective of the majority or high-status member: Whom would they hire? Do they fairly evaluate this individual from a stereotyped group? While it is true that a biased person's perceptions do impact group composition, recognizing agency in the minority targets acknowledges that the interaction has two sides. Outcome dependency research shows that low-status people can hold power over the high-status person. In addition, they face unique cultural tradeoffs (Mor Barak, Findler, and Wind, 2003) and additional barriers due to their minority status (Triandis, Kurowski, and Gelfand, 1994).

Clearly, hiring and promoting are distinct. Some psychological processes operate more commonly at one level than the other (descriptive stereotypes might keep people out, while prescriptive stereotypes might hold them back). Merely complying with legal requirements to provide equal opportunities is but the first step (Thomas and Ely, 1996). Hiring minorities is not the panacea to job discrimination because discrimination continues throughout work life.

Summary

Stereotypes and prejudice are not new phenomena. What is relatively new, however, is our understanding of their origins, persistence, and usage. We discussed categorization processes that explain some origins of stereotypes and prejudice. Then we discussed the utility of stereotypes which help explain why they so stubbornly refuse to go away, revealing the crucial role of attention and motivation in explaining why they can be convenient biases. People resort to category-based perception of others when short on cognitive resources or on motivation; however, when they are able and motivated, they exercise effort and top-down control in perceiving others based on individual attributes. Even then, unfortunately, attentional, memory, and attributional biases cap stereotype utility.

Because of their roots in categorization processes, intergroup phenomena are most evident along physically salient dimensions, such as ethnicity, gender, and age. Therefore, this chapter focused on demographic diversity rather than functional diversity (e.g., skills differences). First, we reviewed theories of contemporary racism: ambivalent, aversive, symbolic, modern, subtle, and implicit, and discussed how conscious expressions of racial attitudes do not neatly map onto their internal and unconscious manifestations. Such a disconnect between overt and covert attitudes masks workplace discrimination prevalence. While contemporary racism might discriminate at the hiring stage, other issues – such as double and shifting standards in evaluation – devalue on-the-job performance.

In gender discrimination, sexism theories explain the role of hostile as well as ambivalent attitudes toward women in creating stereotypes. We also explored descriptive and prescriptive stereotypes' differential impact on female (potential) employees in terms of disparate impact and disparate treatment. Of course, biases in evaluation standards apply to female targets as well.

Next, we investigated lay attitudes toward diversity management. Models of diversity can roughly be grouped into two major categories: one that advocates multiculturalism and the other, color-blindness. Societal majority members favor the color-blind approach and minority members, the multicultural approach, which further complicates diversity management.

The chapter concluded with recommendations for combating intergroup bias at the organizational level. First, we focused on the perceiver: Organizations can remind people of their egalitarian values and emphasize their self-concepts as fair people. Second, organizations can alter the power dynamics between perceiver and target, by creating interdependence. Third, organizations can direct attention to egalitarian norms and increase perpetrators' accountability to third parties. And finally, diversity researchers can emphasize the dynamics in intergroup relations, studying more relational types of diversity, lay attitudes toward diversity, target perspectives, and employee retention in addition to hiring.

References

Alderfer, C. P. (1987). An intergroup perspective on group dynamics. In J. Lorsch (ed.), *Handbook of Organizational Behavior* (pp. 190–222). Englewood Cliffs: Prentice-Hall.

Alexander, M. G., Brewer, M. B., and Herrmann, R. K. (1999). Images and affect: A functional analysis of out-group stereotypes. *Journal of Personality and Social Psychology, 77,* 78–93.

Altemeyer, B. (1988). *Enemies of Freedom.* San Francisco: Jossey-Bass.

Bargh, J. A. (1989). Conditional automaticity: Varieties of automatic influence in social perception and cognition. In J. S. Uleman and J. A. Bargh (eds.), *Unintended Thought* (pp. 3–51). New York: Guilford Press.

Berry, J. W. (1980). Acculturation as varieties of adaptation. In A. M. Padilla (ed.), *Acculturation: Theory, Models, and Some New Findings* (pp. 9–25). Boulder: Westview.

Biernat, M., and Fuegen, K. (2001). Shifting standards and the evaluation of competence: Complexity in the gender-based judgment and decision making. *Journal of Social Issues, 57,* 707–724.

Biernat, M., and Kobrynowicz, D. (1997). Gender- and race-based standards of competence: Lower minimum standards but higher ability standards for devalued groups. *Journal of Personality and Social Psychology, 72,* 544–557.

Biernat, M., Kobrynowicz, D., and Weber, D. L. (2003). Stereotypes and shifting standards: Some paradoxical effects of cognitive load. *Journal of Applied Social Psychology, 33,* 2060–2079.

Biernat, M., and Manis, M. (1994). Shifting standards and stereotype-based judgments. *Journal of Personality and Social Psychology, 66,* 5–20.

Biernat, M., Manis, M., and Nelson, T. E. (1991). Stereotypes and standards of judgments. *Journal of Personality and Social Psychology*, 60, 485–499.

Brewer, M. B. (1998). A dual process model of impression formation. In R. Wyer and T. Srull (eds.), *Advances in Social Cognition* (Vol. 1, pp. 1–36). Hillsdale: Laurence Erlbaum Associates.

Brewer, M. B., and Brown, R. J. (1998). Intergroup relations. In D. T. Gilbert, S. T. Fiske, and G. Lindzey (eds.), *The Handbook of Social Psychology* (Vol. 2, 4th edn, pp. 554–594). New York: McGraw-Hill.

Brickman, P., Rabinowitz, V. C., Karuza, J., Jr., Coates, D., Cohen, E., and Kidder, L. (1982). Models of helping and coping. *American Psychologist*, 37, 368–384.

Brief, A. P., Dietz, J., Cohen, R. R., Pugh, S. D., and Vaslow, J. B. (2000). Just doing business: Modern racism and obedience to authority as explanations for employment discrimination. *Organizational Behavior and Human Decision Processes*, 81, 72–97.

Burgess, D., and Borgida, E. (1999). Who women are, who women should be: Descriptive and prescriptive gender stereotyping in sex discrimination. *Psychology, Public Policy, and the Law*, 5, 665–692.

Chen, C. C., and Eastman, W. (1997). Toward a civic culture for multicultural organizations. *The Journal of Applied Behavioral Science*, 33, 454–470.

Cikara, M., and Fiske, S. T. (2006). Unpublished research, Princeton University.

Clausell, E., and Fiske, S. T. (2005). When do subgroup parts add up to the stereotypic whole? Mixed stereotype content for gay male subgroups explains overall ratings. *Social Cognition*, 23, 161–181.

Cleveland, J. N., and Landy, F. J. (1983). The effects of person and job stereotypes on two personnel decisions. *Journal of Applied Psychology*, 68, 609–619.

Copeland, J. T. (1994). Prophecies of power: Motivational implications of social power for behavioral confirmation. *Journal of Personality and Social Psychology*, 67, 264–277.

Corneille, O., Vescio, T. K., and Judd, C. M. (2000). Incidentally activated knowledge and stereotype based judgments: A consideration of primed construct-target attribute match. *Social Cognition*, 18, 377–399.

Cuddy, A. J. C., Fiske, S. T., and Glick, P. (2004). When professionals become mothers, warmth doesn't cut the ice. *Journal of Social Issues*, 60, 701–718.

Cuddy, A. J. C., Norton, M., and Fiske, S. T. (2005). This old stereotype: The pervasiveness and persistence of the elderly stereotype. *Journal of Social Issues*, 61, 267–285.

Dépret, E., and Fiske, S. T. (1999). Perceiving the powerful: Intriguing individuals versus threatening groups. *Journal of Experimental Social Psychology, 35*, 461–480.

Devine, P. G. (1989). Stereotypes and prejudice: Their automatic and controlled components. *Journal of Personality and Social Psychology, 56*, 5–18.

Devine, P. G., and Elliot, A. J. (1995). Are racial stereotypes really fading? The Princeton trilogy revisited. *Personality and Social Psychology Bulletin, 21*, 1139–1150.

Dijksterhuis, A., Spears, R., and Lepinasse, V. (2001). Reflecting and deflecting stereotypes: Assimilation and contrast in impression formation and automatic behavior. *Journal of Experimental Social Psychology, 37*, 286–299.

Dovidio, J. F., Brigham, J. C., Johnson, B. T., and Gaertner, S. L. (1996). Stereotyping, prejudice, and discrimination: Another look. In N. Macrae, C. Stangor, and M. Hewstone (eds.), *Stereotypes and Stereotyping* (pp. 276–319). New York: Guilford Press.

Dovidio, J. F., and Gaertner, S. L. (1981). The effects of race, status, and ability on helping behavior. *Social Psychology Quarterly, 44*, 192–203.

(1983). The effects of sex, status, and ability on helping behavior. *Social Applied Social Psychology, 13*, 191–205.

(2004). Aversive racism. In M. P. Zanna (ed.), *Advances in Experimental Social Psychology* (Vol. 36, pp. 1–52). San Diego: Elsevier Academic Press.

Duckitt, J. (2001). A dual-process cognitive-motivational theory of ideology and prejudice. In M. P. Zanna (ed.), *Advances in Experimental Social Psychology* (Vol. 33, pp. 41–113). New York: Academic Press.

Eagly, A. H., and Johannesen-Schmidt, M. C. (2001). The leadership styles of women and men. *Journal of Social Issues, 57*, 781–797.

Eagly, A. H., Karau, S. J., and Makhijani, M. G. (1995). Gender and the effectiveness of leaders: A meta-analysis. *Psychological Bulletin, 117*, 125–145.

Eagly, A. H., Makhijani, M. G., and Klonsky, B. G. (1992). Gender and evaluation of leaders: A meta-analysis. *Psychological Bulletin, 111*, 3–22.

Eckes, T. (2002). Paternalistic and envious gender stereotypes: Testing predictions from the stereotype content model. *Sex Roles, 47*, 99–114.

Ely, R. J., and Thomas, D. A. (2001). Cultural diversity at work: The effects of diversity perspectives on work group processes and outcomes. *Administrative Science Quarterly, 46*, 229–273.

Evans, M. D. R., and Kelley, J. (1991). Prejudice, discrimination, and the labor market: Attainments of immigrants in Australia. *American Journal of Sociology, 97*, 721–759.

Fazio, R. H., Jackson, J. R., Dunton, B. C., Williams, C. J. (1995). Variability in automatic activation as an unobtrusive measure of racial attitudes: A bona fide pipeline? *Journal of Personality and Social Psychology, 69,* 1013–1027.

Fazio, R. H., and Olson, M. A. (2003). Implicit measures in social cognition research: Their meaning and their use. In S. T. Fiske, D. L. Schacter, and C. Zahn-Waxler (eds.), *Annual Review of Psychology* (Vol. 54, pp. 297–327). Palo Alto: Annual Reviews.

Finkelstein, L. M., Burke, M. J., and Raju, N. S. (1995). Age discrimination in simulated employment contexts: An integrative analysis. *Journal of Applied Psychology, 80,* 652–663.

Fiske, S. T. (1993). Controlling other people: The impact of power on stereotyping. *American Psychologist, 48,* 621–628.

   (1998). Stereotyping, prejudice, and discrimination. In D. T. Gilbert, S. T. Fiske, and G. Lindzey (eds.), *The Handbook of Social Psychology* (Vol. 2, 4th edn, pp. 357–411). New York: McGraw-Hill.

Fiske, S. T., Cuddy, A. J. C., and Glick, P. (2007). Universal dimensions of social perception: Warmth and competence. *Trends in Cognitive Sciences, 11,* 77–83.

Fiske, S. T., Cuddy, A. J. C., Glick, P., and Xu, J. (2002). A model of (often mixed) stereotype content: Competence and warmth respectively follow from perceived status and competition. *Journal of Personality and Social Psychology, 82,* 878–902.

Fiske, S. T., and Neuberg, S. L. (1990). A continuum model of impression formation: From category-based to individuating processes as a function of information, motivation, and attention. In M. P. Zanna (ed.), *Advances in Experimental Psychology* (Vol. 23, pp. 1–108). San Diego: Academic Press.

Fiske, S. T., and Ruscher, J. B. (1993). Negative interdependence and prejudice: Whence the affect? In D. M. Mackie and D. L. Hamilton (eds.), *Affect, Cognition, and Stereotyping: Interactive Processes in Group Perception* (pp. 239–268). San Diego: Academic Press.

Fiske, S. T., and Stevens, L. E. (1993). What's so special about sex? Gender stereotyping and discrimination. In S. Oskamp and M. Costanzo (eds.), *Claremont Symposium on Applied Social Psychology, Vol. 6. Gender Issues in Contemporary Society* (pp. 173–196). Thousand Oaks: Sage Publications.

Fiske, S. T., and Taylor, S. E. (2008): *Social cognition: From brains to culture* (2nd edn). New York: McGraw-Hill.

Fiske, S. T., and Von Hendy, H. M. (1992). Personality feedback and situational norms can control stereotyping processes. *Journal of Personality and Social Psychology, 62,* 577–596.

Foddy, M., and Smithson, M. (1989). Fuzzy sets and double standards: Modeling the process of ability inference. In J. Berger, M. Zelditch, Jr., and B. Anderson (eds.), *Sociological Theories in Progress: New Formulations*, pp. 73–99. Newbury Park: Sage.

Foschi, M. (1989). Status characteristics, standards, and attributions. In J. Berger, M. Zelditch, Jr., and B. Anderson (eds.), *Sociological Theories in Progress: New Formulations*, pp. 58–72. Newbury Park: Sage.

(1996). Double standards in the evaluation of men and women. *Social Psychology Quarterly*, *59*, 237–254.

(2000). Double standards for competence: Theory and research. *Annual Review of Sociology*, *26*, 21–42.

Foschi, M., Lai, L., and Sigerson, K. (1994). Gender and double standards in the assessment of job applicants. *Social Psychology Quarterly*, *57*, 326–339.

Foschi, M., Sigerson, K., Lebesis, M. (1995). Assessing job applicants: The relative effects of gender, academic record, and decision type. *Small Group Research*, *26*, 328–352.

Frazer, R. A., and Wiersma, U. J. (2001). Prejudice versus discrimination in the employment interview: We may hire equally, but our memories harbour prejudice. *Human Relations*, *54*, 173–191.

Frederickson, G. M. (1999). Models of American ethnic relations: A historical perspective. In D. A. Prentice and D. T. Miller (eds.), *Cultural Divides: Understanding and Overcoming Group Conflict* (pp. 23–34). New York: Russell Sage Foundation.

Gaertner, S. L., and Dovidio, J. F. (1977). The subtlety of white racism, arousal, and helping behavior. *Journal of Personality and Social Psychology*, *35*, 691–707.

(1986). The aversive form of racism. In J. F. Dovidio and S. L. Gaertner (eds.), *Prejudice, Discrimination, and Racism* (pp. 61–89). San Diego: Academic Press.

(2005). Understanding and addressing contemporary racism: From aversive racism to the common ingroup identity model. *Journal of Social Issues*, *61*, 615–639.

Gaertner, S. L., Dovidio, J. F., and Bachman, B. A. (1996). Revisiting the contact hypothesis: The induction of a common ingroup identity. *International Journal of Intercultural Relations*, *20*, 271–290.

Gaertner, S. L., and McLaughlin, J. P. (1983). Racial stereotypes: Associations and ascriptions of positive and negative characteristics. *Social Psychology Quarterly*, *46*, 23–30.

Gaertner, S. L., Rust, M. C., Dovidio, J. F., Bachman, B. A., and Anastasio, P. A. (1994). The contact hypothesis: The role of a common ingroup identity on reducing intergroup bias. *Small Group Research*, *25*, 224–249.

Gilbert, D. T., and Hixon, J. G. (1991). The trouble of thinking: Activation and application of stereotypic beliefs. *Journal of Personality and Social Psychology*, 60, 509–517.

Gilbert, G. M. (1951). Stereotype persistence and change among college students. *Journal of Abnormal and Social Psychology*, 46, 245–254.

Glick, P., Diebold, J., Bailey-Werner, B., Zhu, L. (1997). The two faces of Adam: Ambivalent sexism and polarized attitudes toward women. *Personality and Social Psychology Bulletin*, 23, 1323–1334.

Glick, P., and Fiske, S. T. (1996). The ambivalent sexism inventory: Differentiating hostile and benevolent sexism. *Journal of Personality and Social Psychology*, 70, 491–512.

(1999). The ambivalence toward men inventory: Differentiating hostile and benevolent beliefs about men. *Psychology of Women Quarterly*, 23, 519–536.

(2001). Ambivalent sexism. In M. P. Zanna (ed.), *Advances in Experimental Social Psychology* (Vol. 33, pp. 115–188). Thousand Oaks: Academic Press.

Glick, P., Fiske, S. T., Mladinic, A., Saiz, J. L., Abrams, D., Masser, B., *et al.*, (2000). Beyond prejudice as simple antipathy: Hostile and benevolent sexism across cultures. *Journal of Personality and Social Psychology*, 79, 763–775.

Gordon, M. M. (1971). The nature of assimilation and the theory of the melting pot. In E. P. Hollander and R. G. Hunt (eds.), *Current Perspectives in Social Psychology* (3rd edn, pp. 102–114). New York: Oxford University Press.

Greenwald, A. G., and Banaji, M. R. (1989). The self as a memory system: Powerful, but ordinary. *Journal of Personality and Social Psychology*, 57, 41–54.

Greenwald, A. G., and Banaji, M. R. (1995). Implicit social cognition: Attitudes, self-esteem, and stereotypes. *Psychological Review*, 102, 4–27.

Greenwald, A. G., and Banaji, M. R. (2002). A unified theory of implicit attitudes, stereotypes, self-esteem, and self-concept. *Psychological Review*, 109, 3–25.

Hamilton, D. L., and Gifford, R. K. (1976). Illusory correlation in interpersonal perception: A cognitive basis of stereotypic judgments. *Journal of Experimental Social Psychology*, 12, 392–407.

Hart, A. J., Whalen, P. J., Shin, L. M., McInerney, S. C., Fischer, H., and Rauch, S. L. (2000). Differential response in the human amygdala to racial outgroup vs ingroup face stimuli. *Neuroreport: For Rapid Communication of Neuroscience Research*, 11, 2351–2355.

Heilman, M. E. (1983). Sex bias in work settings: The lack of fit model. *Research in Organizational Behavior*, 5, 269–298.

Heilman, M. E., Block, C., and Stathatos, P. (1997). The affirmative action stigma of incompetence: Effects of performance information. *Academy of Management Journal, 40,* 603–625.

Henry, P. J., and Sears, D. O. (2002). The symbolic racism 2000 scale. *Political Psychology, 23,* 253–283.

Hilton and Darley (1991). The effects of interaction goals on person perception. In M. P. Zanna (ed.), *Advances in Experimental Social Psychology* (Vol. 24, pp. 236–267). San Diego: Academic Press.

Horvath, M., and Ryan, A. M. (2003). Antecedents and potential moderators of the relationship between attitudes and hiring discrimination on the basis of sexual orientation. *Sex Roles, 48,* 115–130.

Jackson, C. J., Potter, A., and Dale, S. (1998). Utility of facet descriptions in the prediction of global job satisfaction. *European Journal of Psychological Assessment, 14,* 134–140.

James, E. H., Brief, A. P., Dietz, J., and Cohen, R. R. (2001). Prejudice matters: Understanding the reactions of whites to affirmative action programs targeted to benefit blacks. *Journal of Applied Psychology, 86,* 1120–1128.

Jost, J. T., and Banaji, M. R. (1994). The role of stereotyping in system justification and the production of false consciousness. *British Journal of Social Psychology, 33,* 1–27.

Jost, J. T., Banaji, M. R., and Nosek, B. A. (2004). A decade of system justification theory: Accumulated evidence of conscious and unconscious bolstering of the status quo. *Political Psychology, 25,* 881–920.

Jost, J. T., and Kay, A. C. (2005). Exposure to benevolent sexism and complementary gender stereotypes: Consequences for specific and diffuse forms of system justification. *Journal of Personality and Social Psychology, 88,* 498–509.

Judd, C. M., and Park, B. (1993). Definition and assessment of accuracy in social stereotypes. *Psychological Review, 100,* 109–128.

Karlins, M., Coffman, T. L., and Walters, G. (1969). On the fading of social stereotypes: Studies in three generations of college students. *Journal of Personality and Social Psychology, 13,* 1–16.

Katz, I. (1981). *Stigma: A Social Psychological Analysis.* Hillsdale: Lawrence Erlbaum.

Katz, D., and Braly, K. (1933). Racial stereotypes of one hundred college students. *Journal of Abnormal and Social Psychology, 28,* 280–290.

Katz, I., and Hass, R. G. (1988). Racial ambivalence and American value conflict: Correlational and priming studies of dual cognitive structures. *Journal of Personality and Social Psychology, 55,* 893–905.

Katz, I., Wackenhut, J., and Hass, R. G. (1986). Racial ambivalence, value duality, and behavior. In J. F. Dovidio and S. L. Gaertner (eds.), *Prejudice, Discrimination, and Racism* (pp. 35–60). San Diego: Academic Press.

Kawakami, K., Dovidio, J. F., Moll, J., Hermsen, S., and Russin, A. (2000). Just say no (to stereotyping): Effects of training in the negation of stereotypic associations on stereotype activation. *Journal of Personality and Social Psychology*, 78, 871–888.

Kawakami, K., Spears, R., and Dovidio, J. F. (2002). Disinhibition of stereotyping: Context, prejudice and target characteristics. *European Journal of Social Psychology*, 32, 517–530.

Kay, A. C., and Jost, J. T. (2003). Complementary justice: Effects of "poor but happy" and "poor but honest" stereotype exemplars on system justification and implicit activation of the justice motive. *Journal of Personality and Social Psychology*, 85, 823–837.

Kinder, D. R., and Sears, D. O. (1981). Prejudice and politics: Symbolic racism versus racial threats to the good life. *Journal of Personality and Social Psychology*, 40, 414–431.

Kinder, D. R., and Sears, D. O. (1996). *Divided by Color: Racial Politics and Democratic Ideals*. Chicago: University of Chicago Press.

Konrad, A. M., and Linnehan, F. (1995). Formalized HRM structures: Coordinating equal employment opportunity or concealing organizational practices? *Academy of Management Journal*, 38, 787–820.

Lee, T. L., and Fiske, S. T. (2008). Not an outgroup, not yet an ingroup: Immigrants in the stereotype content model. *International Journal of Intercultural Relations*, 30, 751–768.

Lepore, L., and Brown, R. (1997). Category and stereotype activation: Is prejudice inevitable? *Journal of Personality and Social Psychology*, 72, 275–287.

Leslie, L. M., Constantine, V. S., and Fiske, S. T. (2006). The Princeton quartet: Does private ambivalence moderate modern stereotype content? Unpublished manuscript.

Leyens, J.-Ph., Dardenne, B., and Fiske, S. T. (1998). Why and under what circumstances is a hypothesis-consistent testing strategy preferred in interviews? *British Journal of Social Psychology*, 37, 259–274.

Li, J. (2005). Mind or virtue: Western and Chinese beliefs about learning. *Current Directions in Psychological Science*, 14, 190–193.

Lin, M. H., Kwan, V. S. Y., Cheung, A., and Fiske, S. T. (2005). Stereotype Content Model explains prejudice for an envied outgroup: Scale of anti-Asian American stereotypes. *Personality and Social Psychology Bulletin*, 31, 34–47.

Madon, S., Jussim, L., Keiper, S., Eccles, J., Smith, A., and Palumbo, P. (1998). The accuracy and power of sex, social class, and ethnic stereotypes: A naturalistic study in person perception. *Personality and Social Psychology Bulletin, 24,* 1304–1318.

Markus, H. R., and Kitayama, S. (1991). Culture and the self: Implications for cognition, emotion, and motivation. *Psychological Review, 98,* 224–253.

Martin, J. (1992). *Cultures in Organizations: Three Perspectives.* New York: Oxford University Press.

Matsouka, J. K., and Ryujin, D. H. (1991). Asian American immigrants: A comparison of the Chinese, Japanese, and Filipinos. *Journal of Sociology and Social Welfare, 18,* 123–133.

McConahay, J. B. (1983). Modern racism and modern discrimination: The effects of race, racial attitudes, and context on simulated hiring decisions. *Personality and Social Psychology Bulletin, 9,* 551–558.

McConahay, J. B., Hardee, B. B., and Batts, V. (1981). Has racism declined in America? It depends on who is asking and what is asked. *Journal of Conflict Resolution, 25,* 563–579.

McConahay, J. B., and Hough, J. C., Jr. (1976). Symbolic racism. *Journal of Social Issues, 32,* 23–45.

Miller, D. T., and Prentice, D. A. (1999). Some consequences of a belief in group essence : The category divide hypothesis. In D. A. Prentice and D. T. Miller (eds.), *Cultural Divides* (pp. 213–238).

Mor Barak, M. E., Cherin, D. A., and Berkman, S. (1998). Organizational and personal dimensions in diversity climate: Ethnic and gender differences in employee perceptions. *Journal of Applied Behavioral Sciences, 34,* 82–104.

Mor Barak, M. E., Findler, L., and Wind, L. H. (2003). Cross-cultural aspects of diversity and well-being in the workplace: An international perspective. *Journal of Social Work Research and Evaluation, 4,* 145–169.

Mucchi-Faina, A., Costarelli, S., and Romoli, C. (2002). The effects of intergroup context of evaluation on ambivalence toward the ingroup and the outgroup. *European Journal of Social Psychology, 32,* 247–259.

Mummendey, A., and Wenzel, M. (1999). Social discrimination and tolerance in intergroup relations: Reactions to intergroup difference. *Personality and Social Psychology Review, 3,* 158–174.

Neuberg, S. L. (1989). The goal of forming accurate impressions during social interactions: Attenuating the impact of negative expectancies. *Journal of Personality and Social Psychology, 56,* 374–386.

Neuberg, S. L., and Fiske, S. T. (1987). Motivational influences on impression formation: Outcome dependency, accuracy-driven attention,, and individuating processes. *Journal of Personality and Social Psychology, 53,* 431–444.

Nisbett, R. E., Peng, K., Choi, I., and Norenzayan, A. (2001). Culture and systems of thought: Holistic versus analytic cognition. *Psychological Review*, *108*, 291–310.

Olian, J. D., Schwab, D. P., and Haberfeld, Y. (1988). The impact of applicant gender compared to qualifications on hiring recommendations: A meta-analysis of experimental studies. *Organizational Behavior and Human Decision Processes*, *41*, 180–195.

Peeters, G. (2002). From good and bad to can and must: Subjective necessity of acts associated with positively and negatively valued stimuli. *European Journal of Social Psychology*, *32*, 125–136.

Pendry, L. F., and Macrae, C. N. (1994). Stereotypes and mental life: The case of the motivated but thwarted tactician. *Journal of Experimental Social Psychology*, *30*, 303–325.

Pettigrew, T. F., and Meertens, R. W. (1995). Subtle and blatant prejudice in western Europe. *European Journal of Social Psychology*, *25*, 57–75.

Phalet, K., and Poppe, E. (1997). Competence and morality dimensions of national and ethnic stereotypes: A study in six eastern-European countries. *European Journal of Social Psychology*, *27*, 703–723.

Phelps, E. A., O'Connor, K. J., Cunningham, W. A., Funayama, E. S., Gatenby, J. C., Gore, J. C., *et al.*, (2000). Performance on indirect measures of race evaluation predicts amygdala activation. *Journal of Cognitive Neuroscience*, *12*, 729–738.

Plaut, V. C. (2002). Cultural models of diversity in America: The psychology of difference and inclusion. In R. A. Shweder, M. Minow, and H. R. Markus (eds.), *Engaging Cultural Differences: The Multicultural Challenge in Liberal Democracies* (pp. 365–395). New York: Russell Sage Foundation.

(2003). Sociocultural models of diversity: The dilemma of difference in America. *Dissertation-Abstracts-International: Section B: The Sciences and Engineering*, *64*(3B), 1553.

Prentice, D. A., and Carranza, E. (2002). What women and men should be, shouldn't be, are allowed to be, and don't have to be: The contents of prescriptive gender stereotypes. *Psychology of Women Quarterly*, *26*, 269–281.

Reszke, I. (1995). How a positive image can have a negative impact: Stereotypes of unemployed women and men in liberated Poland. *Women's Studies International Forum*, *18*, 13–17.

Richards, Z., and Hewstone, M. (2001). Subtyping and subgrouping: Processes for the prevention and promotion of stereotype change. *Personality and Social Psychology Review*, *5*, 52–73.

Ridgeway, C. L. (1982). Status in groups: The importance of motivation. *American Sociological Review, 47,* 76–88.

Rosenberg, S., Nelson, C., and Vivekananthan, P. S. (1968). A multidimensional approach to the structure of personality impressions. *Journal of Personality and Social Psychology, 9,* 283–294.

Rudman, L. A. (1998). Self-promotion as a risk factor for women: The costs and benefits of counterstereotypical impression management. *Journal of Personality and Social Psychology, 74,* 629–645.

Rudman, L. A., Ashmore, R. D., Gary, M. L. (2001). "Unlearning" automatic biases: The malleability of implicit prejudice and stereotypes. *Journal of Personality and Social Psychology, 81,* 856–868.

Schofield, J. W. (1986). Black and White contact in desegregated schools. In M. Hewstone and R. J. Brown (eds.), *Contact and Conflict in Intergroup Encounters* (pp. 79–92). Oxford: Blackwell.

Schopler, J., and Insko, C. A. (1992). The discontinuity effect in interpersonal and intergroup relations: Generality and mediation. *European Review of Social Psychology 3,* 121–151.

Sears, D. O., and Kinder, D. R. (1971). Racial tensions and voting in Los Angeles. In W. Z. Hirsch (ed.), *Los Angeles: Viability and Prospects for Metropolitan Leadership.* New York: Praeger.

Sears, D. O., Van Laar, C., Carrillo, M., and Kosterman, R. (1997). Is it really racism? The origins of white Americans' opposition to race-targeted policies. *Public Opinion Quarterly, 61,* 16–53.

Seijts, G. H., and Jackson, S. E. (2001). Reactions to employment equity programs and situational interviews: A laboratory study. *Human Performance, 14,* 247–265.

Shelton, J. N., and Richeson, J. A. (2006). Ethnic minorities' racial attitudes and contact experiences with white people. *Cultural Diversity and Ethnic Minority Psychology, 12,* 149–164.

Sidanius, J., Feshbach, S., Levin, S., and Pratto, F. (1997). The interface between ethnic and national attachment: Ethnic pluralism or ethnic dominance? *Public Opinion Quarterly, 61,* 102–133.

Sidanius, J., and Pratto, F. (1999). *Social Dominance: An Intergroup Theory of Social Hierarchy and Oppression.* New York: Cambridge University Press.

Sniderman, P. M., and Piazza, T. (1993). *The Scar of Race.* Cambridge: Harvard University Press.

Snyder, M. (1984). When belief creates reality. In L. Berkowitz (ed.), *Advances in Experimental Social Psychology* (Vol. 18, pp. 248–306). New York: Academic Press.

Spence, J. T., Helmreich, R., and Stapp, J. (1973). A short version of the Attitudes toward Women Scale (AWS). *Bulletin of the Psychonomic Society, 2,* 219–220.

Stangor, C. (1995). Content and application inaccuracy in social stereotyping. In Y. Lee, L. Jussim, and C. R. McCauley (eds.), *Stereotype Accuracy: Toward Appreciating Group Differences* (pp. 275–292). Washington, DC: American Psychological Association.

Stangor, C., and McMillan, D. (1992). Memory for expectancy-congruent and expectancy-incongruent information: A review of the social and social developmental literatures. *Psychological Bulletin, 1,* 42–16.

Steele, C. M., and Aronson, J. (1995). Stereotype threat and intellectual test performance of African Americans. *Journal of Personality and Social Psychology, 69,* 797–811.

Swim, J. K., Aikin, K. J., Hall, W. S., and Hunter, B. A. (1995). Sexism and racism: Old-fashioned and modern prejudice. *Journal of Personality and Social Psychology, 68,* 199–214.

Swim, J. K., Borgida, E., Maruyama, G., and Myers, D. G. (1989). Joan McKay versus John McKay: Do gender stereotypes bias evaluations? *Psychological Bulletin, 105,* 409–429.

Swim, J. K., and Sanna, L. J. (1996). He's skilled, she's lucky: A meta-analysis of observers' attributions for women's and men's successes and failures. *Personality and Social Psychology Bulletin, 22,* 507–519.

Tajfel, H., and Turner, J. C. (2004). The social identity theory of intergroup behavior. In J. T. Jost and J. Sidanius (eds.), *Key Readings in Social Psychology. Political Psychology: Key Readings* (pp. 276–293). New York: Psychology Press.

Talaska, C., Fiske, S. T., and Chaiken, S. (2008). Legitimating racial discrimination: A meta-analysis of the racial attitude-behavior literature shows that emotions, not beliefs, best predict discrimination. *Social Justice Research.*

Thomas, D. A., and Ely, R. J. (1996). Making differences matter: A new paradigm for managing diversity. *Harvard Business Review, 74,* 79–90.

Tougas, F., Brown, R., Beaton, A. M., and Joly, S. (1995). Neosexism: Plus ca change, plus c'est pareil. *Personality and Social Psychology Bulletin, 21,* 842–849.

Triandis, H. C., Kurowski, L. L., Gelfand, M. J. (1994). Workplace diversity. In H. C. Triandis, M. D. Dunnette, and L. M. Hough (eds.), *Handbook of Industrial and Organizational Psychology* (pp. 769–827). Palo Alto: Consulting Psychologists Press.

Tsui, A. S., Egan, T. D., and O'Reilly, C. A. (1992). Being different: Relational demography and organizational attachment. *Administrative Science Quarterly, 37,* 549–579.

Turner, J. C., Hogg, M. A., Oakes, P. J., Reicher, S. D., and Wetherell, M. (1987). *Rediscovering the Social Group: A Self Categorization Theory.* Oxford: Blackwell.

Turner, J. C., and Oakes, P. J. (1989). Self-categorization theory and social influence. In P. B. Paulus (ed.), *The Psychology of Group Influence* (pp. 233–275). Hillsdale: Erlbaum.

Van Knippenberg, A., Dijksterhuis, A., and Vermeulen, D. (1999). Judgement and memory of a criminal act: The effects of stereotypes and cognitive load. *European Journal of Social Psychology, 29,* 191–201.

Van Lange, P. A. M., and Kuhlman, D. M. (1994). Social value orientations and impressions of partner's honesty and intelligence: A test of the might versus morality effect. *Journal of Personality and Social Psychology, 67,* 126–141.

Wegner, D. M., Schneider, D. J., Carter, S. R., and White, T. L. (1987). Paradoxical effects of thought suppression. *Journal of Personality and Social Psychology, 53,* 5–13.

Wenzel, M., and Mummendey, A. (1996). Positive-negative asymmetry of social discrimination: A normative analysis of differential evaluations of ingroup and outgroup on positive and negative attributes. *British Journal of Social Psychology, 35,* 493–507.

West, S. L., McMahon, B. T., Monasterio, E., Belongia, L., and Kramer, K. (2005). Workplace discrimination and missing limbs: The national EEOC ADA research project. *Journal of Prevention, Assessment and Rehabilitation, 25,* 27–35.

Wheeler, M. E., and Fiske, S. T. (2005). Controlling racial prejudice: Social-cognitive goals affect amygdala and stereotype activation. *Psychological Science, 16,* 56–63.

Williams, K., and O'Reilly, C. (1998). Demography and diversity in organizations: A review of 40 years of research. In B. Staw and R. Sutton (eds.), *Research in Organizational Behavior* (Vol. 20, pp. 77–140). Greenwich: JAI Press.

Wojciszke, B. (1994). Multiple meanings of behavior: Construing actions in terms of competence or morality. *Journal of Personality and Social Psychology, 67,* 222–232.

Word, C. O., Zanna, M. P., and Cooper, J. (1974). The nonverbal mediation of self-fulfilling prophecies in interracial interaction. *Journal of Experimental Social Psychology, 10,* 109–120.

Younes, N. (2001). Getting corporations ready to recruit workers with disabilities. *Journal of Vocational Rehabilitation, 16,* 89–91.

Zimmer, L. (1988). Tokenism and women in the workplace: The limits of gender-neutral theory. *Social Problems, 35,* 64–77.

3 | Promoting racial diversity at work: Challenges and solutions

WILLIAM T. BIELBY

From social stratification to workplace discrimination: Six decades of sociological inquiry

Studies of social class, social stratification, and social mobility – inquiries into how aspects of one's social origins facilitate or limit one's career success as an adult – have a long and distinguished history in American sociology, dating back to the 1940s (Davis and Moore, 1945; Warner, Meeker, and Bells, 1949; Gordon, 1949; 1958; Lipset and Bendix, 1959; Blau and Duncan, 1967). However, sociological scholarship on how workplace policies and practices limit or promote equal employment opportunity ("EEO") is a relatively recent phenomenon, and the discipline all but ignored workplace racial bias prior to the 1970s.

It should be no surprise that American sociologists began to take notice of racial bias in employment around the same time as the rest of the country. The counts in Figure 3.1 are based on 80% or higher relevancy scores in a JSTOR search in the discipline's premier journals, *American Sociological Review* and *American Journal of Sociology* for the terms "race or racial" and "discrimination or bias" and "employment or jobs or careers" and "organization or firm or workplace." Similar patterns to those in Figure 3.1 are evident when I include other journals or somewhat broader search terms. The civil rights and student movements, urban unrest, and landmark legislation of the 1960s motivated sociological inquiry in much the same way it shaped political discourse. The upturn in the 1970s also reflects the growth of increasingly sophisticated quantitative studies of social inequality and mobility, many of them focusing at least in part on differences by race and ethnicity.

By the 1970s, economists' market-based accounts had become the primary counterpoint to sociological studies of racial inequality. Although not always explicitly framing their scholarship as a critique

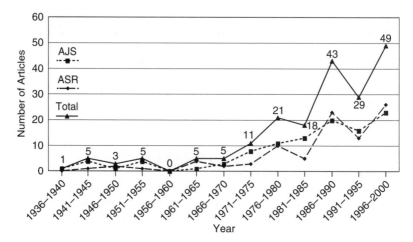

Figure 3.1 *American Sociological Review* and *American Journal of Sociology* articles on workplace racial bias, 1936–2000

of market models, sociologists nonetheless sought to show that racial disparities in occupational status and earnings could not be fully reduced to differences between advantaged and disadvantaged groups in schooling, job experience, and other kinds of human capital. Instead, they emphasized the "dual" or "segmented" nature of labor markets that posed structural barriers to racial parity in career outcomes (e.g., Beck, Horan, and Tolbert, 1980; Kalleberg, Wallace, and Althauser, 1981; Hodson and Kaufman, 1982; Kaufman, 1986; Semyonov, 1988). Although stratification researchers were often skeptical of economists' assumptions about rational, goal-directed, maximizing behavior, they took little notice of research by psychologists on stereotypes, in-group favoritism, conformity, and related cognitive processes that might be linked to workplace bias.[1]

---

[1] A notable exception is Kanter's (1977) research on the dynamics of tokenism in the workplace. Kanter's theory, consistent with psychological research on stereotyping, is based on the notion that tokens – e.g., the sole woman or person of color in a work setting – are perceived and evaluated by supervisors and coworkers based on their social category (gender or race) and not according to personal qualities and contributions. Although Kanter's work is widely cited in sociological studies of racial and gender inequality, it has been used by sociologists primarily as a structural theory about the consequences of relative numbers, not as a way to understand the social psychological mechanisms implicated in workplace discrimination. Similarly, sociologists invoke the

The "new structuralism" of the 1980s gave rise to a focus on specific features of workplaces that shape socioeconomic inequality (Baron, Davis-Blake, and Bielby, 1986; DiPrete and Soule, 1986; Podolny and Baron, 1997; Fernandez and Weinberg, 1997; Bielby and Bielby, 1999; Kalleberg, Reskin, and Hudson, 2000) and disparities in career outcomes by race and gender (Baron and Newman, 1990; Barnett, Baron, and Stewart, 2000; Zwerling and Silver, 2002). By the 1990s, sociologists working in this tradition were much more accepting of economists' perspectives, especially in the application of market concepts and models to understanding how organizational arrangements provide efficient solutions to issues relating to information uncertainty, ambiguity, risk, and trust (Baron and Pfeffer, 1994; Lie, 1997; Menger, 1999; Kalleberg, 2000; Fountain, 2005). In any case, from the 1970s through the 1990s, sociological scholarship on social inequality and on workplace disparities by race, ethnicity, and gender developed largely in isolation from the explosive growth in psychological research on stereotyping and cognitive bias. Keeping an eye on and reacting to economists' claims about having a more complete account of workplace disparities by gender and race, sociologists almost missed the "cognitive turn" illuminated by psychological research on the cognitive basis for unequal treatment.

While structuralist sociologists, both new and old, tended to ignore the cognitive, normative, or "softer" sources of workplace inequality, that was not true of the "new institutionalists," who developed an important line of research in the 1990s on organizational responses to EEO laws and regulations. Unlike the structuralists, who focused on how workplace structures and policies differentially shaped the actual career trajectories of majority and minority groups, these scholars studied how such arrangements were used to signal to external constituencies, especially the courts and government regulators, that the organization was taking an appropriate stance towards its EEO obligations (Edelman, 1990; 1992; Edelman *et al.*, 1991; Sutton *et al.*, 1994; Edelman and Petterson, 1999; Bisom-Rapp, 1999). They showed that once structures such as grievance procedures, affirmative action offices, and formal promotion systems become widely adopted, they

concept of stereotyping to understand the rationale for "statistical discrimination" (hiring and assigning jobs based on assumptions about group attributes rather than individual qualifications and interests), but they rarely study workplace stereotyping as a cognitive process (Bielby and Baron, 1986).

become taken-for-granted, imbued with symbolic meaning, and accepted as rational and appropriate by constituencies both inside and outside the organization (Edelman *et al.*, 1991; Edelman, Uggen, and Erlanger, 1999; Dobbin *et al.*, 1993; Edelman, Fuller, and Mara-Ditra, 2001). Moreover, the presence of such structures comes to be viewed as evidence of EEO compliance by the courts, further reinforcing their widespread adoption, regardless of (or even in spite of) their actual impact on reducing bias and enhancing diversity (Edelman, Erlanger, and Lande, 1993; Edelman, 2005; Kalev, Dobbin, and Kelley, 2005).

The "cognitive turn" – incorporating recent work by psychologists on stereotyping and cognitive bias – finally came to sociology in the new millennium, largely through the writings of Barbara Reskin. In an important article published in 2000, Reskin argued that sociological approaches to workplace bias, which emphasize the impact of workplace structures on personnel outcomes, had ignored *how* the many routine personnel decisions about hiring, job assignment, training, promotion, and compensation made daily in organizations are done in such a way as to disadvantage women and persons of color (Reskin, 2000). She argued that cognitive social psychologists' research on automatic or implicit bias against minorities and women provides unique insights into the proximate causes of workplace discrimination which mediate the impact of organizational structures, policies, and practices. Noting that cognitive biases "occur independently of decision-makers' group interests or their conscious desire to favor or harm others," Reskin recommended that sociologists should direct their research efforts to enhance our understanding of how workplace policies and practices facilitate or minimize the impact of these cognitive processes on personnel decisions (Reskin, 2000, pp. 320–323; also see Bielby, 2000; Reskin, 2003).

The "cognitive turn" in sociology came none to soon. In the past few years psychologists' important and ever-expanding work on implicit, subconscious, or "hidden" bias has been embraced by human resource professionals (Babcock, 2006; Stockdale and Crosby, 2003), attorneys (Harris and Boddy, 2004; Dichter and Burkhardt, 2005); and by legal scholars and the courts (Krieger, 1995; Kang, 2005; Lee, 2005; Bielby, 2005; Hart, 2004, 2005; *Dukes* v. *Wal-Mart Stores Inc.*, 2004), and it is increasingly the focus of attention and scrutiny from the press and electronic media (Orey, 2006; Wax and Tetlock, 2005; Lehrman,

2006; Bower, 2006; Scheck, 2004). Articles such as "Detecting hidden bias: you may not see it, but it's probably lurking among your managers – and perhaps even in you," which appeared in the Society for Human Resource Development's *HR Magazine* (Babcock, 2006), summarize the scientific research on cognitive bias, alert companies to the ways it is manifested in the workplace, and offer interventions for minimizing its impact. In a related genre, law firms that represent employers in discrimination litigation note the potential legal liability due to the impact of hidden bias and suggest policies and practices that are claimed to reduce vulnerability to expensive lawsuits, as in the article appearing in Morrison and Foerster's online newsletter, "Sex discrimination and merit-based compensation: is your system at risk?" (Harris and Boddy, 2004). And for companies that find themselves already in litigation over claims of unconscious bias, attorneys who represent employers are promoting in firm newsletters, webpages, and legal workshops increasingly sophisticated attacks on social science experts. For example, attorneys from Morgan, Lewis and Bockius recently gave a presentation titled "Class certification after Wal-Mart" which included the subsection, "the subjective decision making theory and expert stereotype testimony in class cases: how to attack" (Dichter and Burkhardt, 2005). With social science expert testimony on stereotypes and implicit bias increasingly common in class action discrimination lawsuits, that body of scholarship is now embedded in case law, and legal scholars have begun to analyze both how it is shaping litigation dynamics and how legal doctrine might be reformed to be more consistent with new understandings of the cognitive bases of discrimination (Krieger, 1995; Hart, 2005).

Besides following Reskin's lead and incorporating theory and research on cognitive bias into our own scientific work on workplace bias, sociologists can and should play an important role in explaining to constituencies outside the discipline how and why the social, institutional, and organizational context matters if we are to fully understand how stereotyping and related cognitive processes are implicated in workplace discrimination. Rejecting this role poses four significant risks. First, it reinforces the perception that discrimination occurs simply because of individuals' personal shortcomings, i.e., their inability to overcome the automatic tendency to make categorical judgments based on race or gender, regardless of social context. Second, as a result, it invites reform proposals that focus exclusively on individual and interpersonal processes – training to make people aware of stereotypes, programs to enhance interdependence and teamwork, etc. (see Babcock, 2006). Third, by highlighting automatic or unconscious processes at the level of individual cognition, it avoids addressing the ways organizations act to structure decision-making contexts so that cognitive biases are allowed to affect personnel decisions. Fourth, it avoids addressing the responsibility organizations have for taking steps to ensure that the impact of cognitive bias is minimized and analyzing the effectiveness of any efforts an organization takes along those lines. Sociologists have much to contribute in each of these areas, based on decades of research on the organizational and institutional contexts of workplace bias, but too often our attention is focused narrowly on specific hypotheses defined by the subfields in which we work and not on the implications of our work for those who care about addressing workplace bias and diversity in the "real world." It is indeed ironic that psychologists, who are generally much more oriented towards the "ivory tower" and inclined to avoid being drawn into debates about the social implications of their scientific research, have come to dominate public discourse about workplace bias.

Accordingly, the review that I present here aims to redress this imbalance, at least in part. My primary goal is to explain how work by organizational sociologists and by management studies scholars informs our understanding of workplace racial bias and the challenges of and opportunities for promoting racial diversity at work. In contrast to scholarship on gender and work, the sociological research on workplace racial bias has been less widely reviewed and receives much less attention, apart from studies of urban poverty and low-wage jobs. Thus, while much of what I review applies equally to gender issues in the workplace, a secondary goal of mine is to increase the visibility of sociological work that informs understanding of racial bias and racial diversity in employment.

While I summarize research on stereotypes and cognitive bias, I do so only briefly, since my focus is on the context that shapes how those social psychological processes influence workplace outcomes, not the processes themselves. The scholarship on stereotypes and cognitive bias has been reviewed expertly and thoroughly by Fiske and Lee in chapter 2 of this volume. Besides reviewing the work of sociologists relevant to workplace racial bias and diversity, I review in some detail studies on bias in performance assessment systems, mostly by industrial psychologists, since it too has a focus on systemic features of organizational systems that shape how cognitive bias is manifested in the workplace. A theme I want to emphasize is that scientific literature produced by organizational sociologists, social psychologists, and management scholars provides scientifically valid and practically useful information about how organizational policies and practices create and sustain barriers to equal employment opportunity for persons of color and about the kinds of policies and practices that promote racial diversity in the workplace.

I also cite liberally to professional literature from the fields of human resources and diversity management, highlighting similarities and differences between practitioners' and social scientists' understandings of the sources of workplace racial bias and the kinds of policies and practices that minimize it. Where similarities exist, it is often because the work of organizational professionals charged with addressing equal employment opportunity in the "real world" generates practical knowledge consistent with the findings of social scientists, although practitioners are increasingly turning to the work of social scientists for insights (e.g., Babcock, 2006). At the same time, it is important to understand that parishioners orient to organizational goals and professional agendas that place multiple and conflicting demands on them, often leading to a focus on symbol rather than substance in the area of EEO and racial bias (Edelman *et al.*, 1991; Edelman, 1992; Bisom-Rapp, 1999). Sustained, systematic, peer-reviewed scientific analysis of issues related to workplace racial bias and diversity by scholars who are free from such concerns generates knowledge which is mostly unaffected by those demands and both helps inform the work of practitioners and place it in perspective.

The research I rely upon and cite here has applied multiple methodologies in a variety of contexts, including experiments in controlled laboratory settings; ethnographies and case studies in "real world" organizations both large and small, public and private, and in a range of industries; surveys done with representative samples of workers and employers; and historical studies based on archival materials from the United States and abroad. I believe that the scientific evidence about bias, discrimination, and the structure and dynamics of race in organizations has substantial external validity and provides a sound basis for understanding the sources of subtle racial bias in the workplace and how to minimize it.

I focus on the kinds of "subtle" bias one finds in contemporary workplaces – bias that is sometimes unconscious at the level of individual action, often unintended at the organizational level, and more often than not unexamined by those who formulate, implement, and oversee an organization's human resources system. I am not addressing blatant, racially motivated bias that results in a company never hiring or always favoring white employees over equally qualified minorities. I am not denying that such blatant racism exists in contemporary work settings, with real consequences for those who are subject to it. That kind of racism is relatively easy to detect in the workplace, and the organizational and legal interventions for effectively responding to it are relatively straightforward. In contrast, when it comes to subtle forms of racial bias and barriers to equal employment opportunity, there is a greater gap between social science knowledge and organizational practice. However, that gap has closed in recent years, although the relevant social science expertise comes from different disciplines and across a range of subfields. The review below aims to provide an integrated overview of that diverse work in order to make it more accessible to both human resources practitioners and scholars.

"Subtle bias" in organizational context: How discretionary and subjective practices allow stereotypes and bias to affect personnel decisions

Decades of social science research on stereotypes and other forms of cognitive bias show us how barriers to workplace racial diversity become embedded in workplace policies and practices, often in ways that are not often apparent to those who make personnel decisions. While I emphasize here social science research that addresses racial bias in the workplace, I also cite studies addressing gender bias. In addition, research on racial bias in the workplace and remedies for minimizing it usually generalizes to gender bias, and vice versa.

Sources of workplace racial disparities

Depending on the job, organizational setting, and work environment, there are many reasons why whites and non-whites can have different career trajectories. For example, jobs may have job-related skill and experience requirements that differ, on average, by race or ethnicity.

Racial disparities arising from such factors would not be considered discriminatory, so long as the employer is not responsible for differences in qualifications by race (e.g., by not providing equal access to training). Conversely, employers create racial barriers when they make decisions about individuals' suitability for jobs, training, advancement, or compensation based on beliefs about a person's race or favoritism towards their own racial group rather than on an individual's actual qualifications or performance. Employers also create racial barriers when they ignore (or encourage) an organizational climate that is hostile towards members of racial minorities and inhibits them from performing to their full potential.

Stereotypes, bias, and discretion

A large body of social science research shows that personnel decisions such as decisions about hiring, job assignment, promotion selections, performance assessment, and compensation are vulnerable to stereotyping and bias when they are based on the discretionary use of subjective criteria. A stereotype is a set of beliefs that links personal traits of individuals to specific social groups (Gaertner and Dovidio, 2005; Fiske *et al.*, 2002; Dovidio *et al.*, 1996; Mackie *et al.*, 1996; Evans and Tyler, 1986). The association of such traits as "assertive" and "rational" with the category male, "nurturing" and "emotional" with the category female, "violent" and "hostile" with the category African American, and "gang-banger" and "macho" with Latino, are examples of stereotypes. When stereotypes such as these are allowed to influence social judgments, decisions about members of minority groups will be based on general beliefs about the behaviors, traits, and qualities associated with their gender or race/ethnicity instead of the actual traits of the individuals being judged (Dasgupta, 2004; Dovidio and Gaertner, 1993; Devine, 1989; Devine and Elliot, 1995; Brewer and Brown, 1998; Messick and Mackie, 1989; Nieva and Gutek, 1980; Word, Zanna, and Cooper, 1974).

Substantial discretion in assessing and weighing evaluative criteria invites bias. For example, social psychologists Samuel Gaertner and John Dovidio have conducted research showing that when white evaluators have discretion in how to weigh evaluative criteria, they tend to do so selectively, in a way that biases outcomes in favor of white ratees. In one part of their study, participants were told they were assisting a university in making admission decisions, and they were given information on factors such as test scores and high school grades for (hypothetical) African American and white applicants. When applicants were strong on one dimension and weak on the other, raters tended to give the stronger dimension a greater weight for white applicants and the weaker one a greater weight for African American applicants (Hodson, Dovidio, and Gaertner, 2002). In other words, they exercised their discretion in a way that ensured that whites would rank on top. The authors summarize their findings as follows (Gaertner *et al.*, 2005, p. 384):

White college participants (whom, relative to the general population may be regarded as generally moderate to low prejudiced . . .), give White candidates the "benefit of the doubt," a benefit they do not extend to Blacks.

In a study of gender bias with a similar experimental design, Eric Uhlmann and Geoffrey Cohen found that when given discretion on defining and weighing qualifications, evaluators redefined criteria of success so that men were assigned to stereotypically male jobs and females were assigned to stereotypically female jobs (Uhlmann and Cohen, 2005; also see Norton, Vandello, and Darley, 2004). They concluded (p. 474) that "even without ambiguity in applicants' credentials, the criteria used to assess merit can be defined flexibly in a manner congenial to the idiosyncratic strengths of applicants who belong to desired groups." By acting in this way, decision-makers can justify biased decisions by appealing to seemingly "objective" criteria. In their words (p. 479):

Bias in the construction of job criteria allows evaluators both to discriminate and to maintain a personal illusion of objectivity. Although gender stereotypes encourage discrimination, egalitarian norms compel making hiring decisions on the basis of applicants' merit rather than their group membership. These conflicting pressures can be reconciled by defining and redefining merit in a manner that justifies discrimination.

Although theirs is a study of gender bias, Uhlmann and Cohen conclude their study by linking it to the research of Gaertner and Dovidio described above, noting (p. 479) that it "dovetails with work on aversive racism in suggesting that prejudice often expresses itself in rationalizable ways . . ." In sum, this body of research demonstrates that discretion in the definition and weighing of evaluative criteria, even with regard to ostensibly objective criteria, contributes to bias, and it often does so in a way that allows decision makers to justify to themselves and to others that their actions are fair and nondiscriminatory.

Racial bias in performance assessment

There is ample reason to closely scrutinize any performance review system for potential racial bias. A large body of social science research, including many studies conducted in organizational settings, shows that African Americans tend to receive lower performance evaluations than do whites. For example, a 1985 article by Kraiger and Ford performed a meta-analysis of 84 studies with a total of over 20,000 ratees, including 64 field studies and 10 experimental studies of white raters rating a total of 17,159 African American and white ratees (Kraiger and Ford, 1985). Meta-analysis is a method for quantitatively aggregating results across studies in order to obtain a more precise estimate of the size and reliability of effects than can be obtained from any single study (Hunter and Schmidt, 1990). In addition, a meta-analysis of studies conducted across a variety of settings contributes to establishing the external validity of the research. Kraiger and Ford's meta-analysis found that African Americans, on average, received significantly lower evaluations than did whites. They also found evidence suggesting that white raters give significantly higher ratings to whites than do African Americans; and that African American raters give significantly higher ratings to African Americans than do whites.

A subsequent meta-analysis replicates Ford *et al.*'s finding regarding racial differences in performance measures (Martocchio and Whitener, 1992). The Martocchio and Whitener meta-analysis focused specifically on field studies of performance assessment conducted in private sector firms. The results of their analysis of ten field studies also indicated that race effects were larger on subjective than on objective measures of performance. In an article published in 2003, Roth *et al.* replicated Kraiger and Ford's research on a larger sample of studies, and they found that overall, racial differences in performance ratings between African Americans and whites were comparable to those in the 1985 meta-analysis (Roth, Huffcutt, and Bobko, 2003). However, unlike earlier studies, they found that racial disparities on objective assessments could be as large or larger than those for subjective assessments. The Roth *et al.* research is also the first large-scale meta-analysis of disparities between whites and Hispanics, and they found that Hispanics tend to be rated lower than whites, although the disparities are generally not as large as those between African Americans and whites.

Numerous other studies conducted in organizational settings and published in leading refereed journals report similar findings or racial disparities in performance ratings. For example, Jeffrey Greenhaus and colleagues studied the career experiences of a matched sample of 373 African American and 455 white managers in three companies in the communications, banking, and electronics industry (Greenhaus, Parasuraman, and Wormley, 1990; Greenhaus and Parasuraman, 1993). The African American and white managers included in their study were similar in age, organizational tenure, job function, and organizational level. Their 1990 article in the *Academy of Management Journal* reports (p. 79) that supervisors rate the performance and promotion potential of African American managers significantly lower than whites, findings the authors describe as "remarkably consistent with the results of Kraiger and Ford's (1985) meta analysis." Compared to white managers, African American managers scored lower on a scale of "corporate fit," expressing higher levels of isolation and lower levels of acceptance within the organization. African American managers reported lower career satisfaction and were more likely to report that there careers had reached a plateau, compared to white managers with similar performance evaluations. The 1993 article explored the attributions supervisors made about the reasons for the successful performance of African American and white managers. Their findings were consistent with laboratory studies on this topic: compared to white managers, successful performance by African American managers was less likely to be attributed to ability or effort and more likely to be attributed to help from others (Greenhaus and Parasuraman, 1993, pp. 285–288).[2]

The findings of Greenhaus *et al.* regarding race differences in assessment of promotion potential were replicated in a study by Jacqueline Landau of 682 managerial and professional employees of a Fortune 500 company who had been rated at least "above average" in performance (Landau, 1995). Her study examined the impact of race on

---

[2] For experimental evidence of race bias in attributions of the causes of successful performance, see Yarkin, Town, and Wallston (1982).

supervisors' assessments of promotion potential as recorded in company records from the annual performance appraisal process. Landau found that African American managers and professionals were rated lower in promotion potential than whites of comparable age, education, organizational tenure, salary grade, job type, and satisfaction with career support.

Other studies and reviews suggest that in many organizational settings, performance reviews by supervisors are not subject to racial bias. For example, in a 1994 review article in the *Annual Review of Psychology*, Frank Landy and colleagues (Landy, Shankster, and Kohler) state (pp. 282–283) that "the field has been moving inexorably toward the final conclusion that *well-developed rating procedures accompanied by training of the raters* will produce ratings that are minimally biased by demographic characteristics of raters or ratees" (emphasis added). In a book published that same year, Latham and Wexley (1994) assert that "*when the appraiser uses behaviorally based appraisal scales*, ratee characteristics, such as age, race, and sex, have a negligible effect on the resulting performance appraisal" (emphasis added). The conclusions of Landy *et al.* and of Latham and Wexley are not inconsistent with the research cited above. It is indeed the case that appropriately designed performance appraisal systems, carefully implemented and monitored, can be free of bias, a topic I return to below.

A recent study argues that the widely-cited article by Sackett and DuBois, sometimes cited as evidence of minimal bias in supervisors' ratings of performance (Sackett and DuBois, 1991), has been misinterpreted by many scholars (Stauffer and Buckley, 2005). The 1991 article has received considerable attention because it is a relatively large-scale study based on supervisor ratings in "real world" settings, both civilian and military. In their reexamination of the results, Stauffer and Buckley note that the findings demonstrate convincingly that African American and white supervisors give similar ratings to white employees, but African American employees receive substantially lower ratings from white supervisors.[3]

---

[3] The Sackett and DuBois study, based on both civilian and military data, is a "repeated measure" design, where each ratee was rated by multiple supervisors, both white and African American. Since both white and African American supervisors were rating the same individuals, it is possible to isolate the impact of supervisor's race, independent of race differences in the performance of the ratees.

The studies of racial disparities in assessments of performance and promotion potential are consistent with theory and research on in-group favoritism and outgroup bias. In settings where persons of color are a small minority (e.g., less than 15% of those being evaluated), outgroup bias is likely to influence evaluative judgments made by members of the white majority (Dasgupta, 2004; Brewer and Brown, 1998; Jackson, Thoits, and Taylor, 1995; Kramer, 1991). Negative performance by members of the outgroup are attributed to internal dispositions (e.g., a lack of ability or talent), while positive performance is attributed to situational factors such as assistance from others or luck.[4] In organizational settings, members of the minority group tend to receive less desirable job assignments because of low expectations, and they are also likely to receive unreliable and unrealistic feedback about their performance (McGuire, 2002).[5]

Other studies done in workplace settings document the barriers to effective mentorship and support faced by minority employees in predominately white companies. Cox and Nkomo (1991) report analyses of the early career experiences of a sample of 273 African American and 456 white graduates of MBA programs. Most received their degrees from top 20 business schools in the United States. African Americans reported receiving less support from mentors than did whites of comparable age and experience, with comparable performance ratings, and who were working in organizations of similar size. Cox and Nkomo also report evidence of greater isolation among the African American MBAs, who reported lower levels of job involvement and lower career satisfaction than whites. In a related study of graduates of MBA programs, Dreher and Cox (1996) found that compared to whites, African Americans and Hispanics were less likely to establish mentor relationships with white men and that the disparity in mentorship contributed to the racial gap in salaries. Thomas (1990) analyzed the quality of mentorship received by 88 African American and 109 white managers in a large public utility company. He found that compared to cross-race mentorship relationships, same-race relationships provided African American managers with significantly more

---

[4] For a review of research on this phenomenon, known as the "ultimate attribution error," see M. Hewstone (1990). Also see reviews of outgroup bias by Brewer and Kramer (1985), Messick and Mackie (1989), and Ostrom and Sedikides (1992).

[5] The early experimental and field studies of these phenomena are summarized in Pettigrew and Martin (1987, pp. 55–60).

"psychosocial support," i.e., direction and guidance, affirmation of ideas, role modeling, and mutuality and trust (also see Dreher and Cox, 1996). In a study of white and African American managers in a financial services company, James (2000) found that African Americans were promoted at a slower rate than whites with comparable education and training and that they received less psychosocial support, were more isolated, and benefited less from company training than their white counterparts.

These studies are consistent with the findings of prior research on the experience of African American managers in predominately white organizations. Fernandez's study of 4,202 managers, including over 900 African American managers, employed in ten large companies reports that a majority of African American managers perceive that whites exclude minority managers from informal work groups (Fernandez, 1981). Moreover, over a third of upper-level white male managers agreed with that assessment. Regina Nixon's study of 303 African American managers in middle and upper management in large corporations found that a majority perceive themselves as either alienated from, or marginal to, the formal and informal networks of corporate life (Nixon, 1985a). Nixon also found that a lack of mentorship was one of the most important factors contributing to this perception and to the perception of blocked promotion opportunities (Nixon, 1985a, 1985b). Research on middle managers in a Fortune 500 firm showed that "high potential" minorities tend to have less access to informed and influential others and to be isolated from corporate informal social networks (Ibarra, 1995).

Subtle bias in hiring: Referrals and other informal recruitment methods

A large body of research, using both quantitative and qualitative approaches, conducted in a wide range of industries and occupations, shows that referrals, word of mouth, and similar informal recruitment mechanisms perpetuate the existing racial composition of a workforce and creates barriers for African Americans' entry into white-dominated jobs (Hyde, 2006; Mouw, 2002; Moss and Tilley, 2001; Elliott, 2001; Kasinitz and Rosenberg, 1996; Kirschenman, Moss, and Tilley, 1995; Kirschenman and Neckerman, 1991; Holzer, 1987a; 1987b). For example, in a recent study of labor markets in four large cities, demographer Mouw (2002) found that the use of employee referrals rather than more formal recruitment methods reduced the probability of African Americans being hired in predominately white companies by 74%. The discriminatory impact of word of mouth and other informal referral methods documented in social science studies is also addressed in publications written by and for human resources professionals who devise and implement hiring and EEO policies (Buhler, 2002; Sims, 2002; Block, 1994; Arvey and Faley, 1992; Martin, 1991; LoPresto, 1986).

Minimizing workplace bias

Organizational policies and practices that create barriers to career advancement for women and minorities, once in place, become institutionalized and rarely change in the absence of any substantial change in a firm's business, technical, or legal environment (Stinchcombe, 1965; Hannan and Freeman, 1984; Baron, 1991; Stainback, Robinson, and Tomaskovic-Devey, 2005).[6] However, discrimination in the workplace is by no means inevitable, and social science research shows what kinds of policies and practices effectively minimize bias.

Research studies show that the effects of stereotypes, in-group favoritism and out-group bias on evaluative judgments such as those involved in recruitment, hiring, job assignment, compensation, promotion, and assessments of skills and qualifications can be minimized when decision-makers know that they will be held accountable for the process and criteria used to make decisions, for the accuracy of the information upon which the decisions are based, and for the consequences their actions have for equal employment opportunity. Converging evidence comes from organizational research done by sociologists and management scholars (Kalev, Dobbin and Kelley, 2006; Konrad and Linnehan, 1995; Schreiber, Price, and Morrison, 1993), experimental and field studies done by social psychologists (Uhlmann and Cohen, 2005; Ford *et al.*, 2004; Reskin, 2003; Fiske,

---

[6] The concept of organizational inertia has been applied in scientific studies conducted in a wide range of industrial settings. For reviews, see Kaplan and Henderson (2005) and Gresov, Haveman, and Oliva (1993). For applications of the concept of inertia to a range of organizational issues, see Roggema and Smith (1983), Abrahamson and Fombrun (1994), Gardenswartz and Rowe (1994), Fairhurst, Green, and Courtright (1995), Doucouliagos (1996), and Ruef (1997).

Lin, and Neuberg, 1999; Nelson, Acker, and Manis, 1996; Eberhardt and Fiske, 1996; Pettigrew and Martin, 1987; Salancik and Pfeffer, 1978; Tetlock, 1985; 1992; Tetlock and Kim, 1987), and the lessons learned from research on accountability and bias have been incorporated into "best practices" recommended by human resources professionals (e.g., Aronson, 2002; Gatewood and Field, 2001; Heneman and Judge, 2003; Hubbard 2003).

Formal written policies alone are not sufficient to minimize bias in personnel decisions. Passive organizational approaches to the prevention of harassment and discrimination that rely primarily on posters and policy statements and that take action only after an incident is brought to the attention of management are largely ineffective. A written antidiscrimination policy that is simply reactive and lacks effective accountability is vulnerable to bias against women and minorities. Often, such a system is simply a symbolic exercise in "going through the motions," with little substantive impact on creating organizational policy and practice that is free of bias (Edelman, 1992; Edelman *et al.*, 1991; Edelman, Erlanger, and Lande, 1993; Edelman and Petterson, 1999; Leonard, 1989; Leonard, 1994). Sociologist and legal scholar Lauren Edelman, the leading expert on this topic, summarizes the findings of fifteen years of research on organizational responses to EEO as follows (Edelman, 2005, pp. 345–346):

Because it is generally the form rather than the substance of compliance that attains an institutionalized status, there is variation in how enthusiastically management, as well as the personnel who staff compliance structures, embraces legal ideals. In some cases, structures have both symbolic and substantive significance – their form signals attention to legal ideals and they operate to enhance the workplace status and conditions of legally protected employees. In other cases, however, the structures fit the law in form but lack substantive effect. Organizations may strategically seek to create compliance structures merely as symbolic gestures by "decoupling" those structures from core organizational activities. Organizations may, for example, create affirmative action officer positions but give the officer little or no autonomy or authority or create grievance procedures that are hard to access and known to provide little relief.[7]

---

[7] Also see Krawiec (2003), and on the general issue of decoupling of organizational functions, see Orton and Weick (1990).

lesigning systems to minimize workplace racial bias and promote
;ity, sorting out symbol from substance is a formidable but not
...,ssible task. Drawing on recent work by both social scientists and
human resources professionals, it is possible to provide a roadmap for
reaching this goal. The specific recommendations for EEO accountability and monitoring advocated in the paragraphs that follow are
formulated to address the kind of subtle or "hidden" bias described in
the scientific literature summarized above. They are also formulated
with the recognition that organizations can and should make symbolic
efforts to reassure internal and external constituencies that the policies
and practices in place to address EEO and promote diversity are
appropriate and legitimate. At the same time, building on the scientific
research that helps us understand how EEO efforts can become
decoupled from day-to-day human resources decision making, the
recommendations have been designed to avoid "going through the
motions" and to ensure that the symbol and substance of organizational policy and practice operate together to effectively minimize bias
and promote diversity.

The most effective approaches to minimizing bias rely on proactive
policies and practices, with adequate monitoring and accountability
(Kalev, Dobbin, and Kelley, 2006; Reskin, 2003, pp. 12–13; Sturm,
2001; Bielby, 2000). There are four key elements to effective EEO
policy. The first, *managerial EEO accountability*, begins with recurring and mandatory training of managers and supervisors regarding
their duties and responsibilities relating to equal employment opportunity. Nearly all medium- to large-scale organizations have a written
antidiscrimination policy, and many have a written policy stating that
implementing the objectives of the Affirmative Action Plan is the
responsibility of every employee. However, such policies are merely
symbolic unless they also delineate explicit duties and responsibilities
relating to equal opportunity in each manager's or supervisor's job
description. Effective managerial EEO accountability requires explicit
evaluation of managers and supervisors on their contributions to the
organization's equal opportunity goals. This evaluation should be
incorporated into specific evaluative dimensions in the performance
reviews of those employees and tied in a significant way to the supervisor's or manager's compensation (Aronson, 2002; Kennedy, 2000).
In short, in the area of EEO as well as other aspects of human resources,
"what gets measured gets done" (Giovannini, 2004; Kerr, 1975).

The second, *HR process accountability*, starts with recurring and mandatory training of managers and supervisors regarding their duties and responsibilities as specified in the organization's written policies for making decisions about hiring, job assignment, promotion, compensation, and the like (Aronson, 2002; Bielby, 2000). Key here is the establishment of specific, job-relevant guidelines for the factors and weighting to be used in making these decisions. To assess the effectiveness of training for HR process accountability, the decision-making process for personnel decisions should be audited regularly to ensure that managers and supervisors are carrying out their duties in a manner that is consistent with their training and with the organization's written policies. And again, the compensation of those who make personnel decisions should be linked in a significant way to assessments of their performance in the area of HR processes.

The third element is *organizational EEO assessment*: periodic monitoring and analysis of disparities by race and gender in job assignments, pay, promotion, performance assessment, and turnover as a routine part of an organization's personnel system. Such monitoring assesses whether disparities are greater than what plausibly might be expected based on differences in job-related knowledge, skills, abilities, and interests and other job-related factors that influence an employee's contributions to the organization.[8] While the mere existence of disparities should not be taken as evidence of discriminatory barriers, they are often the most efficient way to identify which aspects of the company's personnel system warrant closer scrutiny (Aronson, 2002; Bielby, 2000; Kennedy, 2000; Stites, 2005; US Department of Labor, 2006).

The fourth is *workplace climate assessment*: systematic analysis of feedback from employees about perceptions of barriers to and opportunities for career advancement. This kind of monitoring of trends in employees' perceptions can be used to identify subtle forms of bias and

---

[8] Organizations with Affirmative Action Plans usually do something like this under the rubric of "availability and utilization analyses," but often such analyses are generic reports generated by off-the-shelf programs with little real connection to a company's overall personnel system. Effective monitoring is not based on the generic formulae and broad occupational categories typically used in Affirmative Action Plans, but instead relies on actual job transitions and is based on the same information used by those who make decisions about hiring, job assignment, training, performance evaluation, promotion, compensation, and the like.

related problems not immediately apparent from analyses of more objective workforce data. Also part of workplace climate assessment is periodic and systematic monitoring of the organization's complaint and discipline procedures to ensure that they are accessible and responsive, that investigations are thorough and well documented, and that responses are timely and consistent whenever it has been determined that illegal discrimination or harassment has taken place (Oppenheimer, 2004; Buhler, 1999; Relyea, 1999; Kobata, 1995; Gregg, 1992).[9] Such monitoring should include analysis of racial and gender disparities in the rates of complaints, types of complaints, and outcomes of investigations. Aggregate statistical analysis over time is essential, because in individual cases discriminatory treatment is not always perceived as such by the person who alleges that she or he was treated unfairly, and when discrimination is perceived, organizations often redefine the complaint as a personal dispute between an employee and supervisor or as a claim of improper treatment having nothing to do with equal employment opportunity. Thus statistical analysis of complaints and discipline that show a pattern by race or gender can provide an early indication of potential discriminatory barriers that are not apparent in a review of the documentary record of from cases (Lengnick-Hall, 1992; Jossem, 1991).

Implementing the four elements of effective EEO policy requires commitment and leadership from senior management that goes beyond pronouncements and policy statements to include structuring the EEO function to be a tightly-coupled component of the organization's human resources system. Those charged with designing, implementing, and monitoring policy and practice pertaining to decisions about hiring, job assignment, compensation, promotion, and the like must have the authority and resources to deliver on the promise of equal employment opportunity, and their work must flow directly from and feed back into the organization's overall goals and strategy.

---

[9] Also see resources for human resource professionals at the Society for Human Resource Management's Knowledge Center, including *Sample Human Resource on Investigating Workplace Conduct*, www.shrm.org/hrtools/policies_published/ CMS_000550.asp, and *Anti-Harassment Policy and Complaint Procedure*, www.shrm.org/hrtools/policies_published/CMS_000534.asp (retrieved February 9, 2006).

Directions for the future: Bringing the firms back in

In 1999, I was asked by the editors of *Contemporary Sociology* to be a contributor for a special issue of "utopian essays" that would explain how sociological research would address important social problems – poverty, residential segregation, interpersonal violence, ethnic conflict, and so on – if only someone would listen to our advice and follow it. My assignment was to write about "how to minimize workplace gender and ethnic bias," and in it I argued that this need not be a utopian project, since we had a good handle on how bias gets created and sustained, and that the same research, "either directly or by implication, indicates the kinds of workplace policies and practices that are likely to minimize bias" (Bielby, 2000, p. 121). The "by implication" part of that statement meant that we often have to draw inferences or "connect the dots" between, for example, what we learn about social cognition from laboratory studies, about the dynamics of tokenism from workplace ethnographies, and about the impact of formalization of human resource practices from organizational surveys. No single study can or should attempt to explore all of these mechanisms relating to subtle bias with a single methodology and set of conceptual tools. In the six years since my essay was published, we've gained considerable new knowledge, which I've cited here (approximately one-third of the works cited in this chapter have been published since 2000), and again, appropriately, it comes from a range of disciplines, using multiple methodologies in a variety of settings.

In recommendations for the future, it is always fashionable to call for more interdisciplinary research that incorporates insights from the theories, concepts, methodologies, and findings of different subfields and disciplines. Such a recommendation would seem to follow naturally here, given the range of scholarship covered in this chapter, from labor economics to organizational sociology to cognitive psychology. However, it is important to acknowledge that social science advances through research programs with theories, methods, and research questions defined by and evaluated within specialized subfields. The important insights about "hidden bias" due to stereotyping, so relevant to contemporary discussions about subtle workplace discrimination, comes out of rigorous and highly technical work in a relatively narrow subfield of cognitive psychology. Many of the contributors to that body of scholarship are much more interested in how the brain functions than in how workplaces generate or minimize bias, yet the results of their research are undeniably important for the latter issue. Similarly, many of those who developed the important sociological scholarship on organizations' symbolic responses to their EEO environments were motivated primarily by an interest in the normative and mythic dimensions of organizational life, not by an interest in discrimination and diversity. Pairing up cognitive psychologists with institutionalist sociologists in most instances will not lead to a productive collaboration, since it is unlikely that scholars with such disparate approaches to behavioral and social science will find much common ground when it comes to the technical details of developing concepts, models, measures, and methods of analysis.

On the other hand, mutual awareness and dialogue among scholars working in different subfields and disciplines has proven to be very productive in generating practical knowledge about how our research is (and is not) relevant to issues of workplace bias and diversity. Indeed, the explosion of interest among social scientists in how cognitive bias and stereotyping affects workplace discrimination has its genesis in inter-disciplinary conferences and forums organized by legal scholars. In the fall of 2003, Joan Williams, at that time on the faculty of American University's Washington College of Law, organized the Cognitive Bias Working Group, which brought together organizational sociologists, cognitive psychologists, legal scholars, and litigators to discuss recent research on cognitive bias and its application to workplace gender discrimination, especially against working mothers and other care-givers. The meetings of the group provided the first in-depth exposure to research on implicit bias for most of the non-psychologists, and their comments assisted the cognitive psychologists in designing studies from within their paradigm to address specifically unconscious bias against caregivers (Williams, 2003). The following year, the American Bar Foundation and Stanford Law School sponsored a three-day conference bringing together sociologists, economists, psychologists, legal scholars, and litigators for research presentations and an exchange of ideas on "legal and social scientific approaches to employment discrimination." Research papers published in the conference volume (Nelson and Neilson, 2005) represent each of the social science traditions discussed in this review. While each contribution is firmly grounded in the author's subfield, they all contribute in significant ways to scholarship on workplace bias. Most recently, the American

Bar Foundation, Ford Foundation, and Center for Advanced Study in the Behavioral Sciences have supported meetings of a group of inter-disciplinary scholars on the topic of "Social Scientific Perspectives on Employment Discrimination in Organizations" (SSPEDO). The SSPEDO group, coordinated by Lauren Edelman of UC Berkeley's Center for the Study of Law and Society, includes organizational sociologists, cognitive psychologists, management studies scholars, and legal scholars who meet semi-annually to discuss ongoing research projects and to receive feedback on ideas for future research. This kind of focused dialogue among scholars working on a similar topic area but from markedly different research traditions seems to be an extremely effective way of identifying common themes in our work and its impli-cations for workplace discrimination in the "real world." It also nurtures collaboration that develops organically out of an interchange of ideas among scholars with overlapping interests relating to work-place bias, which is most likely more effective than programmatic directives from funding agencies or "calls for future research" in review articles like this one. A reasonable prognosis for the next decade is that disciplinary-based social science research that helps us understand the forces that sustain and minimize subtle workplace bias is likely to continue at an accelerated pace, but with even more awareness among scholars working from different perspectives about both the common and complementary themes in our work and their implication for organizational policy and practice designed to enhance workplace equal employment opportunity and diversity.

References

Abrahamson, E., and Fombrun, C. J. (1994). Macrocultures: Determinants and consequences. *Academy of Management Review*, *19*, 728–755.

Aronson, D. (2002). Managing the diversity revolution: Best practices for 21st century business. *Civil Rights Journal*, 6 (Winter 2002), 46–71.

Arvey, R. D., and Faley, R. J. (1992). *Fairness in Selecting Employees*, 3rd edn. New York: Addison-Wesley.

Babcock, P. (2006) Detecting hidden bias. *HR Magazine*, *51* (February).

Barnett, W. P., Baron, J. N., and Stuart, T. E. (2000). Avenues of attainment: Occupational demography and organizational careers in the California Civil Service. *American Journal of Sociology*, *106*, 88–144.

Baron, J. N. (1991). Organizational evidence of ascription in labor markets. In R. Cornwall and P. Wunnava (eds.), *New Approaches to Economic and Social Analyses of Discrimination* (pp. 113–143). Westport: Praeger.

Baron, J. N., Blake-Davis, A., and Bielby, W. T. (1986). The structure of opportunity: How promotion ladders vary within and among organizations. *Administrative Science Quarterly*, 31, 248–273.

Baron, J. N., and Newman, A. E. (1990). For what it's worth: Organizations, occupations, and the value of work done by women and nonwhites. *American Sociological Review*, 55, 155–175.

Baron, J. N., and Pfeffer, J. (1994). The social psychology of organizations and inequality. *Social Psychology Quarterly*, 57, 190–209.

Beck, E. M., Horan, P., and Tolbert, C. M. II. (1980). Social stratification in industrial society: Further evidence for a structural alternative. *American Sociological Review*, 45, 712–719.

Bielby, W. T. (2000). Minimizing workplace gender and racial bias, *Contemporary Sociology*, 29, 120–129.

Bielby, W. T. (2005). Applying social research on stereotyping and cognitive bias to employment discrimination litigation: The case of allegations of systematic gender bias at Wal-Mart Stores. In R. L. Nelson and L. B. Neilson (eds.), *Handbook on Employment Discrimination Research: Rights and Realities.* New York: Springer Publishing.

Bielby, W. T., and Baron. J. N. (1986). Men and women at work: Sex segregation and statistical discrimination. *American Journal of Sociology*, 91, 759–799.

Bielby, W. T., and Bielby, D. D. (1999). Organizational mediation of project-based labor markets: Talent agencies and the careers of screenwriters. *American Sociological Review*, 64, 64–85.

Bisom-Rapp, S. (1999). Bulletproofing the workplace: Symbol and substance in employment discrimination law practice. *Florida State University Law Review*, 26, 959–1038.

Blau, P., and Duncan, O. D. (1967). *The American Occupational Structure.* New York: Wiley.

Block, F. (1994). *Antidiscrimination Law and Minority Employment: Recruitment Practices and Regulatory Constraints.* Chicago: University of Chicago Press.

Bower, B. (2006). The bias finders: A test of unconscious attitudes polarizes psychologists. *Science News*, 169, April 22, 2006, 250–252.

Brewer, M. B., and Brown, R. J. (1998). Intergroup relations. In D. T. Gilbert, S. T. Fiske, and G. Lindzey (eds.), *Handbook of Social Psychology*, 2 (4th edn) (pp. 554–594). New York: Oxford University Press.

Brewer, M. B., and Kramer, R. M. (1985). The psychology of intergroup attitudes and behaviors. *Annual Review of Psychology*, 36, 219–243.

Buhler, P. M. (1999). The manager's role in preventing sexual harassment. *Supervision*, 60 (April 1999), 16–18.

Buhler, P. M. (2002). *Streetwise Human Resources Management*. Avon: Adams Media.

Cox, T. H., and Nkomo, S. M. (1991). A race and gender-group analysis of the early career experience of MBAs. *Work and Occupations*, 18, 431–446.

Dasgupta, N. (2004). Implicit ingroup favoritism, outgroup favoritism, and their behavioral manifestations. *Social Justice Research*, 17, 143–169.

Davis, K., and Moore, W. E. (1945). Some principles of stratification. *American Sociological Review*, 10, 242–49.

Devine, P. G. (1989). Stereotypes and prejudice: Their automatic and controlled components. *Journal of Personality and Social Psychology*, 56, 5–18.

Devine, P. G., and Elliot, A. J. (1995). Are racial stereotypes really fading? The Princeton trilogy revisited. *Personality and Social Psychology Bulletin*, 21, 1139–1150.

Dichter, M. S., and Burkhardt, M. S. (2005). Class certification after Wal-Mart: New approaches to challenging rule 23 class certification. Paper presented at the Thirteenth Annual Meeting of the American Employment Law Council, Santa Barbara, CA, October 19–22, 2005.

DiPrete, T. A., and Soule, W. T. (1986). The organization of career lines: Equal employment opportunity and status advancement in a federal bureaucracy. *American Sociological Review*, 51, 295–309.

Dobbin, F. R., Sutton, J. R., Meyer, J. W., and Scott, W. R. 1993. Equal employment opportunity law and the construction of internal labor markets. *American Journal of Sociology*, 99, 396–427.

Doucouliagos, C. (1996). Conformity, replication of design and business niches. *Journal of Economic Behavior and Organization*, 30, 45–62.

Dovidio, J. F., Bringham, J. C., Johnson, B. T., and Gaertner, S. L. (1996). Stereotyping, prejudice, and discrimination: Another look. In C. N. MacRae, C. Stangor, and M. Hewstone (eds.), *Stereotypes and Stereotyping* (pp. 276–319). New York: Guilford Press.

Dovidio, J. F., and Gaertner, S. L. (1993). Stereotypes and evaluative intergroup bias. In D. M. Mackie and D. L. Hamilton (eds.), *Affect, Cognition, and Stereotyping* (pp. 167–193). New York: Academic Press.

Dreher, G. F., and Cox, T. H. (1996). Race, gender, and opportunity: A study of compensation attainment and the establishment of mentoring relationships. *Journal of Applied Psychology*, 81, 297–308.

Dukes v Wal-Mart Stores Inc., 222 F.R.D. 189, 191–92 (N.D. Cal. 2004) (Admitting social science expert testimony based on social framework analysis).

Eberhardt, J. L., and Fiske, S. L. (1996). Motivating individuals to change: What is a target to do? In C. N. MacRae, C. Stangor, and M. Hewstone (eds.), *Stereotypes and Stereotyping* (pp. 369–415). New York: Guilford Press.

Edelman, L. B. (1990). Legal environments and organizational governance: The expansion of due process in the workplace. *American Journal of Sociology*, 95, 1401–1440.

Edelman, L. B. (1992). Legal ambiguity and symbolic structures: Organizational mediation of civil rights law. *American Journal of Sociology*, 97, 1531–1576.

Edelman, L. B. (2005). Law at work: The endogenous construction of civil rights. In R. L. Nelson and L. B. Neilson (eds.), *Handbook on Employment Discrimination Research: Rights and Realities* (pp. 337–353). New York: Springer Publishing.

Edelman, L. B., and Petterson, S. (1999). Symbols and substance in organizational response to civil rights law. *Research in Social Stratification and Mobility*, 17, 107–135.

Edelman, L. B., Erlanger, H. S., and Lande, J. (1993). Employers' handling of discrimination complaints: The transformation of rights in the workplace. *Law and Society Review*, 27, 497–534.

Edelman, L. B., Fuller, S. R., and Mara-Drita, I. (2001). Diversity rhetoric and the managerialization of the law. *American Journal of Sociology*, 106, 1589–1641.

Edelman, L. B., Patterson, S., Chambliss, E., and Erlanger, H. S. (1991). Legal ambiguity and the politics of compliance: Affirmative action officers' dilemma. *Law and Policy*, 13, 1991, 73–97.

Edelman, L. B., Uggen, C., and Erlanger, H. S. (1999). The endogeneity of legal regulation: Grievance procedures as rational myth. *American Journal of Sociology*, 105, 406–454.

Elliott, J. R. (2001). Referral hiring and ethnically homogeneous jobs: How prevalent is the connection and for whom? *Social Science Research*, 30, 401–425.

Evans, N. E., and Tyler, R. B. (1986). Racial stereotypes: The contents of their cognitive representations. *Journal of Experimental Social Psychology*, 22, 22–37.

Fairhurst, G. T., Green, S., and Courtright, J. (1995). Inertial forces and the implementation of a socio-technical systems approach: A communication study. *Organization Science*, 6, 168–185.

Fernandez, J. P. (1981). *Racism and Sexism in Corporate Life: Changing Values in American Business*, Lexington: Lexington Books.

Fernandez, R. M., and Weinberg, N. (1997). Sifting and sorting: Personal contacts and hiring in a retail bank. *American Sociological Review*, *62*, 883–902.

Fiske, S. T., Cuddy, A. J. C., Glick, P., and Xu, J. (2002). A model of (often mixed) stereotype content: Competence and warmth respectively follow from perceived status and competition. *Journal of Personality and Social Psychology*, *82*, 878–902.

Fiske, S. T., Lin, M., and Neuberg, S. L. (1999). The continuum model: Ten years later. In S. Chaiken and Y. Trope (eds.), *Dual Process Theories in Social Psychology* (pp. 231–254). New York: Guilford Press.

Ford, T. E., Gambino, F., Lee, H., Mayo, E., and Ferguson, M. A. (2004). The role of accountability in suppressing managers' preinterview bias against African American sales job applicants. *Journal of Personal Selling and Sales Management*, *24*, 113–124.

Fountain, C. M. (2005). Finding a job in the internet age. *Social Forces*, *83*, 1235–1262.

Gaertner, S. L., and Dovidio, J. F. (2005). Understanding and addressing contemporary racism: From aversive racism to the common ingroup identity model. *Journal of Social Issues*, *61*, 615–639.

Gaertner, S. L., Dovidio, J. F., Nier, J, Hodson, G., and Houlette, M. A. (2005). Aversive racism: Bias without intention. In R. L. Nelson and L. B. Neilson (eds.), *Handbook on Employment Discrimination Research: Rights and Realities*. New York: Springer Publishing.

Gardenswartz, L., and Rowe, A. (1994). Diversity management: Practical application in a health care organization. *Frontiers of Health Services Management*, *11*, 36–40.

Gatewood, R. D., and Field, H. S. (2001). *Human Resource Selection*, 5th edn. Chicago: Dryden Press.

Giovannini, M. (2004). What gets measured gets done: Achieving results through diversity and inclusion. *Journal for Quality and Participation*, *27*, 21–27.

Gordon, M. M. (1949). Social class in American sociology. *American Journal of Sociology*, *55*, 262–268.

Gordon, M. M. (1958). *Social Class in American Sociology*. Durham: Duke University Press.

Greenhaus, J. H., and Parasuraman, S. (1993). Job performance attributions and career advancement prospects: An examination of gender and race effects. *Organizational Behavior and Human Decision Processes*, *55*, 273–297.

Greenhaus, J. H., Parasuraman, S., and Wormley, W. W. (1990). Effects of race on organizational experiences, job performance evaluations, and career outcomes. *Academy of Management Journal, 33*, 64–86.

Gregg, E. (1992). Sexual harassment: Confronting the issues of the '90s. *Office Systems, 9* (February 1992), 33–36.

Gresov, C., Haveman, H. A., and Oliva, T. A. (1993). Organizational design, inertia, and the dynamics of competitive response. *Organization Science, 4*, 181–208.

Hannan, M. T., and Freeman, J. H. (1984). Structural inertia and organizational change. *American Sociological Review, 43*, 143–164.

Harris, L. E., and Boddy, J. E., Jr. (2004). Sex discrimination and merit-based compensation: Is your system at risk? *Morrison and Foerster Employment Law Commentary, 16* (February 2004), 1–6.

Hart, M. (2005). Subjective decisionmaking and unconscious discrimination. *Alabama Law Review, 56*, 741–791.

Hart, M. (2004). Will employment discrimination class actions survive? *Akron Law Review, 37*, 813–843.

Heneman, H. G., III, and Judge, T. A. (2003) *Staffing Organizations*, 4th edn. Middleton, WI: Mendota House and New York: McGraw-Hill.

Hewstone, M. (1990). The "ultimate attribution error"? A review of the literature on intergroup causal attribution. *European Journal of Social Psychology, 30*, 311–335.

Hodson, G., Dovidio, J. F., and Gaertner, S. L. (2002). Processes in racial discrimination: Differential weighting of conflicting information. *Personality and Social Psychology Bulletin, 28*, 460–471.

Hodson, R., and Kaufman, R. L. (1982). Economic dualism: A critical review. *American Sociological Review, 47*, 727–739.

Holzer, H J. (1987a). Hiring procedures in the firm: Their economic determinants and outcomes. In R. Block *et al.* (eds.), *Human Resources and Firm Performance* (pp. 243–272). Madison: Industrial Relations Research Association.

Holzer, H, J. (1987b). Informal job search and black youth unemployment. *American Economic Review, 77*, 446–452.

Hubbard, E. E. (2003). *The Diversity Scorecard: Evaluating the Impact of Diversity on Organizational Performance*. Boston: Butterworth-Heinemann.

Hunter, J. E., and Schmidt, F. L. (1990). *Methods of Meta-analysis: Correcting Error and Bias in Research Findings*. Newbury Park: Sage Publications.

Hyde, A. (2006). Employment discrimination in a high-velocity labor market: How a meritocracy creates disparate labor market outcomes through demands for skills at hiring, hiring through networks, and rewards to entrepreneurship. In G. M. Gulati and M. Yelnosky (eds.), *Behavioral Science Implications for Employment Discrimination Law: Essays in Memory of David Charny* (forthcoming). Dordrecht, NL: Kluwer Academic Press (also available at http://law.bepress.com/cgi/viewcontent.cgi?article=1013&context=rutgersnewarklwps).

Ibarra, H. (1995). Race, opportunity, and diversity of social circles in managerial networks. *Academy of Management Journal, 38*, 673–703.

Jackson, P. B., Thoits, P. A., and Taylor H. F. (1995). Composition of the workplace and psychological well-being: The effects of tokenism on America's black elite. *Social Forces, 74*, 543–577.

James, E. H. (2000). Race-related differences in promotions and support: Underlying effects of human and social capital. *Organization Science, 11*, 493–208.

Jossem, J. (1991). Investigating sexual harassment complaints. *Personnel, 68* (July 1991), 9–10.

Kalev, A, Dobbin, F., and Kelly, E. (2006). Best practices or best guesses? Diversity management and the reduction of inequality. *American Sociological Review, 71*, 589–617.

Kalleberg, A. L. (2000). Nonstandard employment relations: Part-time, temporary and contract work. *Annual Review of Sociology, 26*, 341–365.

Kalleberg, A. L., Reskin, B. F., and Hudson, K. (2000). Bad jobs in America: Standard and nonstandard employment relations and job quality in the United States. *American Sociological Review, 65*, 256–278.

Kalleberg, A. L., Wallace, M., and Althauser, R. P. (1981). Economic segmentation, worker power, and income inequality. *American Journal of Sociology, 87*, 651–683.

Kang, J. (2005). Trojan horses of race. *Harvard Law Review, 118*, 1491–1593.

Kanter, R. M. (1977). *Men and Women of the Corporation*. New York: Basic Books.

Kaplan, S., and Henderson, R. (2005). Inertia and incentives: Bridging organizational economics and organizational theory. *Organization Science, 16*, 509–521.

Kasinitz, P., and Rosenberg, J. (1996). Missing the connection: Social isolation and employment on the Brooklyn waterfront. *Social Problems, 43*, 180–196.

Kaufman, R. L. (1986). The impact of industrial and occupational structure on black–white employment allocation. *American Sociological Review, 51*, 310–323.

Kennedy, D. (2000). *Accountability: Establishing Shared Ownership*. San Francisco: Berrett-Koehler Communications.

Kerr, S. (1975). On the folly of rewarding A, while hoping for B. *Academy of Management Journal*, *18*, 769–783.

Kirschenman, J., Moss, P., and Tilly, C. (1995). Employer screening methods and racial exclusion: Evidence from new in-depth interviews with employers. Working Paper, Russell Sage Foundation, New York.

Kirschenman, J., and Neckerman, K. M. (1991). We'd love to hire them, but . . .: The meaning of race for employers. In C. Jencks and P. E. Peterson (eds.), *The Urban Underclass* (pp. 203–232). Washington: The Brookings Institution.

Kobata, M. T. (1995). Minimize risk by investigating complaints promptly. *Personnel Journal*, *74* (February 1995), 38–39.

Konrad, A. M., and Linnehan, F. (1995). Formalized HRM structures: Coordinating equal employment opportunity or concealing organizational practices? *Academy of Management Journal*, *38*, 787–829.

Kraiger, K., and Ford, J. K. (1985). A meta-analysis of race effects in performance ratings. *Journal of Applied Psychology*, *70*, 56–65.

Kramer, R. M. (1991). Intergroup relations and organizational dilemmas: The role of categorization processes. *Research in Organizational Behavior*, *13*, 191–228.

Krawiec, J. K. (2003). Cosmetic compliance and the failure of negotiated governance. *Washington University Law Quarterly*, *81*, 487–544.

Krieger, L. H. (1995). The content of our categories: A cognitive bias approach to discrimination and equal employment opportunity. *Stanford Law Review*, *47*, 1161–1232.

Landau, J. (1995). The relationship of race and gender to managers' ratings of promotion potential. *Journal of Organizational Behavior*, *16*, 391–400.

Landy, F. J., Shankster, L. J., and Kohler, S. S. (1994). Personnel selection and placement. *Annual Review of Psychology*, *45*, 261–296.

Latham, G. P., and Wexley, K. N. (1994). *Increasing Productivity through Performance Appraisal*. New York: Addison Wesley.

Lee, A. J. (2005). Unconscious bias theory in employment discrimination litigation. *Harvard Civil Rights-Civil Liberties Law Review*, *40*, 481–504.

Lehrman, S. (2006). The implicit prejudice. *Scientific American*, June 2006, 32–34.

Lengnick-Hall, M. L. (1992). Checking out sexual harassment claims. *HR Magazine*, *37* (March 1992), 77–81.

Leonard, J. S. (1989). Women and affirmative action. *Journal of Economic Perspectives*, *3*, 61–75.

Leonard, J. S. (1994). *Use of enforcement techniques in eliminating glass ceiling barriers*. Report prepared for the US Department of Labor, Glass Ceiling Commission, April 1994.

Lie. J. (1997). Sociology of markets. *Annual Review of Sociology, 23,* 341–360.

Lipset, S. M., and Bendix, R. (1959). *Social Mobility in Industrial Society.* Berkeley: University of California Press.

LoPresto, R. (1986). Recruitment sources and techniques. In J. J. Famularo (ed.), *Handbook of Human Resource Administration,* 2nd edn (pp. 13–26). New York: McGraw-Hill.

Mackie, D. F., Hamilton, D. L., Susskind, J., and Roselli, F. (1996). Social psychological foundations of stereotype formation. In C. N. MacRae, C. Stangor, and M. Hewstone (eds.), *Stereotypes and Stereotyping* (pp. 41–78). New York: Guilford Press.

Martin, L. (1991). *A Report on the Glass Ceiling Initiative.* Washington: US Department of Labor.

Martocchio, J. J., and Whitener, E. M. (1992). Fairness in personnel selection: A meta-analysis and policy implications. *Human Relations, 45,* 489–506.

McGuire, G. M. (2002). Gender, race, and the shadow structure: A study of informal networks and inequality in a work organization, *Gender and Society, 16,* 303–322.

Menger, P. (1999). Artistic labor markets and careers. *Annual Review of Sociology, 25,* 541–574.

Messick, D. M., and Mackie, D. (1989). Intergroup relations. *Annual Review of Psychology, 40,* 49–50.

Moss, P., and Tilly, C. (2001). *Stories Employers Tell.* New York: Russell Sage Foundation.

Mouw, T. (2002). Are black workers missing the connection? The effect of spatial distance and employee referrals on interfirm racial segregation. *Demography, 39,* 507–528.

Nelson, R. L., and Neilson, L. B. (eds.). (2005). *Handbook on Employment Discrimination Research: Rights and Realities.* New York: Springer Publishing

Nelson, T. E., Acker. M., and Manis, M. (1996). Irrepressible stereotypes. *Journal of Experimental Social Psychology, 32,* 13–38.

Nieva, V. F., and Gutek, B. A. (1980). Sex effects on evaluation. *Academy of Management Review, 5,* 267–275.

Nixon, R. (1985a). *Black Managers in Corporate America: Alienation or Integration?* Washington, DC: National Urban League.

Nixon, R. (1985b). *Climbing the Corporate Ladder: Some Perceptions among Black Managers.* Washington, DC: National Urban League.

Norton, M. I., Vandello, J. A., and Darley, J. M. (2004). Casuistry and social category bias. *Journal of Personality and Social Psychology, 87,* 817–831.

Oppenheimer, A. (2004). Investigating workplace harassment and discrimination. *Employee Relations Law Journal, 29,* 55–67.

Orey, M. (2006). White men can't help it: Courts have been buying the idea that they have innate biases. *Business Week,* May 15, 2006, 54–56.

Orton, D. J., and Weick, K. E. (1990). Loosely coupled systems: A reconceptualization. *Academy of Management Review, 15,* 203–223.

Ostrom, T. M., and Sedikides, C. (1992). Out-group homogeneity effects in natural and minimal groups. *Psychological Bulletin, 112,* 536–552.

Pettigrew, T. F., and Martin, J. (1987). Shaping the organizational context for black American inclusion. *Journal of Social Issues, 43,* 41–78.

Podolny, J. M., and Baron J. N. (1997). Resources and relationships: Social networks and mobility in the workplace. *American Sociological Review, 62,* 673–693.

Relyea, G. F. (1999). The four cornerstones of a reasonable investigation. *Human Resources Professional, 12* (May/June 1999), 12–15.

Reskin, B. F. (2000). The proximate causes of employment discrimination. *Contemporary Sociology, 29,* 319–328.

Reskin, B. F. (2003). Including mechanisms in our models of ascriptive inequality. *American Sociological Review, 68,* 1–21.

Roggema, J., and Smith, M. H. (1983). Organizational change in the shipping industry: Issues in the transformation of basic assumptions. *Human Relations, 36,* 765–790

Roth, P. L., Huffcutt, A. I., and Bobko, P. (2003). Ethnic group differences in measures of job performance: A new meta-analysis. *Journal of Applied Psychology, 88,* 694–706.

Ruef, M. (1997). Assessing organizational fitness on a dynamic landscape: An empirical test of the relative inertia thesis. *Strategic Management Journal, 18,* 837–853.

Sackett, P. R., and DuBois, C. L. Z. (1991). Rater-ratee race effects on performance evaluation: Challenging meta analytic conclusions. *Journal of Applied Psychology, 76,* 873–877.

Salancik, G. R., and Pfeffer, J. (1978). Uncertainty, secrecy, and the choice of similar others. *Social Psychology, 41,* 246–255.

Scheck, J. (2004). Expert witness: Bill Bielby helped launch an industry – suing employers for unconscious bias. *The Recorder,* October 28, 2004, 1.

Schreiber, C. T., Price, K. F., and Morrison, A. (1993). Workforce diversity and the glass ceiling: Practices, barriers, possibilities. *Human Resource Planning, 16,* 51–69.

Semyonov, M. (1988). Bi-ethnic labor markets, mono-ethnic labor markets, and socioeconomic inequality. *American Sociological Review, 53,* 256–266.

Sims, R. R. (2002). *Organizational Success through Effective Human Resources Management*. Westport, CT: Quorum Books.

Stainback, K., Robinson, C. L., and Tomaskovic-Devey, D. (2005). Race and workplace integration: A politically mediated process? *American Behavioral Scientist, 48*, 1200–1228.

Stauffer, J. M., and Buckley, K. R. (2005). The existence and nature of racial bias in supervisory ratings. *Journal of Applied Psychology, 90*, 586–591.

Stinchcombe, L. (1965). Social structure and organizations. In J. G. March (ed.), *Handbook of Organizations* (pp. 142–193). Chicago: Rand McNally.

Stites, J. (2005). Equal pay for the sexes: High profile lawsuits make the case for investigating gender pay and promotion equity at your organization. *HR Magazine, 50* (May 2005).

Stockdale, M. S., and Crosby, F. J. (eds.) (2003). *The Psychology and Management of Workplace Diversity*. Maiden: Blackwell.

Sturm, S. (2001). Second generation employment discrimination: A structural approach. *Columbia Law Review, 101*, 458–568.

Sutton, J. R., Dobbin, F. R., Meyer, J. W., and Scott, W. R. (1994). The legalization of the workplace. *American Journal of Sociology, 99*, 944–971.

Tetlock, P. E. (1985). Accountability: The neglected social context of judgment and choice. *Research in Organizational Behavior, 7*, 297–332.

Tetlock, P. E. (1992). The impact of accountability on judgment and choice: Toward a social contingency model. *Advances in Experimental Social Psychology, 25*, 331–376.

Tetlock, P. E., and Kim, J. I. (1987). Accountability and judgment processes in a personality prediction task. *Journal of Personality and Social Psychology, 52*, 700–709.

Thomas, D. A. (1990). The impact of race on managers' experiences of developmental relationships (mentoring and sponsorship): An intra-organizational study. *Journal of Organizational Behavior, 11*, 479–492.

Uhlmann, E. L., and Cohen, G. L. (2005). Constructed criteria: Redefining merit to justify discrimination. *Psychological Science, 16*, 474–480.

United States Department of Labor (2006). Voluntary guidelines for self-evaluation of compensation practices for compliance with nondiscrimination requirements of executive order 11246 with respect to systematic compensation discrimination. *Federal Register, 71* (June 15, 2006).

Warner, W. L., Meeker, M., and Bells, K. (1949). *Social Class in America*. New York: Science Research Associates.

Wax, A., and Tetlock, P. E. (2005). We're all racists at heart. *Wall Street Journal*, December 1, 2005, A16.

Williams, J. (2003). The social psychology of stereotyping: Using social science to litigate gender discrimination cases and defang the "clueless" defense. *Employee Rights and Employment Policy Journal*, 7, 401–458.

Word, C. O., Zanna, M. P., and Cooper, J. (1974). The nonverbal mediation of self-fulfilling prophecies in interracial interaction. *Journal of Experimental Social Psychology*, 10, 109–120.

Yarkin, K. L., Town, J. P., and Wallston, B. S. (1982). Blacks and women must try harder: Stimulus for a person's race and sex attributions of causality. *Personality and Social Psychology Bulletin*, 8, 21–24.

Zwerling, C., and Silver, H. (1992). Race and job dismissals in a federal bureaucracy. *American Sociological Review*, 57, 651–660.

PART II

Emerging theoretical approaches

4 | Identity negotiation processes amidst diversity

JEFFREY T. POLZER AND HEATHER M. CARUSO

Diversity is the industrialized world's perennial underdog. Though decades of research have yet to reveal any consistent main effects of diversity (Webber and Donahue, 2001; Mannix and Neale, 2005), the increasing diversity of schools, neighborhoods, and workplaces presents an unrelenting demand for effective interaction among diverse people (Friedman and DiTomaso, 1996; Johnson and Packer, 1987; Offerman and Gowing, 1990; Triandis, Kurowski, and Gelfand, 1994). In addition, the successful utilization of diversity undergirds core social values of fairness and justice, along with the organizational prospects of greater learning, innovation, problem solving, and performance (Cox, Lobel, and McLeod, 1991; Ely and Thomas, 2001; Jehn, Northcraft, and Neale, 1999; Robinson and Dechant, 1997; Watson, Kumar, and Michaelson, 1993).

The challenge of realizing the potential value in diversity has motivated two popular streams of research. Organizational researchers working in the tradition of self-categorization theory (and social identity theory) have, on the one hand, generally pursued insight into the universal aspects of encounters with diversity – that is, how people view and interact with others who belong to a different social group, regardless of how the group is defined (e.g., by gender, race, nationality, occupation, tenure, or some combination of demographic dimensions, see Chatman *et al.*, 1998; Polzer, Milton, and Swann, 2002). This approach aims to expose those intergroup dynamics that are likely to emerge as the result of any type of difference, making few or no distinctions between the myriad social identities that may differentiate people. Though parsimonious and highly generalizable, this approach ignores substantive differences that systematically shape experiences with certain specific kinds of diversity (e.g., race, gender) as a result of their distinct historical, organizational, and societal context.

The other popular approach to studying diversity takes essentially the opposite tack, investigating single dimensions of diversity in great depth so as to bring their unique implications to light (e.g., Ely, 1994). Researchers using this method of investigation have produced rich and nuanced information showing that race (Ely and Thomas, 2001), age (Finkelstein, Allen, and Rhoton, 2003; Lawrence, 1988; Levinson, 1978), gender (Carli, 1989; Ely, 1991; Guimond *et al.*, 2006), nationality (Chen, 2006), and other specific dimensions of diversity present distinct concerns, challenges, and opportunities for social interaction. Rather than ignoring or controlling for contextual variables, this approach fully explores such factors as power and status differences that accumulate from historical and societal forces. This body of research enables and encourages us to examine how the relationships among categories of people within each dimension of diversity may substantively differ (e.g., Whites and Blacks versus Whites and Asians on the dimension of race). However, the depth and specificity of the insights produced with this approach do not readily lend themselves to piecing together a coherent overarching theory of diversity. It is not clear how the idiosyncratic profiles of each dimension of diversity might layer and interact to shape interactions in diverse groups where people commonly differ on several dimensions, and where the salient dimensions of diversity may shift easily with changes in context or group composition (Lau and Murnighan, 1998).

Despite their apparent opposition, the two approaches we have described are connected by a common and continuing challenge: to accurately predict what will happen when diverse people interact. Even in dyadic interactions, the complexity of intergroup relations among people who have some overlapping and some distinct social identities is not fully accounted for by either approach alone. Consider, for example, two people who differ in gender and nationality but are of the same age and race. Even with information about the wide variety of potentially relevant contextual cues, social categorization theories do not clearly predict the extent to which these people are likely to behave as members of a common ingroup or of distinct out-groups. Moreover, they cannot tell us whether or how these people might behave any differently if instead they shared gender and race, and differed on age and nationality. Alternatively, such nuances might be induced from the separate literatures detailing relevant implications for each of the four dimensions of diversity, but this quickly overwhelms the investigator with the difficulty of parsing out any common and generalizable effects from those which are more unique and context-dependent. Such a task is daunting for even the four dimensions of diversity exhibited by the two people in our simple example, but when one considers the many group boundaries that lattice organizational landscapes and the frequency of interaction among more than two people, the task becomes pragmatically impossible. Thus, neither approach provides a satisfactory theoretical foundation for fully understanding actual experiences among diverse people.

We aim to address this shortcoming by presenting a framework which maps the interpersonal terrain of diverse social interaction and by describing how specific identity group concerns lead people to travel together down particular paths. The basis of this framework lies in identity negotiation, a set of social processes through which people come to understand each other's various identities and make themselves understood (Mead, 1934; Goffman, 1959; Swann, 1987, 2005). These identity negotiation processes are an inevitable, routine feature of everyday social interaction, and are actually necessitated by our pervasive diversity. Because no two individuals are exactly alike, we can never rely solely on egocentric projection or stereotyping to form accurate impressions of each other. As a consequence, people must "negotiate" to establish a working consensus of "who is who" in their social interactions (Goffman, 1959). Whether implicitly or explicitly, automatically or deliberately, the information that people exchange enables each of them to attend to, evaluate, and incorporate (or dismiss) that information with respect to their views of themselves and one another.

In the section below, we will establish this cognitive and behavioral framework of identity negotiation, and then elaborate the ways in which specific social identity concerns might steer individuals through it. For example, when social groups have an especially conflict-ridden or even violent history of integration (much more the case with race than, say, with gender), there may be fewer situations in which explicit disclosure of identities will be perceived as safe, and greater likelihood that such negotiations will consist of implicit cues and inference rather than open discussion. Our biggest emphasis regarding social identity concerns, however, is on the status disparities that people derive from their social category memberships, and how these status differences influence identity negotiation processes. Before analyzing the influence of status differences, though, we first describe the identity negotiation framework.

Identity negotiation

Fundamentally, identity negotiation concerns the cognitions people have about themselves (called *self-views*), the cognitions they have about others (called *appraisals*), the correspondence of the two, and the affective and behavioral manifestations of these cognitions. Though these elements can be remarkably flexible, they also buttress an individual's sense of stability and coherence in the world through self-verification – the individual's experience of having his or her self-view affirmed by others' appraisals (Swann, Rentfrow, and Guinn, 2003). Moreover, when individuals act as perceivers, rather than as the target of perceptions, they require valid and reliable appraisals in order to predict how others will act. When an individual's self-views do not correspond to the treatment they receive, or when an individual's appraisals do not correspond to a target's behavior or espoused self-views, he or she is motivated to correct the situation (e.g., Swann, 1987; Swann and Hill, 1982; Swann and Read, 1981a, 1981b; Swann *et al.*, 2004). Identity negotiation refers to the many and varied activities through which targets and perceivers interactively forge agreements regarding the identities of targets (Goffman, 1959; Swann, 1987, 2005).

This work has its roots in the early work of symbolic interactionists (e.g., Cooley, 1902; Mead, 1934), who proposed that people form self-views to make sense of the world and interpret others' behaviors toward them. A professor, for example, will be much better at understanding her position in society and at predicting how students will respond to her if she has some understanding of her identity with respect to relevant characteristics (e.g., intelligence, eloquence, creativity). Self-views make it possible for individuals to interpret and draw meaning from their past social experiences and interactions, while also guiding them toward new ones (Cross and Markus, 1991; Markus and Nurius, 1986; Swann, Rentfrow, and Guinn, 2003). As volatility or inconsistency in these self-views could render an individual socially dysfunctional, it is essential that individuals maintain reasonably stable and reliable self-views. People are therefore motivated to receive ongoing verification of their self-views, and to bring any perceivers with discrepant appraisals into line (e.g., Lecky, 1945; Carson, 1969; Harvey, Hunt and Schroeder, 1979; Swann and Read, 1981a, 1981b; Swann and Hill, 1982; Secord and Backman, 1964).

Along similar lines, stable and adaptive functioning in the social world requires that people perceive and form appraisals of the people around them. It would be difficult for the professor from our earlier example to put together an effective lecture without appraising the abilities, habits, and preferences of her students. Appraisals enable individuals to interpret the actions they observe from others, to adjust their behavior to the abilities and tendencies of their interaction partners, and to anticipate others' responses. Indeed, appraisals are vital to the success of a wide variety of interaction goals (Swann, 1984), such as courting favor (e.g., E. E. Jones, 1964; E. E. Jones and Pittman, 1982; Schlenker, 1980), preserving a relationship (e.g., Kelley, 1979; Thibaut and Kelley, 1959), establishing relationship roles (e.g., Gill and Swann, 2004; Swann, 1990), and changing a partner's behavior (Gill and Swann, 2004; Swann, 1997). As with self-views, people strive to maintain appraisals with some degree of certainty and consistency (e.g., Festinger, 1957; Fromm, 1947; Heine, Proulx, and Vohs, 2006), and construct their social interactions so as to receive corroboration of those appraisals (e.g., S. C. Jones and Panitch, 1971; Kelley and Stahelski, 1970; Rosenthal and Jacobson, 1968; for a review, see Snyder, 1984; Snyder and Stukas, 1999; Snyder and Swann, 1978a, 1978b; Swann and Snyder, 1980; Word, Zanna, and Cooper, 1974; Zanna and Pack, 1975).

While the (mis)alignment of self-views and appraisals is of clear concern to targets and perceivers individually, recent research has shown that it also has serious implications for their collective attitudes, experiences, and outcomes in the interaction. Group identity, social integration, relationship conflict, and collective performance are all sensitive to the overall degree of correspondence between self-views and appraisals in a group of people, referred to as *interpersonal congruence* (Polzer, Milton, and Swann, 2002; Swann *et al.*, 2003). When high interpersonal congruence exists (i.e., when self-views and appraisals are aligned), positive effects should generally follow. The treatment targets receive from others should validate their self-views and lend greater predictability, coherence, and control to their perspectives on reality (Swann, Stein-Seroussi, and Giesler, 1992). Similarly, perceivers should enjoy the stability and reassurance they experience when their expectations of targets are fulfilled. Congruent understandings of each other's views should enable both targets and perceivers to more accurately infer each other's intentions and meanings, facilitating fluent, efficient interaction and helping them utilize their diverse abilities to accomplish their collective goals (Heine, Proulx, and Vohs, 2006; Polzer *et al.*, 2002). At the opposite end of the spectrum, however, low interpersonal congruence is likely to manifest itself in frequent miscommunication, unintentionally inappropriate or even offensive behavioral patterns, and unpredictable encounters that promote self-doubt, frustration, anxiety, and ultimately poor performance on collective tasks.

It is possible for targets and perceivers whose views are not corroborated by their interaction partners to improve their situations by abandoning identity negotiation altogether – that is, by simply excluding those partners from their interaction or avoiding situations involving those partners. When this is not possible, another alternative is simply to accept the incongruence and suffer through the conflict it inevitably engenders. However, in the many cases where such "solutions" are impractical and undesirable, people must find ways to exchange information that will encourage targets to revise their self-views, perceivers to revise their appraisals, or both.

Fortunately, individuals can call upon an impressive range of behaviors to achieve this end. On the implicit side, individuals may merely allow others to observe indicators of the self-views and appraisals they would like to promote (Swann, 1987). By displaying various personal characteristics (e.g., revealing one's creativity by imaginatively decorating one's office), a target can subtly yet persistently encourage others to recognize those characteristics (Elsbach, 2003). Similarly, perceivers can convey their appraisals to targets through facial expressions (e.g., cheery smiles or menacing stares) and body language (e.g., warm hugs or formal handshakes). Using these rather cryptic forms of communication, individuals depend on others to infer their self-views and appraisals from displayed behaviors without clear guidance or indications of success.

In some instances, however, targets and perceivers are moved to take more overt action. An athletic target might, for example, organize an office basketball tournament as a vehicle for proclaiming his athletic prowess, or the perceiver of a depressed coworker might suggest therapy to the target. Most extreme are instances in which individuals leave no room for doubt by communicating information on their self-views and appraisals through direct and explicit self-disclosure (in the case of self-views) or feedback (in the case of appraisals), perhaps combined with an iterative inquiry to ensure that their statements have been understood.

Yet another class of identity negotiation behaviors are not aimed directly at the intended recipient. Targets and perceivers may opt for indirect identity negotiation when they believe that information delivered through another party may carry more weight or involve less personal risk. A target seeking greater peer recognition may, for example, compete for awards publicly conferred by his boss to shift his peers' appraisals. This indirect strategy may also be attractive to perceivers who want to diminish the risk of potentially offending a target with their appraisal.

The substantial range and variety of identity negotiation behaviors is of particular significance for participants in diverse social interactions. Their relative unfamiliarity with each other's experiences, assumptions, and perspectives favors stereotyping over individuation, reducing the likelihood that perceivers' appraisals will verify targets' self-views from the start (Ames, 2004a, 2004b). Therefore, unlike interaction partners with more homogeneous identities, diverse individuals are especially dependent on identity negotiation activities to inform each other, build mutual understandings, and bring appraisals and self-views into line. It is important, therefore, to study which factors will cause various identity negotiation behaviors to emerge among diverse people. We consider several of these factors below.

Diversity and identity negotiation

There is a long history of research that connects diversity to various elements of identity negotiation. As we detail later, several streams of research examine how different social group memberships influence the way individuals develop and construe their self-views, and demonstrate identity-consistent behavior (Cross and Madson, 1997; Gabriel and Gardner, 1999; Cross, Bacon, and Morris, 2000; Steele and Aronson, 1995). Researchers have also explored how people from various social groups differ in the way they form impressions of others, and the way they attend to information in interpersonal exchanges (Lepore and Brown, 1997). This intellectual foundation makes it clear that self-views and appraisals can develop and function differently for members of different social groups, but little work has been done to examine how differences between social group memberships affect identity negotiation processes.

Recently, however, researchers have begun to explore the contours and consequences of identity negotiation in groups with diverse memberships. Polzer, Milton, and Swann (2002) demonstrated that diverse groups with high congruence were able to outperform similarly congruent homogeneous groups on creative tasks. Furthermore, Swann *et al.* (2003) showed that when group members held positive early impressions of their diverse coworkers, they were more likely to individuate each other as identity negotiation proceeded, leading to increased self-verification in the group and attendant benefits to group creative performance. In this chapter we push this frontier forward, using our identity negotiation framework to illustrate how diverse identities can be better understood by examining how they systematically shape social interaction and, in turn, social and work outcomes. We first address the multilayered nature of diversity, describing how both broad and specific differences between people influence the path of identity negotiation. We then discuss how the stigma or status often attached to specific identities can influence identity negotiation processes.

The multilayered influence of diversity

At the most basic level, the mere existence of identity differences between participants in a social interaction is likely to present stressful risks for identity negotiation (Frable, Blackstone, and Scherbaum, 1990). The possibility that group members will reject each other merely for being different makes active, direct, and explicit disclosure of self-views in the identity negotiation process less safe, and therefore, less likely. Related risks may also cause group members to suppress their appraisals, as their opinions of each other might "out" them, revealing the dissimilar backgrounds and experiences that may have given rise to their views. To the extent that diverse group members really inhabit different "thought worlds" (Dougherty, 1992), both targets and perceivers may avoid these more overt identity negotiations in anticipation of miscommunication, misinterpretation, and interpersonal friction. Thus, participants in diverse social interactions are likely to pursue identity negotiation through mostly passive, indirect, and implicit behaviors, enabling them to more safely and incrementally test others' reactions to select aspects of their identities and appraisals.

Beyond overall diversity, the dynamics of identity negotiation are also influenced by the unique histories, experiences, and concerns of the specific social groups to which individuals belong (Sellers *et al.*,

1998). Consider how unique social group profiles can manifest themselves in the content of self-views. For example, the unique experience of being Black in America makes race likely to be a more significant aspect of the self-concept for Black Americans than for members of other ethnic groups (Sellers *et al.*, 1998). Other research demonstrates that women, more so than men, are likely to hold a relational construal of the self (Cross and Madson, 1997). Appraisals, for their part, are also widely known to be influenced by social category memberships and related stereotypes (Lepore and Brown, 1997). However, using the identity negotiation framework, we can go beyond these individual-level identity differences to explore how specific social group concerns are likely to shape the process by which members negotiate their identities.

Some research has already indicated that women are more likely than men to attend to and try to convey relational information about themselves when negotiating identities (e.g., Gabriel and Gardner, 1999). This could have a variety of effects on identity negotiation in gender diverse groups. On one hand, the relational information women convey may prime their male interaction partners to tune into their own relational strengths, shifting their own self-views in a relational direction. An alternative possibility is that a woman who communicates relational information to men may be pigeon-holed by those men as a stereotypic woman, and once this stereotype is triggered, the men's appraisals of her may incorporate more content from their own stereotypes of women. Yet another alternative is that men may simply fail to attend to relational information conveyed by women, miss the opportunity to communicate about this, and find themselves reaching dead-ends in more direct identity negotiation attempts. In more extreme cases the group may break into same-gender subgroups because their preferred strategies for identity negotiation are dramatically more successful with other members of their own group.

Interpersonal differences in age present a different set of group-specific concerns. One possibility stems from the finding that older adults typically prefer social interactions that are pleasant over those which raise new information (Fung, Carstensen, and Lutz, 1999), a preference which is not shared by younger adults. In negotiating their identities, youngsters may attempt to maximize the amount of new identity-relevant information brought to light by pursuing more proactive and direct negotiations, while their older partners may prefer less direct approaches to avoid the possibility of open confrontation. Along similar lines, younger participants may favor explicit over implicit identity negotiations for the clarity of new information they foster, while older individuals are more likely to use implicit (and less threatening) forms of negotiation to reinforce a generally positive atmosphere.

The stereotypes and unique histories of racial groups have strong implications for the way identity negotiation will unfold between members of different groups. Consider the fact that African Americans are, for example, somewhat uniquely subject to stereotype threat in domains like intellectual performance. This is likely to increase the perceived cost of directly seeking feedback for African Americans, as they may feel that others will take this as an indication of low ability or insecurity (Williams *et al.*, 1999; Roberson *et al.*, 2002). Indeed, researchers have already gathered some evidence indicating that stereotype threat concerns relate to the greater use of passive and implicit monitoring strategies when African Americans seek appraisals from perceivers (Roberson *et al.*, 2002; Lovelace and Rosen, 1996). The relatively hazy information such strategies often yield make it likely that racially diverse groups will struggle to achieve interpersonal congruence, and that African Americans in those groups may be at the particular disadvantage of working with more ambiguous information than their peers.

Our purpose in this section has not been to exhaustively catalogue all of the identity-relevant concerns for age, gender, and racial groups, nor address the specific concerns that might affect every social group's selection of identity negotiation behaviors. Instead, we have tried to identify several ways in which people translate encounters with diversity and their own social group concerns into specific identity negotiation processes during social interaction. To enrich our story, we propose that beyond the mere existence of difference, and beyond the specific content of each social group's unique preferences and tendencies, variation in the status accorded to social groups can systematically influence the process and outcome of identity negotiation. We next discuss the relevance of these status differences in the context of an identity negotiation framework.

Status differences and identity negotiation among diverse people

Membership in various social identity groups (e.g., race, gender) tends to be associated in society with systematic differences in power, status, and access to resources (Nkomo, 1992; Omi and Winant, 1994; Ragins, 1997; Ridgeway and Berger, 1986). These status differences influence social interaction processes and outcomes (Ridgeway and Erickson, 2000; Tiedens and Fragale, 2003), and often afford members of dominant identity groups (such as Whites and men) substantial power over others (Levin *et al.*, 2002; Sidanius and Pratto, 1999). When members of high-status and low-status identity groups interact, this asymmetry in power may significantly shape the course of identity negotiation. For example, those with higher power are likely to talk more and exert more influence, while less powerful people are quieter and more likely to withdraw (Falk and Falk, 1981; Foldy, 2004; Konrad, 2003). Dominant group members also tend to employ both subtle and overt cues to maintain their influence over time, suggesting that even the development or change of group members' identities may be influenced by membership in dominant groups (Elsass and Graves, 1997; Ridgeway, 1997; Smith-Lovin and Brody, 1989). In part this may occur because members of dominant groups often assume that their views are correct, without contemplating or even noticing alternative views put forth by lower-status group members. Conversely, members of nondominant groups are likely to be aware of and receptive to all members' views, and to expect that their own views may be devalued or ignored by others (Billig, 1976).

Though highly suggestive, the literature on the social influence of high-status and low-status people does not translate that influence to the actual negotiation of identities, especially in diverse groups where the bases of status (e.g., identity group stereotypes or social inequity) may be privately disdained. In order to more fully consider how status differences might play out through identity negotiation processes, we will turn to an example of a man and a woman working together in a business context. Status expectations theory and related research predict that the man is likely to have higher status than the woman based on the societal status associated with their gender categories (e.g., Berger, Rosenholtz, and Zelditch, 1980; Ely, 1994; Ridgeway, 1991). (We hasten to note that, although our example will focus on gender as the basis of status differences, the relative status between these two people could also easily be influenced by other demographic categories, organizational positions, prior interaction between them, and other factors). Each of these two will enter their interaction with well-established self-views (which may or may not be consistent with

gender stereotypes; Chen and Welland, 2002) and quickly form appraisals of one another (which may or may not be shaped by gender
stereotypes; Ely and Meyerson, 2000). As their interaction unfolds,
the individuals will reveal a wealth of individuating information to
each other, which in addition to the influence of social category memberships, will allow each to elaborate and revise their appraisals. In
some cases, early appraisals and self-views will be so closely aligned
that little adjustment is necessary, but in the more probable cases in
which at least some incongruence exists, we can ask a variety of novel
questions about the interplay of status differences and the identity
negotiations which will follow. For example, given this initial incongruence, is the high-status person more likely to "win" the identity
negotiation by imposing his self-views and appraisals on the lower
status woman? Is the woman at a disadvantage in the identity negotiation processes because of her low status? If so, what form does this
disadvantage take, and what are potential remedies for the low-status
person?

To analyze this situation, we need to consider the two routes through
which identity negotiation processes can increase congruence between
targets' self-views and perceivers' appraisals. On one side of the coin,
targets try to bring perceivers' appraisals into alignment with their self-
views. When perceivers respond by shifting their appraisals toward
targets' self-views, researchers have labeled this route to congruence a
self-verification effect. On the other side of the coin, perceivers use their
own initial appraisals of targets to shape their behavior toward those
targets. When targets respond to this behavior by shifting their self-
views toward perceivers' appraisals, researchers have labeled this route
to congruence an *appraisal effect*. Congruence can be achieved through
a verification effect or an appraisal effect. Swann, Milton, and Polzer
(2000) found evidence of both types of effects in the diverse groups they
studied, with roughly 30% of the dyads in these groups exhibiting
verification effects, 15% exhibiting appraisal effects, and 17% exhibiting both types of effects (the remaining dyads exhibited neither effect).
Verification effects improved group performance on creative tasks
(independent of the diversity of the group), whereas appraisal effects
improved performance on computational tasks. Given these and
related results, researchers have attempted to determine when appraisal effects or self-verification effects will emerge, along with the consequences of these effects (e.g., Swann *et al.*, 2003). They have not,

however, examined how status differences influence the prevalence and utility of these two routes to congruence.

To understand how status differences contribute to the resolution of interpersonal incongruence, it is necessary to complicate matters further by recognizing that incongruence can occur in two directions, with appraisals being either more flattering (positive) or more derogating (negative) than the target's corresponding self-views. We propose that whether self-views are more positive or more negative may moderate the way high- and low-status people negotiate their identities. For example, whether a high-status person attempts to impose his self-views on another may depend on the desirability of these self-views. This potential contingency is central to the arguments of self-enhancement proponents, but is a moot issue for those who advocate self-verification motives, one example of the distinctions we explore below.

In the rest of this section we systematically assess the various possibilities that could ensue from our example. To simplify our analysis, we describe self-views and appraisals as either positive or negative (dichotomizing continuous variables for expositional ease), and focus on situations of incongruence when the target's self-views are either more positive or more negative than the counterpart's appraisals. Under these assumptions, we have four logical circumstances to consider, arrayed in a 2×2 grid along the dimensions of target status relative to the perceiver (high versus low) and positivity of the target's self-view relative to the perceiver's appraisal (self-views more positive than appraisals versus self-views more negative than appraisals). This grid is depicted in Figure 4.1.

In the analysis that follows, we focus on several questions revolving around the occurrence of verification and appraisal effects in each quadrant. The first question concerns the social psychological mechanisms that are likely to contribute to each effect in each quadrant, along with an overall assessment of the relative likelihood of each effect occurring in each quadrant. A second question is whether either route to congruence aligns with the initial status disparity (e.g., the self-views of a high-status target remain or become positive) or works against this disparity (e.g., the self-views of a low-status target remain or become positive). Put another way, the patterns we explore in these four quadrants always constitute identity negotiation processes that result in greater congruence, but whether this congruence results in alignment between status and self-view valence (e.g., high status associated with

Target's self-views	Target's status (relative to perceiver)	
	High-status target (the man in our example)	*Low-status target (the woman in our example)*
More positive than appraisals	Quadrant 1 The rich get richer	Quadrant 2 The struggle to rise
More negative than appraisals	Quadrant 3 Getting off the pedestal	Quadrant 4 Developmental agenda

Figure 4.1 Combining the target's status and the target's self-views

positive self-views; low status associated with negative self-views) can vary depending on the nature of the effect that occurs in each quadrant. The question here is whether identity negotiation processes reinforce or attenuate the initial status disparity.

A third question addresses the consequences that flow from each route to congruence, in particular for joint productivity on creative tasks (which we view as the gold standard of collaborative interaction). For example, Polzer, Milton, and Swann (2002) relied on the argument that verification is good for group productivity on creative tasks. Swann, Milton, and Polzer (2000) found direct evidence that verification effects, compared to appraisal effects, were more strongly associated with improved group performance on creative tasks. Even if we assume that this is the dominant effect, the question remains as to whether certain conditions exist under which appraisal effects may be of greater benefit to the performance of diverse groups. We consider whether status differences may provide one answer to this question by analyzing each of the four quadrants in sequence.

Quadrant 1: High-status target with positive self-views

In this quadrant, we first note that the target's positive self-views are consistent with conventional positive stereotypes associated with high-status people, whereas the relatively negative appraisals are counter to these stereotypes.

We believe this situation favors a verification effect, as the target in this situation seems well positioned to achieve congruence by leveraging his high status to elevate the appraisals of the perceiver, bringing these appraisals into alignment with his positive self-views. Because the target's high status may allow him to dominate conversation and constrain the low-status person's behavior, the perceiver may have little chance to even make herself heard, let alone persuade the target to revise his self-views.

The congruence resulting from a verification effect in this situation reinforces the existing status disparity, as convergence occurs around the positive self-views of the high-status person. From one perspective, this congruence could benefit collective productivity by allowing the high-status person to more easily and confidently contribute skills that are represented by the newly verified positive self-views. A caveat to this prediction is that the high-status person is already likely to be more dominant in leading a collaborative process, and additional verification could cause the high-status person to become too dominant for the good of the collaboration. In addition, to the extent that this effect is driven by the target's self-enhancement motives, the verification effect may leave the target with increased confidence around self-views that could be inaccurate.

Though relatively unlikely, in some cases perceivers in this situation may succeed in producing an appraisal, rather than verification, effect. Research on minority influence does suggest that repeating a consistent message can be effective in influencing others from a minority position (Nemeth, 1986), but such tactics can put the low-status perceiver at considerable risk of retaliation from the powerful. If successful however, the consequent reduction of the individuals' status disparity could have both negative and positive collective effects. To the extent that the high-status target's positive self-views were driven by valid feedback and high self-awareness, an appraisal effect may invalidate the target's sense of self-efficacy around these self-views, which could impair collective productivity. However, if the appraisal effect helps equate contributions with skill and ability levels rather than with superficial status indicators, the appraisal effect is likely to improve efficiency and performance.

Quadrant 2: Low-status target with positive self-views

This quadrant contains positive self-views that are inconsistent with conventional stereotypes of low-status group members, coupled with relatively negative appraisals that are consistent with such stereotypes.

Diverse sets of people are fairly likely to find themselves in this quadrant, as low-status minorities are increasingly being encouraged to develop positive self-views in their in-groups which are inconsistent with more broadly known negative stereotypes. Meanwhile, perceivers who are unfamiliar with a target may rely more heavily on conventional stereotypes, which in this quadrant lead to unflattering appraisals that undervalue a traget's attributes.

The resolution of this form of incongruence will depend on the relative strength of the opposing forces that are at work. The fundamental motive for self-verification will drive the target to try to elevate the perceiver's appraisals and achieve a verification effect, especially when her self-views have been built up over a lifetime and are therefore held with substantial certainty (Swann, 1987). However, the target cannot draw upon the trappings of high status to make her case. While the target may wish to behave and interact in ways that demonstrate her underappreciated competence (e.g., taking on additional work or innovatively improving her output), her low status may constrain her from contradicting low expectations. For example, the stereotypes associated with her social category may interfere with her ability to produce counter-stereotypical behavior (Steele and Aronson, 1995), especially if these stereotypes are made salient by the perceiver's behavior.

Even if the target succeeds in displaying counter-stereotypical behavior, the perceiver may not sufficiently attend to this information, instead favoring information that confirms his initial category-based appraisals (Plaks *et al.*, 2001). If the target's positive behavior does register with the perceiver, he may subtype the target based on her specific behavior, but retain his stereotypes, which may then come into play on other dimensions. The target is therefore working against a conventional stereotype, from a position of weakness based on her status disadvantage, while trying to change appraisals in a direction that could be threatening to the perceiver because it would weaken his relative status advantage. These obstacles to a verification effect could create significant pressure on the target to succumb to an appraisal effect.

Regarding the consequences of these identity negotiation processes, it is clear that a verification effect would provide far more benefits than an appraisal effect. A verification effect would result in greater congruence that reduces the status disparity by converging around the positive self-views of the low-status woman. In our diverse dyad, this congruence should increase her status (at least as informed by the focal self-view), and benefit productivity by prompting the target to contribute skills that could otherwise go unused. A verification effect can also represent an acknowledgement by the high-status person that his judgment is fallible and that he is willing to change his views, lessening the likelihood that he will attempt to overwhelm or ignore the contributions of the low-status target.

The congruence achieved through an appraisal effect in this quadrant would reinforce the status disparity, aligning the target's low status with negative self-views and negative appraisals. This could hurt productivity by minimizing the target's contribution of skills related to her previously positive self-views. Especially to the extent that the appraisal effects are based on specious indicators of the target's true ability (like test performance under stereotype threat), they can reify inaccurate stereotypes, allow dominant group members to exert disproportionate influence over collaborative projects, and halt or even reverse the personal development of the low-status target.

Quadrant 3: High-status target with negative self-views

We next consider a target whose negative self-views are inconsistent with conventional stereotypes of his high-status group, whereas the perceiver's positive appraisals are consistent with these positive stereotypes. Like Quadrant 2, this situation may also be particularly meaningful and consequential for interactions among diverse individuals, especially where people have become cognizant of the extent to which their own abilities are exaggerated by positive stereotypes. In the domain of athletic or dance ability, for example, Blacks in interaction with Whites may view themselves as significantly less talented than the almost caricatured stereotype of their group would suggest. Indeed, the man and woman in our example could easily find themselves in this quadrant if the man sees himself as less competent at logical and mathematical reasoning than the male stereotype would lead the female perceiver to expect (Benbow, 1988; Osborne, 2001).

This situation involves contrary tensions that could produce either a verification or appraisal effect. On one hand, the need for self-verification, bolstered by the desire to escape the pressure of living up to the flattering stereotype, should prompt the target to press for a verification effect. He could utilize his status advantage to assert his self-view, perhaps through explicit self-disclosure, while encountering little overt resistance. Moreover, because asking a perceiver to downgrade positive appraisals does not present a threat to the perceiver (and in fact boosts the perceiver's relative standing), the target is likely to encounter less resistance with such a request than if he were asking the perceiver to enhance her appraisals of him. These tendencies would favor a verification effect.

On the other hand, by pressing for a verification effect, the target risks invalidating his high status in the eyes of his lower-status counterpart. Concern for maintaining his high status may therefore cause him to press rather lightly, if at all, for a verification effect. Such a concern is likely to be especially acute if the target feels that his high status is tenuous and fragile, whereas if he feels his status is well established and secure, disclosing some negative self-views may pose little threat to his status advantage. From the perceiver's side, if her appraisals are based primarily on positive categorical stereotypes (rather than on, say, piecemeal individuated information about the specific target), they may be more resistant to change. Stereotypical beliefs direct attention away from contradictory evidence and may produce the conviction that a person fits the stereotype at some deep, essential level even if the person is not aware of it. Faced with appraisals and consistent treatment suggesting he is more positive than he thinks, the high-status target may well respond by elevating his self-views, bringing them into alignment with the perceiver's positive appraisals. Of course, if his negative self-views are based on voluminous feedback over a long period of time, he may experience some psychological discomfort and even distress from shifting long-held self-views, but shifting self-views in a positive rather than negative direction may allow him to quickly overcome his discomfort, if there is any merit to a self-enhancement motive (Bernichon, Cook, and Brown, 2003; Brown, Collins, and Schmidt, 1988).

An appraisal effect would bring the target's self-views into alignment with the relevant stereotype of his social category and with his high status in the dyad. This alignment may eventually increase the target's sense of psychological coherence after shifting his self-views (despite the temporary disruption of changing his self-views) (Swann, Rentfrow, and Guinn, 2003). An appraisal effect could therefore allow the target to achieve consistency among his self-views, high status, and positive stereotypes of his relevant social category.

Like Quadrant 2, the benefits of a verification effect far outweigh the likely consequences of an appraisal effect. A verification effect would attenuate the status disparity because congruence around the target's negative self-views should detract from his high status. Productivity could receive a boost here because the influence of the high status person would be dampened on dimensions on which he feels he is not very qualified to contribute. Additionally, this could open the door for the lower status person to contribute more along these dimensions, if she feels qualified to do so. A second order benefit could also arise as a result of the vulnerability exhibited by the high status person, which could contribute to a healthy norm of honesty and psychological safety (Ely, 2006; Edmondson, 1999).

The congruence achieved by an appraisal effect would reinforce the status disparity by aligning the target's high status with positive self-views. This could be especially bad for productivity if the high status person starts to dominate contributions along dimensions for which he is not particularly qualified (in light of his own initially negative self-views). More generally, the reinforcement of high status for this individual is unlikely to foster healthy collaboration, especially because the trend is toward him becoming increasingly dominant. To the extent that this limits the contribution of the low-status person, collaboration and performance may suffer.

Quadrant 4: Low-status target with negative self-views

Because the target is low status, her negative self-views are consistent with the conventional stereotype of her social category. The positive appraisals, however, are counter to the prevailing stereotype, suggesting that they may be based on more individuating information, such as observed behavior. As a result, these appraisals may be considerably robust and influential, making an appraisal effect likely. In addition, during the early stages of a relationship, the target's self-enhancement motive may overwhelm her self-verification motive (Swann, de la Ronde, and Hixon, 1994), favoring a shift of self-views toward the relatively positive appraisals.

Achieving congruence in this quadrant through an appraisal effect should generally attenuate the duo's status disparity by fostering more positive self-views in the target, thereby increasing her status. When the low-status person has substantive contributions to make on the dimensions in question, this kind of appraisal effect should increase her contributions in ways that improve productivity. In addition, the confidence gained from elevating self-views on some dimensions may have broader benefits, increasing her contributions on dimensions that go beyond the self-views she elevated (e.g., by increasing the target's confidence that she need not be constrained by her group's stereotype).

There is abundant research suggesting that the target in this quadrant will frequently succeed in convincing the perceiver to downgrade his appraisals and bring them into alignment with her own relatively negative self-views (Swann, Pelham, and Krull, 1989), particularly if the target has low self-esteem (Bernichon, Cook, and Brown, 2003). Little of this research, however, has investigated the influence of status differences on these identity negotiation processes.

Low status may actually exacerbate the desire to have negative self-views verified, according to research on system justification, whereby members of low-status groups accept and even encourage others to reinforce their low-status position (Jost and Banaji, 1994). Given this target perspective, the perceiver may offer little resistance to lowering his appraisals, aligning them with popular stereotypes of the low-status group while simultaneously bolstering his own relative standing.

A verification effect in this situation would reinforce the status disparity, aligning low status with negative self-views. When the target's self-views are the product of self-stereotyping and unwarranted self-doubt, this should have a negative effect on productivity and collaboration because the high-status person will come to support the low-status person in limiting her contributions. Reinforcing the status disparity may also decrease the target's general sense of self-efficacy beyond the self-views in question, further diminishing collaboration and productivity.

Summary of the effects of status differences

Our analysis of these four quadrants highlights a variety of forces that accompany status differences between people engaged in identity negotiation processes. Three of these forces seem particularly potent in predicting whether a verification or appraisal effect is more likely in each of the four quadrants. The first and most obvious effect is that low-status targets should have more difficulty changing their high-status counterpart's views than vice versa, simply because of the relatively low power and influence associated with their low-status position.

This influence would support the straightforward prediction that the high-status person would "win" the identity negotiation in each quadrant.

Complicating this predication, however, are two additional forces. The second consideration is where a target is working with or against conventional stereotypes associated with their social category. Because this social category is also the basis of their status position, it should be easier for a high-status target to align positive self-views and appraisals, whereas it should be easier for a low-status target to align negative self-views and appraisals. This is consistent with research showing that some social categories such as men and Whites convey high status and positive stereotypes, whereas other social categories such as women or racial minorities convey lower status and more negative stereotypes, particularly along dimensions associated with workplace success (Ellemers and Barreto, chapter 7 of this volume).

Finally, a third consideration is whether the change a target is attempting to elicit presents a threat to the perceiver. In general, perceivers are likely to find it more threatening to elevate their appraisals of a target because raising the standing of the target necessarily decreases the perceiver's relative standing. By the same logic, perceivers should not be threatened by lowering their appraisals of a target, because this necessarily improves their own perceived standing relative to the target.

These three forces help to explain the systematically different challenges targets face across the four quadrants, as displayed in Figure 4.2. If we assume that working from a low-status position is the most difficult of the three challenges, followed by working against a stereotyped appraisal, and that the potential threat of elevating a perceiver's appraisals while a challenge is the least difficult of the three, then Quadrants 1 and 3 pose the least difficulty for achieving a verification effect because of the target's high status. Quadrant 4 is difficult because of the target's low status, but is otherwise amenable to eliciting a verification effect. Quadrant 2, on the other hand, presents the most challenging situation for a target attempting to shift the perceiver's appraisals due to the combination of all three challenges: the target is working from a low-status position, working against conventional stereotypes, and trying to elicit a change that is potentially threatening to the perceiver. Importantly, a verification effect in Quadrant 2 also represents the biggest potential benefit from diversity, whereby a low-status person has positive self-views, which represent a strong contribution to

	Target's obstacles to eliciting a verification effect			
	1 Working from low-status position?	2 Working against a stereotype?	3 Threatening to the perceiver?	Degree of difficulty in eliciting verification
Quadrant 1	No	No	Yes	Least difficult
Quadrant 2	**Yes**	**Yes**	**Yes**	**Most difficult**
Quadrant 3	No	Yes	No	Less difficult
Quadrant 4	Yes	No	No	More difficult

Figure 4.2 Obstacles to eliciting a verification effect by quadrant

collective productivity if those with high status can understand, acknowledge, and be open to the skills and abilities of the low-status person. As this quadrant demonstrates, analyzing status differences and identity negotiation processes simultaneously allows us to isolate several distinct challenges that are at the core of the "diversity paradox."

The consequences of identity negotiation effects portrayed in our analysis also take multiple forms. The first order effects consist of the contributions that flow directly from the skills related to the self-views in question. For example, if a low-status person has positive self-views about her creativity, and her counterpart comes to see her as highly creative, their collaboration should benefit from her creative ability. There are also second order effects to consider, starting with whether the identity negotiation outcomes either reinforce or reduce the overall status disparity within the dyad. We assume that reducing status disparities stemming from social category memberships will benefit collaboration, but also acknowledge that status differences based on legitimate criteria can help people collaborate effectively. The way identity negotiation processes unfold also has implications for the climate and norms of the collective. If high-status people are open to discussing and possibly revising their self-views and appraisals, this can set a tone that helps people utilize their skills and abilities to the fullest.

Finally, the pattern of verification and appraisal effects can powerfully influence personal development. Do identity negotiation processes incorporate and legitimate the developmental aspirations of participants, or do they lock people into a static conception of their capabilities and identities? For example, the target in Quadrant 4 has low status and negative self-views, but this raises the question of whether she has more to contribute than indicated by her current self-views. Perhaps an appraisal effect in this quadrant, whereby the perceiver helps the target to elevate her self-views on particular dimensions, could also help the target elevate her confidence, aspirations, and developmental trajectory.

Moderators of the effects of status on identity negotiation processes

The influence of status may, in some cases, be moderated by differences in the way certain individuals understand their status and its implications. For example, some low-status individuals may persistently focus on stigma associated with their position and anticipate mistreatment by others (Pinel, 2004). Stigma-conscious individuals tend to struggle to maintain self-certainty and refrain from challenging the stereotypical judgments non-stigmatized others might make of them (Pinel, 1999; Brown and Pinel, 2003). By contrast, high-status people with corresponding low stigma consciousness tend to engage in more active, direct, and explicit behaviors. Therefore, the differential stigma consciousness that often accompanies status differences should generally amplify the influence of status on identity negotiation. As social interaction unfolds, this could increase the risk of a negative or antagonistic undertone in the relationship, reducing the likelihood that unjustly ignored low-status voices will gain support.

Tendencies to justify existing hierarchies, like those caused by system justification or social dominance beliefs, can also increase the influence of status differences in guiding identity negotiations. Recent formulations of both sets of beliefs include a generalized support for unequal, hierarchical relationships among groups – support that may be provided by both dominant (high-status) and subordinate (low-status) group members (Jost, Banaji, and Nosek, 2004; Sidanius *et al.*, 2001; see also Tiedens and Fragale, 2003). If diverse individuals seek to justify and maintain the prevailing hierarchy, high-status individuals will find it relatively easy to elevate others' appraisals because positive appraisals are consistent with and reinforce the status differential. Interestingly, hierarchy-justifying beliefs could make it more difficult for the high-status person to *lower* others' appraisals, because doing so might disagreeably flatten the cherished social order.

Of course, people can be every bit as invested in their personal views as they are in the social order, if not more so. As we briefly mentioned in our quadrant analysis, a lifetime of experience and feedback from others can give individuals a substantial degree of certainty in their self-views. The egocentric nature of personal life helps people construe the entirety of their experience as evidence for their self-views (Swann and Ely, 1984). At an extreme, certainty could give individuals' self-views a ring of indisputable truth. If investment in personal views is compounded by the sense that the views are central and important to a person's lifestyle and overall identity, resistance to others' appraisals could dominate any influence associated with relative status. For example, low-status individuals who try to elicit positive appraisals from their high-status peers may find that self-certainty can overcome the disadvantages of their low-status position throughout the identity negotiation process.

Questions for future research

Our analysis of status differences, varying patterns of incongruence, and two different routes to congruence generate many possibilities and questions that could be theoretically developed more fully and empirically tested. Perhaps the most prominent question concerns when appraisal effects are helpful, when verification effects are helpful, and whether and how this depends on diversity (and status differences associated with diversity). Prior research in this domain suggests that verification effects are the dominant path to high performance, especially on the creative tasks for which diverse teams are most often assembled. Our analysis partly agrees with this conclusion, but with the qualification that under some circumstances appraisal effects could boost the contributions of low-status people, curtail the dominance of high-status people, and perhaps enhance the collaboration and productivity of the collective as a result.

A related question concerns the transition from theorizing about two people working as a dyad to three or more people working together as a group. The example we have used above consisted of only two people and yet even this simple social arrangement generated quite a bit of complexity around interpersonal congruence. Given the many possibilities we described above, how do groups of people systematically engage in these identity negotiation processes, especially when status differences among the group members are considered? We can imagine numerous configurations of high- and low-status people having a variety of positive and negative self-views and appraisals. Moreover, people belong to multiple social categories, such that some people may be high status along one dimension but low status along another dimension. Perhaps the fundamental advantage of an identity negotiation framework is that all of this complexity is filtered through people's self-views, appraisals, and social interaction, suggesting that status itself is up for negotiation within any particular group. And, while some predictions become inevitably more complicated when several group members are involved, other predictions may become easier to support in a group than in a dyad. Consider, for example, a situation in which five people from a salient high-status group are teammates with a sixth person who belongs to a low-status group. As a target, this sixth person is much less likely to elicit a verification effect if all five teammates hold similar appraisals that are discrepant in the same direction. In this situation, an appraisal effect seems much more likely because of the number of perceivers who are "lined up" against the solo target. Exploring situations in which multiple group members (compared to a dyad) strengthen the likelihood of either a verification or appraisal effect could be a good starting point for extending research in this direction.

Valuable research could also be done to reveal additional moderators of whether a target's status promotes verification or appraisal effects. One possibility suggested above is that the homogeneity of appraisals may make an appraisal effect more likely, whereas verification effects may be easier to elicit when perceivers' appraisals are not aligned (and especially when they are discrepant from self-views not just in magnitude, but in direction). Another avenue of inquiry concerns the nature of self-views, in particular the extent to which they are based on objective criteria and specific evidence versus more subjective judgments. Ability in math, for example, could be tested and verified, whereas leadership qualities may depend on more subjective judgments. The relative likelihood of verification versus appraisal effects may depend in part on whether objective evidence can be brought to bear on the identity negotiation to convince group members of the veracity of a particular view. This, like self-certainty, may be more important for low-status people who may not have other avenues of influence available to them.

In many respects, these questions are all variations on a theme, which is to identify the processes that foster productive interactions and collaboration, and those that discourage unproductive patterns. Along these lines, we return to the question of how low-status targets can prevail in eliciting verification effects for their positive self-views, which as a classic problem that our preceding analysis identified has particularly difficult to solve. We think the identity negotiation framework helps to identify the difficulties inherent in this problem, but we suspect that going one step deeper in analyzing this problem may help to resolve it. More specifically, we suggest that researchers need to explore the identity negotiation processes which trigger and shape the outcomes of *identity deliberation* – the *intra*personal process through which individuals resolve any perceived discrepancies between themselves and others regarding their own or others' identities. While identity negotiation captures the exchange of identity-relevant information between targets and perceivers that is vital to motivate improvements in interpersonal congruence, changes to self-views are only possible if the target ultimately engages in identity deliberation, where he or she considers incorporating new information (such as treatment received from a perceiver) into his or her identity. Similarly, appraisals cannot be adjusted according to novel information (such as the behavior of a target) unless the perceiver is moved to deliberate on the target's identity. Identity deliberation, then, is the key intrapersonal precursor to changes in interpersonal congruence, and only when this deliberation leads to the closer alignment of self-views and appraisals will interpersonal congruence increase.

Caruso, Polzer, and London (2007) contrasted implicit and explicit forms of identity negotiation and how, under various moderating conditions, they differentially influence identity deliberation and, consequently, the degree of interpersonal congruence in groups. Perhaps the most critical difference they describe is that implicit forms of identity negotiation – that is, strategies that rely heavily on indirect suggestive behavior and unchecked inference – are highly vulnerable to obliviousness, misrepresentation, and misinterpretation. When, for example, a target attempts to communicate her group membership through her style of dress, she cannot be sure that perceivers will (a) recognize clothing as representative of any social group at all, (b) correctly attribute the clothing to the corresponding social group, or (c) understand that the choice of clothing was intended to signal group membership rather than, say, conformity to a clothing trend. Moreover, perceivers too face problems of miscommunication. Efforts to signal appraisals to a target through subtle nonverbal behaviors like hugs or smiles have a wide range of possible interpretations that may vary depending on fleeting factors like a target's mood, recent private experiences, and attentiveness. Implicit identity negotiation processes thus risk triggering identity deliberations based on inaccurate and misleading information, if they even succeed in triggering identity deliberations at all.

In contrast, Caruso, Polzer, and London (2007) assert that explicit identity negotiation behaviors – those that utilize direct dialogue about self-views and appraisals – better promote the exchange of intended information, as targets and perceivers together can iteratively check and refine their understandings of each other's perceptions, intentions, and views. For example, a target who explicitly tells a perceiver that he or she is highly skilled capitalizes on norms of dialogue and conversation that encourage the perceiver to react and reveal their appraisals of that claim and thus, of the target. Based on that reaction, or even the absence of one, the target can further elaborate on their claim or probe for further information on the perceiver's appraisal, both of which should increase the likelihood that any discrepancies between the target's self-views and appraisals become known to the target, perceiver, or both. In the absence of active deception, explicit identity negotiation behaviors like self-disclosure and direct feedback are thus more likely to prompt identity deliberations, and inform those deliberations with highly valid and authentic information on targets' and perceivers' views. This gives identity deliberation the highest possible chance of resulting in true improvements to interpersonal congruence. We should also acknowledge the interpersonal risks associated with such direct self-disclosure, based on the vulnerability incurred by the target, and feedback behaviors, given the threat this might introduce to the target of the feedback. Despite these risks, or perhaps intertwined with them, the potential returns to interpersonal congruence for engaging in these explicit behaviors may make them worth attempting (London, 2003).

It may be that these differences between implicit and explicit identity negotiations help solve the puzzling and erratic pattern of superior and inferior performance for diverse groups (Williams and O'Reilly, 1998; Guzzo and Dickson, 1996). In groups, impressions of coworkers and normative roles are set very early on, and often implicitly (Gersick,

1988; Hackman, 2002; Bettenhausen and Murnighan, 1985). However, because members of diverse groups cannot rely heavily on shared experiences to inform their judgments of one another, they are more likely instead to rely on their stereotypes about each other's social groups (Ames, 2004a, 2004b), especially early in group interaction, when little individuating information has been shared. It may be that this implicit and unchecked stereotyping makes it difficult for diverse groups to establish interpersonal congruence, a difficulty that Polzer, Milton, and Swann (2002) showed impedes their ability to reap the performance advantages of interpersonal congruence. In contrast, early implicit identity and role negotiations among members of homogeneous groups are more likely to rely on informed projection than on stereotypes (Ames, 2004a, 2004b), giving these groups the edge in achieving high interpersonal congruence and associated performance advantages.

This difficulty could potentially be offset, however, when identity and role negotiations are made explicit. Our identity negotiation framework suggests that diverse groups can attempt to achieve high interpersonal congruence by engaging in explicit, rather than the common implicit, forms of identity negotiation. Such behavior should enable these groups to overcome or even circumvent stereotyping, and establish channels of communication through which the varied perspectives that constitute diversity's primary advantages could be expressed, understood, and ultimately valued and utilized.

Key challenges

A number of methodological challenges face researchers interested in empirically investigating identity negotiation processes among diverse individuals. One key challenge is to decide whether to study identity negotiations "live" or to gather recollections (perhaps via interviews or surveys) of identity negotiation processes. Recollections are, of course, subject to biases and gaps in memory, but they can be collected more readily than real-time observational data and allow researchers to study identity negotiations that occur in private, relatively unobservable, or spontaneous settings (e.g., intimate gatherings, hallway conversations, remote locations, phone or email correspondence). Using recollections also ensures that the identity negotiation itself was not altered by the artifacts of an observational setting such as an observer, video camera, or isolated room. However, live observations offer the substantial advantage of comprehensive and relatively unbiased data, as well as the opportunity to intentionally use the observational setting to shape the identity negotiation as it unfolds. In order to take advantage of the differing strengths of retrospective and prospective methods, researchers may want to begin investigations with real-time observations in order to identify and select focal aspects of diverse identity negotiations, and then craft tightly focused interview protocols and surveys to explore individuals' recollections for instances of those elements.

Another important issue concerns whether identity negotiations will be studied in dyadic settings or groups. Identity negotiation processes become substantially more complex when members of a group are able to form impressions of one another not only through direct and mutual communication, but also through bystander observation of other group members' exchanges. Because dyadic identity negotiations allow researchers to isolate or manipulate the flow of information between individuals, they neatly highlight influential behaviors and responses, but also prevent examination of the effects of secondary, indirect information flows. Group settings capture the fuller spectrum of interpersonal influence, but make it more difficult to parse out and measure the critical activities. Even high-quality video recordings of group interactions cannot ensure that a researcher will be able to recognize instances of a group member overhearing other members' conversations. Considering these issues, researchers may want to conduct studies in both dyadic and group settings, using detailed outcome measures to identify what outcomes, if any, vary between settings. This should better focus subsequent observations and coding on identifying those identity negotiation activities which uniquely arise in group settings.

Conclusion

The identity negotiation framework that we have described and used in this chapter provides a valuable lens for studying social interaction among diverse people. It is a dynamic framework that accounts for both the initial conditions that frame a social exchange (in the form of participants' self-views and appraisals), how these initial conditions influence the exchange, and how the dynamics of the exchange shape people's self-views and appraisals over time. Yet, in the context of diversity, this framework overlooks an essential dimension of the interaction, namely the status differences among people that they derive from their different social category memberships. In this chapter we have tried to give a flavor of the rich possibilities that can be explored by combining the identity negotiation framework with research on status differences. This is a natural combination that can enrich both domains of inquiry and, in so doing, move us closer to helping diverse groups realize their full potential.

References

Ames, D. R. (2004a). Inside the mind reader's tool kit: Projection and stereo-typing in mental state inference. *Journal of Personality and Social Psychology*, 87(3), 340–353.

Ames, D. R. (2004b). Strategies for social inference: A similarity contingency model of projection and stereotyping in attribute prevalence estimates. *Journal of Personality and Social Psychology*, 87(5), 573–585.

Benbow, C. P. (1988). Sex differences in mathematical reasoning ability in intellectually talented preadolescents: Their nature, effects, and possible causes. *Behavioral and Brain Sciences*, 11(2), 169–232.

Bernichon, T., Cook, K. E., and Brown, J. D. (2003). Seeking self-evaluative feedback: The interactive role of global self-esteem and specific self-views. *Journal of Personality and Social Psychology*, 84(1), 194–204.

Bettenhausen, K., and Murnighan, J. K. (1985). The emergence of norms in competitive decision-making groups. *Administrative Science Quarterly*, 30(3), 350–372.

Billig, M. (1976). *Social Psychology and Intergroup Relations*. London: New York.

Brown, J. D., Collins, R. L., and Schmidt, G. W. (1988). Self-esteem and direct versus indirect forms of self-enhancement. *Journal of Personality and Social Psychology*, 55(3), 445–453.

Brown, R. P., and Pinel, E. C. (2003). Stigma on my mind: Individual differences in the experience of stereotype threat. *Journal of Experimental Social Psychology*, 39(6), 626–633.

Carli, L. L. (1989). Gender differences in interaction style and influence. *Journal of Personality and Social Psychology*, 56(4), 565–576.

Carson, R. C. (1969). *Interaction Concepts of Personality*. Chicago: Aldine Pub.Co.

Caruso, H. M., Polzer, J. T. and London, M. (2006). *Building Interpersonal Congruence to Enhance Team Effectiveness*. Unpublished manuscript.

Chatman, J. A., Polzer, J. T., Barsade, S. G., and Neale, M. A. (1998). Being different yet feeling similar: The influence of demographic composition and organizational culture on work processes and outcomes. *Administrative Science Quarterly*, *43*(4), 749–780.

Chen, S., and Welland, J. (2002). Examining the effects of power as a function of self-construals and gender. *Self and Identity*, *1*(3), 251–269.

Chen, Y. (ed.) (2006). *Research on Managing Groups and Teams: National Culture and Groups*, Vol. 9. New York: Elsevier.

Cooley, C. H. (1902). *Human Nature and the Social Order*. New York: Scribner.

Cox, T. H., Lobel, S. A., and McLeod, P. L. (1991). Effects of ethnic group cultural differences on cooperative and competitive behavior on a group task. *Academy of Management Journal*, *34*(4), 827–847.

Cross, S. E., Bacon, P. L., and Morris, M. L. (2000). The relational-interdependent self-construal and relationships. *Journal of Personality and Social Psychology*, *78*(4), 791–808.

Cross, S. E., and Madson, L. (1997). Models of the self: Self-construals and gender. *Psychological Bulletin*, *122*(1), 5–37.

Cross, S. E., and Markus, H. R. (1991). Possible selves across the life span. *Human Development*, *34*(4), 230–255.

Curtis, R. C., and Miller, K. (1986). Believing another likes or dislikes you: Behaviors making the beliefs come true. *Journal of Personality and Social Psychology*, *51*(2), 284–290.

Dougherty, D. (1992). Interpretive Barriers to Successful Product Innovation in Large Firms. *Organization Science*, *3*(2), 179–202.

Downey, G., Freitas, A. L., Michaelis, B., and Khouri, H. (1998). The self-fulfilling prophecy in close relationships: Rejection sensitivity and rejection by romantic partners. *Journal of Personality and Social Psychology*, *75*(2), 545–560.

Edmondson, A. (1999). Psychological safety and learning behavior in work teams. *Administrative Science Quarterly*, *44*(2), 350–383.

Elsass, P. M., and Graves, L. M. (1997). Demographic diversity in decision-making groups: The experiences of women and people of color. *Academy of Management Review*, *22*(4), 946–973.

Elsbach, K. D. (2003). Relating physical environment to self-categorizations: Identity threat and affirmation in a non-territorial office space. *Administrative Science Quarterly*, *48*(4), 622.

Ely, R. (1991). Gender difference: What difference does it make? *Academy of Management Proceedings*, 363–367.

Ely, R. J. (1994). The effects of organizational demographics and social identity on relationships among professional women. *Administrative Science Quarterly*, *39*(2), 203–238.

Ely, R. J., and Meyerson, D. E. (2000). Theories of gender in organizations: A new approach to organizational analysis and change. *Research in Organizational Behavior, 22*, 103–151.

Ely, R. J., and Thomas, D. A. (2001). Cultural diversity at work: The effects of diversity perspectives on work group processes and outcomes. *Administrative Science Quarterly, 46*(2), 229.

Falk, G., and Falk, S. (1981). The impact of decision rules on the distribution of power in problem-solving teams with unequal power. *Group & Organization Studies, 6*(2), 211.

Farina, A., Allen, J. G., and Saul, B. B. (1968). The role of the stigmatized person in affecting social relationships. *Journal of Personality, 36*(2), 169–182.

Farina, A., Gliha, D., Boudreau, L. A., Allen, J. G., and Sherman, M. (1971). Mental illness and the impact of believing others know about it. *Journal of Abnormal Psychology, 77*(1), 1–5.

Festinger, L. (1957). *A Theory of Cognitive Dissonance.* Evanston, IL: Row Peterson.

Finkelstein, L. M., Allen, T. D., and Rhoton, L. A. (2003). An examination of the role of age in mentoring relationships. *Group & Organization Management, 28*(2), 249–281.

Foldy, E. G. (2004). Learning from diversity: A theoretical exploration. *Public Administration Review, 64*(5), 529–538.

Frable, D. E., Blackstone, T., and Scherbaum, C. (1990). Marginal and mindful: Deviants in social interactions. *Journal of Personality and Social Psychology, 59*(1), 140–149.

Friedman, J. J., and DiTomaso, N. (1996). Myths about diversity: What managers need to know about changes in the US labor force. *California Management Review, 38*(4), 54.

Fromm, E. (1947). *Man for Himself: An Inquiry into the Psychology of Ethics.* New York: Rinehart.

Fung, H. H., Carstensen, L. L., and Lutz, A. M. (1999). Influence of time on social preferences: Implications for life-span development. *Psychology and Aging, 14*(4), 595–604.

Gabriel, S., and Gardner, W. L. (1999). Are there "his" and "hers" types of interdependence? The implications of gender differences in collective versus relational interdependence for affect, behavior, and cognition. *Journal of Personality and Social Psychology, 77*(3), 642–655.

Gersick, C. J. (1988). Time and transition in work teams: Toward a new model of group development. *Academy of Management Journal, 31*(1), 9–41.

Gill, M. J., and Swann, W. B. J. (2004). On what it means to know someone: A matter of pragmatics. *Journal of Personality and Social Psychology, 86*(3), 405–418.

Goffman, E. (1959). *The Presentation of Self in Everyday Life*. Garden City: NY Doubleday.

Guimond, S., Chatard, A., Martinot, D., Crisp, R. J., and Redersdorff, S. (2006). Social comparison, self-stereotyping, and gender differences in self-construals. *Journal of Personality and Social Psychology, 90*(2), 221–242.

Guzzo, R. A., and Dickson, M. W. (1996). Teams in organizations: Recent research on performance and effectiveness. *Annual Review of Psychology, 47*, 307–338.

Hackman, J. R. (2002). *Leading Teams: Setting the Stage for Great Performances*. Boston: Harvard Business School Press.

Harvey, O. J., Hunt, D. E., and Schroder, H. M. (1979). *Conceptual Systems and Personality Organization*. New York: Wiley.

Heine, S. J., Proulx, T., and Vohs, K. D. (2006). The Meaning Maintenance Model: On the coherence of social motivations. *Personality and Social Psychology Review, 10*(2), 88–110.

Jehn, K. A., Northcraft, G. B., and Neale, M. A. (1999). Why differences make a difference: A field study of diversity, conflict, and performance in workgroups. *Administrative Science Quarterly, 44*(4), 741–763.

Johnson, W. B., and Packer, A. E. (1987). *Workforce 2000: Work and Workers for the 21st Century*. Indianapolis: Hudson Institute.

Jones, E. E. (1964). *Ingratiation, A Social Psychological Analysis*. New York: Appleton-Century-Crofts.

Jones, E. E., and Pittman, T. S. (1982). Toward a general theory of strategic self-presentation. In J. Suls (ed.), *Psychological Perspectives on the Self*. Hillsdale, NJ: Lawrence Erlbaum Associates.

Jones, S. C., and Panitch, D. (1971). The self-fulfilling prophecy and interpersonal attraction. *Journal of Experimental Social Psychology, 7*(3), 356–366.

Jost, J. T., and Banaji, M. R. (1994). The role of stereotyping in system-justification and the production of false consciousness. *British Journal of Social Psychology, 33*(1), 1–27.

Kelley, H. H. (1979). *Personal Relationships: Their Structures and Processes*. Mahwah: Lawrence Erlbaum Associates.

Kelley, H. H., and Stahelski, A. J. (1970). Social interaction basis of cooperators' and competitors' beliefs about others. *Journal of Personality and Social Psychology, 16*(1), 66–91.

Konrad, A. M. (2003). Special issue introduction: Defining the domain of workplace diversity scholarship. *Group & Organization Management, 28*(1), 4–17.

Lau, D. C., and Murnighan, J. K. (1998). Demographic diversity and fault-lines: The compositional dynamics of organizational groups. *Academy of Management Review, 23*(2), 325.

Lawrence, B. S. (1988). New wrinkles in the theory of age: Demography, norms, and performance ratings. *Academy of Management Journal, 31*(2), 309–337.

Lecky, P. (1945). *Self-consistency: A Theory of Personality*. Washington, DC: Island Press.

Lepore, L., and Brown, R. (1997). Category and stereotype activation: Is prejudice inevitable? *Journal of Personality and Social Psychology, 72*(2), 275–287.

Levin, S., Federico, C. M., Sidanius, J., and Rabinowitz, J. L. (2002). Social dominance orientation and intergroup bias: The legitimation of favoritism for high-status groups. *Personality and Social Psychology Bulletin, 28*(2), 144–157.

Levinson, D. J. (1978). *The Seasons of a Man's Life*. New York: Knopf.

London, M. (2003). *Job Feedback: Giving, Seeking, and Using Feedback for Performance Improvement* (2nd edn). Mahwah: Lawrence Erlbaum Associates.

Lovelace, K., and Rosen, B. (1996). Differences in achieving person-organization fit among diverse groups of managers. *Journal of Management, 22*(5), 703–722.

Markus, H. R., and Nurius, P. (1986). Possible selves. *American Psychologist, 41*(9), 954–969.

Mead, G. H. (1934). *Mind, Self and Society from the Standpoint of a Social Behaviorist*. Chicago: The University of Chicago Press.

Miller, C. T., and Myers, A. M. (1998). Compensating for prejudice: How heavyweight people (and others) control outcomes despite prejudice. In J. K. Swim and C. Stangor (eds.), *Prejudice: The Target's Perspective* (pp. 191–218). Palo Alto: Academic Press.

Miller, C. T., Rothblum, E. D., Brand, P. A., and Felicio, D. M. (1995). Do obese women have poorer social relationships than nonobese women? Reports by self, friends, and coworkers. *Journal of Personality, 63*(1), 65–85.

Nemeth, C. J. (1986). Differential contributions of majority and minority influence. *Psychological Review, 93*(1), 23–32.

Nkomo, S. M. (1992). The emperor has no clothes: Rewriting "race in organizations." *Academy of Management Review, 17*(3), 487–513.

Offermann, L. R., and Gowing, M. K. (1990). Organizations of the future: Changes and challenges. *American Psychologist, 45*(2), 95–108.

Omi, M., and Winant, H. (1994). *Racial Formation in the United States: From the 1960s to the 1990s* (2nd edn). New York: Routledge.

Osborne, J. W. (2001). Testing stereotype threat: Does anxiety explain race and sex differences in achievement? *Contemporary Educational Psychology*, 26(3), 291–310.

Pinel, E. C. (1999). Stigma consciousness: The psychological legacy of social stereotypes. *Journal of Personality and Social Psychology*, 76(1), 114–128.

Pinel, E. C. (2002). Stigma consciousness in intergroup contexts: The power of conviction. *Journal of Experimental Social Psychology*, 38(2), 178–185.

Pinel, E. C. (2004). You're just saying that because I'm a woman: Stigma consciousness and attributions to discrimination. *Self and Identity*, 3(1), 39–51.

Plaks, J. E., Stroessner, S. J., Dweck, C. S., and Sherman, J. W. (2001). Person theories and attention allocation: Preferences for stereotypic versus counterstereotypic information. *Journal of Personality and Social Psychology*, 80(6), 876–893.

Polzer, J. T., Milton, L. P., and Swann, W. B., Jr. (2002). Capitalizing on diversity: Interpersonal congruence in small work groups. *Administrative Science Quarterly*, 47(2), 296–324.

Ragins, B. R. (1997). Diversified mentoring relationships in organizations: A power perspective. *The Academy of Management Review*, 22(2), 482–521.

Ridgeway, C. (1991). The social construction of status value: Gender and other nominal characteristics. *Social Forces*, 70(2), 367–386.

Ridgeway, C. L. (1997). Interaction and the conservation of gender inequality: Considering employment. *American Sociological Review*, 62(2), 218–235.

Ridgeway, C. L., and Berger, J. (1986). Expectations, legitimation, and dominance behavior in task groups. *American Sociological Review*, 51(5), 603–617.

Ridgeway, C. L., and Erickson, K. G. (2000). Creating and spreading status beliefs. *American Journal of Sociology*, 106(3), 579–615.

Roberson, L., Deitch, E. A., Brief, A. P., and Block, C. J. (2002). Stereotype threat and feedback seeking in the workplace. *Journal of Vocational Behavior*, 62(1), 176–188.

Robinson, G., and Dechant, K. (1997). Building a business case for diversity. *The Academy of Management Executive*, 11(3), 21.

Rosenthal, R., and Jacobson, L. (1968). *Pygmalion in the Classroom: Teacher Expectation and Pupils' Intellectual Development*. New York: Holt Rinehart and Winston.

Schlenker, B. R. (1980). *Impression Management: The Self-concept, Social Identity, and Interpersonal Relations.* Monterey: Brooks/Cole Pub. Co.

Secord, P. F., and Backman, C. W. (1964). Interpersonal congruency, perceived similarity, and friendship. *Sociometry, 27*(2), 115–127.

Sellers, R. M., Smith, M. A., Shelton, J. N., Rowley, S. A. J., and Chavous, T. M. (1998). Multidimensional model of racial identity: A reconceptualization of African American racial identity. *Personality and Social Psychology Review, 2*(1), 18–39.

Sidanius, J., Levin, S., Federico, C., and Pratto, F. (2001). Legitimizing ideologies: The social dominance approach. In J. T. Jost and B. Major (eds.), *The Psychology of Legitimacy: Emerging Perspectives on Ideology, Justice, and Intergroup Relations.* New York: Cambridge University Press.

Sidanius, J., and Pratto, F. (1999). *Social Dominance: An Intergroup Theory of Social Hierarchy and Oppression.* Cambridge: Cambridge University Press.

Smith-Lovin, L., and Brody, C. (1989). Interruptions in group discussions: The effects of gender and group composition. *American Sociological Review, 54*(3), 424–435.

Snyder, M. (1984). When belief creates reality. In M. P. Zanna (ed.), *Advances in Experimental Social Psychology,* Vol. 18 (pp. 247–305). Orlando: Academic Press.

Snyder, M., and Stukas, A. A. J. (1999). Interpersonal processes: The interplay of cognitive, motivational, and behavioral activities in social interaction. *Annual Review of Psychology, 50,* 273–303.

Snyder, M., and Swann, W. B., Jr. (1978a). Behavioral confirmation in social interaction: From social perception to social reality. *Journal of Experimental Social Psychology, 14*(2), 148–162.

Snyder, M., and Swann, W. B., Jr. (1978b). Hypothesis-testing processes in social interaction. *Journal of Personality and Social Psychology, 36*(11), 1202–1212.

Staw, B. M., Sandelands, L. E., and Dutton, J. E. (1981). Threat-rigidity effects in organizational behavior: A multilevel analysis. *Administrative Science Quarterly, 26*(4), 501–524.

Steele, C. M., and Aronson, J. (1995). Stereotype threat and the intellectual test performance of African Americans. *Journal of Personality and Social Psychology, 69*(5), 797–811.

Swann, W. B., Jr. (1984). Quest for accuracy in person perception: A matter of pragmatics. *Psychological Review, 91*(4), 457–477.

   (1987). Identity negotiation: Where two roads meet. *Journal of Personality and Social Psychology, 53*(6), 1038–1051.

(1990). To be adored or to be known? The interplay of self-enhancement and self-verification. In E. T. Higgins and R. M. Sorrentino (eds.), *Handbook of Motivation and Cognition: Foundations of Social Behavior*, Vol. 2 (pp. 408–448). New York: Guilford Press.

(1997). The trouble with change: Self-verification and allegiance to the self. *Psychological Science*, 8(3), 177–180.

(2005). The self and identity negotiation. *Interaction Studies: Social Behaviour and Communication in Biological and Artificial Systems*, 6(1), 69–83.

Swann, W. B., Jr., de la Ronde, C., and Hixon, J. G. (1994). Authenticity and positivity strivings in marriage and courtship. *Journal of Personality and Social Psychology*, 66(5), 857–869.

Swann, W. B., Jr., and Ely, R. J. (1984). A battle of wills: Self-verification versus behavioral confirmation. *Journal of Personality and Social Psychology*, 46(6), 1287–1302.

Swann, W. B., Jr., and Hill, C. A. (1982). When our identities are mistaken: Reaffirming self-conceptions through social interaction. *Journal of Personality and Social Psychology*, 43(1), 59–66.

Swann, W. B., Jr., Kwan, V. S. Y., Polzer, J. T., and Milton, L. P. (2003). Fostering group identification and creativity in diverse groups: The role of individuation and self-verification. *Personality and Social Psychology Bulletin*, 29(11), 1396–1406.

Swann, W. B., Jr., Milton, L. P., and Polzer, J. T. (2000). Should we create a niche or fall in line? Identity negotiation and small group effectiveness. *Journal of Personality and Social Psychology*, 79(2), 238–250.

Swann, W. B., Jr., Pelham, B. W., and Krull, D. S. (1989). Agreeable fancy or disagreeable truth? Reconciling self-enhancement and self-verification. *Journal of Personality and Social Psychology*, 57(5), 782–791.

Swann, W. B., Jr., Polzer, J. T., Seyle, D. C., and Ko, S. J. (2004). Finding value in diversity: Verification of personal and social self-views in diverse groups. *Academy of Management Review*, 29(1), 9–27.

Swann, W. B., Jr., and Read, S. J. (1981a). Acquiring self-knowledge: The search for feedback that fits. *Journal of Personality and Social Psychology*, 41(6), 1119–1128.

Swann, W. B., Jr., and Read, S. J. (1981b). Self-verification processes: How we sustain our self-conceptions. *Journal of Experimental Social Psychology*, 17(4), 351–372.

Swann, W. B., Jr., Rentfrow, P. J., and Guinn, J. S. (2003). Self-verification: The search for coherence. In M. R. Leary and J. P. Tangney (eds.), *Handbook of Self and Identity* (pp. 367–383). New York: Guilford Press, 2003.

Swann, W. B., Jr., and Snyder, M. (1980). On translating beliefs into action: Theories of ability and their application in an instructional setting. *Journal of Personality and Social Psychology, 38*(6), 879–888.

Swann, W. B., Jr., Stein-Seroussi, A., and Giesler, R. B. (1992). Why people self-verify. *Journal of Personality and Social Psychology, 62*(3), 392–401.

Thibaut, J. W., and Kelley, H. H. (1959). *The Social Psychology of Groups.* New York: John Wiley & Sons.

Tiedens, L. Z., and Fragale, A. R. (2003). Power moves: Complementarity in dominant and submissive nonverbal behavior. *Journal of Personality and Social Psychology, 84*(3), 558–568.

Triandis, H. C., Kurowski, L. L., and Gelfand, M. J. (1994). Workplace diversity. In H. C. Triandis, M. D. Dunnette, and L. M. Hough (eds.), *Handbook of Industrial and Organizational Psychology*, Vol. 4 (2nd edn) (pp. 769–827). Palo Alto, CA: Consulting Psychologists Press.

Watson, W. E., Kumar, K., and Michaelsen, L. K. (1993). Cultural diversity's impact on interaction process and performance: Comparing homogeneous and diverse task groups. *Academy of Management Journal, 36*(3), 590–602.

Williams, J. R., Miller, C. E., Steelman, L. A., and Levy, P. E. (1999). Increasing feedback seeking in public contexts: It takes two (or more) to tango. *Journal of Applied Psychology, 84*(6), 969–976.

Williams, K. Y., and O'Reilly, C. A. (1998). Demography and diversity in organizations: A review of 40 years of research. *Research in Organizational Behavior, 20*, 77–140.

Word, C. O., Zanna, M. P., and Cooper, J. (1974). The nonverbal mediation of self-fulfilling prophecies in interracial interaction. *Journal of Experimental Social Psychology, 10*(2), 109–120.

Zanna, M. P., and Pack, S. J. (1975). On the self-fulfilling nature of apparent sex differences in behavior. *Journal of Experimental Social Psychology, 11*(6), 583–591.

5 | Diversity, conflict, and their consequences

KAREN A. JEHN, LINDRED L. GREER, AND
JOYCE RUPERT

Introduction

In recent years, diversity has come to play a central role in organizational life, due to increased globalization, greater workforce diversity, and the increasing complexity of jobs (Williams and O'Reilly, 1998). Scholars have investigated the impact of diversity on organizational outcomes such as performance or satisfaction, but findings on these effects have been largely inconsistent (for reviews and meta-analyses see Jackson, Joshi, and Erhardt, 2003; Mannix and Neale, 2005; Stewart, 2006; Webber and Donahue, 2001; Williams and O'Reilly, 1998). To better understand how diversity impacts organizational groups, research began to examine the processes underlying the effects of diversity on performance (e.g., Jehn, Northcraft, and Neale, 1999; Pelled, Eisenhardt, and Xin, 1999). Conflict has arisen as a primary process in explaining the effects of diversity upon performance (cf. Williams and O'Reilly, 1998; Lau and Murnighan, 1998). This chapter reviews the literature relating diversity, conflict, and performance and then discusses the new directions the field is heading in.

We will begin by briefly reviewing the theory and findings on diversity's effect on group processes and performance. We will identify the trends found in these studies as well as identify areas of diversity research that have not received as much attention in recent reviews and meta-analyses. We will then expand on recent developments in the diversity field. Then, we will move to the conflict literature. We will describe the intra-group conflict literature as it now stands and then specify the new directions within that field. Following this overview of the separate fields of diversity and conflict, we will then provide the first review that we are aware of which specifically focuses on studies which link the two concepts of diversity and conflict (see Appendix for an overview of studies), differentiating our review from that of others. We will separate this review into two different sections looking at the effects of social category diversity (diversity based on gender, age, race, etc.) on conflict separately from the effects of functional diversity (job function, education, etc.). These two different types of diversity lead to several outcomes, but have different mechanisms explaining the relationship between diversity and these outcomes (see Table 5.1). Following this review of the relationship between diversity and conflict, we will then look more in depth at future directions the field could head in. Specifically, we will present five new directions for research on the relationship between diversity and intra-group conflict in which we respectively discuss diversity and faultline perception and activation (new direction I), the role of subgroup status in conflicts (new direction II), intra-subgroup versus inter-subgroup processes (new direction III), the effects of diversity beliefs and attitudes during conflicts in diverse groups (new direction IV), and the effects of demographic faultlines and conflict on team learning (new direction V). We will discuss how these new directions may help to untangle and understand the relationship between diversity and conflict, and then show how this knowledge can be used to promote the status and welfare of disadvantaged group members.

An historical perspective on diversity

Diversity, in its broadest sense, has been defined as anything people could use to tell themselves that another person is different (Jackson, 1992; Mannix and Neale, 2005; Williams and O'Reilly, 1998). While a plethora of research has examined the effects of diversity on group processes and performance, findings have been largely divergent (Jackson *et al.*, 2003; Mannix and Neale, 2005; Stewart, 2006; Webber and Donahue, 2001; Williams and O'Reilly, 1998). Some studies have found that diversity improves group processes and performance (Bantel and Jackson, 1989; Bunderson and Sutcliffe, 2002; Gruenfeld *et al.*, 1996; Nemeth, 1986; Wiersema and Bantel, 1992) while others have found that it impedes group functioning and performance (Guzzo and Dickson, 1996; O'Reilly, Caldwell, and Barnett, 1989; Triandis, Kurowski, and Gelfand, 1993; Wagner, Pfeffer, and O'Reilly, 1984).

The studies which have found diversity to benefit performance provide support for the "value in diversity" hypothesis (Cox, Lobel, and McLeod, 1991), which proposes that diversity may improve team performance through an increased range of knowledge, expertise, and

Table 5.1 *An overview of the theoretical mechanisms and effects of different diversity conceptualizations*

	Does What		Leads to
Individual Level			
Dissimilarity		Conflict	Outcomes
Social Category	stereotyping/discrimination	RC +	Performance −
	differences in communication style	TC −	Satisfaction −
	differences in knowledge	PC +	OCB/Helping −
	increased misunderstandings	All +	All −
	mistrust	All +	All −
	discomfort	All +	All −
Functional	different backgrounds lead to different task and process approaches	RC−	Performance +
	stereotyping, but no expectancy violation	TC+	Creativity +
		PC+	Innovation +
Dyad/Group Level			
Heterogeneity		Conflict	Outcomes
Social Category	stereotyping/discrimination	RC +	Performance −
	differences in communication style	TC +	Satisfaction −
	differences in knowledge	PC +	OCB/Helping −
	increased misunderstandings	All +	All −
	mistrust, discomfort, tension	All +	All −
	decreased group communication	All +	All −
	exclusion of dissimilar members	All +	All −
Functional	different backgrounds lead to different task and process approaches	RC+	Performance +
	stereotyping, but no expectancy violation	TC+	Creativity +
		PC+	Innovation +

Table 5.1 (*cont.*)

	Does What		Leads to
Faultlines		Conflict	Outcomes
Social Category	subgroup goal orientation	RC +	Performance −
	subgroup polarization	TC −	Satisfaction −
	intersubgroup competition	PC +	OCB/Helping −
Functional	subgroup social support helps expression of ideas	TC +	Performance +
	intersubgroup competition	TC +	Innovation +
	different approaches to the task because of different backgrounds	PC +	Creativity +

perspectives. This perspective proposes that when members with diverse opinions and backgrounds share and constructively debate their unique viewpoints, groups will be able to achieve more creative and innovative solutions than would have been possible with a homogenous group.

However, a number of studies have also found diversity to have a negative impact on group processes and performance (Messick and Massie, 1989; Jackson *et al.*, 2003), lending support to the pessimistic view of diversity (cf. Mannix and Neale, 2005). This school of thought proposes that diversity may result in social divisions and negative intragroup processes, such as dysfunctional forms of conflict, which may detract from group performance (Mannix and Neale, 2005). The pessimistic view of diversity draws on the theories of similarity–attraction (Byrne, 1971) and social categorization theory (Tajfel, 1981; Turner, 1987). The similarity–attraction paradigm proposes that people are attracted to similar others (Byrne, 1971). This can lead individuals to identify more with the group members more similar to themselves in terms of, for example, demographic characteristics or values. This process of social categorization can lead to the formation of in- and out-groups (Tajfel, 1978; Brewer, 1979), which can set an atmosphere of stereotyping, discrimination, and in-group–out-group hostilities, leading to increased dysfunctional conflicts and decreased performance (Pelled *et al.*, 1999; and Ellemers and Barreto, chapter 7 in this volume).

To better understand when diversity is beneficial or detrimental for team performance, researchers began to classify diversity characteristics into different categories. Among the most prominent distinctions is the dichotomous distinction between visible (or surface level) diversity and non-visible (or deep-level diversity) (Harrison *et al.*, 2002; Harrison, Price and Bell, 1998; cf. Jackson, May, and Whitney, 1995; Pelled, 1996; Townsend and Scott, 2001). Visible diversity, which some researchers propose includes social diversity category (Jackson, 1992; Jehn *et al.*, 1999; Pelled, 1996), encompasses demographic traits, such as gender, age, or nationality, which can be seen upon meeting someone. Non-visible diversity encompasses forms of diversity that are not immediately visible to the naked eye, such as functional diversity or value diversity. Functional diversity is based on differences in knowledge bases and perspectives that members bring to a work group based, for example, on their academic background or past work experience (Jehn *et al.*, 1999). Value diversity reflects differences of opinions or norms of group members, related to, for example, what the task, goal, or mission of their group should be (Jehn *et al.*, 1999).

The visibility of certain demographic characteristics can increase the salience of these attributes. It is therefore not surprising that the most frequently used bases for social categorization are the more visible, surface-level, social category characteristics, such as race, gender, and age. These categories are more likely to evoke responses because of stereotyping or bias (see Table 5.1; Milliken and Martins, 1996) than less visible, informational attributes such as functional background, education and experience. In addition to being readily apparent, social category traits often tend to carry more baggage with them. For example, Brief and co-authors (2006) found that the interethnic conflict organizational members perceived in their communities influenced their response to diversity within the workplace. Such background biases may result, for example, in higher levels of relationship conflict (e.g., Alagna, Reddy, and Collins, 1982; Jehn *et al.*, 1997). Functional differences may also play an important role in workgroup conflicts, but are more often linked to work-related task conflicts (see Table 5.1; e.g., Lovelace, Shapiro, and Weingart, 2001; Pelled, Eisenhardt, and Xin, 1999). These underlying differences in functional background, education, or expertise can be very important for complex tasks that require creativity or problem solving (Argote, Gruenfeld, and Naquin, 2001).

To better understand how these different types of diversity affect intra-group conflict, we will first delve into the general diversity literature on the topics. We will then discuss what we feel are often overlooked areas of the diversity literature, including the literatures on minority influence and relational demography, social dominance theory, top management team (TMT) research, and macro-demographic research. Following this, we will discuss new developments in diversity research others have neglected, which can shed further light on the effects of the different types of diversity as well as the role of minority members. We will specifically focus on the emergence of the literatures on cross-categorization and demographic faultlines.

Deeper examination of these literatures may help us to better understand the special status of minority group members. For example, the literature on minority influence specifically focuses on the role of the individual in the group, allowing comparisons of the experiences of low-status members in minority positions or high-status members in minority positions as well as differences in specific demographic traits. This is especially useful in understanding the effects of diversity within groups, as social dominance theory would predict that a group of men with one female would have larger repercussions on the minority (the female in this case) than a group of females with one male. Because of institutional, structural, group-based, and individual factors, certain groups, such as males, tend to be more social dominance oriented than females (Levin, 2004; Pratto, Stallworth, and Sidanius, 1997; Sidanius, Pratto, and Brief, 1995). This orientation may then result in in-group favoritism (Levin, 2004; Levin *et al.*, 2002; Levin and Sidanius, 1999) and towards the out-group, negative effect (Levin and Sidanius, 1999) and even violence (e.g., Henry *et al.*, 2005; Levin *et al.*, 2003). Therefore, literature within diversity research that can help shed more light on the specific role of the individual within the group, which is often ignored in theories and empirical work on diversity and conflict, will help us to better understand the impact of diversity on group conflict and outcomes.

Minority influence and relational demography research

Two important research streams that have influenced diversity researchers in their thinking about the effects of diversity on the intrapersonal and dyadic level are the literature on minority influence (see Choi and Levine, 2004; De Dreu *et al.*, 1999; Moscovici, 1976; Phillips, 2003) and the relational demography literature (Chatman *et al.*, 1998; Chattopadhyay, 1999; Riordan, 2000; Tsui, Egan, and O'Reilly, 1992; Tsui and O'Reilly, 1989). The minority influence literature focuses on the role of proportions in determining the quality of relations between members from demographically different groups. After the groundbreaking work of Moscovici (1976), several researchers have examined the conditions under which numerical minorities exert social influence (Choi and Levine, 2004; Phillips *et al.*, 2004; Wood *et al.*, 1994).

Another theoretical approach that focuses on relationships between individuals is relational demography. Relational demography researchers have largely built their work on the social categorization paradigm in explaining diversity effects at the dyadic level (see Tsui, Xin, and Egan, 1995), thus between supervisors and subordinates or among individual work-group members, who classify each other as members of the in-group or out-group (Mannix and Neale, 2005). Relational demography researchers propose that employees compare themselves with colleagues from their work group or unit, based on demographic characteristics such as gender and race (Chattopadhyay, Tluchowska, and George, 2004). The extent of perceived dissimilarity influences their identification with the work unit or group, which in turn impacts work-related outcomes, such as performance and innovation (Chatman *et al.*, 1998; Riordan and Shore, 1997), citizenship behavior (Chattopadhyay, 1999; Riordan and Shore, 1997), effectiveness, role ambiguity, absenteeism, intent to remain in the firm, and turnover (Tsui *et al.*, 1992).

Social dominance theory

Another research stream that diversity researchers often neglect to consider is social dominance theory. This theory explains social group oppression and processes of discrimination against specific demographic groups by identifying both individual and structural societal factors that can lead to group-based oppression (Sidanius *et al.*, 2004). Examples of forms of group oppression are discriminatory behaviors of individuals, ideologies that legitimize hierarchical structures in social systems, and the disproportionate allocation of certain desired goods. These forms of group oppression can be seen as examples of a more general tendency for individuals to form and maintain group-based hierarchy (Sidanius *et al.*, 2004).

Diversity characteristics that have been most often examined by social dominance researchers are gender and ethnicity (e.g., Levin, 2004; Pratto *et al.*, 1997; Sidanius *et al.*, 1995; Wilson and Lui, 2003). For instance, Haley and Sidanius (2006) compared people's support for and framing of affirmative action policies over cultures and found that cultural minorities had the tendency to frame affirmative action policies in terms that most individuals find morally acceptable, while whites framed affirmative action more, as it were, unacceptable. Additionally, whites were less supportive of affirmative action policies than cultural minorities. This finding illustrates the idea that, according to social dominance theory, affirmative action policies and social or emancipation policies can be regarded as a threat to the group-based hierarchies (Acquino, Stewart, and Reed, 2005). Other studies have shown that social dominance orientation can explain people's support for violence (e.g., Henry *et al.*, 2005; Levin *et al.*, 2003), people's attitudes towards social policies and social allocations (e.g. Pratto, Tatar, and Conway-Lanz, 1999; Pratto, Stallworth, and Conway-Lanz, 1998), and in-group favoritism (Levin *et al.*, 2002; Levin and Sidanius, 1999; Levin, 2004). Thus, by giving more insight into the structure of group-based social systems, social dominance theory can help diversity researchers explain how processes of discrimination and oppression evolve and how status hierarchies in organizations are maintained.

Top management team research

One stream of research often neglected by social psychologists who study diversity is the literature on top management teams (e.g., Bantel and Jackson, 1989; Hambrick, Cho, and Chen, 1996). According to the upper-echelons theory (Hambrick and Mason, 1984), demographic characteristics of upper-echelons managers are determinants of strategic choices and, through these choices, of organizational performance. Studies that have tested the effect of the demography of top management teams on organizational performance have shown mixed results (Edmondson, Roberto, and Watkins, 2003; Carpenter and Fredrickson, 2001). Some studies have shown that top management teams diverse on age, education, function, and tenure were more innovative (e.g., Bantel and Jackson, 1989; Hambrick *et al.*, 1996), more likely to undergo strategic changes in corporate strategy (e.g.,

Wiersema and Bantel, 1992; Boeker, 1997), performed better (Murray, 1989; Smith *et al.*, 1994), were better able to deal with (Keck and Tushman, 1993), and had faster changes (Murmann and Tushman, 1997). Other studies showed, however, that top management team diversity in education, age, and tenure led to greater turnover (e.g., Jackson *et al.*, 1991; Wagner, Pfeffer, and O'Reilly, 1984), less innovation and learning (e.g., Ancona and Caldwell, 1992; O'Reilly, Snyder, and Boothe, 1993), and that heterogeneous top management teams made less comprehensive evaluations of opportunities and threats (Miller, Burke, and Glick, 1998). Carpenter and Fredrickson (2001) found that although educational and tenure heterogeneity positively influenced firms' global strategic postures, functional heterogeneity showed a negative association. In another recent study, Simsek and colleagues (2005) found CEO tenure diversity to be positively associated with behavioral integration, while educational team diversity was negatively associated with behavioral integration. A possible explanation for these mixed effects in TMT demography studies is that these studies, which often rely on upper-echelons theory, have typically ignored the "black box" of processes that links diversity effects to outcomes (Lawrence, 1997; Simons, Pelled, and Smith, 1999). When we review the literature directly examining the relationship between diversity and performance, we will come back to the TMT literature that has looked at the mediating role of intra-group conflict in the relationship between TMT diversity and performance (e.g., Amason, 1996; Knight *et al.*, 1999).

Macro-demographic research – organizational-level effects

Another often overlooked line of research that investigates the effects of diversity characteristics on group processes and outcomes is organizational demography. This line of research examines the disproportionate representation of identity groups over others as an important factor, which influences social interactions at work (Wharton, 1992). In his influential article "Organizational demography," Pfeffer (1983) argued that the demographic composition of organizations influences many processes of social interaction and organizational outcome variables. Pfeffer's theory endorses the pessimistic view of diversity effects on organizational outcomes and suggests that homogeneity is a predictor of successful processes and outcomes and dysfunctional conflict.

Organizational demography researchers have focused mainly on diversity characteristics that are visible, such as age, race, or sex, or job-related attributes such as functional background and tenure (e.g., Bantel and Jackson, 1989; Wagner, Pfeffer, and O'Reilly, 1984; Wiersema and Bird, 1993).

Many organizational demography studies that tested the relationship between the length of service distribution and organizational outcomes were conducted on top management teams and showed that the effects of social category variables, such as gender, age, and race (e.g., Ely, 1994; Ely and Thomas, 2001; Fairhurst and Snavely, 1983; Gutek and Morasch, 1982), were often mixed and depended on proportions (Mannix and Neale, 2005). Organizational demography research has also extensively examined tenure diversity. Tenure diversity was found to positively influence top management teams' turnover (e.g., Wagner *et al.*, 1984; O'Reilly, Caldwell, and Barnett, 1989; O'Reilly *et al.*, 1993; Wiersema and Bird, 1993), and negatively influence innovation (Flatt, 1993) and social integration (O'Reilly *et al.*, 1989). However, other studies showed no significant relationship between heterogeneity in tenure and turnover (Jackson *et al.*, 1991) and innovation (Bantel and Jackson, 1989).

Many of these studies and reviews have shown inconsistent findings on the relationship between diversity and group process and outcomes. In the next section, we will identify areas of diversity research that are utilizing new perspectives to better understand the relationship between diversity and group processes and outcomes. At the close of this chapter, we will offer our ideas on other, new ways of looking at the specific relationships of diversity, conflict, and group outcomes.

Recent developments in diversity research

In the preceding sections, we reviewed the main areas of diversity research as well as several of its more overlooked areas, and found support for both the positive and negative perspectives of diversity. This section discusses two new trends in diversity research, which may shed more light onto understanding when diversity may either positively or negatively impact group outcomes. We will first look at the role of cross-categorization theory and social identity theory in explaining the effects of diversity on group outcomes, and then we will look at the role of demographic faultlines in helping to better understand the impact of diversity on group processes and outcomes.

Cross-categorization theory and social identity theory

Most diversity researchers have based their predictions of the effects of diversity on group processes and performance on the logic of social categorization theory (Tajfel, 1981; Turner, 1987) and social identification or social identity theory (Hogg and Abrams, 1988; Turner, 1982). Social identity (Hogg and Abrams, 1988; Tajfel, 1978) and self-categorization theories (Turner, 1982; 1987) offer theoretical insights about the processes of interaction between members from different social groups at the team level (Mannix and Neale, 2005). According to social identity theory, individuals have a desire to maintain a positive social self, which they acquire through a process of social comparison (Hogg and Abrams, 1988; Turner, 1982). Individuals identify themselves with social categories which give them a positive social self. In turn, individuals seek to maximize intra- or inter-group distinctions and to perceive others as less attractive (Kramer, 1991). This process often results in increased stereotyping, polarization, and anxiety, which in turn can lead to decreased satisfaction with the group, increased turnover, decreased cooperation, and high levels of conflict (Crocker and Major, 1989; Triandis *et al.*, 1993). Diversity can thus promote the creation of in-groups versus out-groups and cognitive biases, based on these social categorization processes (Pelled, 1997; Riordan and Shore, 1997; Tsui *et al.*, 1992; Williams and O'Reilly, 1998). However, individuals do not necessarily categorize themselves in terms of demographic group memberships.

More recently, researchers have started to investigate the importance of organizational identities and work-related subgroup identities for enhancing organizational outcomes (Haslam, 2001; Hogg and Terry, 2000; Hornsey and Hogg, 2000; Tyler and Blader, 2000). Literature on superordinate identity suggests that the identification with a common work-related entity can lessen stereotypes and biases due to in-group–out-group distinctions based on social category diversity (Hornsey and Hogg, 2000). The identification with a work-related entity can be important particularly for disadvantaged people. Social identity theory predicts that when inter-group boundaries appear to be permeable and that individuals believe in social mobility, disadvantaged group members (e.g., women, immigrants, the aged) will attempt to become members of the high-status majority work group (Ellemers, Wilke, and Van Knippenberg, 1993) casting off their disadvantaged status.

Therefore, promoting a superordinate identity can be particularly beneficial for members of these groups.

Another theory highly relevant for diversity, which is based on social categorization and social identity theory, is that of cross-categorization. The underlying assumption of cross-categorization theory is that individuals identify with multiple social identities that can either be formal or informal and that are at least partially non-overlapping (Crisp and Hewstone, 2001; Hogg and Terry, 2001). The basic assumption predicting the effects of cross-categorization is that over-lapping membership reduces the psychological distances between in-group and out-group members (Brewer, 2000). Once there is a high degree of overlap between categories, they are perceived to be conver-gent rather than cross-cutting, creating convergent boundaries (Brewer and Campbell, 1976), which will increase in-group bias (Brewer, 2000). A low degree of overlap decreases in-group–out-group bias and stereotyping. Migdal, Hewstone, and Mullen's (1998) meta-analysis indeed showed that the divergence of social categories accent-uates the differences between and the similarities within subgroups, while crossed categories emphasize the similarities between different categories and differences within each category. Cross-categorization theory may prove useful to understanding the relationship between diversity and conflict, because it can be inferred from the above findings, that if members in a diverse group create a shared identity, they may be more likely to experience the positive side of diversity (including con-structive conflicts and an absence of disruptive, interpersonal issues).

Demographic faultlines

The concept of demographic faultlines (Lau and Murnighan, 1998) has arisen in response to critiques on the traditional conceptualization of diversity. The traditional conceptualization of group-level diversity (i.e., heterogeneity) examines the degree to which employees in a group or department differ on only one demographic characteristic at a time and neglects to consider the interaction with other demographic characteristics (Lau and Murnighan, 1998). For instance, if one is studying race, gender is often ignored, which leads to the assumption that the experiences of black men in a group would be similar to that of black women in an otherwise identical group. While some studies have actually examined more than one demographic characteristic at a time, for example, combining the effects of age, race, and gender and aggregating these effects (e.g., Jehn *et al.*, 1999), these models of aggregation did not accurately reflect the degree of interdependence between the demographic characteristics under study. Specifically, it was still impossible to tell if the black individuals in a group are also women. Demographic faultlines offer a possible solution to this.

Faultline theory (Hambrick *et al.*, 2001; Lau and Murnighan, 1998, 2005; Li and Hambrick, 2005) formulates an answer to the problem described above by arguing that the compositional dynamics of multiple demographic characteristics affect group processes more than separate attributes. In line with the multiform heterogeneity literature (Blau, 1977; Kanter, 1977), faultline theory emphasizes the importance of examining multiple parameters of social structure (e.g., race, age) and how they overlap with each other, creating subgroups based on these differences (Blau, 1977). Attributes that consolidate each other reinforce in-group bonds and group barriers between subgroups, while a low correlation between them promotes group integration. This reasoning is similar to the prediction of cross-categorization theory about convergent categories: categories that align are more likely to create inter-group bias than categories that are overlapping. An important difference between cross-categorization theory and faultline theory is, however, that cross-categorization theory focuses on the alignment of social categories that individuals identify with, while faultline theory examines the alignment of objective demographic characteristics.

Both of these theories may further our understanding of the complex and often contradictory relationship between diversity, conflict, and performance. In the section on the historical perspective on the relationship of diversity and conflict, we will discuss the findings relating group faultlines to intra-group conflict, and we will also in our new directions section discuss how the nuances of faultline theory are helping to further our understanding of the relationship between diversity and conflict. However, we must first define what we mean by intra-group conflict.

An historical perspective on conflict

Intra-group conflict has been defined as the process arising from perceived incompatibilities or differences between team members

(Boulding, 1962; Thomas, 1992; Wall and Callister, 1995). Most research has focused on incompatibilities arising from either task or relationship issues (Amason, 1996; Greer and Jehn, 2005; Guetzkow and Gyr, 1954; Jehn, 1995).

Task conflicts involve disagreements among group members over ideas and opinions relating to the task, such as disagreements over strategic choices or the appropriate information to include in a project report (e.g., De Dreu and Weingart, 2003; Jehn, 1995; 1997). Relationship conflicts, on the other hand, revolve around non-work-related issues between members, such as personality differences or conflicts over political beliefs (e.g., De Dreu and Weingart, 2003; Jehn, 1995; 1997).

In addition to relationship and task conflicts, Jehn (1997) proposed that a third type of conflict exists: process conflict. Process conflicts occur over the logistical issues of task accomplishment, such as disagreements over the delegation of tasks or the allocation of resources (Jehn, 1997). While both task and process conflicts are about work-related issues, research has found that organizational members see task and process issues as distinct because process issues concern planning and task delegation, while task issues focus more on the content or goal of the task itself (Weingart, 1992). Even though process conflicts are about work-related issues, process conflicts have typically been found to behave more like relationship conflicts (Jehn and Bendersky, 2003). To understand this dual nature, researchers have made distinctions between various types of process conflict. Behfar *et al.* (2002) differentiate between task and people-centered process conflicts while Greer and Jehn (2006) delineate between emotional process conflicts and non-emotional process conflicts. In their exploratory study, Behfar *et al.* (2002) found that process conflicts revolving around people coordination seemed to be associated with less effective groups, whereas conflicts about task coordination seemed to be associated with more effective groups. In a separate attempt to understand the dual nature of process conflict, Greer and Jehn (2006) proposed that the emotional component of process conflicts drives process conflicts' similarity to relationship conflicts. They propose that process conflicts may often contain an emotional component, similar to relationship conflicts, because process conflicts are about the allocation of desired resources or undesired assignments. Such allocations may often involve individual assessments which may incite emotive reactions, causing process conflict to behave similarly to relationship conflicts.

Task conflict and group outcomes

The effect of task conflict on group outcomes has stimulated extensive debate in the literature (De Dreu and Weingart, 2003). Research which proposes that task conflict improves performance suggests that task conflicts benefit performance through improved consideration of different alternatives and group problem solving (e.g., Jehn and Bendersky, 2003). This proposition has some support (Amason, 1996; Jehn, 1997; Greer, Jehn, and Thatcher, 2006; Matsuo, 2006; Pelled *et al.*, 1999). Other research proposes that conflict of any sort, including task conflict, interferes with the cognitive processing of group members (e.g., Carnevale and Probst, 1998). Task conflicts may thus impede a group member's ability to adequately process information and make decisions. The cognitive process perspective received support in a recent meta-analysis by De Dreu and Weingart (2003), which found the effects of task conflict on performance to be predominantly negative. De Dreu and Weingart do suggest though, consistent with Jehn (1995; 1997), that under certain conditions task conflicts may still be able to help performance. For example, De Dreu and Weingart suggest that task conflict on non-routine tasks in an open, trusting, and psychologically safe environment may result in improved group performance. There is much less dispute about the effects of task conflict on perceived outcomes, such as satisfaction, commitment, or willingness to work together again. Task conflict seems to reduce satisfaction of group members in most situations. Frustration and dissatisfaction are thought to be normal reactions to conflict, regardless of the subject or outcome of the conflict (Ross, 1989).

Relationship conflict and group outcomes

Relationship conflicts, because of their focus on interpersonal issues, have largely been proposed to detract from group performance because of misspent time and effort (Jehn and Bendersky, 2003). When involved in a personal issue, individuals may waste energy on squabbling, avoiding, or resolving the issue, rather than on task completion. Research on intra-group relationships has found strong support for this proposition, with many studies finding that relationship conflict harmed both effective group processes (Amason, 1996; Evan, 1965; Jehn, 1995), group performance (De Dreu and Weingart, 2003; Jehn, 1995; Li and Hambrick, 2005; Nibler and Harris, 2003; Pelled, 1997; Rau, 2005), and innovation (e.g., Matsuo, 2006). However, recent findings suggest that under certain conditions, limited amounts of relationship conflict may help performance (De Dreu and Weingart, 2003; Greer and Jehn, 2005; Greer *et al.*, 2006; Rispens, Jehn, and Thatcher, 2005). In a study of conflict occurring among activist group members, Greer and Jehn (2005) found that when relationship conflicts were properly managed, relationship conflict was associated with higher levels of performance. In an attempt to better understand the conditions under which such findings may occur, Rispens, Greer, and Jehn (2006) examined and found that when team members had close relationships and were highly interdependent on the task, relationship conflicts actually improved performance. These findings are in line with the family literature on close relationships, which proposes that relationship conflicts may help to clear the air and establish boundaries (Bernstein *et al.*, 1997; Coser, 1965). Future research is needed to better understand the conditions under which relationship conflict may positively or negatively impact group performance.

Process conflict and group outcomes

While process conflict has not yet received as much attention as relationship or task conflict, it has also been the focus of a theoretical debate. Some research has proposed that process conflict would aid performance through improved fit between individual ability and preference, and task requirements (e.g., Jehn *et al.*, 1999). Other research proposes, in line with the cognitive processing perspective, that process conflicts decrease members' cognitive abilities and distract them from more important goal-related issues (Jehn and Bendersky, 2003). Findings on the general construct of process conflict thus far have found process conflict to negatively affect performance (e.g., Behfar *et al.*, 2002; Jehn and Mannix, 2001; Greer and Jehn, 2006; Greer *et al.*, 2006; Vodosek, 2005) and innovation among Japanese sales teams (Matsuo, 2006).

Recent developments in conflict research

In order to better understand when task, relationship, and process conflict help or hurt group performance and perceived outcomes, researchers have begun to examine factors moderating the relationship between the conflict types as well as the interlocking nature of the conflict types. For example, Yang and Mossholder (2004) propose that how group members handle emotion moderates the transformation of task conflict into relationship conflict. Specifically, collective emotional intelligence (the ability to manage one's own emotions and deal with others' emotions in problem solving and decision making; Mayer and Salovey, 1997), intra-group relational ties (relationship quality and history) influence the way emotions are communicated and understood (Gallois, 1994), and conflict-relevant group norms for regulation of emotion may moderate the relationship between task conflict and relationship conflict. Yang and Mossholder (2004) thus propose that when task conflicts are managed so that they are devoid of emotion, they may help performance, but when task conflicts become emotional, they may turn into relationship conflicts, which may harm group performance.

Recent research has also begun to look at the possibility that the presence of conflict could moderate the presence of other group processes. Rau (2005) found that the location dimension of transactive memory (the awareness within the group where expertise lies) had a positive effect on performance when relationship conflict was low, but an insignificant and negligible effect when relationship conflict was high. This finding opens the door to future research which could look at the effects of intra-group conflict as moderating, rather than driving group performance.

In addition to looking at the direct or moderating effects of the tripartite grouping of relationship, task, and process conflict on work-group outcomes, recent research has started to look at other types and conceptualizations of intra-group conflict. For example, work by Jehn and Chatman (2000) introduces the concepts of proportional and relational conflict. These concepts offer more fine-grained approaches to examining the effects of intra-group conflict on performance. Proportional conflict takes into account the proportion of each conflict occurring within a group (Jehn and Chatman, 2000). For example, a group with a high proportion of task conflict compared to relationship conflict may perform better than a group with a higher proportion of relationship conflict. Research by Greer, Jehn, and Thatcher (2005) found that groups characterized by a faultline token split (three white men and a black woman) experienced a higher *proportion* of process conflict than groups with a faultline coalitional split (two white men and two black women). Greer, Jehn, and Thatcher suggest that this occurs because token members may use process conflict as a way to exercise their frustration with their token status and lack of voice in more opinion-related issues. Their finding shows the importance of looking at both the main effects and proportions of intra-group conflict.

Relational conflict, similar to the concept of relational demography, looks at how different an individual's *perception* of conflict level is from other group members (Jehn and Chatman, 2000). When individuals within a group perceive there to be different levels of, for example, process conflict, in their group, this may have important implications for performance. Relational conflict is similar to the new concept of conflict asymmetry (Jehn *et al.*, 2006; Rispens, Jehn, and Thatcher, 2005). Conflict asymmetry describes a situation in which group members have different perceptions of the conflict levels within their group. Jehn and coauthors (2006) found that asymmetric perceptions decrease commitment and satisfaction while Rispens, Jehn, and Thatcher (2005) found that the direction of asymmetric perception (who is perceiving more or less) was critical to understand the effects of asymmetry on group outcomes.

In addition to using different conceptualizations of the existing conflict types, recent work by Jehn and Conlon (2006) proposes that more conflict types may exist than just relationship, task, or process conflict. In their archival study of punk rock bands, Jehn and Conlon (2006) find several new forms of conflict to occur in these groups. Specifically, they find conflicts occurring over financial issues (financial conflicts), political issues (political conflict), and creative issues (creative conflict) to be distinct from the past conflict types. They find political conflict to positively impact production and negatively impact critical success, process conflict to positively impact band performance in terms of critical success but negatively impact the production of the band, financial conflict to detract from popular success, relationship conflict to increase popular success, and creative conflict to have a curve linear relationship with critical success with highest levels of success occurring at moderate levels of creative conflict. Future research is needed to further examine these and other potentially distinct forms of intra-group conflict.

An historical perspective on the relationship between diversity and conflict

The following section views the state of the literature examining the relationship of diversity to conflict (see Appendix for a list of studies), including identifying the main reasoning used by researchers to predict the effects of the different formulations of diversity on each of the three conflict types – relationship, task, and process – (this reasoning is summarized in Table 5.1) as well as summarizing the findings on each of these relationships. We will separate our summary of theorizing and findings by the category and conceptualization of diversity that was of focus in the particular study. We will first review the effects of social category and functional heterogeneity on conflict, and then review the effects of faultlines on conflict.

Social category heterogeneity and conflict

Social category heterogeneity has often been linked to increases in relationship conflicts in groups (Jehn *et al.*, 1999; Pelled *et al.*, 1999; O'Reilly, Williams, and Barsade, 1997). Researchers argue that social identity and social categorization processes in diverse groups can lead to discomfort, hostility, and tension that may result in higher levels of relationship conflict (see Table 5.1; Jehn *et al.*, 1999; Tajfel and Turner, 1986). At a societal level, social category differences have often been associated with differences in social dominance orientation. For example, men have been found to be more socially dominance-oriented than women (Levin, 2004; Pratto *et al.*, 1997; Sidanius *et al.*, 1995). When placed in a group together with women, socially dominance-oriented men may be more likely to favor their in-group (Levin *et al.*, 2002; Levin and Sidanius, 1999; Levin, 2004) and support violence against the out-group (e.g., Henry *et al.*, 2005; Levin *et al.*, 2003). In a small group setting, it seems likely that there would thus be high levels of conflict between men and women. Support has been found for this proposition, as research has found social category diversity to be associated with increased relationship conflict (Alagna *et al.*, 1982; Jehn *et al.*, 1997).

Social category heterogeneity may also influence task conflict in groups (Jehn, Bezrukova, and Thatcher, 2006). Because social category characteristics are a salient basis for in-group/out-group categorizations, social categorization processes in social category diverse groups may prompt hostile interactions (see Table 5.1; Jehn *et al.*, 1999; Pelled *et al.*, 1999) as well as dislike and distancing between members of different demographic categories (Byrne, 1971). Individuals who feel excluded or disliked by other group members may be less likely to share their opinions with other group members, limiting the range of opinions shared during task conflicts. This is consistent with research which has found social category diverse groups to communicate less frequently and more formally than homogenous groups (e.g., Zenger and Lawrence, 1989).

In groups with high levels of social category diversity, process conflict is likely to be high (Table 5.1). When group members have different social category characteristics, they may have different experiences or values (Dougherty, 1992) that may lead to process issues in diverse groups. Different experiences or values may lead to different ideas over how best to coordinate the task at hand (Behfar *et al.*, 2002), which may result in increased process conflict (Jehn *et al.*, 1999).

Results so far suggest mixed effects for these theoretical propositions. Eisenhardt, Kahwajy, and Bourgeois (1997), in their observational study of 12 top management teams, found that heterogeneity in age and background promoted healthy conflict and disagreement. However, O'Reilly, Williams, and Barsade (1997) found no effect of age, race, or gender diversity on relationship or task conflict. Alagna, Reddy, and Collins (1982) compared same sex and mixed sex medical student groups, and found that mixed sex groups reported higher levels of conflict, interpersonal tension, and lower levels of friendliness. Pelled (1997) found gender diversity to be positively associated with relationship conflict. Pelled, Eisenhardt, and Xin (1999) found racial diversity to increase relationship conflict, but age diversity to decrease relationship conflict. Jehn, Northcraft, and Neale (1999) found social category diversity to increase relationship conflict and that relationship conflict mediated the relationship between social category diversity and morale. Vodosek (2005) found intra-group conflict to fully mediate the relationship between cultural diversity and group outcomes (namely, satisfaction, affective commitment, and turnover intentions). Specifically, he found cultural diversity to increase all three conflict types (relationship, task, and process), and he found all three conflict types to decrease subjective performance, satisfaction, and commitment and increase turnover intentions. He also found in his control variables that gender diversity had a negative correlation with task conflict, such that more diverse groups in terms of gender had significantly less task conflicts.

To attempt to better understand the relationship between social category diversity and conflict, researchers have begun to examine moderators of this relationship. Pelled, Eisenhardt, and Xin (1999) found task routineness and group longevity to moderate the relationship between racial heterogeneity and performance, such that when task routineness was high, racial heterogeneity was less strongly related to relationship conflict, and when group longevity reached a certain threshold, the positive effect of racial diversity on relationship conflict was diminished. Ayoko and Hartel (2003) proposed and found that different viewpoints regarding the use of space, the inability to retreat from exposure to others, decreased interpersonal space, and privacy invasion moderated the relationship between cultural diversity in the work group and the type, frequency, and duration of conflict events in culturally heterogeneous work groups. Randel (2002) examined identity salience as either mediating or moderating the relationship between gender numerical distinctiveness (the proportion of men in the group squared) and relationship conflict. Identity salience was found to both mediate and moderate the relationship between gender numerical distinctiveness and relationship conflict, such that identity increased relationship conflict and the interaction of identity salience with gender numerical distinctiveness showed gender numerical distinctiveness to lead more strongly to relationship conflict when identity salience was high. Relatedly, Garcia-Prieto, Bellard, and Schneider (2003) proposed in their theoretical model that identity salience would mediate the relationship between the presence of diversity and behavioral consequences, such as emotions and/or conflicts. Nibler and Harris (2003) found Chinese participants to report higher levels of relationship and task conflict and perform worse than US participants. For the US participants, relationship quality moderated the effects of task conflict on performance, such that when participants were friends rather than strangers, performance benefited from better exchange of ideas and opinions. Relationship conflict was negatively related to performance for the overall study, but no main effects were found within each separated sample. They suggested that the benefits of task conflict may be specific to the US context. Mohammed and Angell (2004) found that team orientation decreased the effect of surface level (gender) diversity on relationship conflict, and that relationship conflict resulted in lower perceived performance by team members.

Functional heterogeneity and conflict

Functional heterogeneity may increase relationship conflict (see Table 5.1 and Appendix). Functional differences, just like social category differences, may elicit in-group/out-group comparisons that can result in tensions and hostilities within the group that can escalate to relationship conflicts. Strauss (1962) found support for this in his study of cross-functional interactions – he found that communication between engineers and purchasing agents was punctuated by annoyance and resentment. Functional heterogeneity may also increase task conflict. Members of different functional backgrounds may bring different education, training, and experience to the group (e.g., Lovelace *et al.*, 2001). These resulting different perspectives may lead to more debates and disagreements about the group task (Pelled *et al.*, 1999). Past research has suggested that members of different functional backgrounds may rely on different working methods (Bantel and Jackson, 1989; Gruenfeld *et al.*, 1996). Differences in functional background may also result in different views of how to coordinate a task (Jehn *et al.*, 1999). When different views over task coordination exist, process conflicts might result (Behfar *et al.*, 2002; Jehn *et al.*, 1999).

Research so far offers some support for these propositions. O'Reilly, Williams, and Barsade (1997) found diversity in tenure to increase conflict, and Pelled (1997) found tenure diversity to be positively associated with relationship conflict, as did Pelled, Eisenhardt, and Xin (1999). Jehn, Northcraft, and Neale (1999) found that functional diversity improved performance, and that this relationship was mediated by task conflict. Knight and coauthors (1999) in their study of 76 top management teams (TMTs) in the United States and Ireland found that functional diversity's effect on strategic consensus was mediated by relationship conflict and agreement seeking, such that functional diversity increased relationship conflict, which was associated with lower agreement seeking, and agreement seeking was positively related to strategic consensus.

Research has also attempted to examine forces that could moderate the relationship between functional, or deep-level diversity, and conflict (see Table 5.1). Mohammed and Angell (2004) found that effective team processes (leadership, communication, coordination) decreased the effect of deep-level diversity (differences in time urgency) on relationship conflict, and that relationship conflict resulted in lower perceived performance by team members. Pelled, Eisenhardt, and Xin (1999) found task routineness and group longevity to moderate the relationship between functional heterogeneity and performance, such that when task routineness was high, tenure diversity was less strongly related to relationship conflict, and when group longevity reached a certain threshold, the positive effect of functional diversity on task conflict was weakened as was the positive effect of tenure diversity on relationship conflict. Lovelace, Shapiro, and Weingart (2001) found that functional diversity increased intra-team task disagreement while leader effectiveness decreased the amount of task disagreement (no moderation was found of leader effectiveness on functional diversity-task disagreement). Their study also showed that the way task conflict is communicated could vary. Specifically, their findings show that, although cross-functional diversity increased the level of task disagreement in the teams in their study, the effect of task disagreement on team's performance was due to how collaboratively or contentiously the task disagreement was communicated.

Research has also compared the effects of social category and functional heterogeneity, as well as examining their interacting effects (see Table 5.1 and Appendix). For example, Pelled (1996) proposed in her intervening process model that visible diversity would lead to relationship conflict while job-relatedness of the diversity variable would lead to task conflict, and that group longevity would reduce both of these relationships. Pelled, Eisenhardt, and Xin (1999) in a study of 45 teams in the electronics industry found functional diversity to have a greater effect on task conflict than social category diversity. In their model of diversity and conflict, Jehn, Northcraft, and Neale (1999) found that value diversity, social category diversity, task complexity, and task interdependence moderated the relationship·between functional heterogeneity and performance, such that functional diversity was more strongly linked to positive performance when value and social category diversity were low and task complexity and interdependence were high. Jehn and coauthors (1999) also introduced in this study a third type of diversity, distinct from social category or functional diversity. They introduced value diversity, as differences in the values that members hold regarding work. Value diversity was found to increase all three conflict types and to decrease perceived and actual performance as well as morale. Process conflict mediated the relationship between value diversity and morale and perceived and actual performance, and relationship conflict mediated the relationship between value diversity and morale.

Faultlines and conflict

Demographic faultlines have been hypothesized to lead to increased levels of relationship conflict (see Table 5.1 and Appendix; e.g., Lau and Murnighan, 1998; 2005; Li and Hambrick, 2005; Thatcher, Jehn, and Zanutto, 2003). When faultlines occur in groups, the resulting subgroups, or coalitions, may increase the salience of in-group/out-group memberships, resulting in strain and polarization (Hogg, Turner, and Davidson, 1990), out-group derogation (Hogg, 1996), and inter-subgroup competition (Lau and Murnighan, 1998). Resulting tensions may intensify relationship conflict within the group (Jehn *et al.*, 2006).

While faultlines are likely to increase relationship conflict, their effects on task conflict within the group are less clear. On the one hand, when in-group and out-group identities are salient, subgroups may polarize (Lau and Murnighan, 1998) and talk less with each other about work issues. When communication between subgroups declines, task conflict is less likely to occur. On the other hand, when members have subgroup members to share their opinion with, they may be more willing to hold to their own opinion during group discussions (Asch, 1952; Lau and Murnigan, 1998). Task conflicts are therefore more likely as members back up by representative subgroups may be more willing to enter into task conflicts, and task conflicts may become even more intense as subgroups each rally around their own unique point of view (Lau and Murnighan, 1998).

The different backgrounds members of different functional subgroups have may lead members to approach process issues differently (Bantel and Jackson, 1989; Pelled, 1996; Gruenfeld *et al.*, 1996). These differences may be accentuated by subgroup dynamics. When subgroups form, inter-subgroup competition may take place (Lau and Murnighan, 1998). When subgroups feel compelled to compete for group resources, higher levels of process conflict may also result.

Findings so far on the effects of faultlines on conflict and performance have been mixed (Table 5.1). Li and Hambrick (2005) found that strong faultlines (based on age, tenure, gender, and ethnicity) led to increased task conflict, relationship conflict, and behavior disintegration, and decreased performance. The relationship between faultline strength and behavioral disintegration (diminishment of interaction, exchange, and collective effort) was entirely mediated by relationship conflict, but not by task conflict. They found relationship conflict to negatively influence performance, but did not find an effect of task conflict on performance. The group processes (relationship conflict, task conflict, and behavioral disintegration) fully mediated the negative relationship between faultline size and performance. Lau and Murnighan (2005) found that faultlines (based on gender and ethnicity) explained more variance in perception of team learning, psychological safety, satisfaction, and expected performance than single-attribute heterogeneity indices. Lau and Murnighan also found strong faultlines to decrease relationship conflict. Thatcher, Jehn, and Zanutto (2003) found that diversity faultlines (based on years of work experience, type of functional background, degree major, sex, age, race, and country of origin) were linearly associated with lower levels of relationship and process conflict, but did not find a linear effect on either task conflict, performance, or morale. In curvilinear tests, they found that faultline strength had a curvilinear effect on relationship conflict, process conflict, performance, and morale. Groups with low faultline strength (where no subgroups existed, i.e., Asian male accountant, black male manager, Native American male salesman, and Hispanic male secretary) and groups with very strong faultline strength (where subgroups clearly align on the basis of multiple characteristics, i.e., two black male managers and two white female assistants) had higher levels of process and relationship conflicts and lower levels of performance and morale than groups where medium faultline strength existed (i.e., one female Asian consultant, one female white consultant, one white male assistant, one black male assistant). Molleman (2005) found that both demographic faultline strength and distance (see Bezrukova, Jehn, and Zanutto, 2002; Thatcher *et al.*, 2003 for overview of faultline strength and distance) increased general intragroup conflict (the average of task and relationship conflict items). He also found faultlines formed on the basis of personality types to significantly interact with team autonomy in predicting intra-group conflict, such that when personality faultline distance was high and team autonomy was high, intra-group conflict was the highest, and when faultline distance was low and team autonomy was low, intra-group conflict was the lowest.

New directions in research on diversity and conflict

Having summarized where the literature relating diversity and conflict stands at the moment, we now turn to the directions we feel the field should be heading to resolve past findings and inconsistencies as well as to better highlight the role of disadvantaged minorities. Past work on the relationship between diversity and intra-group conflict has often focused primarily at group-level processes, ignoring differences in individual experiences or orientations within the group. We propose that multilevel models that better incorporate the role of the unique individual within the group can help us to better understand diversity and conflict. For example, we propose in new direction III that insight can be gained into small group dynamics by looking at dynamics between specific demographic subgroups, rather than the group as a whole. By investigating specific conflicts between, for example, men and women, rather than conflict in the group as a whole, a more detailed understanding of conflict within the group can be gained, and the minority status of, for example, a small female subgroup may be better understood. Thus, in the following sections, we will propose five new directions to help researchers better understand the dynamics of diverse groups and their effects on conflict and performance. Specifically, we will discuss the discrepancies between perception and reality in terms of both diversity and faultlines (new direction I), the role of subgroup status in conflicts (new direction II), intra-subgroup versus inter-subgroup processes (new direction III), the effects of diversity beliefs and attitudes during conflicts in diverse groups (new direction IV), and the effects of demographic faultlines and conflict on team learning (new direction V).

New direction I: Perceived versus actual diversity and faultlines

One key direction in future research that has been largely neglected thus far is the distinction between actual diversity and perceived diversity (for exceptions, see Dooley, Freyxell, and Judge, 2000; Harrison *et al.*, 1998; 2002; Jehn *et al.*, 1999). Most past work on diversity has focused on objective demographic characteristics, such as gender, age, or race (Williams and O'Reilly, 1998) that can *potentially* influence team processes, such as conflict, and team outcomes. However, as seen in the recent reviews and meta-analyses on diversity and group processes and outcomes (Jackson *et al.*, 2003; Mannix and Neale, 2005; Stewart, 2006; Webber and Donahue, 2001; Williams and O'Reilly, 1998), findings on diversity have been largely inconsistent. We propose that one possible way of explaining theses contradictory findings is by proposing that diversity impacts group process and outcomes only when it is perceived or salient. Research has proposed and shown, for example, that individuals are not always accurate when assessing the degree of diversity in their work unit as compared to other work units (Harrison and Klein, 2006). Therefore, considering the perception, as well as the actuality, of diversity may help better understand the effects of diversity on intra-group conflict and outcomes.

This same discrepancy between perceived and actual diversity is also a point of contention in the literature on demographic faultlines. Most work on faultlines conceptualizes faultlines based on objective demographic characteristics that can *potentially* influence team processes and team functioning (Lau and Murnighan, 2005; Li and Hambrick, 2005; Gibson and Vermeulen, 2003; for an exception see Earley and Mosakowski, 2000). However, as Lau and Murnighan (1998) state in their original article on faultline theory, groups may have many potential faultlines, "each of which may activate or increase the potential for particular subgroupings" (p. 328). Since faultlines can remain inactive and go unnoticed for years without influencing the group process (Lau and Murnighan, 1998), it is important to take into account whether team members actually perceive or experience these subgroup splits and to what extent these faultline perceptions determine intra-group processes and outcomes. Recent work on faultline activation (the process by which objective faultlines become perceived within a group; Bezrukova and Jehn, 2006) suggests one possible route towards exploring the relationship between actual and perceived diversity. By understanding the factors that can lead to faultline activation, for example, researchers can increase their understanding of the role of faultlines in the conflicts of real-life working groups. Other work looking at identity salience as a mediator of the relationship between intra-group conflict and outcomes (e.g., Garcia-Prieto *et al.*, 2003; Randel, 2002) may also lend another way to better understanding the effects of diversity on conflict and group outcomes.

New direction II: The role of subgroup status

While faultline research has extended diversity research by identifying subgroup existence in groups on the basis of demographic characteristics, group-level diversity research – either on heterogeneity or on faultlines – has failed to take into account *who* constitutes the diverse subgroups or minorities within a group. We propose that by looking at who composes these subgroups, the relative status of the unique subgroups, for example, can be determined as well as its effects on resulting group dynamics. For example, two groups with equally strong faultlines might have very different dynamics if in one group the members of both subgroups were of equal traditional demographic status (two black male mangers and two white female managers) while in the other group the subgroups were of unequal demographic status (two white managers and two black female assistants).

Subgroup size may also impact subgroup status. Kanter (1977) proposed that the more "skewed" a group is, with minority members constituting 1–15% of the group, the more visible this "token" minority-group member is, the more the member(s) is subject to stereotyping and marginalization. While much research has looked at the organizational and individual-level outcomes of "tokenism," little research has been done on tokenism, or subgroup size, at the group level of research, or on the effects of this on intra-group conflict or performance (for exceptions, see Greer *et al.*, 2006; Randel, 2002). Given that the hostility and negativity associated with intra-group conflicts may be more extreme in groups where discrimination is more likely, such as groups with a low-status subgroup, we propose that investigating the effects of subgroup status on conflict and performance may help to better understand the complex relationship between diversity, conflict, and performance.

New direction III: Intra-subgroup and inter-subgroup processes

With the growing amount of research examining the relationship between faultlines and conflict (e.g., Greer *et al.*, 2006; Lau and Murnighan, 2005; Thatcher *et al.*, 2003) still showing inconclusive findings, we propose that research is needed into the underlying mechanisms in this complex relationship. As mentioned in new direction II, subgroup status, research is lacking on the identification of who subgroups are in diverse groups, and determining whether subgroups are of lower, higher, or equal status. Related to this, research is also lacking on the dynamics between these subgroups – specifically, inter-subgroup processes – as distinct from the general group-level processes. Past faultline research has primarily looked at the role of general group-level processes (e.g., Lau and Murnighan, 2005; Li and Hambrick, 2005; Thatcher *et al.*, 2003), and ignored the processes that could be occurring between subgroups or even just within one particular subgroup.

We suggest that the dynamics between subgroups can be more powerful in explaining the effects of diversity than general group-level processes. For example, perhaps a low-status subgroup feels over-powered by a high-status subgroup, and is thus unable to contribute to the group. If the high-status subgroup was unaware of this, they might report there being, for example, high levels of group task conflict as there is a high level of task debate within their subgroup (i.e., *intra-subgroup* conflict), while low-status subgroup members, who realize their unique opinions are not being debated by the other subgroup (i.e., *inter-subgroup* conflict), would report there to be low levels of group task conflict. As a result, the general intra-group task conflict score would show there to be a moderate level of task conflict in the group. However, by looking at the subgroup scores separately (e.g., intra-conflict scores of the subgroup and the inter-subgroup), a greater insight could be gained into what is going on within the group. By unpacking the relationship between faultlines and intra-group conflict through examining the different levels of conflict occurring in groups split by a demographic faultline, we propose that researchers may be able to explain past mixed findings and better identify how and why faultlines affect conflict and group outcomes.

New direction IV: The influence of diversity beliefs

If group members positively value diversity, we propose that this might impact the effects that diversity, either in terms of heterogeneity or faultlines, has on intra-group conflict and group outcomes. Initial work at the individual-organization level showed that when an organization emphasized the value of diversity for the organization, organizational members reported that they felt more valued and respected, and that there were better inter-group relations and success than when the organization did not explicitly value diversity (Ely and Thomas, 2001). Recent research has introduced the topic of diversity beliefs within the group setting (beliefs about the value of diversity for group functioning; Van Knippenberg and Haslam, 2003).

In the small-group setting, positive diversity beliefs may bring out the positive aspects of diversity through encouraging a feeling of psychological safety within the group (Edmondson, 1999). This, in turn, will encourage the expression of multiple opinions by the team members. In support of this, Homan *et al.* (In Press) found positive diversity beliefs to increase the likelihood of information elaboration in informationally diverse groups. Accordingly, when group members are more willing to express opinions and enter into debates, there will be a higher level of task conflict within the group. Additionally, positive attitudes about diversity may be likely to lead to a stronger team identity (Chattopadhyay *et al.*, 2004) and decreased stereotyping (Bunderson and Sutcliffe, 2002), which will presumably result in reduced levels of relationship conflict (Randel, 2002).

However, no empirical work has examined the role of diversity beliefs in the relationship between diversity and intra-group conflict. We propose that future research would benefit from examining this relationship, especially as positive diversity beliefs may both minimize negative group processes and maximize potentially positive group processes, such as task conflict, through encouraging traditionally disadvantaged group members to participate more in group discussions and activities.

New direction V: Group composition and team learning

Although much research has been done on the effects of diversity on group processes and performance, little research has linked diversity to the concept of team learning. Team learning can be defined as a process of reflection and interaction through which group members actively acquire, process, and share knowledge and information in order to improve team performance (based on Argote, Gruenfeld and Naquin, 2001). We propose that a team's composition in terms of social category and informational characteristics can have an important impact on the processes and outcomes of team learning, and feel this has been a relatively neglected area in diversity research.

Past research on heterogeneity and outcomes related to team learning, such as creative problem solving and innovation, has often confirmed the 'value in diversity hypothesis' (Cox *et al.*, 1991), showing that heterogeneity in knowledge, backgrounds, and perspectives leads to improved problem solving and innovative solutions (e.g., Jackson, 1992; Nemeth and Kwan, 1987). More recently, researchers have started to examine the relationship between group faultlines and team learning. Lau and Murnighan (2005) found that gender and ethnicity faultlines explained more variance in perceptions of team learning than single-attribute heterogeneity indices. Additionally, they found that cross-sex and cross-ethnicity work communications had a positive impact on perceptions of group learning and were particularly effective in the condition of weak faultline groups. In another study, Gibson and Vermeulen (2003) found that the relationship between faultlines and learning behavior was curvilinear. Teams with moderately strong demographic subgroups showed more learning behavior than teams that were characterized by weak or strong subgroups.

However, these studies did not consider the nature of the faultlines, which are crucial to group functioning, nor did they investigate conflict as an explanation mechanism (Jehn *et al.*, 2006). We propose that a more fully specified model including faultline type and conflict will help better explain learning in groups. For instance, alignment based on social category characteristics is likely to set in motion mechanisms such as stereotyping and prejudice (Messick and Mackie, 1989), causing subgroup polarization (Hogg *et al.*, 1990), which can result in higher levels of relationship conflict (e.g., Alagna *et al.*, 1982; Jehn, 1997; Jehn *et al.*, 1997; Pelled, 1996; Tsui *et al.*, 1992). These processes can distract members' attention from the task (Jehn, 1995; 1997) and impede team learning. In contrast, alignment based on informational characteristics may result in coalitions of opposing thoughts and the confrontation of different ideas (Gibson and Vermeulen, 2003), which can lead to task conflict (Jehn, 1995; 1997). This "cross-fertilization of ideas" can in turn lead to team learning (Van der Vegt and Bunderson, 2005). We propose that by studying learning as a group outcome determined by faultlines and conflict, research with the goal of understanding how diverse groups learn and are productive will be improved.

With these five different research directions, we propose means by which researchers can gain improved insight into the complex relationship between diversity, conflict, and group outcomes. Each of these five directions – perceived versus actual diversity and faultlines, subgroup status, intra-subgroup versus inter-subgroup processes, diversity beliefs, and the effects of demographic faultlines and conflict on team learning – may all help to improve understanding of diversity and conflict, and also the combination of any of these directions can be expected to yield even further insight into the dynamics of conflict and performance among diverse teams. In the following section, we will discuss the implications of these new directions for the special role of minorities and disadvantaged group members.

Implications for minorities and disadvantaged groups

In past research exploring the relationship between diversity and conflict, the role of status has been largely ignored. However, in diverse, conflicting groups, minority members may often occupy a very visible and precarious position (e.g., Kanter, 1977). In the preceding sections, we reviewed new areas of research that may help us better understand both the role of and consequences for low-status members in diverse, conflicting groups.

Specifically, by looking at the role of perceived diversity and faultlines, researchers can examine the extent to which harmful processes for disadvantaged group members, such as stereotyping or discrimination, are likely to take place. If group members do not perceive social category diversity to exist and do not look on their group as containing one subgroup (consisting of themselves) against the low-status group members, group processes are likely to be much more positive, and groups are more likely to have healthy conflicts and high performance as disadvantaged group members are able to perform to their full potential within the group.

Furthermore, by looking at the role of demographic status in studies of small-group dynamics, researchers may be able to better understand group dynamics and thus better able to identify the conditions under which low-status subgroups are better able to perform at their best. By identifying the disadvantaged members within groups and then looking at the processes within this low-status group, the dynamics within the high-status group, and then the dynamics between the two subgroups, researchers may be able to get a clearer picture of the processes occurring in diverse groups.

In addition to improving the understanding of the relationship of diversity, conflict, and performance, the position of disadvantaged group members can also be improved through identifying conditions which create a healthy environment, where conflicts can lend to productivity and improved performance. One such condition could be through promoting positive diversity beliefs within diverse groups. By focusing members on the value of diversity, derogatory subgroup dynamics may be overcome.

Finally, our understanding of the position and role of disadvantaged group members can also be improved by looking at non-traditional group outcomes. Looking at the effects of conflict on team learning can show how productively team members are using their differences and growing and learning together, benefiting both low- and high-status group members.

Key challenges

As evidenced by the many contradictory findings on the relationship between diversity, conflict, and performance, more and improved research is needed to better understand this relationship. In the following sections, we will highlight some of the key challenges we see in better crystallizing our understanding of the relationship between diversity, conflict, and performance and pursuing our recommended future directions.

Theoretical challenges

One of the largest theoretical challenges in past and present diversity research is our lack of a multilevel view of diversity. Experiences and orientations at the societal level may affect interactions between diverse people at the group level. Individual differences and orientations at the individual level may also shape how groups interact at the group level. While some research has begun to look at the interaction among these different levels (e.g., Brief *et al.*, 2005; Jackson and Joshi, 2004), more work is needed to integrating the different factors from different levels of analyses that come to shape group interactions.

Another large theoretical challenge facing diversity research is the lack of common definitions and understandings about similar subjects. Multiple terms and definitions often exist for the same, or related, concepts. For example, race has been referred to as a "visible" characteristic, a "surface-level" characteristic, and a "social category" characteristic. Relatedly, a group split in two on the basis of nationality could be said to be suffering from either a "faultline" or a "compositional gap." While recent work by Harrison and Klein (2007) has attempted to synthesize the different ways of looking at diversity into a tripartite framework of dispersion, variety, and alignment, it remains to be seen if the field will follow.

Methodological challenges

While new conceptualizations of diversity, such as faultlines, offer exciting new perspectives on the relationship between diversity and conflict, challenges lie in effectively operationalizing these new conceptualizations. Demographic faultlines, for example, have been particularly hard to operationalize. At the moment of this chapter, at least four different methods are being employed to operationalize faultlines. Different formulas have been developed by Shaw (2004), Thatcher, Jehn and Zanutto (2003), Li and Hambrick (2005), and Gibson and Vermeulen (2003). The use of different operationalizations of faultlines poses challenges for the field in being able to identify trends within faultline research. In addition to using different methods, the demographic variables used to assess faultlines are inconsistent, making comparison across studies difficult. For example, Li and Hambrick (2005) looked at faultlines based on gender, race, age, and tenure, Lau and Murnighan (2005) looked at faultlines based on gender and race, and Thatcher, Jehn and Zanutto (2003) looked at faultlines based on years of work experience, type of functional background, degree major, sex, age, race, and country of origin. Future research would benefit from better understanding and identification of the proper methods to use for constructs such as faultlines.

Within conflict research, challenges are also posed by the operationalizing of new developments in the conflict field. For example, conflict asymmetry can be calculated in numerous ways. Identifying a preferred way of calculating this score would also help researchers to understand the relationship between diversity, conflict, and performance.

Conclusion

While many challenges remain in understanding the relationship of diversity, complex, and group outcomes as well as their relevance to and impact upon the disadvantaged members of groups, there is reason to be optimistic. Advances in the theoretical conceptualizations of diversity, such as the faultline concept, are helping to better identify and understand the special role of diversity and of members of different status in intra-group dynamics. The future directions we specify in this chapter will hopefully help to contribute to this improved understanding, and therefore the identification of processes and strategies that can help realize the potential that diversity has to offer, through the full inclusion and participation of group members from all demographic backgrounds.

Appendix

Studies used in review of literature on the relationship between diversity and conflict

Recent reviews and meta-analyses on diversity and group processes
Jackson, Joshi, and Erhardt (2003)
Mannix and Neale (2005)
Stewart (2006)
Webber and Donahue (2001)
Williams and O'Reilly (1998)

Social category heterogeneity and conflict

Alagna, Reddy, and Collins (1982)
Ayoko and Hartel (2003)
Eisenhardt, Kahwajy, and Bourgeois (1997)
Garcia-Preito, Bellard, and Schneider (2003)
Jehn, Bezrukova, and Thatcher (2006)
Jehn, Chadwick, and Thatcher (1997)
Jehn, Northcraft, and Neale (1999)
Mohammed and Angell (2004)
Nibler and Harris (2003)
O'Reilly, Williams, and Barsade (1997)
Pelled (1997)
Pelled, Eisenhardt, and Xin (1999)
Randel (2002)
Vodosek (2005)

Functional heterogeneity and conflict

Jehn, Bezrukova, and Thatcher (2006)
Jehn, Northcraft, and Neale (1999)

Knight, Pearce, Smith, Olian, Sims, Smith, and Flood (1999)
Lovelace, Shapiro, and Weingart (2001)
Mohammed and Angell (2004)
O'Reilly, Williams, and Barsade (1997)
Pelled (1996)
Pelled (1997)
Pelled, Eisenhardt, and Xin (1999).

Faultlines and conflict

Jehn, Bezrukova, and Thatcher (2006)
Lau and Murnighan (1998)
Lau and Murnighan (2005)
Li and Hambrick (2005)
Molleman (2005)
Thatcher, Jehn, and Zanutto (2003)

References

Acquino, K., Stewart, M. M., and Reed, A. (2005). How social dominance orientation and job status influence perceptions of African-American affirmative action beneficiaries. *Personnel Psychology, 58*(3), 703–744.

Alagana, S., Reddy, D., and Collins, D. (1982). Perceptions of functioning in mixed-sex and male medical training groups. *Journal of Medical Education, 57*, 801–803.

Amason, A. (1996). Distinguishing effects of functional and dysfunctional conflict on strategic decision making, Resolving a paradox for top management teams. *Academy of Management Journal, 39*, 123–148.

Ancona, D. G., and Caldwell, D. D. (1992). Demography and design, Predictors of new product team performance. *Organization Science, 3*, 321–341.

Argote, L. Gruenfeld, D., and Naquin (2001). Group learning in organizations. In M. E. Turner (ed.), *Groups at Work: Advances in Theory and Research*, 369–411. Mahwah: Laurence Erlbaum Associates.

Asch, S. E. (1952). *Social Psychology*. Englewood Cliffs: Prentice-Hall.

Ayoko, O. B., and Hartel, C. E. J. (2003). The role of space as both a conflict trigger and a conflict control mechanism in culturally heterogeneous workgroups. *Applied Psychology – An International Review, 52*(3), 383–412.

Bantel, K. A., and Jackson, S. E. (1989). Top management and innovations in banking: Does the composition of the top management team make a difference? *Strategic Management Journal, 10*, 107–124.

Behfar, K. J., Mannix, E. A., Peterson, R. S., and Trochim, W. M. K. (2002). A multi-faceted approach to intragroup conflict issues of theory and measurement. Paper presented at the 15th Annual Conference of the International Association for Conflict Management, Salt Lake City, Utah.

Bernstein, D. A., Clarke-Stewart, A., Roy, E. J., and Wickens, C. D. (1997). *Psychology*, 4th edn. New York: Houghton Mifflin.

Bezrukova, K., and Jehn, K. (2006). Examining ethnic faultlines in groups: A multimethod study of demographic alignment, leadership profiles, coalition formation, intersubgroup conflict and group outcomes. Working Paper, Rutgers University.

Bezrukova, K., Jehn, K. A., and Zanutto, E. (2002). A field study of group faultlines, team identity conflict, and performance in diverse groups. Working Paper. Wharton: University of Pennsylvania.

Blau, P. (1977). *Inequality and Heterogeneity*. New York: Free Press.

Boeker, W. (1997). Strategic change: The influence of managerial characteristics and organizational growth. *Academy of Management Journal*, *40*, 152–170.

Boulding, K. (1962). *Conflict and Defense*. New York: Harper and Row.

Brewer, M. B. (1979). In-group bias in the minimal intergroup situation, A cognitive-motivational analysis. *Psychological Bulletin*, *86*, 307–324.

Brewer, M. B. (2000). Reducing prejudice through cross-categorization: Effects of multiple social identities. In S. Oskamp (ed.), *Reducing Prejudice and Discrimination*, 165–183. Mahwah: Erlbaum Associates.

Brewer, M. B., and Campbell, D. T. (1976). *Ethnocentrism and Intergroup Attitudes. East African Evidence*. New York: Sage.

Brief, A. P., Umphress, E. E., Dietz, J., Butz, R. M., Burrows, J., and Scholten, L. (2005). Community matters: Realistic group conflict theory and the impact of diversity. *Academy of Management Journal*, *48*, 830–844.

Bunderson, J. S., and Sutcliffe, K. (2002). Comparing alternative conceptualizations of functional diversity in management teams: Process and performance effects. *Academy of Management Journal*, *45*, 875–893.

Byrne, D. E. (1971). *The Attraction Paradigm*. New York: Academic Press.

Carnevale, P. J., and Probst, T. M. (1998). Social values and social conflict in creative problem solving and categorization. *Journal of Personality and Social Psychology*, *74*, 1300–1309.

Carpenter, M. A., and Fredrickson, J. W. (2001). Top management teams, global strategic posture, and the moderating role of uncertainty. *Academy of Management Journal*, *44*, 533–545.

Chatman, J. A., Polzer, J. T., Barsade S. G., and Neale, M. A. (1998). Being different yet feeling similar. The influence of demographic composition and organizational culture on work processes and outcomes. *Administrative Science Quarterly*, *43*(4), 749–780.

Chattopadhyay, P. (1999). Beyond direct and symmetrical effects: The influence of demographic dissimilarity on organizational citizenship behavior. *Academy of Management Journal, 42*, 273–287.

Chattopadhyay, P., Tluchowska, M., and George, E. (2004). Identifying the ingroup, A closer look at the influence of demographic dissimilarity on employee social identity. *Academy of Management Review, 29*(2), 180–202.

Choi, H-S., and Levine, J. M. (2004). Minority influence in work teams. The impact of newcomers. *Journal of Experimental Social Psychology, 40*, 273–280.

Coser, L. (1965). *The Functions of Social Conflict.* Glencoe: Free Press.

Cox, T., Lobel, S., and McLeod, P. (1991). Effects of ethnic group cultural differences on cooperative and competitive behavior on a group task. *Academy of Management Journal, 34*, 827–884.

Crisp, R. J., and Hewstone, M. (2001). Multiple categorization and implicit intergroup bias: Differential category dominance and the positive-negative asymmetry effect. *European Journal of Social Psychology, 31*, 45–62.

Crocker, J., and Major, B. (1989). Social stigma and self-esteem: The self-protective properties of stigma. *Psychological Review, 96*(4), 608–630.

De Dreu, C. K. W., De Vries, N. K., Gordijn, and Schuurman (1999). Convergent and divergent processing of majority and minority arguments, effects on focal and related attitudes. *European Journal of Social Psychology, 29*, 329–348.

De Dreu, C. K. W., and Weingart, L. R. (2003). Task versus relationship conflict, team performance, and team member satisfaction, A meta-analysis. *Journal of Applied Psychology, 88*, 741–749.

Dooley, R. S., Fryxell, G. E., and Judge, W. Q. (2000). Belaboring the not-so-obvious: Consensus, commitment, and strategy implementation speed and success. *Journal of Management, 26*(6), 1237–1257.

Dougherty, D. (1992). Interpretive barriers to successful product innovation in large firms. *Organization Science, 3*(2), 179–202.

Earley, P. C., and Mosakowski, E. (2000). Creating hybrid team cultures: An empirical test of transnational team functioning. *Academy of Management Journal, 43*(1), 26–49.

Edmondson, A. (1999). Psychological safety and learning behavior in work teams. *Administrative Science Quarterly, 44*, 350–383.

Edmondson, A. C., Roberto, M. A., and Watkins, M. D. (2003). A dynamic model of top management team effectiveness: Managing unstructured task streams. *Leadership Quarterly, 14*(3), 297–325.

Eisenhardt, K., Kahwajy, J., and Bourgeois, L. (1997). Conflict and strategic choice. How top management teams disagree. *California Management Review, 39*, 42–62.

Ellemers, N., Wilke, H., and Van Knippenberg, A. (1993). Effects of the legitimacy of low group or individual status on individual and collective status-enhancement strategies. *Journal of Personality and Social Psychology, 64,* 766–778.

Ely, R. J. (1994). The effects of organizational demographics and social identity on relationship among professional women. *Administrative Science Quarterly, 39,* 203–238.

Ely, R. J., and Thomas, D. A. (2001). Cultural diversity at work. The effects of diversity perspectives on work group processes and outcomes. *Administrative Science Quarterly, 46,* 229–273.

Evan, W. (1965). Conflict and performance in R&D organizations. *Industrial Management Review, 7,* 37–46.

Fairhurst, G. T., and Snavely, B. K. (1983). Majority and token minority group relationship. Power acquisition and communication. *Academy of Management Review, 8,* 292–300.

Gallois, C. (1994). Group membership, social rules, and power. A social-psychological perspective on emotional communication. *Journal of Pragmatics, 22,* 301–324.

Garcia-Prieto, P., Bellard, E., and Schneider, S. C. (2003). Experiencing diversity, conflict, and emotions in teams. *Applied Psychology – An International Review, 52*(3), 413–440.

Gibson, C., and Vermeulen, F. (2003). A healthy divide: Subgroups as a stimulus for learning team behavior. *Administrative Science Quarterly, 48,* 202–239.

Greer, L. L., and Jehn, K. A. (2005). Relationship and task conflict in e-mail. Performance effects moderated by verbal style and influence tactic usage. Presented at the International Association of Conflict Management, Seville, Spain.

Greer, L. L., and Jehn, K. A. (2007). The pivotal role of emotion in intragroup process conflict. In E. A. Mannix, M. A. Neale, and C. P. Anderson (eds.), *Research on Managing Groups and Teams,* 10, 23–45, New York: Elsevier.

Greer, L. L., Jehn, K. A., and Thatcher, S. M. B. (2005). Trust, conflict, and faultlines. Paper presented at Trust Within and Between Organizations, Amsterdam, The Netherlands.

Greer, L. L., Jehn, K. A., and Thatcher, S. M. B. (2006). Demographic fault-line token splits, Effects on conflict and performance. Presented at the Academy of Management, Atlanta.

Gruenfeld, D. H., Mannix, E. A., Williams, K. Y., and Neale, M. A. (1996). Group composition and decision making: How member familiarity and information distribution affect processes and performance. *Organizational Behavior and Human Decision Processes, 67,* 1–15.

Guetzkow, H., and Gyr, J. (1954). An analysis of conflict in decision making groups. *Human Relations, 7,* 367–381.

Gutek, B. A., and Morasch, B. (1982). Sex-ratios, sex-role spillover, and sexual harassment of women at work. *Journal of Social Issues, 38,* 55–74.

Guzzo, R., and Dickson, M. (1996). Teams in organizations, Recent research on performance and effectiveness. *Annual Review of Psychology, 47,* 307–338.

Haley, H., and Sidanius, J. (2006). The positive and negative framing of affirmative action: A group dominance perspective. *Personality and Social Psychology Bulletin, 32*(5), 656–668

Hambrick, D., Cho, T., and Chen, M. (1996). The influence of top management team heterogeneity on firms' competitive moves. *Administrative Science Quarterly, 41,* 659–684.

Hambrick, D. C., Li, J. T., Xin, K., and Tsui, A. S. (2001). Compositional gaps and downward spirals in international joint venture management groups. *Strategic Management Journal, 22*(11), 1033–1053.

Hambrick, D., and Mason, P. (1984). Upper echelon, The organization as a reflection of its top managers. *Academy of Management Review, 9,* 193–206.

Harrison, D. A., and Klein, K. J. (2007). What's the difference? Diversity constructs as separation, variety, or disparity in organizations. *Academy of Management Review,* in press.

Harrison, B., Price, K., and Bell, M. (1998). Beyond relational demography. Time and the effects of surface- and deep-level diversity on group functioning. *Academy of Management Journal, 41,* 96–107.

Harrison, B., Price, K., Gavin, J., and Florey, A. (2002). Times, teams, and task performance, Changing effects of surface- and deep-level diversity on work group cohesion. *Academy of Management Journal, 45,* 1029–1045.

Haslam, S. A. (2001). *Psychology in Organizations, The Social Identity Approach.* London: Sage.

Henry, P. J., Sidnaius, J., Levin, S., and Pratto, F. (2005). Social dominance orientation, authoritarianism, and support for intergroup violence between the Middle East and America. *Political Psychology, 26*(4), 569–583.

Hogg, M. (1996). Social identity, self-categorization, and the small group. In J. Davis and E. Witte (eds.), *Understanding Group Behavior,* Vol. 2, 227–254. Mahwah: Lawrence Earlbaum Associates.

Hogg, M. A., and Abrams, D. (1988). *Social Identifications: A Social Psychology of Intergroup Relations and Group Processes.* London: Routledge.

Hogg, M. A., and Terry, D. J. (2000). Social identity and self-categorization processes in organizational contexts. *Academy of Management Review, 25,* 121–140.

Hogg, M. A., and Terry, D. J. (2001) *Social Identity Processes in Organizational Contexts*. Ann Arbor: Sheridan Books.

Hogg, M. A., Turner, J. C., and Davidson, B. (1990). Polarized norms and social frames of reference: A test of the self-categorization theory of group polarization. *Basic and Applied Social Psychology, 11*, 77–100.

Homan, A. C., Knippenberg, D. V., Kleef, G. A. V., and De Dreu, C. K. W. (2007). Bridging faultlines by valuing diversity, the effects of diversity beliefs on information elaboration and performance in diverse work groups. *Journal of Applied Psychology, 92*, 1189–1199.

Hornsey, M. J., and Hogg, M. A. (2000). Assimilation and diversity. An integrative model of subgroup relations. *Personality and Social Psychology Review, 4*(2), 143–156.

Jackson, S. (1992). Team composition in organizations. In S. Worchel, W. Wood, and J. Simpson (eds.), *Group Processes and Productivity*, 138–173. Newbury Park: Sage.

Jackson, S. E., Brett, J. F., Sessa, V. I., Cooper, D. M., Julin, J. A., and Peyronnin, K. (1991). Some differences make a difference: Individual dissimilarity and group heterogeneity as correlates of recruitment, promotions and turnover. *Journal of Applied Psychology, 76*(5): 675–689.

Jackson, S. E., and Joshi, A. (2004). Diversity in social context: a multi-attribute, multilevel analysis of team diversity and sales performance. *Journal of Organizational Behavior, 25*(6), 675–702.

Jackson, S. E., Joshi, A., and Erhardt, N. L. (2003). Recent research on team and organizational diversity, SWOT analysis and implications. *Journal of Management, 29*, 801–830.

Jackson, S., May, E., and Whitney, K. (1995). Understanding the dynamics of diversity in decision-making teams. In R. Guzzo and E. Slaas Associates (eds.), *Team Decision Making Effectiveness in Organizations*, 204–261. San Francisco: Jossey-Bass.

Jehn, K. A. (1995). A multi-method examination of the benefits and detriments of intragroup conflicts. *Administrative Science Quarterly, 40*, 256–282.

Jehn, K. A. (1997). Qualitative analysis of conflict types and dimensions in organizational groups. *Administrative Science Quarterly, 42*, 530–557.

Jehn, K. A., and Bendersky, C. (2003). Intragroup conflict in organizations, A contingency perspective on the conflict-outcome relationship. In B. Staw and L. L. Cummings, *Research in Organizational Behavior, 25*, 189–244. Greenwich: JAI Press.

Jehn, K. A., and Bendersky, C. (2003). Intragroup conflict in organizations, A contingency perspective on the conflict-outcome relationship. *Research in Organizational Behavior, 25*, 187–242.

Jehn, K. A., Bezrukova, K., and Thatcher, S. M. B. (2006). Conflict, diversity and faultlines in workgroups. In C. K. W. De Dreu and M. J. Gelfand (eds.), *The Psychology of Conflict and Conflict Management in Organizations*. Mahwah: Laurence Erlbaum Associates.

Jehn, K. A., and Chatman, J. A. (2000). The influence of proportional and perceptual conflict composition on team performance. *International Journal of Conflict Management, 11*(1), 56–73.

Jehn, K. A., and Conlon, D. (2006). Behind the music: Conflict and performance in punk rock bands. Working Paper, Leiden University.

Jehn, K. A., Greer, L. L., Rispens, S., Barreto, M., and Rink, F. (2006). The roots and effects of asymmetric group conflict. Presented at the Academy of Management, Atlanta.

Jehn, K. A., and Mannix, E. A. (2001). The dynamic nature of conflict. A longitudinal study of intragroup conflict and group performance. *Academy of Management Journal, 44*, 238–251.

Jehn, K. A., Northcraft, G. B., and Neale, M. A. (1999). Why differences make a difference. A field study of diversity, conflict, and performance in workgroups. *Administrative Science Quarterly, 44*(4), 741–763.

Kanter, R. (1977). *Men and Women of the Organization*. New York: Basic Books.

Keck, S. L., and Tushman, M. L. (1993). Environmental and organizational context and executive team structure. *Academy of Management Journal, 36*(6), 1314–1344.

Knight, D., Pearce, C. L., Smith, K. G., Olian, J. D., Sims, H. P., Smith, K. A., and Flood, P. (1999). Top management team diversity, group process, and strategic consensus. *Strategic Management Journal, 20*(5), 445–465.

Kramer, R. (1991). Intergroup relations and organizational dilemmas: The role of categorization processes. In B. Staw and L. Cummings (eds.), *Research in Organizational Behavior*, 13, 191–228. Greenwich: JAI Press.

Lau, D. C., and Murnighan, J. K. (1998). Demographic diversity and faultlines: The compositional dynamics of organizational groups. *Academy of Management Review, 23*(2), 325–340.

Lau, D., and Murnighan, J. K. (2005). Interactions within groups and subgroups: The effects of demographic faultlines. *Academy of Management Journal, 48*, 645–659.

Lawrence, B. (1997). The black box of organizational demography. *Organization Science, 8*, 1–22.

Levin, S. (2004). Perceived group status differences and the effects of gender, ethnicity, and religion on social dominance orientation. *Political Psychology, 25*(1), 144–157.

Levin, S., Federico, C. M., Sidanius, J., and Rabinowitz, J. L. (2002). Social dominance orientation and intergroup bias: The legitimation of favoritism for high-status groups. *Personality and Social Psychology Bulletin*, 28(2), 144–157.

Levin, S., Henry, P. J., Pratto, F., and Sidanius, J. (2003). Social dominance and social identity in Lebanon: Implications for support of violence against the West. *Group Processes and Intergroup Relations*, 6(4), 353–368.

Levin, S., and Sidanius, J. (1999). Social dominance and social identity in the United States and Israel: Ingroup favoritism or outgroup derogation? *Political Psychology*, x(1), 99–126.

Li, J., and Hambrick, D. C. (2005). Factional groups: A new vantage on demographic faultlines, conflict, and disintegration in work teams. *Academy of Management Journal*, 48, 794–813.

Lovelace, K., Shapiro, D., and Weingart, L. R. (2001). Maximizing cross-functional new product teams' innovativeness and constraint adherence: A conflict communications perspective. *Academy of Management Journal*, 24, 779–784.

Mannix, E. A., and Neale, M. A. (2005). What differences make a difference? The promise and reality of diverse teams in organizations. *Psychological Science in the Public Interest*, 6(2), 31–55.

Matsuo, M. (2006). Customer orientation, conflict, and innovativeness in Japanese sales departments. *Journal of Business Research*, 59, 242–250.

Mayer, J. D., and Salovey, P. (1997). What is emotional intelligence? In P. Salovey and D. J. Sluyter (eds.), *Emotional Development and Emotional Intelligence*, 3–31. New York: Basic Books.

Messick, D. M., and Mackie, D. M. (1989). Intergroup relations. *Annual Review of Psychology*, 40, 45–81.

Migdal, M. J., Hewstone, M., and Mullen, B. (1998). The effects of crossed categorization on intergroup evaluations: A meta-analysis. *British Journal of Social Psychology*, 37, 303–324.

Miller, C. C., Burke, L. M., and Glick, W. H. (1998). Cognitive diversity among upper-echelon executives, implications for strategic decision process. *Strategic Management Journal*, 19, 39–58.

Milliken, F. J., and Martins, L. (1996). Searching for common threads: Understanding the multiple effects of diversity in organizational groups. *Academy of Management Review*, 21(2), 402–433.

Mohammed, S., and Angell, L. C. (2004). Surface- and deep-level diversity in workgroups, examining the moderating effects of team orientation and team process on relationship conflict. *Journal of Organizational Behavior*, 25(8), 1015–1039.

Molleman, E. (2005). Diversity in demographic characteristics, abilities, and personality traits, Do faultlines affect team functioning? *Group Decision and Negotiation*, 14, 173–193.

Moscovici, S. (1976). *Social Influence and Social Change*. London: Academic Press.

Murray, A. I. (1989). Top management group heterogeneity and firm performance. *Strategic Management Journal, 10*, 125–141.

Nemeth, C. J. (1986). Differential contributions of majority and minority influence. *Psychological Review, 93*, 23–32.

Nemeth, C. J., and Kwan, J. L. (1987). Minority influence, divergent thinking and detection of correct solutions. *Journal of Applied Social Psychology, 17*, 788–799.

Nibler, R., and Harris, K. L. (2003). The effects of culture and cohesiveness on intragroup conflict and effectiveness. *The Journal of Social Psychology, 143*, 613–631.

O'Reilly, C. A., Caldwell, D. F., and Barnett, W. P. (1989). Work group demography, social integration, and turn over. *Administrative Science Quarterly, 34*, 21–37.

O'Reilly, C. A., Snyder, R. C., and Boothe, J. N. (1993). Effects of organizational demography on organizational change. In G. P. Huber and W. H. Glick (eds.), *Organizational Change and Redesign,* 147–175. New York: Oxford University Press.

O'Reilly, C., Williams, K., and Barsade, S. (1997). Group demography and innovation, Does diversity help? In E. Mannix and M. Neale (eds.), *Research in the Management of Groups and Teams,* Vol. 1. Greenwich: JAI Press.

Pelled, L. H. (1996). Demographic diversity, conflict, and work group outcomes. An intervening process theory. *Organization Science, 6*, 615–631.

Pelled, L. H. (1997). Relational demography and perceptions of group conflict and performance. A field investigation. *International Journal of Conflict Resolution, 22*(1), 54–67.

Pelled, L. H., Eisenhardt, K. M., and Xin, K. R. (1999). Exploring the black box. An analysis of work group diversity, conflict, and performance. *Administrative Science Quarterly, 44*(1), 1–28.

Pfeffer, J. (1983). Organizational demography. In B. Staw and L. Cummings (eds), *Research in Organizational Behavior, 5*, 299–357. Greenwich: JAI Press.

Phillips, K. W. (2003). The effects of categorically based expectations on minority influence, The importance of congruence. *Personality and Social Psychology Bulletin, 29*, 3–13.

Phillips, K., Mannix, E., Neale, M., and Gruenfeld, D. (2004). Diverse groups and information sharing in groups: The effect of congruent ties. *Journal of Experimental Social Psychology, 40*, 497–510.

Pratto, F., Stallworth, L. M., and Conway-Lanz, S. (1998). Social dominance orientation and the ideological legitimization of social policy. *Journal of Applied Social Psychology, 28*(20), 1853–1875.

Pratto, F., Stallworth, L. M., and Sidanius, J. (1997). The gender gap: Differences in political attitudes and social dominance orientation. *British Journal of Social Psychology, 36*, 49–68.

Pratto, F., Tatar, D. G., and Conway-Lanz, S. (1999). Who gets what and why: Determinants of social allocations. *Political Psychology, 20*(1), 127–150.

Randel, A. E. (2002). Identity salience, a moderator of the relationship between group gender composition and work group conflict. *Journal of Organizational Behavior, 23*(6), 749–766.

Rau, D. (2005). The influence of relationship conflict and trust on the transactive memory. *Small Group Research, 36*(6), 746–771.

Riordan, C. M. (2000). Relational demography within groups. Past developments, contradictions, and new directions. *Research in Personnel and Human Resource Management, 19*, 131–173.

Riordan, C., and Shore, L. (1997). Demographic diversity and employee attitudes. An empirical investigation of relational demographic within work units. *Journal of Applied Psychology, 82*, 342–358.

Rispens, S., Greer, L. L., and Jehn, K. A. (2006). Can relationship conflict be positive? Exploring the moderating role of interdependence on the link between relationship conflict and workgroup performance. Presented at the International Association of Conflict Management Conference, Montreal, Canada.

Rispens, S., Jehn, K. A., and Thatcher, S. M. B. (2005). An examination of three perspectives on conflict in workgroups: Constructive debate, cognitive processing, and asymmetric perceptions. Paper presented at the Association for Researchers in Work and Organizational Psychology, The Netherlands: Rotterdam.

Ross, R. (1989). Conflict. In R. Ross and J. Ross (eds.), *Small Groups in Organizational Settings*, 139–178. Englewood Cliffs: Prentice-Hall.

Shaw, J. B. (2004). The development and analysis of a measure of group faultlines. *Organizational Research Methods, 7*(1), 66–100.

Sidanius, J., Pratto, F., and Brief, D. (1995). Group dominance and the political psychology of gender: A cross-cultural comparison. *Political Psychology, 16*(2), 381–396.

Sidanius, J., Pratto, F., Van Laar, C., and Levin, S. (2004). Social dominance theory: Its agenda and method. *Political Psychology, 25*(6), 845–880.

Simons, T., Pelled, L. H., and Smith, K. A. (1999). Making use of difference: Diversity, debate, and decision comprehensiveness in top management teams. *Academy of Management Journal, 42*, 662–673.

Simsek, Z., Veijga, J. F., Lubatkin, M. J., and Dino, R. N. (2005). Modeling the multilevel determinants of top management team behavioral integration. *Academy of Management Journal, 48,* 69–84.

Smith, K. G., Smith, K. A., Olian, J. D., Sims, H. P., O'Bannon, D. P., and Scully, J. (1994). Top management team demography and process: The role of social integration and communication. *Administrative Science Quarterly, 39,* 412–438.

Stewart, G. L. (2006). A meta-analytic review of relationships between team design features and team performance. *Journal of Management, 32*(1), 29–54.

Strauss, G. (1962). Tactics of lateral relationships. The purchasing agent. *Administrative Science Quarterly, 7,* 161–186.

Tajfel, H. (1978). Social categorization, social identity, and social comparison. In H. Tajfel (ed.), *Differentiation between Social Groups, Studies in the Social Psychology of Intergroup Relations,* 61–76. London: Academic Press.

Tajfel, H. (1981). *Human Groups and Social Categories: Studies in Social Psychology.* Cambridge: Cambridge University Press.

Tajfel, H., and Turner, J. C. (1986). The social identity theory of intergroup behavior. In S. Worchel and W. G. Austin (eds.), *Psychology of Intergroup Relations,* 7–24. Chicago: Nelson-Hall.

Thatcher, S. M. B., Jehn, K. A., and Zanutto E. (2003). Cracks in diversity research, The effects of diversity faultlines on conflict and performance. *Group Decision and Negotiation, 12*(3), 217–241.

Thomas, K. W. (1992). Conflict and negotiation process in organizations. In M. Dunette and L. Hough (eds.), *Handbook of Industrial and Organizational Psychology,* 651–718. Palo Alto: Consulting Psychologists Press.

Tinsley, C. H. (2001). How negotiators get to yes, Predicting the constellation of strategies used across cultures to negotiate conflict. *Journal of Applied Psychology, 86*(4), 583–593.

Toren, N., and Kraus, V. (1987). The effects of minority size on women's position in academia. *Social Forces, 65,* 1090–1100.

Townsend, A. M., and Scott, K. D. (2001). Team racial composition, member attitudes, and performance: A field study. *Industrial Relations, 40*(2), 317–337.

Triandis, H., Kurowski, L., and Gelfand, M. (1993). Workplace diversity. In H. Triandis, M. Dunette, and L. Hough (eds.), *Handbook of Industrial and Organizational Psychology,* Vol. 4, 769–827. Palo Alto: Consulting Psychologists Press.

Tsui, A. S., Egan, T. D., and O'Reilly, C. A. (1992). Being different: Relational demography and organizational attachment. *Administrative Science Quarterly, 37*(4), 549–579.

Tsui, A. S., and O'Reilly, C. A. (1989). Beyond simple demographic effects: The importance of relational demography in superior-superordinate dyads. *Academy of Management Journal, 32*, 402–423.

Tsui, A. S., Xin, K., and Egan, T. D. (1995). Relational demography: The missing link in vertical dyad linkage. In S. Jackson and M. Ruderman (eds.), *Productivity and Interpersonal Relations in Work Teams Characterized by Diversity*, 97–130. Washington, DC: American Psychological Association.

Turner, J. C. (1982). *Social Identity and Intergroup Relations*. Cambridge: Cambridge University Press.

Turner, J. C. (1987). A self-categorization theory. In J. C. Turner, M. A. Hogg, P. J. Oakes, S. D. Reicher, and M. S. Wetherell (eds.), *Rediscovering the Social Group: A Self-categorization Theory*, 42–67. Oxford: Basil Blackwell.

Turner, J. C., Hogg, M. A., Oakes, P. J., Reicher, S. D., and Wetherell, M. S. (1987). *Rediscovering the Social Group: A Self-categorization Theory*. Oxford: Blackwell.

Tyler, T. R., and Blader, S. (2000). *Co-operation in Groups, Procedural Justice, Social Identity and Behavioral Engagement*. Philadelphia: Psychology Press.

Van der Vegt, G., and Bunderson, S. (2005). Learning and performance in multidisciplinary teams: The importance of collective team identification. *Academy of Management Journal, 48*, 532–547.

Van Knippenberg, D., and Haslam, S. A. (2003). Realizing the diversity dividend – exploring the subtle interplay between identity, ideology, and reality. In S. A. Haslam, D. Van Knippenberg, M. Platow, and N. Ellemers (eds.), *Social Identity at Work, Developing Theory for Organizational Practice*, 61–77. New York: Psychology Press.

Vodosek, M. (2005). Cultural diversity, intragroup conflict, and group outcomes. *Academy of Management Conference Proceedings*, Honolulu, HI.

Wagner, W. G., Pfeffer, J., and O'Reilly, C. A. (1984). Organizational demography and turnover in top management groups. *Administrative Science Quarterly, 29*, 74–92.

Wall, J. A., and Callister, R. R. (1995). Conflict and its management. *Journal of Management, 21*(3), 515–558.

Webber, S. S., and Donahue, L. M. (2001). Impact of highly and less job-related diversity on work group cohesion and performance, a meta-analysis. *Journal of Management, 27*, 141–162.

Weingart, L. R. (1992). Impact of group goals, task component complexity, effort, and planning on group performance. *Journal of Applied Psychology, 77*, 682–693.

Wharton, A. S. (1992). The social construction of gender and race in organizations, A social identity and group mobilization perspective. In

P. S. Tolbert and S. B. Bacharach (eds.), *Research in the Sociology of Organizations*, 10, 55–84. Greenwich, CT: JAI Press.

Wiersema, M., and Bantel, K. (1992). Top management team demography and corporate strategic change. *Academy of Management Journal*, 35, 91–121.

Wiersema, M. F., and Bird, A. (1993). Organizational demography in Japanese firms: Group heterogeneity, individual dissimilarity, and top management team turnover. *Academy of Management Journal*, 36, 996–1025.

Williams, K., and O'Reilly, C. A. (1998). Demography and diversity in organizations, A review of 40 years of research. In B. Staw and L. L. Cummings (eds.), *Research in Organizational Behavior*, 20, 77–140. Oxford, UK: Elsevier Science Inc.

Wilson, M. S., and Liu, J. H. (2003). Social dominance orientation and gender: The moderating role of gender identity. *British Journal of Social Psychology*, 42, 187–198.

Wittenbaum, G. M., and Stasser, G. (1996). Management of information in small groups. In J. L. Nye and A. M. Brower (eds.), *What's Social about Social Cognition? Social Cognition Research in Small Groups*, 3–28. Thousand Oaks: Sage.

Wood, W., Lundgren, S., Oullette, J. A., Buscene, S., and Blackstone, T. (1994). Minority influence, A meta-analytic review of social influence processes. *Psychological Bulletin*, 115, 323–345.

Yang, J. X., and Mossholder, K. W. (2004). Decoupling task and relationship conflict, the role of intragroup emotional processing. *Journal of Organizational Behavior*, 25(5), 589–605.

Zenger, T., and Lawrence, B. (1989). Organizational demography: The differential effects of age and tenure distributions on technical communications. *Academy of Management Journal*, 32, 353–376.

6 | Shifting frames in team-diversity research: From difference to relationships

ROBIN J. ELY AND LAURA MORGAN ROBERTS

Shifting frames in team-diversity research: From difference to relationships

Organizational research on cultural diversity in teams has tended to focus both theoretically and empirically on differences. In this research stream, diversity is typically defined as the degree of heterogeneity among team members on specified demographic dimensions; theory aims to explain how such heterogeneity affects team processes and performance (for review, see Williams and O'Reilly, 1998). An assumption underlying much of this research has been that difference *per se* is a source of conflict and hence that teams must minimize members' experience of different-ness from others so as to mitigate diversity's negative effects (Chatman *et al.*, 1998; Dovidio, Kawakami, and Gaertner, 2000; Jehn, Northcraft, and Neale, 1999).

In this chapter, we reframe diversity research from a paradigm that emphasizes difference to one that emphasizes relationships. In our approach, while difference remains a defining feature of diversity, it is no longer the principle feature. Rather, our relational approach highlights the personal, interpersonal, and intergroup dynamics that influence how people interpret and act on their differences. From this perspective, difference can also be a source of creativity and resilience. This reframing has implications for how scholars conceptualize and measure diversity and for how they theorize about the conditions that influence whether diversity becomes an asset or a liability.

We define cultural diversity as differences among team members in race, ethnicity, gender, religion, nationality, or other dimensions of social identity *that are marked by a history of intergroup prejudice, discrimination, or oppression*. The intergroup component of our definition is key; it constructs diversity as a relation of power and provides the theoretical grounding for our relational approach. In this chapter, we explore how societal power disparities between identity groups are manifested at the personal and interpersonal levels, hindering the effective functioning of culturally diverse teams. We then consider how team members can extricate themselves and their relationships from the grip of these dynamics to leverage the benefits diversity has to offer.

Specifically, we argue that stereotypes and power imbalances between groups at the societal level pose threats to people's identity, such as the threat of being misjudged or mistreated due to their social identity group membership. Negative team dynamics follow from people's defensive responses to such threats. People's defensive responses involve a preoccupation with protecting the image of themselves they wish others to see – an inward-focused goal – which prevents teams from realizing their potential.

This chapter's central premise is that teams whose members submit to outward-focused goals – for example, the goal of advancing broad social ideals, furthering an organization's mission, or enhancing the quality of their relationships – can overcome these negative dynamics. Team members using this strategy resist the impulse to validate a desired image and instead regard threats to identity as signaling an opportunity to learn – about themselves, the other, or the task – in service of larger goals. Applying this framework to classic diversity-related dilemmas in teams, we explore the challenges and opportunities of shifting one's orientation from inward- to outward-focused goals as a strategy for constructively engaging across cultural differences (see also Ely and Meyerson, 2006, and Ely, Meyerson, and Davidson, 2006).

Below, we identify some of the limitations of the traditional, difference frame on diversity. We then present an alternative that places relationships front and center. Finally, we explore the implications of this alternative framing for future research on culturally diverse teams.

Culturally diverse teams: A difference frame

The difference frame on cultural diversity has been largely informed by social categorization (Turner, 1987) and social identity theories (Hogg and Abrams, 1988; Tajfel, 1981; 1982) as well as the similarity/attraction paradigm (Byrne, 1971) (for a review of these approaches, see Williams and O'Reilly, 1998). These approaches' underlying premise is that people prefer and have an easier time interacting with similar others, such as those who share membership in the same social identity groups. Interactions with people who are different, such as those belonging to different social identity groups, are difficult at best (similarity/attraction paradigm) and hostile at worst (social categorization and identity theories).

From this perspective, researchers focus "on visible differences in themselves rather than on their content" (Chatman and Flynn, 2001: 962). What matters in this frame is whether and on how many dimensions team members differ from one another. On any given dimension – whether age, gender, race, or sex, for example – a team member scores as "different" or "the same" relative to other team members. Composite measures of diversity, in which multiple demographic dimensions are aggregated to form a single index, reflect this framing and are commonly used in difference-oriented research (e.g., Chatman and Flynn, 2001; Chatman *et al.*, 1998; Colquitt, Noe, and Jackson, 2002).

While this approach has produced some important insights into the effects of group heterogeneity, it has several drawbacks. First, emphasizing the binary distinction of difference versus sameness treats all identity group memberships as if they were equal, ignoring the meaning society or the immediate setting confers on group membership. Some demographic dimensions, such as race, are marked by societal power disparities and a history of intergroup conflict, whereas others, such as age, are more variably marked at the local level. Given the different historical, cultural, and local circumstances surrounding race relations and intergenerational relations, for example, we would not expect racial diversity to yield the same team resources nor generate the same team dynamics as age diversity. Thus, understanding the impact of different dimensions of diversity on team processes and performance requires some knowledge of these dimensions' societal and local meanings.

An emphasis on different-ness *per se* also misses the dynamics of "simultaneity" (Collins, 1993; Collins and Thorne, 1995; Crenshaw, 1997; Holvino, 2001). Simultaneity refers to the fact that people hold multiple identities, some culturally marginalized (e.g., women, racial "minorities," gays and lesbians) and some privileged (e.g., men, Whites, heterosexuals), and that the meaning and impact of each depends in part on the others. Thus, for example, a gay white man and a straight black man are likely to have different experiences of their maleness because maleness takes on different cultural meanings and power-status positions for people of different races and sexual orientations. Likewise, a straight Puerto Rican man and a straight Puerto Rican woman may have different experiences of their presumably shared ethnic and sexual identities because of their different gender positions. In other words, the meaning and experience of one identity is interpreted through the lens of other identities. From this perspective, shared group memberships do not necessarily translate into shared experiences nor promote the same in-group and out-group sentiments. Moreover, power positioning matters: shared marginalized identities (e.g., being Black) may create a greater subjective sense of similarity and connection than shared privileged identities (e.g., being male or straight) partly because the former tend to be more salient than the latter (Cox, 1993; Ely, 1995; Tajfel, 1982). Clearly, a difference framing, which would consider difference or sameness on each dimension separately and additively, would miss these nuances, yet they are crucial factors influencing the dynamics of culturally diverse teams.

Another drawback of the difference framing on cultural diversity is that, in attending primarily to *inter*group dynamics, it tends to overlook important *intra*group dynamics – interactions between members of the same social identity group – which are often shaped by the intergroup relationships in which they are embedded. People sometimes pay as much attention to people who are similar to them as to those who are different to determine how aligned in-group members' goals and orientations are with out-groups. For example, a black woman might monitor how her black coworker interacts with their non-black teammates in order to judge if her behavior is "black enough" to warrant her respect and inclusion in the black community (see, e.g., Branscombe *et al.*, 1999). Alternatively, she may be concerned that her coworker's behavior is "too black" (e.g., she confirms negative racial stereotypes or radical political beliefs), which she fears may jeopardize the status of both black women on the team. Aware of this possibility, her black coworker may be guarded in her expression of certain attitudes and behaviors, so as to manage her black colleague's impression of her, perhaps hoping to prove that she is a fit "ambassador" for their racial group. As this example illustrates, the presence of the out-group influences in-group interactions and vice versa. In short, sameness is more than just the absence of difference; it has its own dynamics that influence how diversity plays out in teams.

Finally, a focus on difference has led many diversity researchers to treat cultural diversity as relevant only insofar as it triggers tensions and conflict to be avoided, thus neglecting how cultural diversity can also be a team asset (Roberts, 2006b). Conditions that mitigate the negative dynamics associated with diversity usually center on minimizing people's felt different-ness from others in the group by, for example, encouraging identification with a superordinate category (e.g., the team) or with communal values. Such interventions increase the salience of team members' shared fate, fostering a sense of themselves as one unified group rather than as individuals differentiated by demographic characteristics (Chatman *et al.*, 1998; Harrison *et al.*, 2002). The drawback of this approach is that it mitigates liabilities associated with diversity by suppressing differences. Such suppression discards the very source of benefits that diversity is supposed to provide. In addition, suppressing differences can take an emotional toll in teams as some members – particularly those from traditionally marginalized identity groups – strive to prove their commitment to, or legitimacy in, the superordinate category. In short, if group members suppress their differences, then they may have difficulty mobilizing them as resources in service of the group's work (Ely and Thomas, 2001; Ely, Thomas, and Padavic, 2006; Polzer, Milton, and Swann, 2002).

In sum, a difference framing suggests hypotheses that are insufficiently nuanced to adequately capture the full range of diversity effects. We turn now to an alternative framing to address some of these shortcomings.

Shifting the paradigm: A relationship frame on culturally diverse teams

Framing cultural diversity in relational terms focuses attention on the nature of people's encounters with one another in culturally diverse teams and on the relational dynamics within which such encounters are embedded. These dynamics operate at multiple levels of analysis (Alderfer, 1987; Alderfer and Smith, 1982). At the broadest level is the history of societal relations between identity groups, including the distribution of power, which shapes social roles, expectations, and hence, meanings at the group level. Individuals draw a sense of collective identity from the societal meanings associated with group membership and, to varying degrees, internalize the group's positive and negative aspects (for a review, see Ashmore, Deaux, and McLaughlin-Volpe, 2004). Whereas a difference frame depicts diversity as a static dimension characterized in simple, binary terms (different versus the same), a relational frame highlights diversity's dynamic aspects: diversity from a relational perspective is constituted by multiple and intersecting relations of power that manifest at several, mutually reinforcing (and sometimes conflicting) levels of analysis.

Importantly for our purposes, a relational approach directs attention not only to people's reactions to others' identity group memberships, but to people's concerns about their own identity group memberships as well – particularly, their concerns about how others view them as members of such groups. Below, we explicate how power-status asymmetries between social identity groups influence such concerns and how these concerns, in turn, influence interactions in culturally diverse teams.

Public image and social identity threats

Social psychological research on the self suggests that people consistently seek evidence of their merit and strive to demonstrate such evidence to others (Crocker and Park, 2004). The domains, or areas of life, in which people seek evidence vary. Some people stake their self-worth on being popular, slender, or strong; others on being competent or morally virtuous; and still others on having accumulated wealth or power. Personal self-worth is contingent on demonstrating – to oneself and to others – that one possesses desirable traits and abilities in one's chosen domains. This constellation of desirable characteristics constitutes one's desired public image (see Roberts, 2005, on the concept of desired image). On the flip side is one's dreaded public image – those characteristics that belie the desired image. We use the general term "public image"[1] to capture the host of characteristics that reflect the desired image and defy the dreaded one. Success and failure in validating one's public image can generalize to one's sense of value as a whole

---

[1] The concept of "public image" was adapted from material developed for a personal mastery seminar by Learning as Leadership, Inc., San Rafael, CA. (www.learnaslead.com). See Ely (2006) for a further explanation of this construct.

person (Crocker and Park, 2004). Thus, people are deeply invested in proving to themselves and to others that they *are* their public image.

People's social identity affiliations, such as their race, gender, nationality, and social class, influence the characteristics they choose to emphasize in their public image (Roberts, 2005). The social identity component of people's public image refers to the image they wish to convey as members of their social identity groups. It is typically influenced by a wish to be seen as associated with or distanced from the societal stereotypes that characterize their groups. The domains of one's public image, therefore, are shaped in large measure by stereotypes.

When situations, events, or encounters trigger people's fears of being misjudged or mistreated because of their membership in a social identity group, they experience a "social identity threat" (for a review, see Steele, Spencer, and Aronson, 2002). Such threats are especially apt to arise in multicultural settings where stereotypes are likely to be activated (Branscombe *et al.*, 1999; Ethier and Deaux, 1994; Roberts, 2005). Although the literature on social identity threat has tended to focus on people with marginalized social identities (e.g., women; gays or lesbians; or members of minority racial, ethnic, religious, or national groups), people with privileged social identities (e.g., men; heterosexuals; those in majority racial, ethnic, religious, or national groups) also experience such threats. Membership in both kinds of groups can cause people to fear being judged according to negative cultural stereotypes, on the one hand, and to worry about failing to live up to positive cultural stereotypes, on the other. We call situations that trigger such concerns "devaluation threats" and "legitimacy threats," respectively. Because stereotypes that attach to marginalized groups are more likely to be negative, their members tend to experience more devaluation than legitimacy threats, whereas the opposite is true for members of privileged groups.

Devaluation threats

Devaluation threats are situations, events, or encounters that people interpret as signaling social identity-based negative evaluations of them and that thus compromise their public image. Because different stereotypes attach to different social identity groups, the domains in which people fear others' devaluation vary.

Two common scenarios illustrate devaluation threats from both marginalized and privileged perspectives. In the first scenario, an Asian-American is routinely mistaken for his Asian-American coworker.

When his white teammate calls him by his coworker's name, he worries that he is not seen as an individual but rather as a stereotypical Asian – a quiet, shy, nonentity on the team (a devaluation threat). Aware that Whites frequently apply such stereotypes, he is especially invested in demonstrating non-stereotypical attributes, such as being extroverted (his desired public image) and in fending off the perception that he is quiet or shy (his dreaded public image). Hence, when coworkers call him by the wrong name, he feels particularly threatened. A second scenario involves a woman whose ideas are repeatedly misattributed to male teammates, which causes her to worry that her coworkers do not expect her to make useful or insightful contributions. Aware of the stereotype that women's contributions are less valuable than men's, being seen as smart is a central part of her public image; hence, she is particularly anxious about these misattributions. In each scenario, offense at the perceived slight may or may not be well-founded, but to discuss it poses further risk, such as the risk of being labeled "overly sensitive," "strident," or "not a team player" – characterizations that may also be part of these workers' dreaded images. To raise the issue, therefore, could introduce yet another threat to their public image.

At the same time, raising such issues can trigger devaluation threats for members of privileged identity groups as well. (Indeed, labeling others as "overly sensitive," for example, is often a defensive reaction by those in privileged groups to fend off such threats.) In the first example, when the white person realizes she has called her Asian-American colleague by the wrong name, she may fear that he and others will accuse her of being racist. In the second example, if the woman points out that her ideas are repeatedly misattributed to her teammates, male colleagues may hear her as accusing them of being sexist. For many people with privileged identities, to be seen as "racist" or "sexist" – stereotypes that often attach to Whites and men, respectively – is a dreaded public image. To appear fair and supportive to those from marginalized groups may even be an explicit part of privileged group members' desired public image.

Although research suggests that the structure of devaluation threats is similar regardless of one's particular identity group affiliation (for review, see Crocker *et al.*, 2006), the frequency, severity, and consequences of such threats clearly vary. Those with marginalized or stigmatized identities may experience more – and more severe – devaluation threats than their privileged counterparts. Indeed, some members of marginalized groups may experience chronic devaluation threats, and are constantly besieged with worries that their public image will be compromised by negative stereotypes. Settings that may foster chronic threat experiences include those in which one is a token (Kanter, 1977), members of one's group are underrepresented in senior positions (Ely, 1994; 1995), and the dominant culture is antithetical to one's group's interests (Meyerson and Kolb, 2000). In contrast, people with privileged identities are likely to experience devaluation threats only intermittently – typically when in the company of marginalized group members – and in more circumscribed domains. For example, the threat to a Latino of being stereotyped as lazy or unintelligent is more likely to arise, because work settings are more likely to be White-dominated, and more likely to be debilitating, because the domain of those stereotypes strike at the heart of one's value as a coworker, compared to the more circumscribed threat of being seen as racist.

Legitimacy threats

Just as confirming negative stereotypes can threaten one's sense of self-worth, so too can the prospect of failing to live up to positive ones. Legitimacy threats are situations, events, or encounters that people interpret as signaling that they fail to live up to the culture's idealized images of their social identity group and thus are not fully legitimate members. As with devaluation threats, legitimacy threats strike both privileged and marginalized group members.

People with privileged identities are especially susceptible to legitimacy threats because the positive traits associated with their group help to justify the group's privileged status. Status accrues to the most prototypical members, and such traits are therefore frequently central to privileged group members' desired public image. In its idealized and stereotypical forms, male identity, for example, connotes authority, autonomy, and strength, which is often seen as justification for their overrepresentation in leadership roles (Heilman *et al.*, 1989; Powell, Butterfield, and Parent, 2002). Many men seek to demonstrate their masculine credentials, look for affirmation of their masculine status, and feel threatened when they do not receive it (Barrett, 1996; Connell, 1995; Kerfoot and Knights, 1993).

Legitimacy threats to members of marginalized identity groups often arise in intragroup interactions as members police each other's actions to assess loyalty to the group or authenticity of identity (Anderson, 1999; Branscombe *et al.*, 1999). For example, a gay team member may worry that to criticize a gay colleague would be seen as disloyal, costing him the support and acceptance of other gays and lesbians in the company. The impulse to criticize thus summons a threat to identity.

People with marginalized identities may also experience pressure from out-groups to fulfill stereotypes that, although positive, nevertheless justify their group's marginalized status. For example, a white woman may be reluctant to enact her leadership role in too assertive a manner for fear of violating men's – and the broader culture's – idealized image of women as nice. As this example suggests, deviating from gender roles can evoke identity threats for women as well as for men.

In sum, people from both privileged and marginalized identity positions can experience threats to the social identity components of their public images, and such threats influence how people relate to each other. Social identity threats are pivotal points in the life of culturally diverse teams: defensive reactions can seriously derail the team's work, but when team members replace their need to defend themselves with an outward-focused goal, the team can become stronger from the experience. What differentiates people is not whether they have a public image or even whether their public image has a social identity component, but rather, how aware they are of these dynamics and what strategies they use to respond to them. Below, we describe two kinds of strategies for responding to social identity threats – one involving the pursuit of inward-focused goals and the other the pursuit of outward-focused goals – and how each influences team effectiveness.

Common strategies for responding to identity threats: Pursuing inward-focused goals

The most common strategies for responding to social identity threats are defensive reactions intended to protect or validate one's desired public image. We identify four such strategies: distancing, dispelling, living up to idealized images, and feigning indifference. When experiencing a devaluation threat, people tend either to *distance* themselves personally from their social identity group and its stereotypes or to *dispel* negative stereotypes about the group more generally. When experiencing a legitimacy threat, they try to *live up to idealized images* of their group. Finally, to address both types of threats, people may *feign indifference* to how others view them.

Distancing and dispelling

Distancing as a strategy for countering the threat of social identity devaluation involves disassociating from one's social identity group (Roberts, 2005; Tajfel, 1978), a strategy that members of both marginalized and privileged identity groups employ. An example of a marginalized group member using this strategy is an Arab-American man who fears being stereotyped as a terrorist and thus avoids discussing his Islamic faith and publicly repudiates Muslim extremists. This strategy suppresses one's marginalized identity to avoid social rejection, harassment, or loss of social status.

Members of privileged groups also use distancing tactics to reduce the likelihood that others will view them according to negative stereotypes. For example, a liberal-minded straight person who mistakenly assumes his gay male coworker is straight may try to counteract his *faux pas* by mentioning a gay bar he has been to – atypical behavior for straight people – to protect his public image as tolerant and progressive. Other examples include Whites who withhold negative feedback from coworkers of color or who support job candidates of color regardless of their qualifications to distinguish themselves as "good" white people. Importantly, the goal of these behaviors is inward-focused – to validate one's moral character by proving that the negative stereotypes associated with one's group do not personally apply – despite one's apparent altruistic intent.

An alternative to the distancing strategy for addressing devaluation threats is dispelling negative stereotypes, not just about oneself as illustrated above, but about one's group more generally. People using this strategy often take the role of group representative, holding themselves to a standard of perfection in order to demonstrate the group's capabilities. Others may attempt to educate their coworkers about their group; for example, they may attribute a group member's questionable work habits to the group's cultural norms. When people undertake this strategy primarily to protect their public images, however, their efforts to educate fail to enlighten. Instead, they can come off as self-righteousness, condescending, and judgmental. Still others may take the role of group advocate, for example, indiscriminantly defending group members whose performance may be lacking.

Living up to idealized images

Defensive reactions to legitimacy threats involve demonstrating that one can live up to the culture's idealized images of one's social identity groups. For example, a Chinese-American who wishes to live up to the "model minority" image of Asian-Americans might avoid conflict and work tirelessly to demonstrate that she is a technical genius who does not challenge authority (Oyserman and Sakamoto, 1997). Or, male medical residents seeking to prove their masculine credentials may take unnecessary risks, avoid asking for help, and cover up their mistakes to be seen as heroic and invulnerable (Kellogg, 2005). When a group's idealized characteristics are conflated with task requirements, the threat associated with nonconformity increases (Bailyn, 1993; Fletcher, 2003).

Feigning indifference

Some people respond to social identity threats by acting as if they are indifferent to how others view them. Ironically, this strategy entails carefully crafting a public image of indifference (Schlenker and Weigold, 1992). It involves adopting a detached, even antisocial stance to appear autonomous and independent, while in fact shielding oneself from the pain of rejection. Acting in a detached manner signals that one is unwilling to invest time or effort into making a good impression on others. Another way to create the image of indifference is to intentionally defy group norms by expressing one's willful deviance from the dominant culture. For example, a young woman might wear several tattoos and body piercings or dye her hair purple to symbolize her unwillingness to conform to mainstream notions of femininity. Her male counterpart might appear conservative in his dress and hair, but express controversial opinions to flaunt his indifference to cultural expectations for the well-behaved gentleman. People using this strategy justify their behavior by insisting that being authentic is more important than appearances or social acceptance. Despite such claims to authenticity, the striving quality of one's nonconformity belies the actor's *in*dependence from group norms and illustrates instead his or her *counter*-dependence, a stance as beholden to cultural norms as is conformity.

Costs of pursuing inward-focused goals

Despite some short-term benefits, these strategies exact many costs (for review of benefits and costs, see Crocker and Park, 2004). When people successfully demonstrate their public images in the face of social identity threats, they temporarily feel good: self-esteem creates the illusion of belongingness, competence, and optimism. But when self-esteem rests on efforts to prove oneself, it does not actually increase social inclusion, competence, efficacy, or relatedness, nor does it lead to improved performance. Rather, the pursuit of inward-focused goals in the face of social identity threats interferes with learning and performance, leads to poor self-regulation, increases tension and stress, and undermines autonomy and relationships. Research shows that when people have the goal of validating their self-worth, they interpret mistakes and failures as threats rather than as opportunities to learn and improve; they challenge criticism; they are preoccupied with themselves, losing sight of the implications of their own actions for others; and when success is uncertain, they feel anxious and do things that decrease the probability of success, while building in excuses for failure. In short, while managing others' impressions is a natural part of life, problems arise when people are *driven* by concerns about others' assessments of them (Crocker and Park, 2004; Crocker *et al.*, 2006; Ely and Meyerson, 2006).

When people are preoccupied with protecting their image – whether validating a desired image, dispelling a dreaded one, or feigning indifference – they are distracted from the work at hand, ultimately hampering both individual and team effectiveness (Baumeister, 1999; Baumeister *et al.*, 1998; Steele, 1997). Ironically, this distraction often leads people to confirm the very stereotypes they had hoped to dispel (Steele and Aronson, 1995). For example, when women or African-Americans fear that their math test performance will confirm a negative stereotype of incompetence, they are less able to focus on the test itself and are more likely to perform poorly than when they are less concerned about social identity threats (for a review of relevant study results, see Steele, Spencer, and Aronson, 2002).

Many defensive strategies entail creating an image of perfection to deflect identity threats. To appear perfect, a person must cover up weaknesses, mistakes, and other vulnerabilities (Hewitt *et al.*, 2003). Instead of owning his shortcomings, he may attempt to derogate others and blame them for his failures in order to prove his personal value or the worthiness of his group (Branscombe *et al.*, 1999; Cialdini and Richardson, 1980; Crocker and Luhtanen, 1990). These behaviors can incite dysfunctional competition (Ely, 1994; Jehn, Northcraft, and Neale, 1999) and instigate identity threats to others. They compromise personal and team learning, interfere in the team's ability to work effectively together, and risk the safety, well-being, and effectiveness of those who depend on the team's work (Ely and Meyerson, 2006).

In addition, when people suppress aspects of their identities or sequester themselves away from the team, they withhold potentially important resources, such as insights and perspectives that may derive from their social identity group memberships (Ely and Thomas, 2001). Superficial engagement and lack of self-disclosure also interfere in the development of trust among team members and often generate additional threats, because people jump to false conclusions about others' intentions (Davidson and James, 2006; Roberts, 2006a).

Finally, these strategies, even when ostensibly geared to changing the relative status of an individual or group, may ultimately reinforce the status quo. When marginalized group members suppress their identities and disassociate from their identity groups, they also tend to avoid conflicts with members of privileged groups to prove their fit with the dominant culture. Conflicts fester beneath the surface, constraining people's ability to form the kinds of relationships necessary to advance change (Davidson and James, 2006). Likewise, striving to conform to idealized images reifies group stereotypes and the status positions associated with them (e.g., dominant, masculine leaders; submissive, feminine caretakers). Finally, when self-focused, even attempts to dispel negative stereotypes through advocacy and education can end up reinforcing the status quo. Their defensive quality translates to judgment and condescension, which poses identity threats to others. Others are likely to respond defensively, resisting the advocate/educator's message in order to protect themselves. Both sides become self-righteous, creating more distance, fear, and judgment, further undermining mutual respect and understanding.

Specifying these costs is not to deny that social identity threats are often real. Threats range from the infliction of intentional harm, as when people commit hate crimes, intentionally undermine their co-workers, or verbally abuse them, to more subtle manifestations of unconsciously held stereotypes, as when members of certain social identity groups are held to higher or lower performance standards (Schultz, 1998; Wilkins and Gulati, 1996). Clearly, such threats can be damaging. But research suggests that defensive reactions are rarely effective ways to respond and may even cause further damage (Crocker and Park, 2004). We propose a more effective response below.

Alternative strategies: Pursuing outward-focused goals

Research suggests that outward-focused goals, such as advancing broad social ideals, contributing to a task, or striving to achieve an organization's mission, may guide a more effective response to social identity threats. Such goals can provide the impetus for resisting the impulse to react defensively (Crocker *et al.*, 2006; Ely and Meyerson, 2006). Outward-focused goals infuse people's lives with meaning by connecting them with others (Grant, forthcoming). Such goals remind people of what is at stake, giving them a reason to engage with other people, rather than defend themselves, even as they feel threatened. When driven by outward-focused goals, people regard felt-threats as signaling an opportunity to learn – about themselves, the other, or the task (Ely, Meyerson, and Davidson, 2006). Although pursuing these goals may not quell fears about rejection or incompetence in the short term, outward-focused goals provide a powerful reason to constructively move forward despite such fears.

We illustrate this strategy with examples from members of both marginalized and privileged social identity groups. In the following example, Bridget Heller, an African-American and former Vice President and General Manager at Kraft, describes how, as a college student, her commitment to mutual intellectual growth – an outward-focused goal – enabled her to respond nondefensively when identity threats arose:

Northwestern [University] was all about intellectual growth. We challenged each other openly on so many levels, and we were all being enlightened. Everyone thought very differently, and it was cool to ask questions. That's how we all grew, through questions and long discussions and arguments. One of my friends was a freckle-faced Jewish woman from Wisconsin who had never met anyone black. She asked me, "Are you black all over?" If she had asked me that in junior high, I'd have just decked her. If she asked me that in high school, same thing. But by college, it was okay. I'd gotten through a lot of that. She just didn't know. And you know what? The truth was, I'd never met a person with freckles, and I said to her, are there freckles all over you? . . . She was just curious. And the truth was, I was curious about freckles. So that was the environment. It was safe to ask questions. (Cobbs and Turnock, 2003: 15)

We draw a second example from Milton Irvin, former executive director at UBS Warberg, also an African-American, who describes a social identity threat he experienced as an MBA student at Wharton and how he used it as a signal to learn.

One day, everyone was running into the auditorium, and I asked a guy, "What's going on?" He said, "Gus Levy from Goldman Sachs is making a presentation." So I said, "Who's Gus Levy and what's Goldman Sachs?" And the guy looked at me and said, "If you have to ask that question, you shouldn't be here." And I said, "Oh my goodness." I felt so bad. The next day I went to the placement director. I said, "I'll be honest with you. The only reason I'm at Wharton is somebody told me it was a good school. I don't know what to do once I graduate. I just have no idea. I was embarrassed yesterday because I didn't know who Gus Levy was, I didn't know what Goldman Sachs was, and I was told I shouldn't be here." He took me under his wing, maybe because he'd never seen someone with such brutal honesty. He set me up at General Motors, Bankers Trust, and Goldman Sachs, just for informational meetings, to learn context, to ask questions, just to talk to them. I ended up getting summer job offers from all three. (Cobbs and Turnock, 2003: 45)

By addressing his identity threat nondefensively, Irvin not only launched a highly successful career; his reaction also enabled him to develop a generative relationship with Wharton as an institution. While there, he founded the Whitney M. Young conference, an African-American student-run national conference to support economic development in the black community. More recently, he led a successful campaign to fund the Whitney M. Young Endowed Professorship at Wharton, a position to be filled by a faculty member whose research on workforce diversity honors Dr. Young's humanitarian efforts in civil rights, education, and advocacy for African-Americans.

Members of privileged identity groups have also used this strategy in the face of social identity threats. Consider the example of workers on two offshore oil platforms – a workplace that has traditionally rewarded men for masculine displays of prowess while punishing them for appearing weak – in which masculine displays were markedly absent (Ely and Meyerson, 2006; Meyerson and Ely, forthcoming). Whereas men in dirty, dangerous work environments are often motivated by the goal of proving their masculinity (see Chetkovich, 1997, for examples in the fire service, and Barrett, 1996, for military examples), workers on these platforms were largely motivated by goals larger than themselves: the safety and well-being of their coworkers and the effective accomplishment of their work. The organization's self-conscious focus on increasing safety and effectiveness compelled workers to adopt a set of work practices that supported deep and ongoing learning in the service of these outward-focused goals. These practices had the secondary consequence of disrupting and revising the hyper-masculine codes of behavior that were normal within the oil industry, thus quelling legitimacy threats to male workers' identity. A production operator, who described the platform environment of the past as "macho," noted that now "there's room for both the softer side and the other one. But the change was very hard," he explained.

[We had to be taught] how to be more lovey-dovey and more friendly with each other and to get in touch with the more tender side of each other type of thing. And all of us just laughed at first. It was like, man, this is never going to work, you know? But now you can really tell the difference. Even though we kid around and joke around with each other, there's no malice in it. We are a very different group now than we were when we first got together – kinder, gentler people. (Ely and Meyerson, 2006: 26)

Finally, a study of gay and lesbian workplace activism illustrates how activists' ability to anchor on the outward-focused goal of changing their organizations not only kept them from becoming defensive in the face of social identity threats, but also helped out-group members (i.e., their heterosexual coworkers) to remain nondefensive as well (Creed and Scully, 2000). A heterosexual male vice president and a lesbian employee activist in one company describe an "educative encounter" that enabled the vice president to deal with his personal fears concerning gays and lesbians and her group to win dependent-partner benefits (Creed and Scully, 2000: 399). Initially he had turned down the group's request for such benefits, writing a hostile letter to them. Rather than responding defensively to the letter, the lesbian activist "counseled patience to the group" and wrote to the vice president acknowledging that "the issues were not easy" but stressing how important they were to the group's members (Creed and Scully, 2000: 400). She emphasized her availability as a resource and proposed a lunch, which she described as giving him the opportunity "to ask questions. It wasn't a pitch . . . We talked about all of the things that people . . . [have questions about but don't have someone they can ask] in a safe place" (Creed and Scully, 2000: 400). The encounter became a catalyst for the vice president's coming to see the group's concerns as legitimate workplace issues and for his dealing with his own "'biases and 'baggage'": "My kids all think . . . and my wife will tell you, it was like this personal transformation took place, and I say I just dealt with the fear" (Creed and Scully, 2000: 400). After the meeting, the lesbian activist reflected on "how lucky" she felt to have been given that opportunity, and how it answered for her the question of why she had "come out" as a lesbian in her workplace: "If I'm going to change anyone's mind, well what a great mind to change, somebody who was in a place where he could have a huge influence on the lives of gay and lesbian employees at our company." Both parties' willingness to shift from self-protection goals to the goal of learning in service of making the organization more equitable was key to their success.

In these examples, actors' commitment to achieving goals larger than themselves enabled them to override the self-protective impulse they might otherwise have felt in these situations. Their outward-focused goals motivated them to respond instead by engaging others – even those who posed threats – in a mutual learning process that would ultimately serve their goals. Importantly, this strategy entails neither being indifferent to the threat experience itself nor being indifferent to how one comes across to others. Rather, it involves no longer being *driven* by such concerns. Managing the image one conveys can still be of value, especially as a means to a larger goal rather than as a goal in itself.

Benefits of pursuing outward-focused goals

When members of culturally diverse teams use this strategy for dealing with social identity threats, their teams stand to gain in at least two ways. First, because such threats are treated as a signal to inquire rather than to defend, they can be a springboard for building stronger inter-personal relationships within the team (for a description and examples of this process, see Ely, Meyerson, and Davidson, 2006). People using this strategy respond to felt-threats by asking such questions as: What am I missing in the way I'm seeing this situation? How might my felt-need to protect myself be distorting my view of reality and of the other person? To what extent are my interpretations of the situation driven by my desire to be proven right or innocent? Seeking transparency in oneself and clarification from others involves taking risks at precisely the moment when one feels most in need of protection. Yet taking the risks of interrogating oneself and asking another for clarification cre-ates safety for the other person, encouraging him or her to take similar risks (Aron, 2003; Roberts, 2006a). Mutual risk-taking undermines defensive identity-related processes and allows a task-focus to re-emerge, enabling the team to move forward in its work (Edmondson and Smith, 2006; Ely and Meyerson, 2006).

Second, because they are less focused on defending themselves, team members using this strategy can more easily draw on their cultural knowledge to rethink the team's primary tasks, increasing the team's ability to leverage its diversity for performance gains (Ely and Thomas, 2001; Ely, Thomas, and Padavic, 2006). Teams taking this approach are receptive to the notion that cultural differences may underlie team members' expectations, norms, and assumptions about work and that these differences are worth exploring as a source of insights into how the group might improve its effectiveness. Because this approach legitimates discussion of cultural experiences, it gives traditionally under-represented groups validation for their cultural self-identities and diminishes social identity threats (Steele, 1997). It also frees up majority-group members who no longer need to fear being misunderstood with no hope of clarification. Again, these actions entail taking risks (Edmondson, 1999), but when team members receive affirmation, trust builds and relationships become stronger (Dutton and Heaphy, 2003; Kramer, 1999). Hence, the outward-focused strategy for responding to social identity threats creates a virtuous cycle in which building trust across cultural differences further enhances the team's capacity to experiment, learn, and solve problems creatively (Davidson and James, 2006).

In sum, culturally diverse teams whose members anchor on outward-focused goals when faced with social identity threats are well equipped to reap the benefits diversity has to offer. If the competitive advantage of a culturally diverse team lies in the capacity of its members to learn from each other and to develop within each other a range of cultural competencies, then this strategy can be a tool for leveraging diversity.

Implications for research on culturally diverse teams

The relational framing we propose in this chapter points team diversity researchers in several new directions. First, it turns their attention to research questions about relational dynamics at multiple levels of analysis. In this chapter, for example, we consider how stereotypes and power disparities between groups in the wider society give rise to social identity threats in team interactions. We argue that many of the conflicts and tensions that arise in culturally diverse teams involve members' defensive reactions to such threats and that nondefensive reactions can lead to better relationships and greater effectiveness. From this perspective, societal stereotypes influence not only how one relates to in-groups and out-groups, but also how one relates to the self and manages one's identity in relation to others. Investigating how these dynamics affect team functioning is one example of relationally framed diversity research that spans several levels of analysis.

Second, a relational framing calls for research and theory about particular, rather than generic, intergroup relations. Different dimensions of difference, such as race, gender, and age, are associated with distinct social histories and cultural arrangements, and these distinctions matter for how diversity on these dimensions plays out in teams. For example, communities and households tend to be segregated along racial but not gender or generational lines. Contact among racial groups, therefore, is both less frequent and less intimate than contact between men and women or across people of different ages. The frequency and nature of intergroup contact outside of work in turn influences how people encounter one another at work. Another distinction is that different group memberships have more or less widely shared cultural meanings. The connotations of being older or younger, for example, tend to be locally determined and thus more malleable than the connotations of being male or female (but see Ely and Padavic, forthcoming, and Ely and Meyerson, 2006, for how gender meanings can be reinterpreted locally).

Likewise, we argue that to understand interactions between specific social identity groups, even within a single dimension of difference (such as race), requires attention to the historical, cultural, and local contexts within which such groups are embedded. Consider, for example, Black–White relations in the US. Most people who have been educated in the US from an early age share a deep awareness of the country's history of slavery, Black–White segregation, and the Civil Rights Movement. Although a history of oppression is not unique to black Americans, it may be more clearly etched in the psyche of US-American minds, making Black–White interactions a potentially more cathected – and more identity-threatening – experience for both Whites and Blacks compared to other cross-race encounters. Another example concerns religious groups. Relations between, for example, Muslims and non-Muslims in the US have become more strained since the September 11, 2001, terrorist attacks, increasing the threat potential of that line of difference relative to the period preceding the attacks when other religious differences may have been more salient than this one. In short, historical, cultural, and local circumstances influence how different group memberships play out in team interactions, and team diversity research should consider such effects.

Third, our relational frame directs attention to the simultaneous – and potentially asymmetrical – effects of a person's multiple identities. One experiences different kinds of threats in different domains depending on whether the threat strikes a privileged or marginalized identity. A white woman encountering a black male teammate, for example, may worry from her privileged position about being perceived as racist, on the one hand, while on the other, worrying from her marginalized position that he is discounting her input because of her gender. The frequency, severity, and consequences of such threats may, however, be asymmetric. Threats to privileged identities probably occur less frequently and cause less personal harm than threats to marginalized ones, though defensive reactions to both types of threats may be equally detrimental to the team. Research documenting the relative frequency, severity, and consequences of social identity threats from privileged versus marginalized identity positions is warranted.

Finally, our perspective calls for research on how organizations can facilitate members' shift from inward-focused to outward-focused goals. At the individual level, this shift requires recognizing when social identity threats are at play, identifying the costs of defensive reactions, and developing tactics for responding differently. Organizations, for their part, can support – or impede – this process. In many organizations, systems of reward and censure reinforce employees' pursuit of self-focused goals, but alternative practices can help them redirect their energies toward outward-focused goals that better serve organizational ends (see Ely and Meyerson, 2006, for a case example). Although our argument is based in research (see Crocker *et al.*, 2006), these ideas remain to be tested in the context of culturally diverse teams.

In sum, we propose that cultural differences – and the conflicts and tensions that arise from them – are a potential resource for learning that can strengthen the quality of team members' relationships as well as the quality of their work. A team's resilience in the face of social identity threats can be a source of satisfaction in its own right, perpetuating a virtuous cycle: engaging productively across potentially divisive group differences begets satisfaction, further engagement, success, and so on. From this perspective, the potential benefits of cultural diversity may be as much relational and emotional as they are directly task-related.

References

Alderfer, C. P. (1987). An intergroup perspective on group dynamics. In J. Lorsch (ed.), *Handbook on Organizational Behavior*: 190–222. Englewood Cliffs: Prentice-Hall.

Alderfer, C. P., and Smith, K. K. (1982). Studying intergroup relations embedded in organizations. *Administrative Science Quarterly*, 27: 35–65.

Anderson, E. (1999). The social situation of the black executive: Black and white identities in the corporate world. In M. Lamont (ed.), *The Cultural Territories of Race: Black and White Boundaries*: 3–29. Chicago: The University of Chicago Press.

Aron, A. (2003). Self and close relationships. In M. R. Leary, and J. P. Tangney (eds.), *Handbook of Self and Identity*: 442–461. New York: The Guilford Press.

Ashmore, R., Deaux, K., and McLaughlin-Volpe, T. (2004). An organizing framework for collective identity: Articulation and significance of multi-dimensionality. *Psychological Bulletin, 130*(1): 80–114.

Bailyn, L. (1993). *Breaking the Mold: Women, Men, and Time in the New Corporate World*. New York: Free Press.

Barrett, F. J. (1996). The organizational construction of hegemonic masculinity: The case of the US Navy. *Gender, Work, and Organization, 3*(3): 129–141.

Baumeister, R. F. (1999). The self. In D. T. Gilbert, S. T. Fiske, and G. Lindzey (eds.), *The Handbook of Social Psychology*, 4th edition: 680–740. Boston: McGraw-Hill.

Baumeister, R. F., Bratslavsky, E., Muraven, M., and Tice, D. M. (1998). Ego depletion: Is the active self a limited resource? *Journal of Personality and Social Psychology, 74*(5): 1225–1237.

Branscombe, N. R., Ellemers, N., Spears, R., and Doosje, B. (1999). The context and content of social identity threat. In N. Ellemers, R. Spears, and B. Doosje (eds.), *Social Identity Context, Commitment, Content*: 35–58. Blackwell: London.

Byrne, D. (1971). The ubiquitous relationship: Attitude similarity and attraction: A cross-cultural study. *Human Relations, 24*(3): 201–207.

Chatman, J. A., and Flynn, F. J. (2001). The influence of demographic composition on the emergence and consequences of cooperative norms in groups. *Academy of Management Journal, 44*(5): 956–974.

Chatman, J. A., Polzer, J. T., Barsade, S. G., and Neale, M. A. (1998). Being different yet feeling similar: The influence of demographic composition and organizational culture on work processes and outcomes. *Administrative Science Quarterly*, 43(4): 749–780.

Chetkovich, C. (1997). *Real Heat: Gender and Race in the Urban Fire Service*. New Brunswick: Rutgers University Press.

Cialdini, R. B., and Richardson, K. D. (1980). Two indirect tactics of image management: Basking and blasting. *Journal of Personality and Social Psychology*, 39: 406–415.

Cobbs, P. M., and Turnock, J. L. (2003). *Cracking the Corporate Code: The Revealing Success Stories of 32 African-American Executives*. New York: American Management Association.

Collins, P. H. (1993). Towards a new vision: Race, class and gender as categories of analysis and connection. In P. H. Collins (ed.), *Race, Sex, Class*: 25–46. Memphis: The Center of Research on Women.

Collins, P. H., and Thorne, B. (1995). On West and Festermaker's "Doing Difference." *Gender and Society*, 9: 491–506.

Colquitt, J. A., Noe, R. A., and Jackson, C. L. (2002). Justice in teams: Antecedents and consequences of procedural justice climate in teams. *Personnel Psychology*, 55: 83–109.

Connell, R. W. (1995). *Masculinities*. Berkeley: University of California Press.

Cox, T. H. (1993). *Cultural Diversity in Organizations: Theory, Research, and Practice*. San Francisco: Berrett-Koehler.

Creed, D., and Scully, M. (2000). Songs of ourselves: Employees' deployment of social identity in workplace encounters. *Journal of Management Inquiry*, 9(4): 391–412.

Crenshaw, K. (1997). Intersectionality and identity politics: Learning from violence against women of color. In M. L. Shanley and U. Narayan (eds.), *Reconstructing Political Theory: Feminist Perspectives*: 178–193. University Park: Pennsylvania State University Press.

Crocker, J., and Luhtanen, R. (1990). Collective self-esteem and ingroup bias. *Journal of Personality and Social Psychology*, 58(1): 60–67.

Crocker, J., Nuer, N., Olivier, M. A., and Cohen, S. (2006). Egosystem and ecosystem: Two motivational orientations for the self. Working Paper, University of Michigan, Ann Arbor.

Crocker, J., and Park, L. E. (2004). The costly pursuit of self-esteem. *Psychological Bulletin*, 130: 392–414.

Davidson, M. N., and James, E. H. (2006). The engines of positive relationships across difference: Learning and conflict. In J. Dutton, and B. R. Ragins (eds.), *Exploring Positive Relationships at Work: Building a Theoretical and Research Foundation*. Mahwah: Lawrence Erlbaum.

De Dreu, C. K. W., and De Vries, N. K. (1993). Numerical support, information processing and attitude change. *European Journal of Social Psychology, 23*, 647–662.

Deaux, K., and Major, B. (1990). A social-psychological model of gender. In D. Rhode (ed.), *Theoretical Perspectives on Sexual Difference*: 89–100. New Haven: Yale University Press.

Dovidio, J. F., Kawakami, K., and Gaertner, S. L. (2000). Reducing contemporary prejudice: Combating explicit and implicit bias at the individual and intergroup level. In S. Oskamp (ed.), *Reducing Prejudice and Discrimination*: 137–163. Mahwah: Lawrence Erlbaum Associates.

Dutton, J. E., and Heaphy, E. D. (2003). The power of high quality connections at work. In K. Cameron, J. Dutton, and R. E. Quinn (eds.), *Positive Organizational Scholarship: Foundations of a New Discipline*: 263–278. San Francisco: Berrett-Koehler Publishers.

Edmondson, A. C. (1999). Psychological safety and learning behavior in work teams. *Administrative Science Quarterly, 44*: 350–383.

Edmondson, A. C., and Smith, D. M. (2006). Too hot to handle? Engaging hot conflict to make better decisions and build resilient management teams. Working Paper, Harvard Business School, Boston, MA.

Ely, R. J. (1994). The effects of organizational demographics and social identity on relationships among professional women. *Administrative Science Quarterly, 39*: 203–238.

Ely, R. J. (1995). The role of dominant identity and experience in organizational work on diversity. In S. E. Jackson and M. N. Ruderman (eds.), *Diversity in Work Teams: Research Paradigms for a Changing Workplace*: 161–186. Washington, DC.: American Psychological Association.

Ely, R. J. (2006). Managing a public image. Teaching Note # 5–406–099, Harvard Business School.

Ely, R. J., and Meyerson, D. E. (2006). Unmasking manly men: The organizational reconstruction of men's identity. Working Paper, Harvard Business School, Boston, MA.

Ely, R. J., Meyerson, D. E., and Davidson, M. N. (2006). Rethinking political correctness. *Harvard Business Review, 84*: 79–87.

Ely, R. J., and Padavic, I. A feminist analysis of organizational research on sex differences. *Academy of Management Review*, forthcoming.

Ely, R. J., and Thomas, D. (2001). Cultural diversity at work: The effects of diversity perspectives on work group processes and outcomes. *Administrative Science Quarterly, 46*: 229–273.

Ely, R. J., Thomas, D., and Padavic, I. (2006). Team racial learning environment and the link between racial diversity and performance. Working Paper, Harvard Business School, Boston, MA.

Ethier, K. A., and Deaux, K. (1994). Negotiating social identity when contexts change: Maintaining identification and responding to threat. *Journal of Personality & Social Psychology*, 67(2): 243–251.

Flatt, S. (1993). The innovative edge. How top management team demography makes a difference. Unpublished doctoral thesis. University of California at Berkeley.

Fletcher, J. K. (2003). The greatly exaggerated demise of heroic leadership: Gender, power, and the myth of the female advantage. In R. J. Ely, E. G. Foldy, and M. A. Scully (eds.), *Reader in Gender, Work, and Organization*: 204–210. Victoria, Australia: Blackwell Publishing, Ltd.

Grant, A. Relational job design and the motivation to make a prosocial difference. *Academy of Management Review*, forthcoming.

Harrison, D. A., Price, K. H., Gavin, J. H., and Florey, A. T. (2002). Time, teams and task performance: Changing effects of surface- and deep-level diversity on group functioning. *Academy of Management Journal*, 45, 1029–1045.

Heilman, M. E., Block, C. J., Martell, R. F., and Simon, M. C. (1989). Has anything changed? Current characterizations of men, women, and managers. *Journal of Applied Psychology*, 74(6): 935–942.

Hewitt, P. L., Flett, G., Sherry, S., Habke, M., Parkin, M., Lam, R., McMurty, B., Ediger, E., and Stein, M. (2003). The interpersonal expression of perfection: Perfectionistic self-presentation and psychological distress. *Journal of Personality and Social Psychology*, 84(6): 1303–1325.

Hogg, M., and Abrams, D. (1988). *Social Identification*. London: Routledge.

Holvino, E. (2001). Complicating gender: The simultaneity of race, gender and class in organizational change(ing). Simmons School of Management, Center for Gender in Organizations.

Jehn, K. A., Northcraft, G. B., and Neale, M. A. (1999). Why differences make a difference: A field study of diversity, conflict and performance in workgroups. *Administrative Science Quarterly*, 44: 741–763.

Kanter, R. M. (1977). *Men and Women of the Corporation*. New York: Basic Books.

Kellogg, K. (2005). *Challenging operations: Changing interactions, identities, and institutions in a surgical teaching hospital*. Unpublished doctoral dissertation. Cambridge MA: MIT Sloan School of Management.

Kerfoot, D., and Knights, D. (1993). Management, masculinity and manipulation: From paternalism to corporate strategy in financial services in Britain. *Journal of Management Studies*, 30: 659–678.

Kramer, R. M. (1999). Trust and distrust in organizations: Emerging perspectives, enduring questions. *Annual Review of Psychology*, 50: 569–598.

Meyerson, D. E., Ely, R., and Wernick, I. (2007). Disrupting gender, revising leadership. In B. Kellerman and D. L. Rhode (eds.), *Women and Leadership: The State of Play and Strategies for Change*: 453–473. San Francisco: Jossey-Bass.

Meyerson, D. E., and Kolb, D. (2000). Moving out of the "armchair": Developing a framework to bridge the gap between feminist theory and practice. *Organization*, 7: 589–608.

Murmam, P., and Tushman, M. (1997). Organization responsiveness to environmental shock as an indicator of organizational foresight and oversight: The role of executive team characteristics and organization context. In R. Garud, P. Nogyar, and Z. Shapira (eds.), *Technological Innovation: Foresights and Oversights*: 261–278. New York: Cambridge University Press.

Oyserman, D., and Sakamoto, I. (1997). Being Asian American: Identity, cultural constructs, and stereotype perception. *Journal of Applied Behavioral Science*, 33: 435–453.

Phillips, K. W., and Lloyd, D. L. (2006). When surface and deep-level diversity collide. The effect on disserting group members. *Organizational Behavior and Human Decision Processes*, 99, 143–160.

Polzer, J. T., Milton, L. P., and Swann, W. B., Jr. (2002). Capitalizing on diversity: Interpersonal congruence in small work groups. *Administrative Science Quarterly*, 47: 296–324.

Powell, G. N., Butterfield, D. A., and Parent, J. D. (2002). Gender and managerial stereotypes: Have the times changed? *Journal of Management*, 28(2): 177–193.

Roberts, L. M. (2005). Changing faces: Professional image construction in diverse organizational settings. *Academy of Management Review*, 30: 685–711.

Roberts, L. M. (2006a). From proving to becoming: How positive relationships create a context for self-discovery and self-actualization. In J. Dutton and B. R. Ragins (eds.), *Exploring Positive Relationships at Work: Building a Theoretical and Research Foundation*. Mahwah: Lawrence Erlbaum Associates.

Roberts, L. M. (2006b). Shifting the lens on organizational life: The added value of positive scholarship. *Academy of Management Review*, 31: 241–260.

Schlenker, B., and Weigold, M. (1992). Interpersonal processes involving impression regulation and management. *Annual Review of Psychology*, 43: 133–168.

Schultz, V. (1998). Reconceptualizing sexual harassment. *The Yale Law Journal*, 107: 1682–1805.

Steele, C. M. (1997). A threat in the air: How stereotypes shape intellectual identity and performance. *American Psychologist*, 52(6): 613–629.

Steele, C. M., and Aronson, J. (1995). Stereotype threat and the intellectual test performance of African Americans. *Journal of Personality and Social Psychology*, 69(5): 797–811.

Steele, C. M., Spencer, S. J., and Aronson, J. (2002). Contending with group image: The psychology of stereotype and social identity threat. In M. P. Zanna (ed.), *Advances in Experimental Social Psychology*: 379–440. San Diego, CA: Academic Press, Inc.

Tajfel, H. (1978). *Differentiation between Social Groups: Studies in the Social Psychology of Intergroup Relations*. New York: Academic Press.

Tajfel, H. (1981). *Human Groups and Social Categories*. Cambridge: Cambridge University Press.

Tajfel, H. (1982). *Social Identity and Intergroup Relations*. Cambridge: Cambridge University Press.

Turner, J.C. (1987). *Rediscovering the Social Group: A Self-categorization Theory*. Oxford: Basil Blackwell.

Wilkins, D., and Gulati, G. M. (1996). Why are there so few black lawyers in corporate law firms? An institutional analysis. *California Law Review*, 84: 493–625.

Williams, K. Y., and O'Reilly, C. A., III. (1998). Demography diversity in organizations: A review of 40 years of research. In B. Staw and L. L. Cummings (eds.), *Research in Organizational Behavior*, Vol. 20: 77–140. Greenwich: JAI Press.

7 | Putting your own down: How members of disadvantaged groups unwittingly perpetuate or exacerbate their disadvantage

NAOMI ELLEMERS AND MANUELA BARRETO

Group-based disadvantage in organizations

One of the great challenges contemporary work organizations face, is the increasing diversity of the labor force. It is generally acknowledged that, in addition to a variety of practical issues that may play a role, there are a number of relevant psychological processes that affect the well-being, motivation, and career performance of workers with different ethnic or demographic backgrounds. For instance, in relation to personnel selection, it has been established that the same job application is rated differently, depending on whether or not the person who submitted it uses an ethnic name (Bovenkerk, Gras, and Ramsoedh, 1995; see also Riach and Rich, 2002). Likewise, the same product is evaluated less favorably when people think it is made by a female worker than when they think it is produced by a male (e.g., Bartol, 1999; Davison and Burke, 2000; Graves, 1999). When the quality of a particular work performance is established objectively, people still draw different conclusions about the actual competence of the person, or hold different expectations about future possibilities, depending on their ethnic or gender identity (Deaux, 1976; 1984; Deaux and Emswiller, 1974; Swim et al., 1989). As a result of such psychological biases, individual workers may experience discrimination in employment situations, on the basis of their age (Bendick, Jackson, and Romero, 1996), race and gender (Hitt, Zikmund, and Pickens, 1982; McIntrye, Moberg, and Posner, 1980), physical disabilities (Ravaud, Madiot, and Ville, 1992), or sexual orientation (Weichselbaumer, 2003).

Substantial efforts have been made to address these biased judgments and behaviors to optimize the use of the available potential in the labor force. Legal measures have been taken to prevent discrimination, personnel procedures have been adapted to enhance equal employment opportunities, and governmental and organizational measures have introduced affirmative action policies (Konrad and Linnehan, 1999). What these efforts have in common, is that they focus on the perspective of the manager or employer who has to judge the abilities of individual workers, to decide about employment or career opportunities. We agree that this represents an important perspective, which should inform legal and political guidelines as well as organizational policy (Fiske *et al.*, 1991). At the same time, it has become clear that there are limits in the extent to which this approach can resolve the problem of stereotyping and discrimination in the workplace.

Among the individual managers or personnel workers who deal with these issues on a day-to-day basis, there is often a lack of perceived urgency or motivation to deal with the possibility that discriminatory judgments affect their decisions in employment situation. A case in point is the well-publicized address of Lawrence Summers, President of Harvard University, who argued that differential career success of male and female academics primarily stems from innate gender differences – not discrimination (*Boston Globe*, January 17, 2005). Furthermore, even if they acknowledge the possibility that biased judgments affect personnel decisions, people seem unable to prevent stereotypical judgments, or to reverse discriminatory decisions. There are a number of psychological mechanisms that can explain why this is the case. At the cognitive level, a first difficulty is that stereotyping and discrimination at least partly consist of automatic and unconscious processes (e.g., Eagly, Makhijani, and Klonski, 1992). They are the result of functional mechanisms that help people deal with complex social information, and as such they are difficult to change (Oakes, Haslam, and Turner, 1994). Furthermore, even if specific instances of unfair judgment may be obvious, stereotyping and discrimination are group-level phenomena, which are not easily inferred from the accumulation of individual-level experiences (e.g., Crosby *et al.*, 1986).

At the motivational level, acknowledging the possibility that biased judgments affect individual opportunities and outcomes at work, challenges just world views (Hafer and Olson, 1989; Lerner and Miller, 1978) and undermines the perceived legitimacy of current procedures. That is, people tend to believe that employment opportunities are based on individual merit only, implying that those who are less successful at work, are by definition less able or motivated to perform well.

Thus, they tend to resist drawing the conclusion that unfair biases may play a role, particularly when they may have benefitted from these procedures (Schmitt, Ellemers, and Branscombe, 2003). Furthermore, even when they are privately convinced that certain groups of workers are disadvantaged due to group-based discrimination people may be reluctant to call public attention to this, because they fear being seen as complainers or troublemakers (Kaiser and Miller, 2001). Finally, strong beliefs in the individual mobility ideology (Ellemers and Barreto, in press) easily raise the concern that any attempts to improve the plight of those who are disadvantaged implies reverse discrimination (Konrad and Linnehan, 1999). For instance, in a public speech the Chancellor of Erasmus University in Rotterdam stated that contemporary university culture actually discriminates against men, not women (*Erasmus Magazine*, November 14, 2005).

Focus on targets of disadvantage

Because of these difficulties in changing the cognitions, motivations, or behaviors of those who (unwittingly) stereotype and discriminate against others in the workplace, and because we think this approach only addresses part of the problem, we take a different perspective in the present contribution. That is, instead of examining the biased judgments and behaviors that can disadvantage particular groups of workers, we address the mechanisms that determine the behavior of those who are *subject* to these judgments and behaviors, as we focus on the responses of (potentially) disadvantaged workers. In doing this, we specify a number of psychological processes that are likely to induce responses and behaviors that may seem to justify or even contribute to their disadvantage.

Our purpose in this is not to blame the victims of discrimination in the workplace, instead of the perpetrators. However, we do think it is important to identify which cognitions and behaviors displayed by members of disadvantaged groups are most likely to perpetuate the disadvantage encountered by themselves and other members of their group, as this may help them to realize what they can do to change this state of affairs. In this way, we aim to contribute a different perspective to scientific knowledge about diversity issues in the workplace, but also hope to raise the awareness of the people who are likely to suffer most from group-based disadvantage. Indeed, we think that greater awareness of the mechanisms that play a role, may help to empower those workers who are most vulnerable to the mechanisms that currently prevent them from achieving optimal work performance and career success.

In the remainder of this chapter we will address four distinct phenomena that are relevant to this discussion. *First*, we will draw on theory and research on social identity and intergroup differentiation, to explain that members of disadvantaged groups may come to internalize their inferior position as a defining group feature. *Second*, we will address the problem that due to legal and social sanctions, prejudice and discrimination tend to be expressed in increasingly subtle and ambiguous ways. This makes it more difficult for those who are subjected to such treatment to realize that they are being discriminated by others, leading them instead to respond to failure with self-doubt and suboptimal performance. *Third*, we will connect to the literature on stereotype confirmation, to show how the possibility that others hold negative group-based expectations about the self may lead individuals to express stereotypical emotions, endorse stereotypical self-descriptions, and behave in stereotypical ways, so that negative expectations are confirmed instead of challenged. *Fourth*, we will examine how individual attempts to escape group-based disadvantage may contribute to the illusion of meritocracy and make it more difficult for other group members to be successful.

Disadvantaged groups see their inferior position as a defining group feature

In this section we aim to explain how processes of intergroup differentiation, which imply a search for distinctive group norms and characteristic group features, can lead to the internalization of status differences between groups. As a result, members of disadvantaged groups often fail to challenge the current state of affairs, and may even come to emphasize and nurture their inferior standing.

A prominent theoretical perspective in the study of intergroup perceptions is offered by social identity theory (Tajfel, 1978; Tajfel and Turner, 1979; Turner, 1999). Essentially, this perspective is based on the assumption that people often think of themselves and others in terms of social group memberships, instead of as separate individuals. As a result, they should be motivated to perceive the groups to which they belong as positively distinct from other relevant groups, whereas they are expected to be reluctant to acknowledge the ways in which their group memberships might reflect negatively upon them. Some interpretations of this perspective (e.g., Jost and Elsbach, 2001) have argued that this implies that the default strategy is for people to maintain that their group is superior to other groups. According to this view, members of devalued groups in particular should compensate for the identity threat implicated in their group membership by increasing the positive bias showed when judging their own group. Indeed, a range of observations pertaining to different types of groups and allowing for the expression of in-group bias in different ways revealed empirical evidence in support of this general hypothesis (for an overview see Ellemers and Barreto, 2000; Mullen, Brown, and Smith, 1992). However, this is not the full story.

Social creativity as an identity management strategy

Social identity scholars (e.g., Haslam and Ellemers, 2005; Spears *et al.*, 1997; Turner, 1999) have emphasized that displays of in-group bias only constitute *one* of the possible strategies people may use to cope with a devalued group identity (see also Ellemers, 1993a). Original statements of social identity theory never advanced the hypothesis that there should be a direct causal connection between the extent to which people see themselves as a group member on the one hand, and their tendency to display in-group bias on the other. Instead, in the early writings on social identity theory (Tajfel, 1978; Tajfel and Turner, 1979) *different possible strategies* were distinguished that might help people achieve a positive social identity. In addition to the possibility to compete with members of other groups for material resources or more symbolic indicators of social standing (*social competition*), members of disadvantaged social groups can also use "*social creativity*" strategies to cope with the inferior standing of their group (Ellemers, Barreto, and Spears, 1999). Specifically, when individuals come to the conclusion that their group is less successful than a focal comparison group, it is possible that there are specific reality constraints (e.g., a lack of specific resources or abilities) implying that it is highly unlikely that they will be able to effectively challenge this group in social competition, or even to credibly maintain that their group is actually superior to the other group (Ellemers *et al.*, 2000; Ellemers and Van Rijswijk, 1997). Under such circumstances, the

theory predicts that group members will start searching for other comparison targets or introduce alternative comparative dimensions. Both
these social creativity strategies can help them to develop a favorable
view of their group, albeit in different ways.

Different studies have been carried out to illustrate how this might
work. To examine whether circumstances that challenge a positive
view of one's group may lead people to shift their focus to a different
comparison *target*, Spears and Manstead (1989) compared students
from educational institutions that differed in terms of overall prestige.
Their data revealed that students from the university with lower standing acknowledged their inferiority to students from the more prestigious university. However, they responded to this identity threat by
focusing on the way their group compared to a different comparison
group. That is, after having acknowledged their disadvantage vis-à-vis
the more prestigious university, research participants started to compare themselves with students from a nearby polytechnic which had an
even lower standing (Spears and Manstead, 1989). Importantly, while
such a downward comparison may relieve the negative feelings associated with an inferior performance, it is unlikely to raise future ambitions or to result in performance improvement (Ouwerkerk and
Ellemers, 2002; Wills, 1981).

In a similar vein, people who come to the conclusion that their group is
objectively disadvantaged, may cope with this identity threat by ceasing
to compare themselves with members from the advantaged group.
Instead, they will tend to limit their comparisons to those who are
'comparable' to them in terms of related attributes, for instance by
comparing their own outcomes with those of other members of the
disadvantaged group. For instance, it was established that female
employees who were invited to evaluate the pay they received for the
work they did, did not focus on the way they were under-rewarded
compared to men. Instead, they compared different subgroups of female
workers, and came to the conclusion that their pay was a valid reflection
of their relative ability (see Crosby *et al.*, 1986; Major, 1994). This
represents another shift in comparison focus that people are likely to
use to creatively cope with a devalued identity, rather than maintaining
that their group is actually superior to other groups where concrete
evidence suggests otherwise.

Other research has addressed the possibility that people introduce
different comparative *dimensions* when they are reminded of the

inferior standing of their group. In an early study that compared different occupational groups, hospital-trained nurses acknowledged the greater theoretical knowledge which justified the higher status of nurses with a college education. At the same time, they pointed out that their practical nursing skills were superior to nurses with a college degree, presumably to help them derive a positive view about their own professional group despite their inferior standing in the hospital (Van Knippenberg and Van Oers, 1984; see also Mummendey and Schreiber, 1983). More recently, when examining the effects of organizational mergers in hospitals and scientific organizations, Terry and her colleagues also found that employees of the lower status organization entering the merger were inclined to acknowledge their group's inferiority on status-relevant dimensions. At the same time, however, they accentuated that they were superior in other dimensions which were unrelated to the status difference between the two organizations (for an overview see Terry, 2003). Similar results were obtained by Ashforth and Kreiner (1999), who investigated the ways in which people who do what these authors refer to as "dirty work" (e.g., garbage collectors, dog catchers, or exotic dancers) respond to the challenge this poses for their work-based identity. They also observed that these workers cope by defining their work along those dimensions that convey a positive rather than a negative image (e.g., having flexible hours, working outdoors, or meeting new people). Finally, Lupton (2006) describes how men who do "women's work" tend to reconstruct the nature of their occupation, to bring it more in line with their gender identity.

Both types of social creativity strategies – focusing on a different comparison group and focusing on different comparative dimensions – emerged in an investigation carried out by Elsbach and Kramer (1996) among the faculty of eight "top-20" business schools. They examined how these academics responded to rankings that challenged their beliefs about the relative standing of their school. The researchers found that academics at business schools that were ranked lower than they had anticipated, selectively focused on comparative categories (e.g., making regional instead of national comparisons) and dimensions (e.g., level or basis of funding) that would yield a favorable outcome for their own school. Thus, the results of different studies converge in that they show how members of groups that are commonly devalued or objectively disadvantaged do not necessarily challenge the view that their group is inferior to other relevant groups on these status-defining dimensions. That is, instead of maintaining the unrealistic claim that they are actually superior in terms of status defining dimensions, they will tend to focus on alternative comparison targets and/or introduce alternative comparative dimensions which may yield them a positive identity in a different way.

Now how does the operation of these social creativity strategies help us to understand the ways in which members of disadvantaged groups in organizations, such as ethnic minority employees, can unwittingly internalize and even reproduce their inferior standing? We think the knowledge about social creativity is relevant in this respect because it reminds us that even though people have a general desire to achieve or maintain a positive identity, this does not imply that they will mechanically claim in-group superiority or compete with other groups for more favorable outcomes. For instance, when ethnic minority employees perceive that members of their group generally are less successful in their professional careers, it is unlikely that they will directly argue that their minority group actually has superior professional skills. Instead, they will tend to reproduce the external view that their group is less likely to be competent or successful on status-defining dimensions. This is the case for instance, when female workers indicate that although women may be equally smart as men, they are less likely to be competitive or ambitious, which explains why they are less likely to get ahead in their career. Shifting to other target groups or comparative dimensions may then help them maintain a positive view of their group (as when women point to their superior communicative skills). However, it is important to note that such social creativity strategies are unlikely to result in objective position improvement on the dimensions that matter (Van Knippenberg and Ellemers, 1990). As a result, while the use of social creativity strategies may help members of disadvantaged groups to cope with their plight, it does not really challenge current intergroup differences in perceived competence or potential on status-defining dimensions.

The importance of distinctiveness

In addition to the notion that a positive social identity may be established through social creativity strategies which lead group members to concede the ways in which their group is inferior to others, more recent formulations of social identity theory (Oakes, Haslam, and Turner,

1994; Turner, 1999) have pointed out that under some circumstances intergroup *distinctiveness*, not superiority, is key. This occurs particularly when the relations between groups are not yet clearly defined, as when representatives of "new" ethnic groups or demographic categories enter a particular profession or organization – the primary motive of the individuals in this situation might be to establish the distinct identity of their group (Ellemers, Spears, and Doosje, 2002; Jetten, Spears, and Manstead, 1999; 2000). This will cause them to focus in the first place on the characteristic *differences* between members of their group and other relevant groups (Mullin and Hogg, 1998; Spears, Doosje, and Ellemers, 1997; Spears, Jetten, and Scheepers, 2000; Van Rijswijk and Ellemers, 2002). This may be the case even when a positive view of their group might be more easily established by pointing out the ways in which the groups are similar to each other (Mlicki and Ellemers, 1996).

One possible outcome of the search for intergroup distinctiveness is that members of different groups come to mutually acknowledge each other's strengths and weaknesses. Under such circumstances, each group is likely to uphold the conviction that their group's characteristic strengths are the one's that count most, or should be valued most highly (Ellemers *et al.*, 1997; Ellemers and Van Rijswijk, 1997). As is the case with social creativity strategies more generally, this may help newcomers or minority group members in the work context to derive a positive sense of self and social identity. However, an important consequence is that the behavior that is enacted as being characteristic for the minority group is likely to be valued less by the majority. In fact, characteristics and behaviors that are seen as distinctive and valued within the minority group (such as the observance of certain religious practices) can easily be seen as deviant, uncooperative, or even antisocial by the majority (e.g., Ellemers *et al.*, 1999; Jetten, Postmes, and McAuliffe, 2002; Postmes and Spears, 1998).

In other words, while the search for a distinct identity may direct the efforts of minority group members toward behaviors that set them apart from other groups (Van Rijswijk, Haslam, and Ellemers, 2006), it is important to take into account that the adoption of behavioral norms that characterize the group as distinct from other groups does not necessarily result in superior performance on the dimensions that can help them achieve better outcomes (Ellemers, De Gilder, and Haslam, 2004). On the one hand, this is the case because – as noted above – when achieving distinctiveness is the main motive, groups may come to focus on the ways in which they are different from others, even if this results in an emphasis on traits that are generally devalued (Mlicki and Ellemers, 1996) or elicits behavior that seems less desirable for the organization as a whole (Barreto and Ellemers, 2000). On the other hand, the focus on distinctive group features often implies that behaviors that are characteristic for and valued by the majority group are regarded as less important and self-relevant by minority group members (Major *et al.*, 1998; Schmader and Major, 1999; Schmader, Major, and Gramzow, 2001). Such domain disengagement in turn tends to result in motivational withdrawal from status-defining dimensions and underperformance on tasks that most likely determine individual standing in the organization (Derks, Van Laar, and Ellemers, 2006). This is the case, for instance, when African-American students turn away from academic performance as a relevant domain for achievement and invest their efforts in developing their sporting ability or musical talents instead. Again, while this may help them cope with their relative lack of educational and employment opportunities, and can enhance their well-being and sense of value, this focus on distinctive group traits will not help them to actually improve their standing in society to the extent that this is defined by educational success and achievement in employment contexts.

How then, can this be resolved – is there a way for minority group members to protect themselves against identity threat, without losing the motivation to perform well on status-defining dimensions? A possible solution may be to emphasize the relevance of different comparative dimensions at the same time. This was demonstrated in a recent program of research (Derks, Van Laar, and Ellemers, 2006; 2007) which investigated the responses of women in a simulated job application procedure. In this context, participants were led to believe that their performance on a test that measured typically masculine abilities would determine their chances of being selected. Results from a series of studies using this paradigm revealed that when the importance of these masculine abilities was emphasized, this only served to increase feelings of threat and inadequacy. By contrast, when experimental manipulations led research participants to focus on an alternative ability which was regarded as more characteristic for women (although it would be less useful in helping them be selected), this relieved feelings of threat and enhanced well-being. However, this also decreased the motivation to perform well on the status-defining ability test.

The only condition under which participants actually showed greater motivation and improved their performance on the status-defining (masculine) task, was when *both* in- and out-group dimensions were considered important, i.e., where feelings of threat were reduced by reassurance that typically feminine abilities were valued but they were also reminded that displaying their ability on the typically masculine task was crucial to achieve success. In this case, they were more likely to focus on the achievement of success than on the avoidance of failure (Derks *et al.*, 2006). Accordingly, only when the importance of both in-group and out-group defining dimensions was emphasized did these women show evidence of increased task motivation (persistence), and actually showed a superior performance on the test that would assess the typically masculine ability (Derks *et al.*, 2007). Thus, this research suggests that when people engage in social creativity strategies to cope with their inferior standing, a loss of motivation to perform well on status-defining dimensions may be prevented by acknowledging the importance of the alternative domains in which their group is superior, while continuing to emphasize that they can only achieve better outcomes by performing well on status-defining dimensions.

In sum, in this section we have presented theory and research indicating that there is no universal tendency to emphasize positive features of one's group. Instead, people can use a variety of (cognitive) strategies to cope with a devalued identity, and objective intergroup differences or other reality constraints determine which of several possible identity management strategies people are likely to use. As a result, those who belong to a group that is in some sense inferior or objectively disadvantaged compared to other groups in the workplace do not necessarily uphold the conviction that their group actually is superior by displaying in-group bias. Instead, they will tend to acknowledge their group's lack of achievement or disadvantage in the organizational context (e.g., Baron and Pfeffer, 1994). Under these circumstances, we have argued that they will try to establish a positive view of their group in an alternative way, namely by using social creativity strategies. However, the resulting focus on distinct group features that can help define what is characteristic for the group may at the same time imply that group members internalize negative group traits as self-defining, and withdraw from societally important dimensions of achievement and performance, with the result that their group is further marginalized, instead of becoming more integrated. We have presented recent empirical evidence suggesting that such motivational withdrawal may be prevented by emphasizing that *both* in-group defining traits and out-group defining traits are important.

Members of disadvantaged groups fail to perceive themselves as targets of discrimination

Members of disadvantaged groups often fail to see themselves as targets of discrimination, especially in modern societies, where more old-fashioned and blatant expressions of prejudice are legally and socially sanctioned, giving place to more subtle and ambiguous forms of prejudice and discrimination (e.g., Devine, Plant, and Blair, 2001; Dovidio, 2001; Glick and Fiske, 2001; McConahay, 1983; Pettigrew and Meertens, 1995). By failing to detect personal discrimination, members of disadvantaged groups can hurt not only themselves individually, but also the disadvantaged group as a whole. In fact, if group members do not recognize that they are victims of discrimination, and do not report the discriminatory treatment they receive, they (unwittingly) communicate agreement with the existing social system and thereby contribute to the maintenance of social inequalities (Taylor, Wright, and Porter, 1994). Failing to perceive personal discrimination also reduces the group's chances of improving its position by impairing collective action (Crosby *et al.*, 1989; Major, 1994). In fact, perceiving personal discrimination increases group identification (Branscombe, Schmitt, and Harvey, 1999), which is an important predictor of collective action and social change (e.g., Simon *et al.*, 1998). In addition, since group identification can be seen to increase support to other group members, failing to perceive discrimination lets fellow in-group members down by reducing interpersonal support within the group (Branscombe *et al.*, 1999). Given the demonstrated importance of perceiving discrimination for the likelihood that social inequalities are addressed, we will now consider why people may fail to do so, and under what conditions people are likely to detect discriminatory treatment.

Failing to perceive discrimination

Research into this phenomenon was sparked in the 1980s by the results of a survey that Crosby (1982; 1984) carried out among working women. The female respondents to this survey indicated concern about discrimination against women as a group within American society. However, ratings of personal discrimination (i.e., the extent to which each woman saw herself as discriminated against) were comparatively very low. The discrepancy between these two ratings – later designated as the personal-group discrimination discrepancy by Taylor *et al.* (1990) – meant that individual respondents were either underestimating the extent to which they personally were victims of discrimination, or overestimating the extent to which women as a group were discriminated against. A comparison between these women's ratings and more objective indexes of their working conditions led Crosby (1982) to conclude that women were minimizing personal discrimination.

This effect has since been replicated several times with several different samples (e.g., men, Kobrynowicz and Branscombe, 1997; whites, Operario and Fiske, 2001). Although researchers called attention to the fact that ratings of personal and group discrimination are not entirely comparable as they are the result of quite different psychological processes (Kessler, Mummendey, and Leisse, 2000; Postmes *et al.*, 1999), evidence for minimization of personal discrimination has also been obtained within quite different research paradigms. For example, Vorauer and Kumhyr (2001; see also Ruggiero and Taylor, 1995; 1997) found that when minority group members (Canadian Aboriginals) interacted with highly prejudiced majority group members they did not perceive the interaction partner as prejudiced, even though they experienced the interaction as distressing (they felt uncomfortable and expressed self-anger). Magley *et al.* (1999) reported a similar effect in yet another context. These authors found that although their female respondents reported that they had experienced a range of outcomes that qualify as sexual harassment, only a small amount of these respondents actually indicated that they had been victims of sexual harassment when directly asked about this experience. Work by Foster (e.g., Foster *et al.*, 2004) also reveals that people not only minimize their exposure to discrimination, but they also minimize its pervasiveness, that is, the extent to which discrimination affects their lives in a number of situations.

However, researchers in this domain have also pointed out that individuals may gain by perceiving themselves as victims of discrimination, or rather by attributing negative outcomes they receive to discriminatory treatment rather than to their lack of ability (see Major,

Quinton, and McCoy, 2003 for a review). If so, then in some contexts people may actually be motivated to see themselves as targets of discrimination, and thus it is possible that in some contexts members of disadvantaged groups actually over-estimate the extent to which they are victims of discrimination (see also Feldman-Barrett and Swim, 1998). Although past research found little direct evidence for this over-estimation effect when comparing estimates of personal discrimination to objective indexes or base-rates, members of disadvantaged groups have been found to be ready to point out discriminatory treatment even when it is highly ambiguous (see also Major and O'Brien, 2005 for a review). In fact, the mixed evidence in this domain has led several authors to conclude that it makes less sense to talk about under- or over-estimation of personal discrimination, and more sense to identify the factors that can hinder or facilitate detection of discrimination (e.g., Major *et al.*, 2003; Postmes *et al.*, 1999).

Factors that hinder or facilitate perceptions of discrimination

The question that has caught the attention of researchers in this area is why and under what circumstances disadvantaged group members fail to perceive discrimination as a cause of their disadvantage. Broadly speaking, the answer to this question appears to be that sometimes detecting discrimination is simply quite hard (e.g., because characteristics in the situation make it difficult), while other times it is not in the interest of members of disadvantaged groups to do so (e.g., because it threatens a treasured feeling of belonging to society at large). Accordingly, in this section we will review some of the cognitive and motivational factors that contribute to hindering or facilitating perceptions of discrimination. Although some of these factors are likely to function by affecting both cognitive and motivational processes, this classification reflects the main theoretical argument that has been put forward as the underlying process through which each of these factors affects perceptions of discrimination.

Cognitive factors

Information availability and processing
A first set of factors that affect the *cognitive processes* involved in detecting discrimination refer to information availability and information

processing limitations. Crosby (1984) pointed out that inferring discriminatory treatment on the basis of individual cases is hard due to the
multitude of potential causes that can account for any negative outcome. For example, rejection after a job interview can be due to
discrimination, but it can also be due to poor self-presentation skills
on the part of the candidate. Further research demonstrated that people
have difficulty inferring discriminatory treatment even when they have
more information, as when they are confronted with several cases, as
long as they were presented in a case-by-case format (Crosby *et al.*,
1986). However, perceptions of discrimination were facilitated when
the *same* information was presented in aggregate form (e.g., in a table
where outcomes were classified according to gender; see also Rutte
et al., 1994). This is because aggregated information provides the
opportunity to observe repeated patterns, thereby reducing the likelihood that similar outcomes may be due to individual idiosyncrasies.
In addition, when providing information about several cases, isolated
exceptions can impede the perception of a consistent pattern of
discriminatory treatment against one's group, and thereby hinder
perceptions of personal discrimination. This is what happens, for
example, when there is evidence that some individual in-group
members – tokens – have been selected to particular positions in an
otherwise discriminatory social system (Barreto, Ellemers, and
Palacios, 2004; Wright, Taylor, and Moghaddam, 1990).

Also, providing aggregated information may facilitate perceptions of
discrimination by directing them towards social comparisons that are
otherwise rarely made. In fact, people are unlikely to make comparisons with members of other groups, and instead tend to compare their
own input and outcomes to those of other members of their (disadvantaged) group (see Major, 1994 for a review). In fact, work by Major
and colleagues showed that women tend to compare their work-related
outcomes to those obtained by other women, rather than to those
obtained by men, and this led to entitlement standards that were
lower than they would have been had they compared their situation
to that of their male colleagues (e.g., Bylsma and Major, 1994; Major
and Forcey, 1985; Major and Testa, 1989). However, this effect is only
obtained when people are not provided with explicit performance
feedback and clear comparison standards (Bylsma and Major, 1992;
Major, McFarlin, and Gagnon, 1984). In sum, the particular comparisons people make when left to choose their comparison targets can

cover intergroup differences and thereby hinder perceptions of discriminatory treatment, but this can be counteracted by providing explicit information and clear comparison standards.

Identity salience

A set of other factors can also affect the cognitive interpretation of events involving discrimination and thereby interfere with perceptions of discrimination by determining the cognitive salience of membership in the disadvantaged group. Indeed, salience of group membership determines the extent to which one interprets the behavior of others as targeting one's group membership (Tajfel and Turner, 1979; Turner *et al.*, 1987), and in this way it can increase perception of discrimination. Group identification can be seen as a chronic tendency, defining individual differences, but the extent to which particular individuals identify with a given group varies across contexts or characteristics of the stimuli they encounter. Research has provided both correlational (Branscombe *et al.*, 1999; Crosby *et al.*, 1989; Dion, 1975; Eccleston and Major, 2006; Schmitt *et al.*, 2002) and experimental (Major, Quinton, and Schmader, 2003; Operario and Fiske, 2001; see also Sellers and Shelton, 2003) evidence in support of this idea. A similar process has been documented with other related concepts, such as stigma consciousness (Pinel, 1999; 2004), group consciousness (Gurin, Miller, and Gurin, 1980), and feminist beliefs (Swim *et al.*, 2001). However, group identification appears to only increase perceptions of discrimination when the context includes cues to prejudicial treatment, and not when it is unreasonable to make such inferences (Major, Quinton, and Schmader, 2003). It is important to note that group identification (and related concepts) can be seen not only as an antecedent to perceptions of discrimination, but also as a coping strategy, resulting from such perceptions (Branscombe *et al.*, 1999), and this direction of causality has also been experimentally demonstrated (Redersdorff, Martinot, and Branscombe, 2004).

Prototypes of discriminatory events

Characteristics of the stimulus – i.e., the event which may or not be perceived as involving discriminatory treatment – can also affect perceptions of discrimination through cognitive processes. In particular, events which match people's mental prototypes of discriminatory events are more likely to be recognized as discriminatory than events that deviate from this prototype (Feldman-Barrett and Swim, 1998). For example, perceptions of prejudice are strongly influenced by whom we expect to be the perpetrators of discrimination. Indeed, a remark is more likely to be seen as sexist if the source is male than if the source is female (Baron, Burgess, and Kao, 1991; Dion, 1975; Inman and Baron, 1996), especially if it is ambiguous (Barreto and Ellemers, 2005). Also, perpetrators who belong to powerful or high-status groups are more expected to express prejudice against powerless or low-status targets, increasing perceptions of prejudice when the perpetrator is powerful rather than when it is powerless (Inman, Huerta, and Oh, 1998; Rodin *et al.*, 1990).

People also have expectations (or mental prototypes) concerning the way in which prejudice is expressed. However, researchers have identified a number of forms of prejudice that are expressed in current times but which do not conform to the traditional images people have when they think of prejudice expressions. For example, it has been pointed out that although people expect prejudice expressions to be clearly negative (see also Allport, 1954), often prejudice is expressed in seemingly positive ways – for example, in jokes (LaFrance and Woodzicka, 1998; Swim and Hyers, 1999), or when it is accompanied by protectiveness and flattery (Glick and Fiske, 1996; Jackman, 1994). As a result of this expectation, people have difficulty recognizing prejudice when it assumes a relatively positive tone (Barreto and Ellemers, 2005a). This is one of the reasons why people are reluctant to confront others who tell sexist jokes (see also Greenwood and Isbell, 2002), who cover their prejudice with flattery (Pryor and Whalen, 1996), as well as those who make unwanted sexual advances (e.g., Magley *et al.*, 1999). Moreover, denying the existence of discrimination has been defined as a modern form of prejudice, if this is done in the context of existing gender inequalities (McConahay, 1983; Swim *et al.*, 1995). However, people have difficulty recognizing this as a form of sexism, as compared to when they are confronted with a more typical form of sexism such as a clear statement about women's inferior cognitive abilities (Barreto and Ellemers, 2005b).

Taken together, the evidence reviewed in this section suggests that cognitive limitations responsible for the failure to detect discriminatory treatment may be addressed by searching for clear information about individual outcomes and comparison standards, by nurturing and encouraging in-group identification, as well as by increasing awareness about the various forms that prejudice and discrimination can take in modern societies.

Motivational factors

Self-protection

When considering people's motivation to perceive or not to perceive themselves as targets of discrimination, the most researched question has been whether perceptions of discrimination are self-protective or are damaging to the individual's well-being. On the one hand, it has been argued that pointing out that one has been a target of discrimination can be in an individual's self-interest, implying that for that reason people may be generally motivated to do so. At the individual level, research has indeed shown that identifying discrimination as the cause of a negative outcome can have self-protective effects (e.g., Crocker *et al.*, 1991; Dion, 1975; Inman, 2001; Kaiser and Miller, 2001; Major, Kaiser, and McCoy, 2003; see Major, Quinton, and McCoy, 2003 for a review). For example, negative feedback after a job interview can hurt an individual's self-esteem, but if the individual is able to blame the negative outcome on prejudice from the interviewer, this may leave the individual's self-esteem undamaged (see also Crocker and Major, 1989). More recently, these researchers have clarified that this should not be taken to mean that people will be ready to make attributions to discrimination even when it is not plausible. Indeed, a study by Major, Quinton, and Schmader (2003) demonstrates that attributions to discrimination are only self-protective when they are a plausible cause of one's negative outcomes. A set of studies from our own laboratory also helps specify under which conditions perceiving discrimination can be expected to be self-protective. Specifically, we found that being able to attribute a negative outcome to discrimination is mainly beneficial for those individuals who have a weak belief in their own abilities, as compared to those individuals who do not have such a need to self-protect in this domain (Cihangir, Barreto, and Ellemers, 2006a).

Perceiving discrimination is not always self-protective – it may, in fact, be quite costly. Indeed, perceiving oneself as a victim of discrimination implies a devaluation of an important part of oneself – one's social group membership – implying exclusion from society at large (see Schmitt and Branscombe, 2002b for a review). Consistent with this view, perceiving oneself as a target of discrimination is associated with feelings of social exclusion (such as loss of collective self-esteem; e.g., Branscombe *et al.*, 1999). In fact threats to feelings of inclusion can reduce the extent to which people see themselves as targets of discrimination by increasing people's need to see themselves as respected and accepted by others (Carvallo and Pelham, 2006). As a consequence, perceiving oneself as a target of discrimination has been associated with a number of psychological and physiological responses indicative of stress experiences (Clark *et al.*, 1999), as well as with psychiatric symptoms, and low personal and collective self-esteem (e.g., Branscombe *et al.*, 1999; Kobrynowicz and Branscombe, 1997; see also Dion and Earn, 1975; Landrine and Klonoff, 1997; see Schmitt and Branscombe, 2002b for a review).

Much of this research has compared the effects of being or not being exposed to discrimination, confounding exposure and perceptions of discrimination (and lack of exposure with lack of perceptions; cf. Major, Quinton, and Schmader, 2003). Research directly comparing the effects of perceiving or not perceiving discrimination when controlling for exposure to discriminatory treatment indicates that both detecting and not detecting discrimination have negative psychological effects, but of quite a different nature (Barreto and Ellemers, 2005b; Cihangir *et al.*, 2006a). Indeed, we found that female participants exposed to sexism that was expressed in a subtle way reported more negative self-directed emotions (i.e., anxiety, self-anger) than female participants who were exposed to clearly sexist remarks (see also Vorauer and Kumhyr, 2001). By contrast, female participants exposed to clearly sexist remarks reported more negative other-directed emotions (i.e., hostility) than those exposed to subtle sexism. Besides demonstrating the harmful effects of both detecting and failing to detect discriminatory treatment, this evidence shows that when one is exposed to discrimination, detecting that this is the case can be important to direct one's negative affective responses to the other not the self, and potentially guide restorative behavior. Such actions can make a real difference between promoting the status quo, thereby hurting the disadvantaged in-group as a whole, or instead contributing to social change.

Loss of control

It has been argued that attributing one's outcomes to discrimination threatens an important feeling of control over one's outcomes (Ruggiero and Taylor, 1997). Consistent with this view, these authors found that feelings of personal control were higher when people were able to attribute a negative outcome to internal causes than when people made attributions to discrimination. However, the opposite finding was reported by Sechrist, Swim, and Stangor (2004). These authors found that the need for personal control increased with discrimination attributions and suggested that the need to maintain control over one's outcomes should facilitate, rather than hinder prejudice perceptions. These authors argue that this is the case because even though attributions to discrimination are relatively external, they are often unstable – i.e., tied to particular contexts (e.g., a particular employment situation) which are not necessarily repeated and can be avoided in other contexts. By contrast, attributions to ability are not necessarily under the individual's control – people who fail a job interview may or may not believe that they can change their performance in the future. Work by Schmitt and Branscombe (2002a; Schmitt *et al.*, 2002) further clarifies that attributions to discrimination can be seen as stable (true across time and contexts) or as unstable (tied to particular situations), and that this importantly determines their psychological effects. This points to the possibility that disadvantaged groups may facilitate perceptions of discrimination among its members by stressing that discriminatory treatment can be changed, thus also reducing the extent to which it threatens feelings of personal control.

Social norms

Some social norms promote the belief that existing social inequalities are justly deserved and should not be seen as the product of social discrimination. Examples of these ideologies are prejudiced beliefs, as well as beliefs more directly related to the distribution of resources such as the Protestant work ethic, or the meritocratic ideology. Individuals endorse these beliefs because they are motivated to see the world as just (Lerner and Miller, 1978), and this image of the world as just is indeed positive for individual well-being (see also Taylor and Brown, 1988; Tomaka and Blascovich, 1994). The more individuals endorse these so-called system-justifying ideologies, the less they are likely to perceive themselves as targets of discrimination (e.g., Jost and Banaji 1994; Jost and Major, 2001). For example, the more people endorse prejudice against their own group, the less they are able to identify discrimination (Swim and Cohen, 1997; Swim, Mallet, and Stangor,

2004). Also, the more people believe that society is meritocratic, the less they see themselves as targets of discrimination (Major *et al.*, 2002). Although these processes are generally seen as motivational (Lerner and Miller, 1978), it is important to note that these beliefs can also be more situationally promoted by particular characteristics of the social structure. Specifically, the belief that society is meritocratic and fair is promoted by social contexts where a small number of individuals of disadvantaged groups are allowed entry into higher status positions (i.e., token systems; Barreto *et al.*, 2004; Wright *et al.*, 1990).

In this section we reviewed some research suggesting that individuals may be motivated to see themselves as targets of discrimination, as well as research clearly demonstrating that individual self-interest may often be best served by failing to acknowledge discriminatory treatment. Although it is clear that perceiving oneself as a target of discrimination has costs and benefits, in the interest of social change, more research is needed to determine the conditions under which the relative benefits of recognizing discrimination surpass its costs. Once those conditions are known, it may be possible to create conditions that encourage detection of discriminatory treatment and thereby help address social inequalities.

Failure to report discrimination

Although most research in this area has examined the factors that determine the extent to which people perceive themselves as targets of discrimination, some recent research has focused on the factors that determine public reports of discrimination. Empirical evidence demonstrates that even when people perceive themselves as targets of discrimination, they may not report that to others. In fact, people indicate more discrimination when they can do so in private conditions, and when their claims are known only to other in-group members (Stangor *et al.*, 2001 but cf. Ruggiero, Taylor, and Lydon, 1997). However, when their claims of discrimination are known to members of the advantaged group, individuals tend to minimize the extent to which they experience discrimination (Stangor *et al.*, 2001).

The reasons underlying this hesitation in making public reports of discrimination are fear of retaliation (Swim and Hyers, 1999) and the social costs of being seen as oversensitive, rude, or as a complainer (Crosby, 1982; Feagin and Sikes, 1994; Kaiser and

Miller, 2001). For example, a study by Kaiser and Miller (2001) showed that individuals who quite evidently had been discriminated against, were seen as complainers when they pointed this out to others.

Despite the fact that the findings by Stangor *et al.* (2001) seem to suggest that people expect more costs when reporting discrimination to an out-group member, recent work indicates that these social costs are in reality greater when the audience is the in-group. In fact, Garcia *et al.* (2005) show that people are more negative about in-group members who complain about discrimination than about out-group members who do the same. This is in fact another way in which individuals "put their own down" – by being overly rejecting of in-group members who behave in ways they disapprove of (see also Marques and Paez, 1994). Keeping in mind that those who point out discrimination are seen as complainers, this group membership effect may stem from the fact that what in-group members do or say is likely to have stronger implications for the self than what out-group members do or say. If so, then in-group members who claim discrimination are likely to make individuals feel worse about themselves than out-group members who do the same. In support of this argument, research from our own lab shows that in-group members who claim discrimination elicit more negative self-views than out-group members who acknowledge discrimination against one's group (Cihangir *et al.*, 2006b).

Conclusions

The findings reviewed in this section demonstrate that a range of cognitive and motivational factors conspire to lead individuals to fail to detect discriminatory treatment of which they are targets. In addition, empirical evidence demonstrates that individuals may put their own down not only by failing to perceive themselves as targets of discrimination, but when they do perceive it, by failing to report it. On a practical level, these findings also point to the fact that existing inventories of discriminatory treatment within organizations are seriously flawed, as they are based on limited perceptions and constrained reports. In the section below, we will further illustrate how failing to detect prejudice and discrimination can harm the group by leading to behavior that confirms stereotypical group perceptions, thereby legitimizing group inequalities.

Individual group members behave in ways that confirm the group's stereotype

In this section we review evidence demonstrating that at times members of disadvantaged groups unwittingly confirm the group's stereotype by expressing stereotypical emotions, endorsing stereotypical self-descriptions, and performing in stereotype consistent ways. Stereotype confirmation by individual group members hurts the group because it legitimizes intergroup distinctions and in this way constitutes an obstacle to social change (Claire and Fiske, 1998; Jussim and Fleming, 1996; Klein and Snyder, 2003). In this section we review evidence of stereotype confirmation processes and discuss the conditions under which targets of stereotypes may instead behave in ways that help to counter them.

Behavioral confirmation

Behavioral confirmation occurs when targets of stereotypical expectations are led to behave in ways that confirm those expectations (see, Snyder, 1992 for a review). For example, research has shown that people who interact with a target whom they believe is an extrovert can lead the target to confirm this expectation by posing questions that make the target behave as an extrovert (e.g., do you enjoy going to parties?). By contrast, if the person believes the target to be an introvert, he is more likely to ask questions that lead the target to describe herself and behave as an introvert (e.g., do you like reading books?). Importantly, behavioral confirmation processes are not caused only by biased expectations on the part of interaction partners. In fact, the targets of such expectations can also contribute to this cycle by choosing reciprocity as an interaction strategy. Reciprocal interaction strategies are followed when targets deliberately match the other's expectation to ensure a smooth and positive social interaction, such as when targets are motivated to impress an attractive partner (e.g., Snyder, Tanke, and Berscheid, 1977).

Early research in this area focused mainly on behavioral confirmation in dyadic interaction contexts and referred to the confirmation of expectations based on information provided prior to the interaction (see also Olson, Roese, and Zanna, 1996). However, expectations about other people are not only based on information we may have about them, but they may also be based on existing stereotypes about social groups (Klein and Snyder, 2003). Research on behavioral confirmation of stereotypical expectations has provided evidence for a similar process: targets often confirm the stereotype-based expectations that their interaction partners have of them (see Jussim *et al.*, 2000; Klein and Snyder, 2003; Miller and Turnbull, 1986 for reviews). This has also been shown to happen most often when targets choose to adopt reciprocity as an interaction strategy to ensure they make a positive impression on their interaction partner. For example, women undergoing job interviews confirmed the gender stereotypes held by a sexist interviewer by expressing strong interest in marriage and children, dressing attractively, and displaying submissive non-verbal behavior, even if doing so may have actually decreased their chances to be regarded as competent for the job (Von Baeyer, Sherk, and Zanna, 1981; see also Zanna and Pack, 1975).

While research on the behavioral confirmation of stereotypes refers mainly to stereotype confirmation through *social interaction* with a partner who holds stereotypical expectations, social interaction is not necessary for stereotype confirmation to occur. Indeed, stereotype confirmation can also occur when a particular *situation* makes stereotype-based expectations salient. This process has been examined mainly in performance contexts where socially held stereotypes lead to low-performance expectations about members of particular groups (see Steele, Spencer, and Aronson, 2002 for a review). For example, presenting a math test as usually showing gender differences leads to weaker performance among women – but not among men who are not negatively stereotyped in the math domain – relative to presenting the same test as usually revealing no gender differences (Steele, Spencer, and Quinn, 1999). This effect has been replicated with a range of other groups about which negative stereotypes are held in a series of other domains (e.g., with African-Americans in the math domain, see Blascovich *et al.*, 2001; with members of a lower social class in the language domain, see Croizet and Claire, 1998; with white athletes in the sports domain, see Stone *et al.*, 1998).

The theoretical argument proposed to account for these effects is that low stereotype-based expectations create a pressure on members of the stereotyped groups – a *stereotype threat* – who worry they may end up performing in ways that confirm the applicability of the stereotype to themselves, and that they may thereby contribute to further accentuating the stereotype held about their group (Steele and Aronson, 1995).

Moreover, this pressure leads to cognitive and emotional costs that interfere with task performance and lead to under-performance among members of negatively stereotyped groups in contexts where this stereotype is made salient. Indeed, investigations of this effect have shown that it is determined by anxiety (Blascovich *et al.*, 2001; Spencer *et al.*, 1999), increased salience of the negative stereotype (Steele and Aronson, 1995), cognitive load due to attempts at stereotype suppression (Spencer *et al.*, 2001), and cognitive load due to attempts to reduce anxiety (Schmader and Johns, 2003). It is important to note that there is no evidence that this under-performance may be caused by lower effort or dis-investment from the task. On the contrary, stereotype threat effects appear to lead to behavioral confirmation of the negative stereotype despite people's attempts to perform to the best of their abilities (Aronson and Salinas, 2001).

Stereotype disconfirmation

Although evidence that members of devalued or disadvantaged groups often behave in ways that further increase their own disadvantage has accumulated in the past years, stereotype disconfirmation can also occur. Early research on behavioral confirmation demonstrated that targets of negative expectations can choose to compensate for other people's behavior, instead of simply reciprocating it. For example, a study by Burgoon, Le Poire, and Rosenthal (1995) showed that under certain conditions targets chose to be friendly when the other behaved in a cold way (see also Hilton, and Darley, 1985). Importantly, targets chose to compensate instead of reciprocating mainly when their interaction partner clearly violated the target's expectations, raising the possibility that clear awareness of the expectations of which one is target may actually lead to behavioral disconfirmation (see also Swann and Ely, 1984).

Although this has been less researched with regard to behavioral confirmation of *stereotype-based* expectations, a similar process seems to hold in this case. For example, one study showed that women exposed to subtle sexist beliefs expressed stereotype-consistent emotions (anxiety), while women who were exposed to blatant sexist beliefs were more inclined to express counter-stereotypical emotions (anger) (see Barreto and Ellemers, 2005a,b). Also, research by Kray, Thomson, and Galinsky (2001) examining stereotype confirmation in a negotiation setting showed that women only tended to confirm stereotype-based expectations by under-performing on a negotiation task when the gender stereotype was implicitly activated, but not when it was explicitly activated. When the gender stereotype of women was explicitly activated, women were able to defend themselves against the activation of the stereotype, which actually led them to be more successful than men in their negotiation behavior. Consistent with the research on individual-level behavioral confirmation, these results point to the role of clear awareness of (stereotype-based) expectations in facilitating behavioral disconfirmation by targets.

Research at our own lab examined the extent to which targets confirm stereotype-based expectations once they have been exposed to discriminatory treatment (Cihangir *et al.*, 2006a,b; see also Barreto and Ellemers, 2005a,b; Barreto *et al.*, 2004). In line with the suggested importance of awareness of stereotype-based treatment in this process, we also directly examined whether in this context failure to detect discriminatory treatment at an earlier time would be associated with more stereotype confirmation during a subsequent task. Our results indicate that, compared to women who had been targets of blatant discrimination, women who had been targets of subtle discrimination – which was left undetected – tended to confirm stereotype-based expectations by expressing stereotype-consistent emotions (e.g., anxiety), and by endorsing more stereotypical self-descriptions. Moreover, women who had been subject to subtle discrimination also self-handicapped more and ended up performing less well than women who had been targets of blatant discrimination. Importantly, failing to detect discrimination only led to stereotype confirmation among women who were low in performance self-esteem, not among those who were high in performance self-esteem, suggesting that stereotype confirmation processes may depend on the extent to which the individual feels capable of doing his or her best in a given performance context (Cihangir *et al.*, 2006a).

Taken together, these results suggest that exposure to more blatant stereotypes is likely to limit stereotype confirmation by targets. However hopeful this may sound, it is important to note that prevailing stereotypes are less and less blatant, due to the normative pressures that are prevalent in modern societies. Still, and keeping in mind that particular expressions of stereotypical beliefs are only subtle until they are publicly exposed as prejudicial, one solution seems to be to persist in identifying and exposing new forms of prejudice and discrimination, thereby rendering them blatant and reducing their insidious effects on disadvantaged individuals and groups.

Disconnecting the self from the group does not break the cycle

Targets of negative stereotypes can try to control their vulnerability to stereotype confirmation processes by downplaying or hiding their membership in the disadvantaged group. In fact, group membership salience not only increases the extent to which targets behave on the basis of that identity (Turner *et al.*, 1987), but also the extent to which they expect others to stereotype them (Vorauer *et al.*, 2000). Indeed, prior research has shown that when the negatively stereotyped group membership is not salient in a given context, confirmation of the negative stereotype does not occur (Shih, Pittinsky, and Ambady, 1999). Therefore, in principle it seems possible that if targets of stereotype-based expectations choose to reduce the salience of their group membership in a given context, they may escape the cycle that leads to stereotype confirmation. People can try to break this cycle by making sure their group membership is not known to others, i.e., by covering their disadvantaged group membership or passing as a member of a more positively stereotyped group (Croteau, 1996; Goffman, 1963; Jones *et al.*, 1984; Katz, 1981; Link, 1982; Tajfel and Turner, 1979; see also Clair, Beatty, and MacLean, 2005; Ostfield and Jehn, 1999). Thus it would seem that those for whom the stigmatized identity is not immediately visible have an advantage when trying to disconnect the self from the group, in that they have the option to hide their stigmatized identity, so they can simply avoid the negative expectations others may have about them because of that identity.

Early empirical examinations of the potential of this strategy suggested it may indeed protect individuals from stereotype confirmation. For example, Farina *et al.* (1971) showed that members of a devalued group (psychiatric patients) performed better on a task, and were rated by others as better adjusted and less anxious, when they thought the others were not aware of their social stigma than when they thought they were (see also Quinn, Kahng, and Crocker, 2004; Waldo, 1999). However, these empirical studies did not examine the consequences of actively hiding the stigmatized identity, and instead focused on the effects of not mentioning it to others. While these two processes may have some similar effects, active hiding and passing are likely to involve more costs. Empirical examinations of the effects of actively hiding or passing paint a less rosy picture of the self-protective potential of this strategy.

Passing is accompanied by costs as well as benefits, because passing involves two simultaneous acts: an act of deceit (lying about membership in the negatively stereotyped group) and an act of self-presentation (presenting oneself as member of a more valued group membership). While presenting oneself on the basis of a positively stereotyped group membership may be beneficial, deceit is accompanied by psychological costs. Specifically, people who pass report worse physical health (Cole *et al.*, 1996; Pennebaker, Kiecolt-Glaser, and Glaser, 1988) and more negative emotions (such as shame and guilt) than people who choose to reveal a devalued identity (Harris, 2001; Major and Gramzow, 1999; Paxton, 2002). Those who pass also experience apprehension about the possibility of being exposed as impostors and, as a consequence, carefully and painstakingly monitor their thoughts and behaviors to avoid revealing their true identity (Frable, 1993; Smart and Wegner, 1999). This increased self-monitoring can actually lead to thought intrusion, which is in itself disturbing and also leads to the increased salience of the devalued identity (Smart and Wegner, 1999). Finally, those who pass in the work context report lower work satisfaction, lower productivity, and lower loyalty to the organization. In fact, the costs of hiding are so high that people often prefer to project an authentic but negative view of themselves than to present themselves positively (e.g., Swann, 1990).

Although most previous research on the effects of passing follows a correlational methodology, researchers have begun to uncover these effects with resort to experimental methods. For instance, the negative cognitive consequences of passing have been thoroughly and experimentally examined by Smart and Wegner (1999). The emotional and performance-related consequences of passing have been recently examined at our own lab. In a series of studies we experimentally examined the effects of passing on emotional well-being. For instance, we approached a sample of lesbian, gay, and bisexual individuals (Barreto, Ellemers, and Tiemersma, 2005), and randomly asked them either to reflect on their experiences with revealing their homosexuality at work, or to describe their experiences with passing as heterosexual in the work context. Results of this study confirmed the emotional costs of passing: those who described an experience with passing reported feeling less positive and more negative affect, as well as more anxiety and depression. Additionally, although they expected passing to increase their feelings of acceptance in the work context, participants who passed felt less accepted and more isolated than participants who revealed their homosexuality. Finally, passing had negative work-related consequences: participants who passed reported lower work satisfaction, as well as lower organizational and team commitment than participants who revealed their homosexual identity.

In another set of studies we specifically focused on feelings about the self as a consequence of passing (Barreto, Ellemers, and Banal, in press). Based on past research showing that the operation of self-fulfilling prophecies leads members of devalued groups to report low self-confidence (e.g., Biernat *et al.*, 1998; Cadinu *et al.*, 2003; Stangor, Carr, and Kiang, 1998), we explored the possibility that when passing as a member of a positively evaluated group similar self-fulfilling prophecies might result in an increase of self-confidence. Our results showed that even though passing led participants to think others had more positive expectations regarding their own performance, participants who passed reported lower (performance-related) self-confidence than participants who revealed the devalued identity. In addition, participants who passed reported feeling more guilt and shame than participants who revealed, and these emotions actually mediated the effect of passing on self-confidence. Furthermore, no performance benefits of passing could be observed in these studies.

Thus, at first sight, having a stigma that is not immediately visible seems to offer an advantage, in that it enables people to escape negative group-based expectations about the self by trying to pass as a member of a more highly valued group – a strategy that is not available for those whose stigmatized identity is clearly visible. Nevertheless, passing involves the act of hiding one's stigmatized identity, the cognitive and emotional consequences of which still impact negatively upon their performance and well-being, albeit in a different way. In other words, while different processes may play a role in the case of visible vs non-visible stigmas, the relevant issue in view of our present argument is that in both cases it appears quite difficult for individuals to escape the negative behavioral conse-quences of their stigmatized identity.

Conclusion

In this section we reviewed evidence showing that individual group members can "put their own down" by expressing emotions, endorsing self-definitions, and displaying behavior that is consistent with negative stereotypes. We also showed that individual group members are more likely to do this when they fail to perceive the prejudice or discrimination of which they are targets. Finally, we demonstrated that even though individuals may attempt to escape this self-fulfilling cycle by disconnecting themselves from the devalued group, deliberate attempts to hide the devalued identity are not a successful way to reduce behavioral confirmation effects.

Attempts to escape group-based disadvantage backfire at the self or the rest of the group

In this section we will address a final way in which the behavior of disadvantaged group members can contribute to the perpetuation of group-based disadvantage. Specifically, we will examine how individual attempts to escape negative group-based expectations not only sustain the illusion that advancement at work is primarily based on individual merit, but also make it more difficult for other members of the disadvantaged group to be successful. This then, is the ultimate way in which those who are disadvantaged can "put their own down," as we demonstrate that whereas they are more likely than others to discriminate against other members of disadvantaged groups, their behavior is less likely to be identified or challenged as a form of group-based discrimination.

Despite statistical and legal data clearly documenting the ongoing disadvantage encountered by minority group members (e.g., Hopkins, 1996; Lawler, 1999), there is a strong belief that the current workplace offers equal chances for everyone, and that discrimination on the basis of gender or ethnicity no longer occurs (Ellemers and Barreto, in press; Glick and Fiske, 1996; Jackman, 1994; Swim *et al.*, 1995). That is, neither those who are privileged by the current system, nor those who are disadvantaged, like to think of the ways in which their outcomes may be determined by their group membership instead of reflecting their individual efforts, performance, or the life choices they make (Branscombe, 1998; Major *et al.*, 2002; Major and Schmader, 2001;

Schmitt and Branscombe, 2002). As a result, the assumption is that it is unnecessary to make special provisions for minority group members in the workplace (Heilman and Herlihy, 1984). In fact, some even feel that if anything, affirmative action policies have tipped the balance the other way, resulting in the reverse discrimination against white men (Branscombe, 1998; Konrad and Linnehan, 1999).

According to these meritocracy beliefs then, individual upward mobility is the ideal way to achieve better outcomes (Taylor and McKirnan, 1984; Wright *et al.*, 1990; Wright, 2000). In line with "the American Dream," the assumption here is that each individual who displays sufficient competence, effort, or merit, will be offered appropriate educational, employment, and career opportunities. By implication, then, those who turn out to be less successful in completing their professional training, securing a job, or advancing in their careers only have themselves to blame (Bobo and Hutchings, 1996; Hafer and Olson, 1989; Kluegal and Smith, 1986). As we have argued in previous sections of this chapter, we think these beliefs do not accurately reflect the current state of affairs in employment situations. Indeed, we have reviewed empirical evidence to show that minority group members encounter specific challenges and have to cope with unique circumstances that make it more difficult for them to succeed. That having been said, we now will consider what happens when individual members from disadvantaged groups overcome these difficulties, and *are* successful in a work context. Will this help others to achieve the same, can they act as mentors and role models for fellow group members, or will their success help redress stereotypic views of their group? We argue that this is unlikely to be the case. On the contrary, given the cognitive, motivational, and behavioral implications of individual upward mobility, the success of individual group members does not necessarily facilitate the emancipation of other group members. In fact, we think there is reason to believe that it will even have the opposite effect, in legitimizing and stabilizing outcome inequalities between members of different social groups.

Individual success legitimizes group-based disadvantage

In order to understand why individual mobility may legitimize the status quo, let us take a closer look at the individual mobility strategy as a way to address social disadvantage. In the early writings on how the membership in disadvantaged social groups may threaten people's self-views as well as the way they are treated by others (Tajfel, 1978; Tajfel and Turner, 1979), different strategies were specified that might be used to cope with this identity threat. In doing this, a distinction was made between group-level strategies on the one hand (such as social competition for scarce resources, or social creativity to re-define inter-group comparisons) and individual-level strategies on the other (i.e., individual mobility: dissociating the self from the disadvantaged group, to individually gain access to valued outcomes). Additionally, specific characteristics of the situation were identified that might help predict which of these strategies would be most likely to be used. The perceived permeability of group boundaries was seen as the main reason to attempt individual mobility, whereas the perceived stability and legitimacy of current intergroup differences would be the primary cause for people to engage in some form of collective action that might achieve social change (see Ellemers, 1993a; Van Knippenberg and Ellemers, 1990, for overviews).

Empirical research aiming to investigate the impact of perceived situational characteristics on the use of different identity management strategies revealed that a focus on the perceived permeability of group boundaries, and the scope for individual upward mobility this seemed to offer, distracted people from the possibility that existing differences between groups might be illegitimate or that it might be possible to achieve larger scale social change. For instance, it was established that even when members of disadvantaged groups had a very small chance (of 2% or less) of being successful in gaining access to a position that would yield them better outcomes, they continued to pursue this possibility for individual position improvement. Only when it was clear that group boundaries were completely closed did they focus on the group-level disadvantage that they suffered, as was evident for instance from attempts to protest against the general procedure that was followed (Barreto *et al.*, 2004; Pettigrew and Martin, 1987; Wright *et al.*, 1987; Wright, 2000; 2001; Wright and Taylor, 1999; see also Taylor and McKirnan, 1984).

In view of these findings, is has been argued that selectively allowing for (token) mobility may be strategically used by members of currently privileged groups. That is, the (ever so slight) possibility that individual position improvement may be achieved deflects people's attention from the broader problems that their group encounters or the collective disadvantage that they may suffer (Ellemers and Barreto, in press; Hogg and Abrams, 1988). At the same time, the example set by a few successful individuals makes it more difficult to argue that the system is biased or that minority group members generally suffer from prejudice and discrimination, and hence this helps to legitimize and stabilize the status quo (Ellemers, 2001; Jost and Banaji, 1994). For instance, the high political office held by Condoleezza Rice in the Bush administration has been put forward as an example to illustrate that everybody has equal chances to play a role in US politics, and to argue that special provisions for particular groups are unnecessary. In sum, the pursuit of individual mobility sustains meritocracy beliefs, as it suggests that group boundaries are permeable, and prevents people from focusing on group-based disadvantage as a broader societal problem.

Successful individuals are not seen as representative group members

In addition to these more systemic effects that the focus on individual mobility is likely to have, there are significant cognitive and behavioral mechanisms that prevent the success of individual group members from reflecting upon the rest of their group. To be able to escape stereotypic views others may have about one's group, individuals who pursue upward mobility have to distance themselves from the group. That is, they have to emphasize the ways in which they are different from other group members, and demonstrate that they do not conform to the group prototype.

To illustrate how this may work, a study was carried out among women who had been successful in their academic career, and had become full professors at a university in the Netherlands. At the time of this investigation, this was still quite exceptional, as only 3% of all full professors in the Netherlands were women (Becker and Beekes, 1990; Ellemers, 1993b; Hawkins and Noordenbos, 1991). In this study it was established that these individually successful women tended to avoid self-descriptions that entailed stereotypically feminine traits, regardless of whether these traits were generally evaluated positively (considerate) or negatively (shy). At the same time, the professionally successful women emphasized that they possessed a range of stereotypically masculine characteristics, which encompassed positive (independent) as well as negative (aggressive) traits (Ellemers, 1993b). As a result, whereas regular samples of men and women tend to endorse gender-role consistent self-descriptions, these female academics showed the reverse pattern. That is, they described themselves in *more masculine* and *less feminine* terms than did their male colleagues (see also Ellemers *et al.*, 2004). In addition to the traits they selected to describe themselves, these individuals were not representative of the group of women in a different way. That is, although the vast majority of the male professors that were examined had both a partner and children, about half of the female professors indicated that they did not live with a partner and did not have children. The female professors also connected this way of life to their employment status, as they cited the fact that they did not have a family as a significant factor in their career success (Ellemers, 1993b).

These findings are consistent with the notion that the achievement of upward mobility requires that individual group members establish themselves as being different from the rest of their group. This can apply to the way they perceive and present themselves, as well as to the life choices they make. An important consequence is that these successful individuals are no longer seen as prototypical group members. That is, the emphasis on their exceptional characteristics or behaviors implies that it is more difficult for others to see that the qualities they demonstrate may also apply to other members of their group (Weber and Crocker, 1983; Wilder, 1984). This makes it less likely that their success helps combat negative expectations people have about other members of the group, or redresses inappropriately held stereotypical views.

Furthermore, this implies that these successful individuals are unlikely to be seen as suitable or attractive role models by other members of their group. In fact, the individual mobility strategy they pursue implies that they tend to become disconnected from their own group in terms of professional activities as well as social interactions (Branscombe and Ellemers, 1998; Ethier and Deaux, 1994). Thus, it is quite easy for others to notice that the professional success of these individuals comes at the price of displaying particular behaviors, or making certain life choices. Additionally, when those who have been successful emphasize the difficulties they encountered, this can further discourage others from making similar attempts (Pettigrew and Martin, 1987). As a result, other members of the disadvantaged group may come to the conclusion that they are unwilling to make similar sacrifices, or that they are unable to realize such behavioral changes for themselves.

Further, when individual success requires members of disadvantaged groups to renounce qualities that are seen as essential for their group membership, this tends to be seen as a negative thing, and may even be cause for scorn. For instance, professional women are often seen as "bitches" or "dragon ladies," and African-Americans who have succeeded in penetrating into the corporate hierarchy run the risk of being called "oreo's." This is another factor that makes it less likely that they are seen as suitable or desirable role models. In sum, because successful individuals are not seen as typical group members, the success of a few isolated individuals does not reflect on the rest of the group, nor does it inspire other group members to do the same.

Successful individuals are unlikely to help others to achieve

A final mechanism associated with individual mobility as a way to cope with group-based disadvantage is that individual success induces unconscious as well as a more deliberate reluctance to favor other members of the disadvantaged group. Unconscious processes involve the internalization of dominant views on the group, and stem from the tendency to set oneself apart from other group members when pursuing individual mobility. Additionally, successful individuals are likely to experience a more deliberate reluctance to act as a representative or spokesperson of the disadvantaged group (which would emphasize their group identity), and are disinclined to attract attention to ongoing discrimination implied in a system in which they have been successful.

As we have seen above, the pursuit of individual mobility requires people to emphasize the ways in which they differ from the group stereotype, and makes them present the self as a non-prototypical group member. At the same time, however, this emphasis on differences between the self and the group implies that *other* group members continue to be seen in a stereotype-consistent way. Indeed, stereotypes are consensually defined views on characteristic group traits which tend to be shared by those who consider these groups from the outside, as well as those who belong to these groups (Oakes, Haslam, and Turner, 1994). We argue that individual mobility and its implications for the perception of self and others reinforces the tendency to perceive other members of the disadvantaged group in stereotypical terms.

The emergence of this phenomenon was examined in another study of male vs. female academics in the Netherlands and Italy (Ellemers *et al.*, 2004). This time, not only the self-views of senior academics (full professors) were examined, but also the way in which they viewed their more junior male and female colleagues (PhD students). In this research, subjective self-reports and performance indicators showed that male and female academics at the early stages of their academic career were equally ambitious and committed. However, when the senior academics were asked to indicate how they perceived their junior colleagues, female professors were more likely than male professors to hold gender-stereotypic expectations of other women. That is, female professors were inclined to think that female PhD students are generally less career-oriented than male PhD students, while the judgments of male professors more accurately reflected the self-report data we obtained from the PhD students, as these considered male and female PhD students to be equally career-oriented (Ellemers *et al.*, 2004). Importantly, further analyses indicated that the tendency for successful women to hold stereotypic views of other women is related to their own individual career experiences. That is, gender-stereotypic views of female PhD students were mainly endorsed by the group of female professors that had encountered most difficulties in their own career, and that was most inclined to describe themselves in counter-stereotypical terms. This is consistent with the notion that it is the pursuit of individual mobility which requires individual group members to emphasize how they differ from the group stereotype, resulting in the perception of self as a non-prototypical group member on the one hand, and the insistence that stereotypical characteristics continue to apply to the rest of the group on the other.

Thus, we have seen that individual mobility not only prevents the success of individual group members to reflect positively on those who belong to the same group, but can also cause successful individuals to stereotype against others who belong to their group. The fact that negative group-based expectations are internalized and endorsed even by those who belong to the group is a very powerful mechanism that makes it even more difficult for other group members to succeed. That is, when people stereotype against members of their own group, this is unlikely to be detected as a form of group-based discrimination. Indeed, according to the common prototype, discriminatory views are held by members of one group about members of another (Baron *et al.*, 1991). Thus, when people are negatively biased against their *own group*, this is not easily recognized as an expression of stereotypical views (Inman and Baron, 1996). Accordingly, in our research we have observed that the endorsement of gender stereotypic views is less likely to be recognized as a form of sexism when expressed by a woman, rather than a man (Barreto and Ellemers, 2005a; 2005b).

As a result of this process, the inclination of successful individuals to underestimate the abilities or ambitions of other members of their group is likely to be seen as valid information about these individuals, instead of being exposed as stemming from group-based expectations. This is all the more relevant, as it goes against the common belief that minority group members are generally less likely to discriminate against their own group. Indeed, a common policy measure intended to avoid stereotyping and discrimination is to have a minority group representative involved in all employment or career decisions that are made. Given the reasoning presented here, this practice should be seriously questioned. That is, those who are selected as minority representatives are the ones who have been individually successful, despite their group-based disadvantage. This implies that they are likely to suffer from the mechanisms we have described above, in that they are more likely (not less likely) than majority group members to endorse stereotypical views about their group, while chances are small that these views are exposed as discriminatory judgment. Thus, this is another mechanism through which the success of isolated individuals may backfire at the rest of the group: if *they* think other minority group members are not sufficiently competent, then this must really be so.

A final consequence of the perceptual and behavioral effects associated with individual mobility, is that successful individuals tend to be less than willing to act as mentors for other members of their group. Although there is general consensus that mentorship often constitutes a crucial factor in individual career success, it has also been established that it is relatively difficult for minority group members to find a suitable mentor at work (Kirchmeyer, 1998). For instance, it has been established that successful women are generally reluctant to provide instrumental support to other women (Ibarra, 1992). As a result, it seems that an increasing representation of minority group members at higher levels in the organization does not necessarily imply that it is easier for them to find an appropriate role model or mentor (Gibson and Cordova, 1999).

In sum, this section has examined the ways in which the success of isolated individuals can make it more difficult for other minority group members to succeed. Those who are individually successful are seen by others and by themselves as non-representative group members. This not only reinforces the group stereotype, and emphasizes existing intergroup differences, but also makes successful minority group members reluctant to speak for other members of their group, or to act as a mentor for them. Furthermore, the expression of discrimination by minority group members is unlikely to be recognized, as it does not fit the prototype that we have about discrimination.

While we have mainly considered how individual mobility and token status can affect other members of the same group, it is likely that similar mechanisms can also affect people's views on other, unrelated, minority groups. That is, token mobility that sustains meritocracy beliefs is harmful for any disadvantaged group, as it prevents people from noticing the existence of group-based disadvantage more generally. Further, the failure to recognize that minority group members can also discriminate against others who are disadvantaged can be harmful, when minority representation in personnel decisions is seen as a primary tool to combat group-based discrimination. Finally, the general lack of evidence for solidarity among those who suffer similar group-based disadvantage implies that members of other minority groups are equally unlikely to receive support from successful minority group members.

Practical implications and future directions

In this chapter we have considered the ways in which members of disadvantaged groups can "put their own" down in educational and employment contexts. That is, complementary to the view that group-based discrimination and biased judgment generally makes it more difficult for minority group members to be successful at work, we have focused on the cognitive and behavioral responses of the *targets* of such group-based discrimination, in order to examine how these may (unwittingly) contribute to and perpetuate their disadvantage.

We have first pointed out that the tendency to hold positive views of one's group does not necessarily imply that members of disadvantaged groups believe in their superior competence, or that they compete with more privileged groups on status-defining dimensions. Instead the search for positive self-views and group distinctiveness may lead them to focus on alternative, less socially valued dimensions of achievement.

While this may help relieve the stress associated with their group membership, this generally does not improve their position in society or result in better outcomes. The knowledge that disadvantaged group members may need alternative dimensions to secure their feelings of self-worth, but also need to remain motivated to perform well on status-defining dimensions, can help develop the awareness that the importance of *both* types of dimensions needs to be acknowledged to enable minority group members not only to feel well but also to perform well.

Then we have examined the different ways in which group-based discrimination can be expressed, focusing on more implicit forms of discrimination in particular. We have argued and shown the pervasive effects of such implicit discrimination, in that they tend to lead to loss of self-confidence and suboptimal performance on the part of those who are exposed to it, while they usually fail to recognize it as a source of group-based disadvantage. On a more practical level, our analysis also has some important implications. For instance, we have argued and shown that under some circumstances people have great difficulty perceiving themselves as targets of discrimination and even more so (publicly) reporting it. This calls attention to the fact that judging disadvantage cannot rely solely on victims' opinions and on their reports (as is often the case in legal procedures) but that organizations must provide independent and thorough assessments of the fairness of their procedures.

For instance, human resources departments can collect aggregate data on the development opportunities provided to, and the promotions realized by, members of different demographic or ethnic groups, to be able to see whether or not these are proportionate to the representation of these workers in the organization. Indeed, in some cases this has already been introduced as standard policy, and has helped to make organizations more aware of the possibility that members of certain groups are systematically disadvantaged in employment contexts. The social costs of reporting discrimination may be reduced by working towards an organizational culture and climate in which people are encouraged to report observations of discriminatory judgments or behaviors they observe, even if they are not personally involved, and by providing the opportunity to report instances of discrimination anonymously. Even in formal complaint procedures, the burden of proof to establish whether discrimination has played a role may be reversed. For instance, instead of expecting individual employees to prove that they have been discriminated against, the responsibility can be placed on the organization to show that human resources decisions are made on the basis of objective performance criteria, and to demonstrate that these are non-discriminatory. In fact, in European equal rights legislature, this has been proposed as a concrete measure that might be introduced to help prevent discrimination in the workplace.

We continued by showing how behavioral confirmation processes may lead minority group members to behave in stereotype-consistent ways, thus unwittingly confirming and perpetuating stereotypical expectations. Furthermore, we presented recent evidence to show that even when people try to evade such expectations by hiding their devalued identity, they are likely to fall prey to self-defeating cognitions and behaviors. In the examination of these issues, is has become clear that these self-fulfilling processes come into play when people *individually* try to escape negative group-based expectations. In other words, meritocracy beliefs, and the conviction that individual upward mobility is the preferred strategy to cope with group-based disadvantage, lie at the root of this problem. We argue that even though these self-defeating behavioral cycles often occur implicitly and unconsciously, they can be broken by altering the ideology that gives rise to them.

Thus, instead of continuing to endorse individual meritocracy beliefs (implicitly denying the problem of group-based discrimination), it would be better if public and organizational policies would aim to systematically identify and acknowledge instances of prejudice and discrimination in the workplace as a *group-level* problem. This would alleviate individual members of disadvantaged groups from the burden of disconfirming the negative expectations we derive from their group membership, and prevent them from engaging in the self-defeating behavioral cycles we have described. Indeed, members of stigmatized groups have a better chance of overcoming their disadvantage when they support each other, instead of renouncing their common identity, and public policy should facilitate the organization of such support, to empower them to work towards social change as a group.

Finally, we demonstrated how even those individuals who are successful can unwittingly contribute to the perpetuation of the disadvantage for other members of their group. That is, by pursuing individual mobility, these individuals sustain meritocracy beliefs, while they fail to change the view people have about members of their group more generally, nor do they function as attractive role models for other members of their group. Furthermore, as a result of their tendency to set themselves apart from the rest of their group, these successful individuals tend to hold biased views against them, but this is unlikely to be detected as an instance of group-based discrimination.

These insights indicate that a more active policy is necessary for minority group members to benefit from individual success. For instance, quota procedures can help to put minority group representatives in a less isolated position. Furthermore, organizations may set up a mentoring program that more explicitly invites and motivates successful individuals to help others achieve similar successes. Additionally, if through these or other measures the representation of minorities at all levels of the organization is increasing (instead of being embodied in a few token representatives), this will also broaden the behavioral repertoire that is associated with success, and may help others come to the conclusion that perhaps it is possible to be succesful at work without renouncing one's cultural heritage or to changing one's behavioral style.

Previous work in this area mainly focused on those who discriminate against others, in the hope to find ways to prevent such biased judgments and behaviors. In this chapter, we have approached this issue differently, in that we have systematically taken the perspective of those who are disadvantaged, and examined how their perceptions and behaviors can contribute to the perpetuation of the status quo. A recurring theme throughout this chapter has been that the acknowledgment of social disadvantage as a group-level problem is necessary to challenge the legitimacy of current differences, and to develop measures that might help achieve a more equal basis for individual competition in the workplace. Thus, we think it is important to take the target's perspective into account, as it warns those who are disadvantaged against the pittfalls that they may encounter, and may help them find new ways to address their plight.

However, for the future, we think it is important not to focus on one perspective or the other but to start developing a more integrated view that is informed by both perspectives. That is, future analyses should try to capture the mutual influence that members of advantaged and disadvantaged groups have on each other and combine these in a more interactive analysis. For instance, video-taping and content-analyzing specific interactions (e.g., job interviews, performance evaluations), either in field settings or in experimental simulations (using confeder-ates or actors), are likely to enhance our understanding about how members of advantaged and disadvantaged groups mutually influence each other's responses. These materials may also be used to help people in organizations realize how their own behavioral interaction patterns unfold (e.g., in the context of behavioral skills courses for human resource workers or managers), as a first step towards consciousness raising and social change.

Additionally, in this area of research the development of methodol-ogies that allow for the assessment of more implicit and indirect responses that may be displayed, offers further scope for the achieve-ment of novel insights. That is, the reluctance to admit to the endorse-ment of stereotypical views, self-protective mechanisms that prevent people from reporting feelings of threat, and the inability to capture unconscious processes with self-report measures have all plagued pre-vious research in this area. Now that there is a greater acknowledgment that experimental methodologies can help to isolate and examine psychological processes that also play a role in real-life situations, it has become possible to use a range of different laboratory-based meth-odologies and measures that provide a novel way to study these pro-cesses (e.g., Scheepers and Ellemers, 2005).

For instance, response-latencies and word-associations can inform us about the operation of biased judgments or implicit expectations, even when overt responses remain the same. Likewise, facial expressions of emotions (or electromyographic measures of face muscle contractions) provide insight into immediate emotional responses people have, even if they are not consciously aware that they experience these emotions, or are unwilling to report these truthfully. Finally, changes in heart rate and blood pressure can be used to determine whether people are threatened or challenged by specific circumstances or requirements. In sum, we think future research in this area should benefit from these methodolo-gical advances, as they enable us to address important questions that have previously remained unanswered.

In closing, we want to emphasize that although we have focused on responses of targets of discrimination that unwittingly can contribute to the perpetuation of their disadvantage, this is not to say that the onus is on the victim. Clearly, much of the change that is necessary must be introduced by those in power, and those are seldom the disadvantaged. However, the disadvantaged do have an important role in this – because they need to close ranks and make their plight visible, and they need to make better use of the structural remedies that are available to them. This requires that they acknowledge the group-based nature of their disadvantage, and let go of their beliefs in the meritocratic nature of society. Even though this is likely to make them suffer more in terms of well-being in the short term, this offers the only way to achieve actual social change in the long run. Thus, policy makers and organizations should invest in the development of external measures designed to address inequalities (such as affirmative action), to help members of disadvantaged groups achieve equal chances in society. To be able to do this well, they should truly accept that these measures have to be taken, even if this implies having to go through a (temporary) phase of reverse discrimination.

References

Allport, G. (1954). *The Nature of Prejudice*. Cambridge, MA: Perseus Books.

Aronson, J. and Salinas, M. F. (2001). *Stereotype threat, attributional ambiguity, and Latino underperformance*. Unpublished manuscript, New York University.

Ashforth, B. E. and Kreiner, G. E. (1999). "How can you do it?": Dirty work and the challenge of constructing a positive identity. *Academic of Management Review*, 24, 413–434.

Baron, R. S., Burgess, M. L., and Kao, C. F. (1991). Detecting and labeling prejudice: Do female perpetrators go undetected? *Personality and Social Psychology Bulletin*, 17, 115–123.

Baron, J. and Pfeffer, J. (1994). The social psychology of organizations and inequality. *Social Psychological Quarterly*, 57, 190–207.

Barreto, M. and Ellemers, N. (2000). You can't always do what you want: Social identity and self-presentational determinants of the choice to work for a low status group. *Personality and Social Psychology Bulletin*, 26, 891–906.

Barreto, M. and Ellemers, N. (2005a). The burden of "benevolent" sexism: How it contributes to the maintenance of gender inequalities. *European Journal of Social Psychology*, 35, 633–642.

Barreto, M. and Ellemers, N. (2005b). The perils of political correctness: Responses of men and women to old-fashioned and modern sexism. *Social Psychology Quarterly*, 68, 75–88.

Barreto, M., Ellemers, N., and Banal, S. (2006). Working under cover: Performance-related self-confidence among members of contextually devalued groups who try to pass. *European Journal of Social Psychology*, *36*, 337–352.

Barreto, M., Ellemers, N., and Palacios, M. (2004). The backlash of token mobility: The impact of past group experiences on individual ambition and effort. *Personality and Social Psychology Bulletin*, *30*, 1433–1445.

Barreto, M., Ellemers, N., and Tiemersma, J. (2005). The effects of passing on emotional well-being and work-related outcomes. Manuscript in preparation.

Bartol, K. M. (1999). Gender influences on performance evaluations. In G. N. Powell (ed.), *Handbook of Gender and Work* (pp. 165–178). Thousand Oaks: Sage.

Becker, H. A. and Beekes, A. M. G. (1990). *Loopbanen van mannelijke en vrouwelijke academici aan Nederlandse universiteiten. Een studie naar de ontwikkelingen tussen 1974 en 1986* [Career development among male and female academics at universities in the Netherlands. A study into developments between 1974 and 1986]. Utrecht: ISOR.

Bendick, M. Jr., Jackson, C., and Romero, J. (1996). Employment discrimination against older workers: An experimental study of hiring practices. *Journal of Aging and Social Policy*, *8*, 25–46.

Biernat, M., Crandall, C. S., Young, L. V., Kobrynowicz, D., and Halpin, S. M. (1998). All that you can be: Stereotyping of self and others in a military context. *Journal of Personality and Social Psychology*, *75*, 301–317.

Blascovich, J., Spencer, S. J., Quinn, D. M., and Steele, C. M. (2001). Stereotype threat and the cardiovascular reactivity of African-Americans. *Psychological Science*, *12*, 225–229.

Bobo, L. and Hutchings, V. L. (1996). Perceptions of racial group competition: Extending Blumer's theory of group composition to a multiracial social context. *American Sociological Review*, *61*, 951–972.

Bovenkerk, F., Gras, M., and Ramsoedh, D. (1995). Discrimination against migrant workers and ethnic minorities in access to employment in the Netherlands. *International Migration Papers*, *4*. Geneva: International Labour Office.

Branscombe, N. R. (1998). Thinking about one's gender-group's privileges or disadvantages: Consequences for well-being in women and men. *British Journal of Social Psychology*, *37*, 167–184.

Branscombe, B. and Ellemers, N. (1998). Use of individualistic and group strategies in response to perceived group-based discrimination. In J. Swim and C. Stangor (eds.), *Prejudice: The Target's Perspective* (pp. 243–266). New York: Academic Press.

Branscombe, N. R., Schmitt, M. T., and Harvey, R. D. (1999). Perceiving pervasive discrimination among African-Americans: Implications for group identification and well-being. _Journal of Personality and Social Psychology, 77_, 135–149.

Burgoon, J. K., Le Poire, B. A., and Rosenthal, R. (1995). Effects of preinteraction expectancies and target communication on perceiver reciprocity and compensation in dyadic interaction. _Journal of Experimental Social Psychology, 31_, 287–321.

Bylsma, W. H. and Major, B. (1992). Two routes to eliminating gender differences in personal entitlement: Social comparison and performance evaluations. _Psychology of Women Quarterly, 16_, 193–200.

(1994). Social comparisons and contentment: Exploring the psychological costs of the gender wage gap. _Psychology of Women Quarterly, 18_, 241–249.

Cadinu, M., Maass, A., Frigerio, S., Impagliazzo, L., and Latinotti, S. (2003). Stereotype threat: The effect of expectancy on performance. _European Journal of Social Psychology, 33_, 267–285.

Carvallo, M. and Pelham, B. W. (2006). When fiends become friends: The need to belong and perceptions of personal and group discrimination. _Journal of Personality and Social Psychology, 90_, 94–108.

Cihangir, S., Barreto, M., and Ellemers, N. (2006a). _Dealing with discrimination: The moderating role of self-efficacy in responses to subtle and blatant discrimination._ Manuscript under review.

Cihangir, S., Barreto, M., and Ellemers, N. (2006b). _The role of social influence in moderating perceptions of subtle discrimination and their impact on the self._ Manuscript in preparation.

Clair, J. A., Beatty, J. E., and MacLean, T. L. (2005). Out of sight but not out of mind: Managing invisible social identities in the workplace. _Academy of Management Review, 30_, 78–95.

Claire, T. and Fiske, S. T. (1998). A systemic view of behavioral confirmation: Counterpoint to the individualistic view. In C. Sedikides and C. Schopler (eds.), _Intergroup Cognition and Intergroup Behavior_ (pp. 205–231). Mahwah: Lawrence Erlbaum.

Clark, R., Anderson, N. B., Clark, V. R., and Williams, D. R. (1999). Racism as a stressor for African Americans: A biopsychosocial model. _American Psychologist, 54_, 316–322.

Cole, S. W., Kemeny, M. E., Taylor, S. E., and Visscher, B. R. (1996). Elevated physical health risk among gay men who conceal their homosexual identity. _Health Psychology, 15_, 243–251.

Crocker, J. and Major, B. (1989). Social stigma and self-esteem: The self-protective properties of stigma. _Psychological Review, 96_, 608–630.

Crocker, J., Voekl, K., Testa, M., and Major, B. (1991). Social stigma: The affective consequences of attributional ambiguity. _Journal of Personality and Social Psychology, 60_, 218–228.

Croizet, J. C. and Claire, T. (1998). Extending the concept of stereotype threat to social class : The intellectual underperformance of students from low socioeconomic backgrounds. *Personality and Social Psychology Bulletin*, *24*, 588–594.

Crosby, F. (1982). *Relative Deprivation among Working Women*. New York: Oxford University Press.

Crosby, F. (1984). The denial of personal discrimination. *American Behavioral Scientist*, *27*, 371–386.

Crosby, F., Clayton, S., Alksnis, O., and Hemker, K. (1986). Cognitive biases in the perception of discrimination: The importance of format. *Sex Roles*, *14*, 637–646.

Crosby, F., Pufall, A., Snyder, R. C., O'Connell, M., and Whalen, P. (1989). The denial of personal disadvantage among you, me, and all the other ostriches. In M. Crawford, and M. Gentry (eds.), *Gender and Thought* (pp. 79–99). New York: Springer-Verlag.

Croteau, J. M. (1996). Research on the work experiences of lesbian, gay, and bisexual people: An integrative review of methodology and findings. *Journal of Vocational Behavior*, *48*, 195–209.

Davison, H. J. and Burke, M. J. (2000). Sex discrimination in simulated employment contexts: A meta-analytic investigation. *Journal of Vocational Behavior*, *56*, 225–248.

Deaux, K. (1976). Sex: A perspective on the attribution process. In J. H. Harvey, W. J. Ickes, and R. J. Kidd (eds.), *New Directions in Attribution Research* (Vol. 1, pp. 335–352). Hillsdale: Lawrence Erlbaum.

Deaux, K. (1984). From individual differences to social categories: Analysis of a decade's research on gender. *American Psychologist*, *39*, 105–116.

Deaux, K. and Emswiller, T. (1974). Explanations for successful performance on sex-linked tasks: What is skill for the male is luck for the female. *Journal of Personality and Social Psychology*, *29*, 80–85.

Derks, B., Van Laar, C., and Ellemers, N. (2006). Striving for success in outgroup settings: Effects of contextually emphasizing ingroup dimensions on stigmatized group members' social identity and performance styles. *Personality and Social Psychology Bulletin*, *32*, 576–588.

Derks, B., Van Laar, C., and Ellemers, N. (2007). Social creativity strikes back: Improving low status group members' motivation and performance by valuing ingroup dimensions. *European Journal of Social Psychology*, *37*, 470–493.

Devine, P. G., Plant, E. A., and Blair, I. V. (2001). Classic and contemporary analyses of racial prejudice. In R. Brown and S. Gaertner (eds.), *Blackwell Handbook of Social Psychology: Intergroup Processes* (pp. 198–217). Oxford: Blackwell.

Dion, K. L. (1975). Women's reactions to discrimination from members of the same or opposite sex. *Journal of Research in Personality, 9,* 294–306.

Dion, K. L. and Earn, B. M. (1975). The phenomenology of being a target of prejudice. *Journal of Personality and Social Psychology, 32,* 944–50.

Dovidio, J. F. (2001). On the nature of contemporary prejudice: The third wave. *Journal of Social Issues, 57,* 829–849.

Eagly, A. H., Makhijani, M. G., and Klonsky, B. G. (1992). Gender and the evaluation of leaders: A meta-analysis. *Psychological Bulletin, 111,* 3–22.

Eccleston, C. P. and Major, B. (2006). Attributions to discrimination and self-esteem: The role of group identification and appraisals. *Group Processes and Intergroup Relations, 9,* 147–162.

Ellemers, N. (1993a). The influence of socio-structural variables on identity enhancement strategies. *European Review of Social Psychology, 4,* 27–57.

Ellemers, N. (1993b). Sociale identiteit en sekse: Het dilemma van succesvolle vrouwen [Social identity and gender: The dilemma of successful women]. *Tijdschrift voor vrouwenstudies, 14,* 322–336.

Ellemers, N. (2001). Individual upward mobility and the perceived legitimacy of intergroup relations. In J. T. Jost and B. Major (eds.), *The Psychology of Legitimacy: Emerging Perspectives on Ideology, Justice, and Intergroup Relations* (pp. 205–222). Cambridge: Cambridge University Press.

Ellemers, N. and Barreto, M. (2000). The impact of relative group status: Affective, perceptual and behavioral consequences. In R. Brown and S. Gaertner (eds.), *The Blackwell Handbook of Social Psychology, Volume 4: Intergroup Processes* (pp. 324–343). Oxford: Basil Blackwell.

Ellemers, N. and Barreto, M. (in press). Maintaining the illusion of meritocracy. In S. Demoulin, J. P. Leyens, and J. F. Dovidio (eds.). *Intergroup Misunderstandings: Impact of Divergent Social Realities.* Philadelphia: Psychology Press.

Ellemers, N., Barreto, M., and Spears, R. (1999). Commitment and strategic responses to social context. In N. Ellemers, R. Spears, and B. Doosje (eds.), *Social Identity: Context, Commitment, Content* (pp. 127–46). Oxford: Blackwell.

Ellemers, N., De Gilder, D., and Haslam, S. A. (2004). Motivating individuals and groups at work: A social identity perspective on leadership and group performance. *Academy of Management Review, 29,* 459–478.

Ellemers, N., Spears, R., and Doosje, B. (2002). Self and social identity. *Annual Review of Psychology, 53,* 161–186.

Ellemers, N., Van den Heuvel, H., De Gilder, D., Maass, A., and Bonvini, A. (2004). The underrepresentation of women in science: Differential commitment or the queen-bee syndrome? *British Journal of Social Psychology*, 43, 315–338.

Ellemers, N., Van Dyck, C., Hinkle, S., and Jacobs, A. (2000). Intergroup differentiation in social context: Identity needs versus audience constraints. *Social Psychology Quarterly*, 63, 60–74.

Ellemers, N. and Van Rijswijk, W. (1997). Identity needs versus social opportunities: The use of group-level and individual-level identity management strategies. *Social Psychology Quarterly*, 60, 52–65.

Ellemers, N., Van Rijswijk, W., Roefs, M., and Simons, C. (1997). Bias in intergroup perceptions: Balancing group identity with social reality. *Personality and Social Psychology Bulletin*, 23, 186–198.

Elsbach, K. D. and Kramer, R. D. (1996). Members' responses to organizational identity threats: Encountering and countering the Business Week rankings. *Administrative Science Quarterly*, 41, 442–476.

Ethier, K. and Deaux, K. (1994). Negotiating social identity when contexts change: Maintaining identification and responding to threat. *Journal of Personality and Social Psychology*, 67, 243–251.

Farina, A., Gliha, D., Boudreau, L. A., Allen, J. G., and Sherman, M. (1971). Mental illness and the impact of believing others know about it. *Journal of Abnormal Psychology*, 77, 1–5.

Feagin, J. R. and Sikes, M. P. (1994). *Living with Racism: The Black Middle-class Experience*. Boston: Beacon Press.

Feldman-Barrett, L. and Swim, J. K. (1998). Appraisals of prejudice and discrimination. In J. K. Swim and C. Stangor (eds.), *Prejudice: The Target's Perspective* (pp. 12–37). San Diego: Academic Press.

Fiske, S. T., Bersoff, D. N., Borgida, E., Deaux, K., and Heilman, M. E. (1991). Social science research on trial: Use of sex stereotyping research in Price Waterhouse v. Hopkins. *American Psychologist*, 46, 1049–1060.

Foster, M. D., Jackson, L. C., Hartmann, R., and Woulfe, S. (2004). Minimizing the pervasiveness of women's personal experiences of gender discrimination. *Psychology of Women Quarterly*, 28, 224–232.

Frable, D. E. S. (1993). Being and feeling unique: Statistical deviance and psychological marginality. *Journal of Personality*, 61, 85–110.

Garcia, D. M., Reser, A. H., Amo, R. B., Redersdorff, S., and Branscombe, N. R. (2005). Perceivers responses to in-group and out-group members who blame a negative outcome on discrimination. *Personality and Social Psychology Bulletin*, 31, 769–780.

Gibson, D. C. and Cordova, D. I. (1999). Women's and men's role models: The importance of exemplars. In R. J. Ely, A. J. Murrell, and F. J. Crosby (eds.), *Mentoring Dilemmas: Developmental Relationships within Multicultural Organizations*. Mahwah: Lawrence Erlbaum Associates.

Glick, P. and Fiske, S. T. (1996). The ambivalent sexism inventory: Differentiating hostile and benevolent sexism. *Journal of Personality and Social Psychology, 70,* 491–512.

Glick, P., and Fiske, S. T. (2001). Ambivalent sexism. In M. P. Zanna (ed.), *Advances in Experimental Social Psychology.* San Diego: Academic Press.

Goffman, E. (1963). *Stigma: Notes on the Management of Spoiled Identity.* Englewood Cliffs: Prentice-Hall.

Graves, L. M. (1999). Gender bias in interviewers' evaluations of applicants: When and how does it occur? In G. N. Powell (ed.), *Handbook of Gender and Work* (pp. 145–165). Thousand Oaks: Sage.

Greenwood, D. and Isbell, L. M. (2002). Ambivalent sexism and the dumb blonde: Men's and women's reactions to sexist jokes. *Psychology of Women Quarterly, 26,* 341–350.

Gurin, P., Miller, A. H., and Gurin, G. (1980). Stratum identification and consciousness. *Social Psychology Quarterly, 43,* 30–47.

Hafer, C. L. and Olson, J. M. (1989). Beliefs in a just world and reactions to personal deprivation. *Journal of Personality, 57,* 799–823.

Harris, C. (2001). Cardiovascular responses of embarrassment and effects of emotional suppression in a social setting. *Journal of Personality and Social Psychology, 81,* 886–897.

Haslam, S. A. and Ellemers, N. (2005). Social identity in industrial and organizational psychology. *International Review of Industrial and Organizational Psychology, 20,* 39–118.

Hawkins, A. and Noordenbos, G. (1991). The "Matthew Effect" in the relative position of women in academe. *Universiteit en Hogeschool, 38,* 124–135.

Heilman, M. E. and Herlihy, J. M. (1984). Affirmative action, negative reaction? Some moderating conditions. *Organizational Behavior and Human Performance, 33,* 204–213.

Hilton, J. L. and Darley, J. M. (1985). Constructing other persons: A limit on the effect. *Journal of Experimental Social Psychology, 21,* 1–18.

Hitt, M., Zikmund, W., and Pickens, B. (1982). Discrimination in industrial employment: An investigation of race and sex bias among professionals. *Work and Occupations, 9,* 217–231.

Hogg, M. A. and Abrams, D. A. (1988). *Social Identifications: A Social Psychology of Intergroup Relations and Group Processes.* London: Routledge.

Hopkins, A. B. (1996). *So Ordered: Making Partner the Hard Way.* Amherst: University of Massachusetts Press.

Ibarra, H. (1992). Homophily and differential returns: Sex differences in network structure and access in an advertising firm. *Administrative Science Quarterly, 37*, 422–447.

Inman, M. L. (2001). Do you see what I see? Similarities and differences in victims' and observers' perceptions of discrimination. *Social Cognition, 19*, 521–546.

Inman, M. L. and Baron, R. S. (1996). Influence of prototypes on perceptions of prejudice. *Journal of Personality and Social Psychology, 70*, 727–739.

Inman, M. L., Huerta, J., and Oh, S. (1998). Perceiving discrimination: The role of prototypes and norm violation. *Social Cognition, 16*, 418–450.

Jackman, M. R. (1994). *The Velvet Glove: Paternalism and Conflict in Gender, Class, and Race Relations*. Berkeley: University of California Press.

Jetten, J., Postmes, T., and McAuliffe, B. (2002). We're *all* individuals: Group norms of individualism and collectivism, levels of identification, and identity threat. *European Journal of Social Psychology, 32*, 189–207.

Jetten, J., Spears, R., and Manstead, A. S. R. (1999). Group distinctiveness and intergroup discrimination. In N. Ellemers, R. Spears, and B. Doosje (eds.), *Social Identity: Context, Commitment, Content* (pp. 107–126). Oxford: Blackwell.

Jetten, J., Spears, R., and Manstead, A. S. R. (2000). Similarity as a source of differentiation: The role of group identification. *European Journal of Social Psychology, 31*, 621–640.

Jones, E. E., Farina, A., Hastorf, A. H., Markus, H., Miller, D. T., and Scott, R. A. (1984). *Social Stigma: The Psychology of Marked Relationships*. New York: Freeman.

Jost, J. T. and Banaji, M. R. (1994). The role of stereotyping in system-justification and the production of false consciousness. *British Journal of Social Psychology, 33*, 1–27.

Jost, J. T. and Elsbach, K. D. (2001). How status and power differences erode personal and social identities at work: A system justification critique of organizational applications of social identity theory. In M. A. Hogg and D. J. Terry (eds.), *Social Identity Processes in Organizational Contexts* (pp. 181–196). Philadelphia: Psychology Press.

Jost, J. T. and Major, B. (eds.) (2001). *The Psychology of Legitimacy: Emerging Perspectives on Ideology, Justice, and Intergroup Relations*. Cambridge: Cambridge University Press.

Jussim, L. and Fleming, C. (1996). Self-fulfilling prophecies and the maintenance of social stereotypes: The role of dyadic interactions and social forces. In C. N. Macrae, C. Stangor, and M. Hewstone (eds.),

Foundations of Stereotypes and Stereotyping (pp. 161–193). New York: The Guilford Press.

Jussim, L., Palumbo, P., Chatman, C., Madon, S., and Smith, A. (2000). Stigma and self-fulfilling prophecies. In T. F. Heatherton and R. E. Kleck (eds.), *The Social Psychology of Stigma* (pp. 374–418). New York: The Guildford Press.

Kaiser, C. R. and Miller, C. T. (2001). Stop complaining! The social costs of making attributions to discrimination. *Personality and Social Psychology Bulletin, 27,* 254–263.

Katz, I. (1981). *Stigma: A Social Psychological Analysis.* Hillsdale: Erlbaum Associates.

Kessler, T., Mummendey, A., and Leisse, U. K. (2000). The personal group discrepancy: Is there a common information basis for personal and group judgment? *Journal of Personality and Social Psychology, 79,* 95–109.

Kirchmeyer, C. (1998). Determinants of managerial career success: Evidence and explanation of male/female differences. *Journal of Management, 24,* 673–692.

Klein, O. and Snyder, M. (2003). Stereotypes and behavioral confirmation: From interpersonal to intergroup perspectives. In M. P. Zanna (ed.), *Advances in Experimental Social Psychology* (Vol. 35). New York: The Guilford Press.

Kluegal, J. R. and Smith, E. R. (1986). *Beliefs about Inequality: American's View of What Is and What Ought to Be.* Hawthorne: Aldine de Gruyer.

Kobrynowicz, D. and Branscombe, N. R. (1997). Who considers themselves victims of discrimination? Individual difference predictors of perceived gender discrimination in women and men. *Psychology of Women Quarterly, 21,* 347–363.

Konrad, A. M. and Linnehan, F. (1999). Affirmative action: History, effects and attitudes. In G. N. Powell (ed.), *Handbook of Gender and Work* (pp. 429–452). Thousand Oaks: Sage.

Kray, L. J., Thompson, L., and Galinsky, A. (2001). Battle of the sexes: Gender stereotype confirmation and reactance in negotiations. *Journal of Experimental Social Psychology, 12,* 942–958.

LaFrance, M. and Woodzicka, J. A. (1998). No laughing matter: Women's verbal and nonverbal reactions to sexist humor. In. J. Swim and C. Stangor (eds.), *Prejudice: The Target's Perspective* (pp. 62–79). San Diego: Academic Press.

Landrine, H. and Klonoff, E. A. (1997). *Discrimination against Women: Prevalence, Consequences, Remedies.* Thousand Oaks: Sage.

Lawler, A. (1999). Tenured women battle to make it less lonely at the top. *Science, 286,* 1272–1278.

Lerner, M. J. and Miller, D. T. (1978). Just world research and the attribution process: Looking back and ahead. *Psychological Bulletin, 85,* 1030–1051.

Link, B. G. (1982). Mental patient status, work, and income: An examination of the effects of a psychiatric label. *American Sociological Review, 47,* 202–215.

Lupton, B. (2006). Explaining men's entry into female-concentrated occupations: Issues of masculinity and social class. *Gender, Work, and Organization, 13,* 103–128.

Magley, V. J., Hulin, C. L., Fitzgerald, L. F., and DeNardo, M. (1999). Outcomes of self-labeling sexual harassment. *Journal of Applied Psychology, 84,* 390–402.

Major, B. (1994). From social inequality to personal entitlement: The role of social comparisons, legitimacy appraisals, and group membership. In M. P. Zanna (ed.), *Advances in Experimental Social Psychology* (Vol. 26, pp. 293–348). San Diego: Academic Press.

Major, B. and Forcey, B. (1985). Social comparisons and pay evaluations: Preference for same-sex and same-job wage comparisons. *Journal of Experimental Social Psychology, 21,* 393–405.

Major, B. and Gramzow, R. H. (1999). Abortion as stigma: Cognitive and emotional implications of concealment. *Journal of Personality and Social Psychology, 77,* 735–745.

Major, B., Gramzow, R. H., McCoy, S. K., Levin, S., Schmader, T., and Sidanius, J. (2002). Perceiving personal discrimination: The role of group status and legitimizing ideology. *Journal of Personality and Social Psychology, 82,* 269–282.

Major, B., Kaiser, C. R., and McCoy, S. K. (2003). It's not my fault: When and why attributions to prejudice protect self-esteem. *Personality and Social Psychology Bulletin, 29,* 772–781.

Major, B., McFarlin, D. B., and Gagnon, D. (1984). Overworked and underpaid: On the nature of gender differences in personal entitlement. *Journal of Personality and Social Psychology, 47,* 1399–1412.

Major, B. and O'Brien, L. (2005). The social psychology of stigma. *Annual Review of Psychology* (Vol. 56). Chippewa Falls, WI: Annual Reviews.

Major, B., Quinton, W. J., and McCoy, S. K. (2003). Antecedents and consequences of attributions to discrimination: Theoretical and empirical advances. In M. P. Zanna (ed.), *Advances in Experimental Social Psychology* (Vol. 35, pp. 251–329). San Diego: Academic Press.

Major, B., Quinton, W. J., and Schmader, T. (2003). Attributions to discrimination and self-esteem: Impact of group identification and situational ambiguity. *Journal of Experimental Social Psychology, 39,* 220–231.

Major, B. and Schmader, T. (2001). Legitimacy and the construal of social disadvantage. In J. Jost and B. Major (eds.), *The Psychology of Legitimacy: Emerging Perspectives on Ideology, Justice, and Intergroup Relations* (pp. 176–204). Cambridge: Cambridge University Press.

Major, B., Spencer, S., Schmader, T., Wolfe, C., and Crocker, J. (1998). Coping with negative stereotypes about academic performance: The role of psychological disengagement. *Personality and Social Psychology Bulletin, 24*, 34–50.

Major, B. and Testa, M. (1989). Social comparison processes and judgments of entitlement and satisfaction. *Journal of Experimental Social Psychology, 25*, 101–120.

Marques, J. M. and Paez, D. (1994). The "black sheep effect": Social categorization, rejection of ingroup deviates, and perception of group variability. In W. Stroebe and M. Hewstone (eds.), *European Review of Social Psychology, 5*, 38–68.

McConahay, J. B. (1983). Modern racism and modern discrimination: The effects of race, racial attitudes, and context on simulated hiring decisions. *Personality and Social Psychology Bulletin, 9*, 551–558.

McIntrye, S., Moberg, D., and Posner, B. (1980). Preferential treatment in preselection decisions according to sex and race. *Academy of Management Journal, 23*, 738–749.

Miller, D. T. and Turnbull, W. (1986). Expectancies and interpersonal processes. *Annual Review of Psychology, 37*, 233–256.

Mlicki, P. and Ellemers, N. (1996). Being different or being better? National stereotypes and identifications of Polish and Dutch students. *European Journal of Social Psychology, 26*, 97–114.

Mullen, B., Brown, R., and Smith, C. (1992). Ingroup bias as a function of salience, relevance, and status: An integration. *European Journal of Social Psychology, 22*, 103–122.

Mullin, B. and Hogg, M. A. (1989). Dimensions of subjective uncertainty in social identification and minimal group discrimination. *British Journal of Social Psychology, 37*, 345–365.

Mummendey, A. and Schreiber, H. J. (1983). Better or just different? Positive social identity by discrimination against or differentiation from outgroups. *European Journal of Social Psychology, 13*, 389–397.

Oakes, P. J., Haslam, S. A., and Turner, J. C. (1994) *Stereotyping and Social Reality*. Oxford: Blackwell.

Olson, J. M., Roese, N. J., and Zanna, M. P. (1996). Expectancies. In E. T. Higgins and A. W. Kruglanski (eds.), *Social Psychology: Handbook of Basic Principles* (pp. 211–238). New York: The Guilford Press.

Operario, D. and Fiske, S. T. (2001). Ethnic identity moderates perceptions of prejudice: Judgments of personal versus group discrimination and subtle versus blatant bias. *Personality and Social Psychology Bulletin*, *27*, 550–561.

Ostfield, M. L. and Jehn, K. A. (1999). Personal revelation and conflict in organizational settings: The gay individual as social perceiver of power and safety. *Research on Negotiation in Organizations*, *7*, 179–202.

Ouwerkerk, J. W. and Ellemers, N. (2002). The benefits of being disadvantaged: Performance-related circumstances and consequences of intergroup comparisons. *European Journal of Social Psychology*, *32*, 73–91.

Paxton, S. (2002). The paradox of public HIV disclosure. *AIDS-Care*, *14*, 559–567.

Pennebaker, J. W., Kiecolt-Glaser, J. K., and Glaser, R. (1988). Disclosure of traumas and immune function: Health implications for psychotherapy. *Journal of Consulting and Clinical Psychology*, *56*, 239–245.

Pettigrew, T. F. and Martin, J. (1987). Shaping the organizational context for black American inclusion. *Journal of Social Issues*, *43*, 41–78.

Pettigrew, T. F. and Meertens, R. W. (1995). Subtle and blatant prejudice in Western Europe. *European Journal of Social Psychology*, *25*, 57–75.

Pinel, E. C. (1999). Stigma consciousness: The psychological legacy of social stereotypes. *Journal of Personality and Social Psychology*, *76*, 114–128.

Pinel, E. C. (2004). You're just saying that because I'm a woman: Stigma consciousness and attributions to discrimination. *Self and Identity*, *3*, 39–51.

Postmes, T., Branscombe, N. R., Spears, R., and Young, H. (1999). Comparative processes in personal and group judgments: Resolving the discrepancy. *Journal of Personality and Social Psychology*, *76*, 320–338.

Postmes, T. and Spears, R. (1998). Deindividuation and anti-normative behavior: A meta-analysis. *Psychological Bulletin*, *123*, 238–259.

Pryor, J. B. and Whalen, N. J. (1996). A typology of sexual harassment: Characteristics of harassers and social circumstances under which sexual harassment occurs. In W. O'Donohue (ed.), *Sexual Harassment: Theory, Research, and Treatment*. Needham Heights: Allyn & Bacon.

Quinn, D. M., Kahng, S. K., and Crocker, J. (2004). Discreditable: Stigma effects of revealing a mental illness history on test performance. *Personality and Social Psychology Bulletin*, *30*, 803–815.

Ravaud, J. R., Madiot, B., and Ville, I. (1992). Discrimination towards disabled people seeking employment. *Social Science and Medicine*, *35*, 951–958.

Redersdorff, S., Martinot, D., and Branscombe, N. R. (2004). The impact of thinking about group based disadvantages or advantages on women's well-being: An experimental test of the rejection-identification model. *Current Psychology of Cognition*, *22*, 203–222.

Riach, P. and Rich, J. (2002). Field experiments of discrimination in the market place. *The Economic Journal*, *112*, 480–518.

Rodin, M. J., Price, J. M., Bryson, J. B., and Sanchez, F. J. (1990). Asymmetry in prejudice attribution. *Journal of Experimental Social Psychology, 26,* 481–504.

Ruggiero, K. M. and Taylor, D. M. (1995). Coping with discrimination: How disadvantaged group members perceive the discrimination that confronts them. *Journal of Personality and Social Psychology, 68,* 826–838.

Ruggiero, K. M., and Taylor, D. M. (1997). Why minority group members perceive or do not perceive the discrimination that confronts them: The role of self-esteem and perceived control. *Journal of Personality and Social Psychology, 72,* 373–389.

Ruggiero, K. M., Taylor, D. M., and Lydon, J. E. (1997). How disadvantaged group members cope with discrimination when they perceive that social support is available. *Journal of Applied Social Psychology, 27,* 1581–1600.

Rutte, C. G., Diekmann, K. A., Polzer, J. T., Crosby, F., and Messick, D. M. (1994). Organization of information and detection of gender discrimination. *Psychological Science, 5,* 226–231.

Scheepers, D. and Ellemers, N. (2005). When the pressure is up: The assessment of social identity threat in low and high status groups. *Journal of Experimental Social Psychology, 41,* 192–200.

Schmader, T. and Johns, M. (2003). Converging evidence that stereotype threat reduces working memory capacity. *Journal of Personality and Social Psychology, 85,* 440–452.

Schmader, T. and Major, B. (1999). The impact of ingroup vs. outgroup performance on personal values. *Journal of Experimental Social Psychology, 35,* 47–67.

Schmader, T., Major, B., and Gramzow, R. H. (2001). Coping with ethnic stereotypes in the academic domain: Perceived injustice and psychological disengagement. *Journal of Social Issues, 57,* 93–111.

Schmitt, M. T. and Branscombe, N. R. (2002a). The internal and external causal loci of attributions to prejudice. *Personality and Social Psychology Bulletin, 28,* 484–492.

Schmitt, M. T. and Branscombe, N. R. (2002b). The meaning and consequences of perceived discrimination in disadvantaged and privileged social groups. *European Review of Social Psychology, 12,* 167–199.

Schmitt, M. T., Branscombe, N. R., Kobrynowicz, D., and Owen, S. (2002). Perceiving discrimination against one's gender group has different implications for well-being in women and men. *Personality and Social Psychology Bulletin, 28,* 197–210.

Schmitt, M. T., Ellemers, N., and Branscombe, N. (2003). Perceiving and responding to gender discrimination at work. In A. Haslam, D. Van

Knippenberg, M. Platow, and N. Ellemers, *Social Identity at Work: Developing Theory for Organizational Practice* (pp. 277–292). Philadelphia: Psychology Press.

Sechrist, G., Swim, J. K., and Stangor, C. (2004). When do the stigmatized make attributions to discrimination occurring to self and others? The roles of self-presentation and need for control. *Journal of Personality and Social Psychology, 87,* 111–122.

Sellers, R. M. and Shelton, J. N. (2003). The role of racial identity in perceived racial discrimination. *Journal of Personality and Social Psychology, 84,* 1079–1092.

Shih, M., Pittinsky, T. L., and Ambady, N. (1999). Stereotype susceptibility: Identity salience and shifts in quantitative performance. *Psychological Science, 10,* 80–83.

Simon, B., Loewy, M., Stuermer, S., Weber, U., Freytag, P., Habig, C., Kampmeier, C., and Spahlinger, P. (1998). Collective identification and social movement participation. *Journal of Personality and Social Psychology, 74,* 646–658.

Smart, L. and Wegner, D. M. (1999). Covering up what can't be seen: Concealable stigma and mental control. *Journal of Personality and Social Psychology, 77,* 474–486.

Snyder, M. (1992). Motivational foundations of behavioral confirmation. In M. P. Zanna (ed.), *Advances in Experimental Social Psychology* (Vol. 25, pp. 67–114). San Diego: Academic Press.

Snyder, M., Tanke, E. D., and Berscheid, E. (1977). Social perception and interpersonal behavior: On the self-fulfilling nature of social stereotypes. *Journal of Personality and Social Psychology, 35,* 656–666.

Spears, R., Doosje, B., and Ellemers, N. (1997). Self-stereotyping in the face of threats to group status and distinctiveness: The role of group identification. *Personality and Social Psychology Bulletin, 23,* 538–553.

Spears, R., Jetten, J., and Scheepers, D. (2000). Distinctiveness and the definition of collective self: A tripartite model. In A. Tesser, J. V. Wood, and D. A. Stapel (eds.), *Psychological Perspectives on Self and Identity*, Vol. 2. Lexington: APA.

Spears, R. and Manstead, A. S. R. (1989). The social context of stereotyping and differentiation. *European Journal of Social Psychology, 19,* 101–121.

Spears, R., Oakes, P. J., Ellemers, N., and Haslam, S. A. (eds.) (1997). *The Social Psychology of Stereotyping and Group Life.* Oxford: Blackwell.

Spencer, S. J., Iserman, E., Davies, P. G., and Quinn, D. M. (2001). *Suppression of Doubts, Anxiety, and Stereotypes as a Mediator of the Effect of Stereotype Threat on Women's Math Performance.* Unpublished manuscript, University of Waterloo.

Spencer, S. J., Steele, C. M., and Quinn, D. M. (1999). Stereotype threat and women's math performance. *Journal of Experimental Social Psychology*, *35*, 4–28.

Stangor, C., Carr, C., and Kiang, L. (1998). Activating stereotypes undermines task performance expectations. *Journal of Personality and Social Psychology*, *52*, 613–629.

Stangor, C., Swim, J. K., Van Allen, K., and Sechrist, G. (2001). Reporting discrimination in public and private contexts. *Journal of Personality and Social Psychology*, *82*, 69–74.

Steele, C. M. and Aronson, J. (1995). Stereotype threat and the intellectual test performance of African Americans. *Journal of Personality and Social Psychology*, *69*, 797–811.

Steele, C. M., Spencer, S. J., and Aronson, J. (2002). Contending with group image: The psychology of stereotype and social identity threat. In M. Zanna (ed.), *Advances in Experimental Social Psychology* (Vol. 34, pp. 379–440). San Diego: Academic Press.

Stone, J., Lynch, C. I., Sjomeling, M., and Darley, J. M. (1998). Stereotype threat effects on black and white athletic performance. *Journal of Personality and Social Psychology*, *77*, 1213–1227.

Swann, W. B. (1990). To be adored or to be known: The interplay of self-enhancement and self-verification. In R. M. Sorrentino and E. T. Higgins (eds.), *Handbook of Motivation and Cognition* (Vol. 2, pp. 408–448). New York: The Guildford Press.

Swann, W. B. Jr. and Ely, R. J. (1984). A battle of wills: Self-verification versus behavioral confirmation. *Journal of Personality and Social Psychology*, *46*, 1287–1302.

Swim, J. K., Aikin, K. J., Hall, W. S., and Hunter, B. A. (1995). Sexism and racism: Old-fashioned and modern prejudices. *Journal of Personality and Social Psychology*, *68*, 199–214.

Swim, J. K., Borgida, E., Maruyama, G., and Myers, D. G. (1989). Joan McKay versus John McKay: Do gender stereotypes bias evaluations? *Psychological Bulletin*, *105*, 409–429.

Swim, J. K. and Cohen, L. L. (1997). Overt, covert and subtle sexism: A comparison between the Attitudes Toward Women and Modern Sexism scales. *Psychology of Women Quarterly*, *21*, 103–118.

Swim, J. K. and Hyers, L. L., (1999). Excuse me – what did you just say?! Women's public and private responses to sexist remarks. *Journal of Experimental Social Psychology*, *35*, 68–88.

Swim, J. K., Hyers, L. L., Cohen, L. L., and Ferguson, M. J. (2001). Everyday sexism: Evidence for its incidence, nature, and psychological impact from three daily diary studies. *Journal of Social Issues*, *57*, 31–53.

Swim, J. K., Mallet, R., and Stangor, C. (2004). Understanding subtle sexism: Detection and use of sexist language. *Sex Roles*, *51*, 117–128.

Tajfel, H. (ed.) (1978). *Differentiation between Social Groups: Studies in the Social Psychology of Intergroup Relations*. London: Academic Press.

Tajfel, H. and Turner, J. C. (1979). An integrative theory of intergroup conflict. In W. G. Austin and S. Worchel (eds.), *The Social Psychology of Intergroup Relations* (pp. 33–47). Monterey: Brooks/Cole.

Taylor, D. M. and McKirnan, D. J. (1984). A five-stage model of intergroup relations. *British Journal of Social Psychology*, *23*, 291–300.

Taylor, D. M., Wright, S. C., Moghaddam, F. M., and Lalonde, R. N. (1990). The personal/group discrimination discrepancy: Perceiving my group, but not myself, to be a target of discrimination. *Personality and Social Psychology Bulletin*, *16*, 254–262.

Taylor, D. M., Wright, S. C., and Porter, L. E. (1994). Dimensions of perceived discrimination: The personal/group discrimination discrepancy. In M. Zanna and J. M. Olson (eds.), *The Psychology of Prejudice: The Ontario Symposium*. Hillsdale: Lawrence Erlbaum.

Taylor, S. E. and Brown, J. D. (1988). Illusion and well-being: A social psychological perspective on mental health. *Psychological Bulletin*, *103*, 193–210.

Terry, D. J. (2003). A social identity perspective on organizational mergers: The role of group status, permeability, and similarity. In S. A. Haslam, D. van Knippenberg, M. J. Platow, and N. Ellemers (eds.), *Social Identity at Work: Developing Theory for Organizational Practice* (pp. 223–240). Philadelphia: Psychology Press.

Tomaka, J. and Blascovich, J. (1994). Effects of justice beliefs on cognitive appraisal of and subjective physiological and behavioral responses to potential stress. *Journal of Personality and Social Psychology*, *67*, 732–740.

Turner, J. C. (1999). Some current issues in research on social identity and self-categorization theories. In N. Ellemers, R. Spears, and B. Doosje (eds.), *Social Identity: Context, Commitment, Content* (pp. 6–34). Oxford: Blackwell.

Turner, J. C., Hogg, M. A., Oakes, P. J., Reicher, S., and Wetherell, M. S. (1987). *Rediscovering the Social Group: A Self-categorisation theory*. Oxford: Blackwell.

Van Knippenberg, A. and Ellemers, N. (1990). Social identity and intergroup differentiation processes. *European Review of Social Psychology*, *1*, 137–169.

Van Knippenberg, A. and Van Oers, H. (1984). Social identity and equity concerns in intergroup perceptions. *British Journal of Social Psychology*, *23*, 351–361.

Van Rijswijk, W. and Ellemers, N. (2002). Context effects on the application of stereotype content to multiple categorizable targets. *Personality and Social Psychology Bulletin, 28*, 90–101.

Van Rijswijk, W., Haslam, S. A., and Ellemers, N. (2006). Who do we think we are? The effects of social context and social identification on ingroup stereotyping. *British Journal of Social Psychology, 45*, 161–174.

Von Baeyer, C. L., Sherk, D. L., and Zanna, M. (1981). Impression management in the job interview: When the female applicant meets the male (chauvinist) interviewer. *Personality and Social Psychology Bulletin, 7*, 45–51.

Vorauer, J. D., Hunter, A. J., Main, K. J., and Roy, S. A. (2000). Meta-stereotype activation: Evidence from indirect measures for specific evaluative concerns experienced by members of dominant groups in intergroup interaction. *Journal of Personality and Social Psychology, 78*, 690–707.

Vorauer, J. and Kumhyr, S. M. (2001). Is this about you or me? Self- versus other-directed judgments and feelings in response to intergroup interaction. *Personality and Social Psychology Bulletin, 27*, 706–719.

Waldo, C. R. (1999). Working in a majority context: A structural model of heterosexism as minority stress in the workplace. *Journal of Counseling Psychology, 46*, 218–232.

Weber, R. and Crocker, J. (1983). Cognitive processes in the revision of stereotypic beliefs. *Journal of Personality and Social Psychology, 45*, 961–977.

Weichselbaumer, D. (2003). Sexual orientation discrimination in hiring. *Labour Economics, 10*, 629–642.

Wilder, D. A. (1984). Intergroup contact: The typical member and the exception to the rule. *Journal of Experimental Social Psychology, 20*, 177–194.

Wills, T. A. (1981). Downward comparison principles in social psychology. *Psychological Bulletin, 90*, 245–271.

Wright, S. C. (2000). Strategic collective action: Social psychology and social change. In R. Brown and S. Gaertner (eds.), *Blackwell Handbook of Social Psychology: Intergroup Processses*. Oxford: Blackwell.

Wright, S. C. (2001). Restricted intergroup boundaries: Tokenism, ambiguity, and the tolerance of injustive. In J. T. Jost and B. Major (eds.), *The Psychology of Legitimacy: Emerging Perspectives on Ideology, Justice, and Intergroup Relations* (pp. 223–256.) Cambridge: Cambridge University Press.

Wright, S. C. and Taylor, D. M. (1999). Success under tokenism: Co-option of the newcomer and the prevention of collective protest. *British Journal of Social Psychology, 38*, 369–396.

Wright, S. C., Taylor, D. M., and Moghaddam, F. M. (1990). Responding to membership in a disadvantaged group: From acceptance to collective protest. *Journal of Personality and Social Psychology, 58,* 994–1003.

Zanna, M. P. and Pack, S. J. (1975). On the self-fulfilling nature of apparent sex differences in behavior. *Journal of Experimental Social Psychology, 11,* 583–591.

PART III

Moving ahead: Agendas for practice and research

8 Diversity initiative effectiveness: What organizations can (and cannot) expect from diversity recruitment, diversity training, and formal mentoring programs

CAROL T. KULIK AND LORIANN ROBERSON

The organizational literature began emphasizing the "business case" for diversity in the late 1980s (Cox and Blake, 1991; Johnston and Packer, 1987; Robinson and Dechant, 1997). The business case predicted a range of benefits resulting from greater workforce diversity within organizations (Jayne and Dipboye, 2004; Konrad, 2003). Specifically, an organization making maximum use of the talent available in the labor pool would select a diverse group of employees. These diverse employees would be more effective in dealing with a diverse customer base, and the diverse employees would bring a greater range of perspectives to bear on organizational decision making. In sum, "a more diverse workforce, [managers] say, will increase organizational effectiveness. It will lift morale, bring greater access to new segments of the marketplace, and enhance productivity" (Thomas and Ely, 1996: 79). The business case for diversity, and its optimistic expectations of the benefits achieved through employee diversity, has been enthusiastically embraced by managers. In a Catalyst-sponsored study of 15 *Fortune* 500 companies, every corporate executive interviewed by the researchers cited the business case as the primary rationale for their organizations' diversity efforts (Giscombe and Mattis, 2002). And there is evidence of a trickle-down effect to the employee level: a diversity program accompanied by a "competitive advantage" justification is likely to generate the most positive employee attitudes (Kidder *et al.*, 2004).

Given the widespread acceptance of the business case, it is ironic that the academic literature has documented so many negative outcomes associated with workforce diversity. Diverse organizations are associated with less employee commitment (Tsui, Egan, and O'Reilly,

1992), greater employee dissatisfaction and higher turnover (Jackson *et al.*, 1991), and greater intergroup conflict (Jehn, Northcraft, and Neale, 1999; Zenger and Lawrence, 1989). A recent comprehensive report concluded that organizations are rarely able to leverage diversity and capitalize on its potential benefits (Kochan *et al.*, 2003). Describing these findings, a *Workforce* cover story concluded that the business case for diversity "doesn't add up" (Hansen, 2003).

As academic researchers, we understand that the business case for diversity is not wrong, but incomplete. Diversity *can* lead to better organizational performance (e.g., O'Reilly, Williams, and Barsade, 1998; Jehn *et al.*, 1999) – but only if it is effectively managed. Diversity initiatives are the specific activities, programs, policies, and other formal efforts designed to promote organizational culture change related to diversity (Arredondo, 1996; Wentling and Palma-Rivas, 2000). Since the business case was put forward, we have seen a proliferation of these initiatives. Organizations have expended millions (perhaps even billions) of dollars on their diversity efforts (Grossman, 2000).

A diversity initiative can encompass a wide range of specific activities – from recruitment programs or changes in employee benefits, to standalone language training or organization-sponsored social events, to large-scale career development programs and mentoring relationships. Unfortunately, organizations have received little practical guidance on how to choose from the many possibilities available when designing their own diversity management strategy. Practitioner-focused diversity articles warn managers not to succumb to consultant pitches and buy programs "off the shelf" (e.g., Diamante, Reid, and Giglio, 1995; Gochman, 1989). HR managers and diversity managers are urged to conduct a needs analysis to identify their organization's own particular issues which need to be addressed (e.g., Koonce, 2001; Larkin Ford, 2004). Other recommendations commonly seen in the diversity literature include "get top management support" (e.g., Hayes, 1999; Schmidt, 2004) and "establish metrics" (e.g., Anonymous, 2004; Babcock, 2006). While sound advice for any organizational change effort, these recommendations do not address the critical question of *which* diversity interventions will lead to *which* desired diversity outcomes. As a result, a manager's choice of diversity intervention may be based on inaccurate assumptions about "what leads to what." In these situations, organizations may choose a diversity program based on "best practice" lists, competitor practices, employee preferences, or other dubious reasons (Pfeffer and Sutton, 2006; Williams, 2004).

Part of the problem is that there is little published research assessing the effectiveness of diversity interventions or their results. Rigorous academic research on diversity interventions, while clearly relevant to organizations engaged in diversity efforts, is not easily accessed by HR practitioners or diversity managers. An electronic search using the keywords "diversity" and "employee" elicits more than 2,000 hits – but only 20% of these are associated with articles in refereed academic outlets. Our goal in this chapter is to focus on that elusive 20%. We present the "needle in the haystack" academic findings on three common diversity initiatives (diversity recruitment, diversity training, and formal mentoring programs) and explain the outcomes that result (and do not result) from each type of initiative. We discuss these outcomes in light of the diversity literature's assumptions and expectations about what each diversity intervention can accomplish. We present empirical evidence (when available) demonstrating the extent to which those assumptions are warranted, and use theory to explain when and why the data do not conform to expectations.

What organizations want from diversity initiatives

Organizations get involved with diversity for many different reasons. Gentile (1996) suggested eight different motivators that simulate an organization's interest in diversity including: legal and regulatory pressures, labor market demographics, globalization, diverse customer bases, external pressures (e.g., community, religious, or political groups), internal employee pressures (e.g., employee complaints or demands), and the personal commitment of business leaders to diversity. In theory at least, different motivators should lead organizations to adopt different types of diversity interventions and assess the success of their interventions using distinctly different metrics. For example, an organization that launches a diversity effort in response to its diverse customer base might hope to see market share increase, while an organization that initiates a diversity program in response to employee pressures might look for a decline in employee grievances.

In practice, however, the strongest motivators of organizational diversity initiatives may be the threat of a lawsuit and forceful top-down commands (Langevoort, 2004; Sturm, 2001). Organizations are more frequently "pushed" by external forces into launching diversity initiatives than they are "pulled" by their internal strategic objectives. These motivators may discourage organizations from engaging in any kind of systematic evaluation of their diversity initiatives. Organizations reap symbolic rewards from having diversity initiatives in place and demonstrating that they are "doing something" to address diversity challenges. Evaluating the programs could jeopardize these benefits, especially if the evaluation identifies negative outcomes either for the organization or for program participants (Jayne and Dipboye, 2004). A recent survey of HR professionals conducted by the Society for Human Resource Management (SHRM) suggests that only about one-third of organizations engaging in diversity initiatives evaluate their practices and only about 14% measure their diversity return on investment (Esen, 2005).

When evaluations are conducted, the outcomes considered tend to be limited to a narrow set of quantitative measures: the number of diverse employees recruited, the number of diverse employees retained, and evidence of diversity at all levels of the organization (Esen, 2005). These outcomes have the advantage of being easy to measure and report but they may be very distant from the actual "deliverables" resulting from a diversity intervention. For example, a diversity training program may result in managers having better diversity skills and more positive attitudes toward diversity, but managers' skills and attitudes may be only one of many factors influencing the hiring and retention of the diverse employees they supervise.

Further, these outcomes tell us little or nothing about the processes by which diversity interventions affect demographic composition. High levels of employee diversity may reflect an underlying diversity-functional organizational system, but they do not directly yield any information about how or why the system is working (Sturm, 2001). Simply categorizing the percentage of women and minorities in an organization falls woefully short of assessing an organization's overall diversity culture or diversity sensitivity (Hoobler, 2005). Organizations that constrain their diversity effectiveness measures to these demographic variables may be motivated to hire "by the numbers" without creating internal structures to support a diverse workforce or to enable productive conflict resolution in diverse work groups (Sturm, 2001). As a result, an organization may maintain high diversity recruiting numbers while simultaneously experiencing considerable "churn" as diverse employees turn over (McKay and Avery, 2005).

Organizations need to consider a broad range of process and outcome variables in addition to demographic indices (Hoobler, 2005). Jayne and Dipboye (2004) recommend that human resource professionals responsible for diversity initiatives should first develop a well-defined diversity strategy that is tied to business results in a realistic way and does not over-promise results. Our chapter is designed to facilitate that recommendation, by focusing on the immediate outcomes associated with different diversity initiatives so that human resource professionals can form realistic expectations of what each initiative can and cannot deliver. At the end of the chapter, we summarize the state of our knowledge about outcomes of the individual initiatives, and provide research recommendations that will help in linking the immediate outcomes into broader organizational goals and strategies. We turn now to our review of three common diversity initiatives: diversity recruitment, diversity training, and formal mentoring programs.

Diversity recruitment

SHRM's Workplace Diversity Practices Survey Report found that 79% of HR professionals surveyed reported that their organization employed recruiting strategies designed to help increase diversity within the organization, making it the second most highly ranked diversity practice (only "allowing employees to take unpaid leave to observe a religious or cultural holiday" was a more popular diversity practice) (Esen, 2005). Diversity recruiting strategies are consistent with the tenets of the business case for diversity, since they are designed to capture underutilized aspects of the labor pool and make a diverse set of perspectives available to the organization for customer outreach and internal decision making.

Diversity recruiting is part of a strategic HRM approach which views recruitment as the dominant tool for attracting applicants (Rynes and Barber, 1990). The focus is on making strategic choices among recruiting activities to either increase the number or change the characteristics of individuals who are willing to consider applying for or accepting a job (Rynes and Barber, 1990). Organizational recruitment strategies are one of the primary ways that applicants gain information about the organization, and the goal is to get applicants to view the organization as a positive place to work (Ehrhart and Ziegert, 2005). Women and members of racial minority groups rate diversity as more important in a prospective employer than men and Whites (Backhaus, Stone, and Heiner, 2002; Freeman, 2003; Thomas and Wise, 1999). Therefore, highlighting an organization's workforce diversity and its diversity initiatives should increase its attractiveness for members of these demographic groups.

Research suggests that recruitment through informal networks (e.g., through employee referrals) tends to reproduce an organization's demographic composition because current employees usually tell people who are similar to them about jobs (see Reskin, McBrier, and Kmec, 1999 for a review of this literature). Women and members of racial minority groups generally have less access to informal sources of job information (Giscombe and Mattis, 2002; Kirnan, Farley, and Geisinger, 1989) and tend to rely on the messages presented in formal job ads as a basis for forming expectations of the job and the organization. As a result, organizations wishing to increase the diversity of its applicants can do so by modifying the signals they send through formal recruiting channels. Research has examined three specific diversity recruiting tactics: (1) the use of recruiting advertisement photos or text that highlights the diversity of the organization's workforce; (2) the inclusion of statements that communicate the organization's equal employment opportunity (EEO) or diversity management policies in recruiting materials; and (3) the use of female and racial minority recruiters.

Depicting organizational diversity in recruiting materials

According to social identity theory, demographic similarity promotes attraction and liking (Tajfel, 1982). Applicants should be most attracted to organizations whose workforces reflect their own demographic characteristics. A workforce that includes employees with the applicant's demographic profile conveys a message to the applicant that people like him or her are valued at the organization and makes the organization a more attractive place to work (Spence, 1973). Messages about an organization's diversity can be conveyed through pictures of representative employees or through text that describes an organization's demographic composition.

In one of the first studies examining the effect of pictures in recruiting ads, Perkins, Thomas, and Taylor (2000) created four versions of a recruitment advertisement for a fictitious organization. All four ads pictured 10 employees, but the ads varied in the racial mix of the employees (0, 1, 3, or 5 Black employees pictured among White colleagues). Students were asked to rate the attractiveness of the organization, their perception of their compatibility with the organization, and the favorability of the organization's image. For Black students, ratings on all three variables became more favorable as the proportion of Black employees pictured in the ad increased; the diversity of the employees had no effect on ratings made by White students. A later study by Avery (2003) varied the racial mix of employees presented in website ads at two hierarchical levels (coworkers and supervisors) and asked students to rate the attractiveness of the organization. For Black students, organizations were seen as more attractive when the ad depicted Blacks in both the higher and lower status positions; the diversity of the employees had no effect on White students' perceptions of organizational attractiveness. Finally, Avery, Hernandez, and Hebl (2004) suggested that the positive effects of picturing minorities in recruiting advertising holds even if the applicant is from a different minority group than the one featured in the ad. Black and Hispanic adults were more attracted to organizations with recruiting materials depicting either a Black or Hispanic representative rather than a White representative; White adults' attractiveness was unaffected by the race of the organizational representative.

Umphress *et al.* (2007) conveyed diversity information in a recruitment letter to potential job applicants. In a series of studies the researchers manipulated information about the racial or gender composition of the organization's recruiters and its board of directors. Their findings suggest that applicant-organization demographic similarity is not sufficient to predict an applicant's attraction to the organization. Specifically, an individual difference variable ("social dominance orientation") played a significant role. Individuals who are members of low-status groups (e.g., women or members of racial minority groups) but who value and support group-based social hierarchies (i.e., who are high on social dominance orientation) may be repelled by demographically similar organizations, because organizations comprised of people "like themselves" are likely to be low-status organizations.

Affirmative action, EEO or diversity management program advertising

Affirmative action is an umbrella term encompassing a variety of diversity activities including "identity-blind" and "identity-conscious" practices. Both program types are legally defensible versions of affirmative action with a common purpose – to ensure that hiring outcomes are based on individual merit regardless of group identity (Konrad and Linnehan, 1995). However, identity-blind practices recruit a diverse applicant pool and then ignore group identity during the actual decision-making process. For example, an organization might expand the number and type of publication outlets in which its "help wanted" ads appear in an effort to make a larger segment of the labor market aware of its job opportunities – but not use demographic information to make hiring decisions. Identity-conscious affirmative action programs encourage organizational decision-makers to hire non-White and female applicants instead of White or male applicants scoring equally ("tiebreak" affirmative action) or higher ("preferential treatment") on non-demographic hiring criteria. The decision-maker may consciously and deliberately use an applicant's group identity as input into the hiring decision.

A large body of research has documented the economic and social benefits associated with affirmative action (e.g., Bowen and Bok, 1998; Crosby, 2004; Crosby, Iyer, and Sincharoen, 2006). These benefits are more likely to accrue from identity-conscious practices, because "stronger" affirmative action programs are more effective in achieving a diverse organizational workforce (Konrad and Linnehan, 1995). However, identity-blind practices are evaluated more favorably by both Whites (Kravitz, 1995; Kravitz, and Platania, 1993) and people of color (e.g., Cropanzano, Slaughter, and Bachiochi, 2005; Slaughter, Sinar, and Bachiochi, 2002), although attitudes toward affirmative action vary as a function of experience with discrimination (Son Hing, Bobocel, and Zanna, 2002), personal prejudice (Bobo, 1998; Bobo and Kluegel, 1993), and other personal factors. Identity-conscious practices can have adverse consequences for their intended beneficiaries. Employees may believe that coworkers hired under identity-conscious affirmative action programs lack relevant qualifications, leading to perceptions of lower competence and greater stigmatization in the workplace for diverse hires (Carter, 1991; Heilman, Block, and Lucas, 1992; Heilman, Block, and Stathatos, 1997).

Only a few studies have examined the impact of advertising different affirmative action plans on an organization's ability to attract diverse job applicants. In two studies, Black engineering students were asked about their interest in organizations advertising six different types of affirmative action plans. Cropanzano *et al.* (2005) found that the nature of the plans had no effect on intentions to apply for jobs at the organization, and Slaughter *et al.* (2002) found only a few cross-plan differences. However, Highhouse *et al.* (1999) asked Black engineers for their reactions to ads describing the organization as either an identity-blind "equal opportunity employer" or an identity-conscious "affirmative action employer" and found that the engineers were more attracted to the organization when the staffing policy was identity conscious.

Affirmative action statements signal an organization's attention to race and gender, but diversity statements might signal an organization's concerns about a broader range of differences. Some research has examined the effect of organizations placing explicit diversity statements in their recruiting materials. Williams and Bauer (1994) contrasted recruiting materials describing the organization as an "affirmative action/equal opportunity employer" with materials describing the organization as taking a more proactive diversity stance. Students participating in their research consistently rated the diversity-proactive organization as more attractive, and there were no interactions involving the students' race or gender. McNab and Johnston (2002) compared three ads for a trainee manager position: one contained no EEO information (control condition), a second contained a minimal EEO statement, and the third contained an extensive description of the organization's pro-diversity stance. Students reviewing the ads rated the organization in the two experimental conditions as more attractive than the organization in the control condition. But the effect was small and only appeared as marginally significant in a planned comparison. Rau and Hyland (2003) contrasted organizational brochures that featured a statement highlighting the organization's commitment to diversity vs. the organization's commitment to "traditional values." A three-way interaction suggested that the organization with a diversity commitment was most attractive to minority men and non-minority women.

Kim and Gelfand (2003) suggest that an individual difference variable might impact reactions to recruiting materials – ethnic identity. Ethnic identity reflects the strength and centrality that an individual's membership in an ethnic group has on the individual's overall self-concept (Phinney, 1996). Kim and Gelfand (2003) demonstrated that, regardless of the individual's race, people with stronger ethnic identities were more attracted to organizations that described a diversity initiative in their recruiting materials than to organizations that did not describe a diversity initiative.

Female and racial minority recruiters

The research reviewed above suggests that presenting diverse employees and pro-diversity statements in recruiting materials sends a signal to the applicant that the organization values diversity (Spence, 1973). A similar logic is applied in research on recruiter characteristics. According to social identity theory, demographic similarity promotes attraction and liking (Tajfel, 1982). Applicants should be most attracted to recruiters who are demographically similar. Further, the recruiter's similarity to the applicant conveys a message to the applicant that people like him or her are valued at the organization and makes the organization a more attractive place to work (Spence, 1973).

Unfortunately, research on applicant-recruiter similarity has produced results that are inconsistent, confusing, and sometimes counterintuitive (Avery and McKay, 2006; Goldberg, 2003). For example, Turban and Dougherty (1992) reported that gender similarity between recruiter and applicant positively influenced organizational attraction among male but not female job seekers, while Taylor and Bergmann (1987) found that gender similarity between recruiter and applicant negatively influenced job attractiveness and offer acceptance for female (but not male) applicants. Wyse (1972) found that Black applicants preferred Black recruiters while White applicants were not influenced by race, but Young *et al.* (1997) found that Black applicants' preference for Black recruiters was moderated by the recruiter's gender and the content of the recruiting message delivered by the recruiter. In a more recent study of applicant-recruiter demographics, Goldberg (2003) examined the effects of race, sex, and age similarity and found that race similarity affected perceptions of the recruiter's likability and effectiveness but not perceptions of either the job's or the organization's attractiveness; neither sex nor age similarity affected any outcome variables.

What organizations can (and cannot) expect from diversity recruiting initiatives

Including visual presentations of organizational diversity and text presentations of diversity commitment in recruiting materials may be low-cost diversity strategies for organizations to pursue, especially since there seems to be very little backlash from non-targeted groups.

Pictures of diverse employees appear to be effective in attracting members of racial minority groups and have little effect on Whites; pro-diversity statements usually are found to be equally effective (or ineffective) in increasing perceptions of organizational attractiveness across applicant demographic groups. And because pro-diversity statements are unassociated with preferential treatment based on race or gender, they are less likely to trigger the concerns about stigma evoked by affirmative action plans. In contrast, the effects of applicant-recruiter similarity are too mixed to provide any clear recommendations to organizations (see Avery and McKay, 2006, for a convergent conclusion). While there is probably little harm to an organization's image by providing diverse recruiters, there seems to be little benefit in proactively trying to "match" recruiter demographics to target applicants.

However, even the relatively consistent results associated with pictorial diversity and the inclusion of diversity messages in recruitment ads have to be interpreted with several grains of salt. First, this research tends to use students as subjects, and all of the research relies on a self-report measure of applicant interest in the organization or intention to pursue a job opportunity. It is not clear whether the effects are strong enough to impact actual job choice behavior in real decision contexts. We need more longitudinal studies of the effects of actual organizational recruiting campaigns to really assess the effectiveness of variability in diversity recruiting materials. Unfortunately, few organizations systematically compare the applicant "yields" resulting from different recruiting strategies (Kulik, 2004).

Second, the research tends to present relatively straightforward diversity messages, and there has been little attention to whether more subtle manipulations might be effective, or how one practice might interact with others. In a recent study, Rau and Adams (2005) varied the benefits presented to retirees in a fictitious advertising campaign, predicting that retirees would be particularly attracted to organizations communicating an EEO commitment and offering benefits targeted to needs associated with senior career stages (opportunities for flexible part-time work and opportunities to mentor other employees). Their fully-crossed design generated a significant three-way interaction: mentoring opportunities were attractive to retirees, but only when the other two practices (part-time work and an EEO policy) were in place. Communicating a diversity message to job applicants may be an effective recruiting tactic, but the message may be bolstered or diluted by other organizational benefits or practices (Becker *et al.*, 1997; Johns, 2006). Organizations need to consider the effectiveness of their entire recruiting initiative in attracting diverse applications.

Third, applicants themselves are more complex than their demographic profiles might indicate. Other variables (e.g., ethnic identity or social dominance orientation) impact how applicants perceive and interpret the diversity messages communicated by organizations. And applicants are becoming more sophisticated consumers of this organizational information (see, for example, the *Wall Street Journal*'s advice to minority job applicants in Dunham, 2003). Applicants increasingly have access to diversity-relevant information from other sources (e.g., *Fortune* magazine's ratings of the best places for women and members of racial minority groups to work; Vault.com's organizational "snapshots" that describe an organization's climate and culture) that may be perceived as more credible and less biased than an organization's own promotional materials. A diverse workforce alone may be seen as window-dressing unless it is accompanied by evidence that diverse employees are thriving and succeeding in the organization. For example, Avery (2003) found that the actual positions occupied by employees in organizations are important in helping applicants to interpret the diversity message conveyed by a picture of employees.

A final cautionary note needs to be sounded in relation to diversity recruiting: Recruiting tactics may attract diverse applicants, but they play no role in retention. Recruiting practices serve a signaling function by helping applicants to form a pre-hire impression of what life in the organization will be like. However, a variety of theoretical perspectives including the person-organization fit literature (Kristof, 1996), the realistic job preview literature (Hom *et al.*, 1998; Phillips, 1998), and the psychological contract literature (Rousseau, 1995) all suggest that pre-hire expectations will be "trumped" by actual on-the-job experiences with the organization. It is important that an organization ensure that its policies and practices support the climate portrayed in their ads (Avery and McKay, 2006). If the recruiting message results in an overly positive and unrealistic expectation of the organization's diversity climate, diverse recruits will be disappointed and leave the organization (McKay and Avery, 2005).

Diversity training

If an organization has a diversity management strategy, diversity training is very likely to be one of the program components. Diversity training is often seen as the cornerstone of diversity initiatives. Cox (Cox, 1994; Cox and Beale, 1997), for example, views education and training as a primary driver of organizational change, and recommends that training *always* be included in a diversity strategy. Organizations seem to have heeded this advice. Training is one of the most common diversity activities, used in 67% of US organizations (Esen, 2005).

Diversity training is recommended as a way to achieve two distinct goals (Jayne and Dipboye, 2004). First, training is often used early in a diversity effort as a vehicle for disseminating information about the strategy and initiatives. Organizations use diversity training to stress the importance of diversity goals, to describe the potential benefits to the organization in an effort to achieve employee buy-in to diversity programs, and to signal a change in the status quo (Ford and Fisher, 1996; Holvino *et al.*, 2004). Training may also be used to define diversity, to establish a common language for talking about diversity, and to create interest and positive feelings about other parts of the diversity strategy (Gentile, 1996).

Second, diversity training is frequently intended to change employee behavior to improve relations among organizational members. Sometimes diversity training programs tackle behavior change and skill development directly. For example, an organization may use diversity training to try to improve competencies believed to be critical to effective diversity management, such as conflict management, team-building, or decision-making skills (Government Accountability Office [GAO], 2005). Alternatively, a training program may be designed to change behavior indirectly, by first changing stereotypes to reduce their impact on organizational interactions and decision making (Bendick, Egan, and Lofhjelm, 2001).

Diversity training has been soundly criticized in the literature (e.g., Lynch, 1997), but, as many authors have observed (e.g., Nemetz and Christensen, 1996; Sanchez and Medkik, 2004), there is little empirical evidence to demonstrate diversity training's effectiveness or ineffectiveness. Nonetheless, articles in the practitioner literature regularly provide recommendations to human resource and diversity managers about how to make the best use of diversity training. As noted by Roberson, Kulik, and Pepper (2003), some of these articles present contradictory advice. Further, the basic question about whether diversity training can deliver its intended outcomes is left unexamined in the practitioner literature. Setting aside the practical questions associated with training program design and content, choice of trainer, length of program, etc., we ask whether a diversity training initiative can accomplish its major goals. Can training deliver diversity effort buy-in and behavior change?

Training to disseminate information

Sometimes, an organization's goal in initiating diversity training is simple and straightforward: to impart information, explain the organization's diversity strategy, align expectations for the initiatives, and create positive interest by describing the intended benefits to employees. There is ample evidence in the training literature that training can achieve these kinds of outcomes. Orientation programs, for example, have long been used in organizations for similar purposes. As noted by Ford and Fisher (1996), the purpose of orientation training is to socialize newcomers, align their expectations, and provide them with basic information about the organization, its goals and values. Training programs for new employees provide a context where the organization's norms and values can be communicated to newcomers (Feldman, 1989).

There is also some empirical evidence that diversity training, in particular, can achieve this goal. Adler (1986) found that after diversity training, trainees were able to identify the advantages of workforce diversity for the organization. Hanover and Cellar (1998) reported that managers who participated in diversity training rated diversity management practices as significantly more important than those in a control group. Ellis and Sonnenfeld (1994) reported similar results: sixty percent of employees who attended diversity training felt that it increased their understanding of the benefits of diversity. Training appears to be an effective way to transmit information about diversity and its importance.

Training to create behavioral change

Achieving behavior change was listed as a training goal by 95% of the diversity trainers surveyed by Bendick *et al.* (2001). There are two types of training programs designed to change behavior. In *skill training* (Holvino *et al.*, 2004), the training program is intended to directly impart new skills. A wide variety of behavioral competencies or skill sets are mentioned in the literature as important for diversity: communication skills (Holvino *et al.*, 2004), conflict resolution skills (Holvino *et al.*, 2004), and sexual harassment management (Jayne and Dipboye, 2004). In *awareness training* (Holvino *et al.*, 2004), the immediate goal of training is an increased awareness of the cognitive processes that may lead to discrimination and differential treatment. This increased awareness is intended to lay the foundation for subsequent behavior change.

Skill training

There is little doubt that skill training can deliver skill improvements (Noe, 1999). Much organizational training activity is directed toward increasing skills and changing behavior in the training context and, later, on the job. But the voluminous training literature also cautions that the amount of skill learning and behavior change resulting from training is contingent on certain factors. First, a needs assessment is critical, both to identify the skills that need improvement, and to determine if training is the appropriate solution (Noe, 1999). Formal training is warranted only if trainees lack the skills and knowledge to perform. However, poor performance or non-performance of desired behaviors can occur for other reasons. Employees may not engage in desired behaviors because the work environment provides few positive consequences for the behavior, limited opportunities to use skills, or little feedback related to effective performance (Mager and Pipe, 1984). These environmental factors are also important in establishing the transfer climate (Rouiller and Goldstein, 1993) that determines the extent to which trained skills and knowledge will be exhibited in the job setting. Thus, before a formal training program is launched, the needs assessment should verify that these factors are not responsible for employees' failure to engage in desired diversity behavior and will not constrain the transfer of diversity training to the job.

A needs assessment should also determine trainees' readiness or motivation to learn, to ensure that trainees will benefit from training. Noe (1986; 1999) identified two important aspects of trainee motivation: self-efficacy and self-awareness of a skill deficit. Self-efficacy refers to trainees' confidence that they can learn from the program and improve their skills. Pre-training self-efficacy has been associated with learning in the training context, and subsequent transfer of learning from the training context to the job (Colquitt, LePine, and Noe, 2000). Trainees' self-awareness of their skill deficits establishes a perceived need for training and motivates trainees to learn. Trainees who think they have no need for training are unlikely to attend a voluntary program, and, if the training is mandatory, they are unlikely to benefit from it (Noe, 1999).

The importance of environmental conditions and trainee readiness for training has recently been examined in the context of diversity training. Roberson, Kulik, and Pepper (in press) found evidence for the importance of the transfer climate for behavior change. Trainees reported more attempts to use their skills and knowledge from diversity training on the job when supervisors and peers provided positive consequences for exhibiting diversity knowledge. A study by Sanchez and Medkik (2004) indicated the importance of pre-training trainee beliefs and attitudes about training on diversity training outcomes. They compared a group that received diversity training with a control group who received no training. Post-training, the researchers asked coworkers to rate the differential treatment exhibited by trainees and non-trainees toward culturally different others. Surprisingly, in the training group, non-White coworkers rated trainees as exhibiting more differential treatment than White coworkers. In the control group, there was no difference between non-White and White coworker ratings. Follow-up interviews suggested that some trainees believed that their non-White coworkers had reported them as being insensitive, and were responsible for their being sent to the training (in fact, trainees had been selected based on their organizational seniority). After training, trainee resentment toward these coworkers was visible.

Kulik *et al.* (2006) found that trainee pre-training diversity competence predicted participation in voluntary diversity training – trainees with greater diversity competence were more likely to attend a voluntary training session. The authors suggested that trainees with low competence in the diversity domain may be unaware of their low competence levels, or have low self-efficacy for improving their competence. Either factor would decrease low-competence trainees' motivation to participate in a training program designed to increase diversity competence.

Thus, while skill training for diversity competence can be successful, a lack of attention to the needs assessment phase (in particular, a lack of attention to assessing the work environment and trainee factors) can limit its effectiveness in changing behavior. Although diversity specialists stress the importance of needs assessment prior to a diversity initiative (Arredondo, 1996; Jayne and Dipboye, 2004), these discussions tend to focus on its value in identifying diversity issues and training content relevant to the organizational context and the trainee audience. Using needs assessment to identify organization, job, and person factors that might limit training effectiveness is rarely mentioned (Roberson *et al.*, 2003).

Awareness training

The second type of diversity training for behavior change does not teach skills directly. These training programs are often described as "awareness training," because the immediate goal of training is to increase the trainee's awareness of social perception biases such as stereotyping (Sanchez and Medkik, 2004). Awareness of the perception process is seen as a first step in motivating the trainee to inhibit the automatic or mindless use of stereotypes when interacting with different others. A decrease in stereotyping should subsequently result in less differential treatment and discrimination in the organization. For example, trainers in an awareness training program might provide factual information about the cognitive processes that result in bias, and discuss how diversity affects social perception and influences decision making. Trainees might be asked to reflect on and discuss their own stereotypes and the effects of these stereotypes on interactions with others (Holvino *et al.*, 2004; Sanchez and Medkik, 2004). The assumption behind this intervention is that both stereotyping and discrimination are largely unintentional and result from automatic processes of which people are unaware. Once people become aware of these processes, they can begin to change.

The available research casts doubt on the ability of awareness training to increase trainee awareness or knowledge. The awareness training program studied by Sanchez and Medkik (2004) did not increase trainees' knowledge of perception biases. Chrobot-Mason (2004) examined the impact of diversity training on an individual difference measure reflecting self-awareness: manager ethnic identity development. Higher levels of ethnic identity means acknowledging implications of one's ethnicity and replacing stereotypes with more accurate information about others (Chrobot-Mason, 2004; Helms, 1990).

Therefore, awareness training should encourage higher levels of ethnic identity. However, diversity training had no impact on trainee ethnic identity development.

The results of Sanchez and Medkik (2004) also cast doubt on a key assumption underlying the use of awareness training – that increased awareness will, in turn, lead to behavioral change. In their study, trainees' knowledge of biases was unrelated to post-training behavior. Coworkers rated the extent to which trainees engaged in differential treatment of employees, but these ratings were not significantly related to trainee knowledge (Sanchez and Medkik, 2004). Further, research in social psychology raises questions about the validity of another key assumption underlying the use of awareness training – that reduction in stereotype use mediates the relationship between increased awareness and change in behavior. This literature indicates that individuals *can* regulate their cognitive processes to reduce the use of stereotypes (Devine *et al.*, 1991; Monteith, 1993). However, these self-regulatory activities result from a motivation to be fair (a motivation to avoid prejudice), not from an awareness of biases. Awareness training alone is insufficient, because trainees will not act upon their awareness without motivation.

What organizations can (and cannot) expect from diversity training

Our review suggests that diversity training can meet some of its intended objectives. Training programs *can* disseminate information about diversity goals and their importance to the organization. Training *can* also teach specific diversity management skills. The use of training for these purposes seems justified. However, diversity training for the purpose of skill acquisition must be accompanied by a needs assessment that considers the climate for transfer and pre-training motivation to learn.

In contrast, the use of awareness training to reduce discriminatory behavior is unlikely to be effective in organizations. Reducing discrimination is an important goal, but simply raising awareness of cognitive biases seems unable to accomplish this. Research on diversity training has moved from examinations of practitioner perceptions of success (e.g., Rynes and Rosen, 1995) or trainee reactions to training (e.g., Ellis and Sonnenfeld, 1994) to evaluations of learning from training (e.g., Roberson, Kulik, and Pepper, 2001). Recently, research has examined the basic assumptions underlying awareness training (Sanchez and Medkik, 2004), individual and organizational variables that influence training outcomes (Chrobot-Mason, 2004; Roberson *et al.*, in press), and the effects of training on behavioral outcomes (Chrobot-Mason, 2004; Sanchez and Medkik, 2004). However, scholars have concentrated their research efforts on diversity awareness training programs. Perhaps this research activity reflects the popularity of these programs in organizations, but studies that examine the effectiveness of other types of diversity training are needed, especially since organizations are becoming disenchanted with awareness training and increasing their use of diversity skill training (Egodigwe, 2005).

We have argued here that awareness training is likely to have little impact on its intended outcomes, as the assumptions about reduction in stereotype use and behavior change resulting from such training are questionable. Writers have begun to recommend training programs more deeply grounded in theory. For example, Combs (2002) proposes diversity training based on self-efficacy theory, and Wiethoff (2004) suggests the theory of planned behavior (Azjen, 1991) as a basis for the design of diversity training programs. Research should begin to develop theoretically-based training programs and examine their effectiveness for reducing the use of stereotypes and changing behavior. In addition, research should continue to examine the effects of environmental and individual variables on pre-training motivation, learning in training, and post-training behavior change. Diversity training is unlikely to disappear. We need to build a knowledge base to help human resource managers and diversity managers use diversity training more effectively.

Formal mentoring programs

Formal mentoring programs, initiated and managed by the organization, are another common activity used in diversity initiatives. Mentoring programs were ranked fifth in SHRM's survey of organizational diversity practices (Esen, 2005). Ragins and Cotton (1999) estimated that a third of US firms and organizations have some kind of mentoring program in place.

Mentoring programs can take a variety of forms – from programs that establish a traditional dyadic relationship between a junior person and a more senior member, to group or team mentoring programs that involve groups of junior employees meeting with a senior person (Douglas and McCauley, 1999; Hegstad and Wentling, 2004). In Douglas and McCauley's (1999) survey of 246 firms, 21% offered a formal program to facilitate developmental relationships, with 70% of those involving the pairing of junior and senior people. Most often, formal mentoring programs are aimed at managerial/professional employees (Douglas and McCauley, 1999; Noe, Greenberger, and Wang, 2002). When part of a diversity initiative, mentoring programs target (but are not limited to) women and people of color. Hegstad and Wentling (2004) interviewed participants from mentoring programs in 17 *Fortune* 500 companies. 53 percent of participants reported that the mentoring programs in their organizations were begun as part of a diversity strategy.

Mentoring programs have two major related goals. The first goal is career development and advancement (Blake-Beard, 2001; Kilian, Hukai, and McCarty, 2005). Studies have found that women and people of color no longer report barriers at the organizational entry stage, but rather barriers to subsequent advancement (Kilian *et al.*, 2005). Lack of mentoring is consistently mentioned as one of the important advancement barriers (Kilian *et al.*, 2005). Years of research have shown that protégés in informal mentoring relationships experience higher job and career satisfaction, larger salaries, and faster promotion rates (Eby and Lockwood, 2005; Noe *et al.*, 2002). Employees experiencing career success frequently report that a mentor was a critical influence on their development and advancement, providing coaching, sponsorship, and exposure. In addition to these career functions, mentors also provide psychosocial functions such as friendship, emotional support, and role modeling (Noe *et al.*, 2002). However, studies also show that women and people of color report greater difficulty than White males in finding mentors at higher organizational levels (Noe *et al.*, 2002). Thus, mentoring programs are intended to increase access to mentors for members of these groups. For women, the structure of a formal program is believed to remove some of the perceived sexual tensions related to initiating a cross-gender mentoring relationship (Kilian *et al.*, 2005). For people of color, the formal program can provide more access to mentors across racial and ethnic lines.

A second important goal of mentoring programs is retention (Kilian *et al.*, 2005). A recent study of more than 400,000 managerial/professional employees in large companies found that women quit more frequently than men, and low tenure African-Americans turn over at a rate significantly higher than that of low tenure Asians or Whites (Hom, Roberson, and Ellis, in press). If mentoring programs facilitate advancement, they should also reduce turnover among diverse employees, as studies consistently point to lack of advancement for women and minorities as a major reason for turnover within these groups. Exit surveys with women and people of color have revealed career blocks as a primary reason for quit behavior (Hom and Griffeth, 1995). The Federal Glass Ceiling Commission also named turnover as one of the most important consequences of lack of advancement for people of color (Roberson, 2004).

While many studies have linked informal mentoring to pay, advancement, and retention, studies of formal mentoring generally have been limited to job attitudes and self-reported outcomes. The participants in Hegstad and Wentling's (2004) study perceived positive effects of their organizations' mentoring programs on overall retention rates and employee performance, but they did not examine effects within targeted groups. What's the likelihood that mentoring programs can deliver hoped-for outcomes? First, we consider the ability of formal mentoring programs to provide the benefits associated with informal mentoring. Then we examine what is known about improving the advancement and retention of women and minorities to see if mentoring programs are likely to achieve their goals.

Formal vs. informal mentoring

Formal mentoring programs have been initiated because of the proven benefits of informal mentoring (Eby and Lockwood, 2005), but the ability of formal programs to deliver the benefits of informal mentoring has been questioned (Blake-Beard, 2001; Ragins and Cotton, 1999). Formal mentoring relationships differ from informal relationships on several important dimensions. Informal mentoring relationships develop on the basis of mutual identification and perceived similarity between mentor and protégé (Ragins and Cotton, 1999). In contrast, in formal mentoring programs, the organization matches the pair. Therefore, formal mentors may be less motivated than informal mentors to develop a deep relationship because they identify less with the protégé at the outset (Ragins and Cotton, 1999). Informal mentoring relationships tend to be long term, spanning three to six years (Blake-Beard, 2001; Ragins and Cotton, 1999). In contrast, most formal mentoring relationships are defined for a much shorter period, such as one year or six months (Ragins and Cotton, 1999). Finally, formal and informal mentors may have different motivations for entering the relationship (Ragins and Cotton, 1999). Informal mentors typically enter a mentoring relationship to fulfill their own career needs, while formal mentors may be more likely to participate in a mentoring program as an organizational citizenship behavior.

In empirical research comparing the outcomes resulting from formal and informal mentoring, several studies have found that protégés in formal relationships report fewer career-related or psychosocial benefits than those in informal relationships (Chao, Walz, and Gardner, 1992; Fagenson-Eland, Marks, and Amendola, 1997; Ragins and Cotton, 1999). In Ragins and Cotton's (1999) research, this difference in favor of informal mentors was also seen on protégés' self-reported compensation. However, recent work suggests that it is not the mere presence of a mentor, but the quality of the mentoring relationship that is most important for outcomes (Ragins, Cotton, and Miller, 2000). The voluntary nature of informal mentoring relationships tends to ensure high quality, but formal mentoring relationships show greater variability in relationship quality (Ragins et al., 2000). Research suggests that mentor training and participant input into the matching of protégés and mentors contributes to the development of effective formal mentoring relationships (Allen, Eby, and Lentz, 2006; Ragins et al., 2000).

Demographic similarity (e.g., on race and gender) is believed to facilitate identification and liking and to deliver greater psychosocial benefits to protégés (Lankau, Riordan, and Thomas, 2005; Ragins, 1997). However, in terms of career outcomes, demographic similarity may not be an advantage for women and people of color. Dreher and Cox (1996) found that protégés with White male mentors reported significantly higher compensation than those with female or nonWhite mentors. Available research suggests that a demographic match between protégé and mentor is not critical to the quality of the mentoring experience. In several studies, demographic similarity with the mentor did not affect protégés' satisfaction with their mentors (Lyons and Oppler, 2004; Raabe and Beehr, 2003). Lankau et al. (2005) found that demographic similarity affected mentors more than protégés. Demographic similarity (on race and gender) was associated with mentors' liking for their protégés and with their perceptions of the level of role modeling they provided. For protégés, perceptions of deep-level similarity (on values, interests, and personality) were more important than demographic similarity for perceptions of the mentoring (career support, psychosocial support, and role modeling) they received. Although more research on compensation and advancement outcomes is needed, it does not appear that demographic similarity is critical for perceptions of mentoring quality.

Mentoring to enhance advancement

Is the provision of a formal mentor enough to have a significant impact on advancement of women and people of color? Besides a lack of mentoring, stereotypes and few visible or challenging job assignments are also frequently mentioned as major barriers to advancement (Kilian *et al.* 2005). Decision-maker stereotypes can result in biased performance evaluations and underestimation of an employee's potential (Chen and DiTomaso, 1996). As a result, women and people of color may be overlooked for promotions, resulting in career stagnation. Decision-maker stereotypes can also lead to differential treatment and discrimination (Dovidio and Hebl, 2005), which can lower the level of performance displayed by an employee. For example, a biased supervisor may withhold important job information or fail to provide feedback to women or minority subordinates, limiting their ability to perform. A reluctance to give women and people of color visible and challenging job assignments may be part of the differential treatment resulting from stereotypes (Roberson and Block, 2001).

Mentoring programs would have a greater impact on the advancement of women and people of color if they influenced decision-maker stereotypes. Formal mentoring may have the potential to decrease stereotype usage for the parties involved in cross-gender or cross-racial/ethnic relationships. Such relationships provide opportunities to learn more about members of another group and increase friendships and respect – and these interpersonal processes are associated with stereotype reduction (Fiske, 2002). However, the stereotypes having the greatest impact on the advancement of members of diverse groups are those of their immediate supervisors, because supervisors are responsible for evaluating performance, giving job assignments, and making recommendations for promotion. Even if stereotypes decrease within mentoring relationships, the mentoring program may have little or no impact on the stereotypes of the immediate supervisor.

Stereotype threat is another possible cause of lack of advancement, as it depresses true performance levels (Roberson and Kulik, 2007). People who experience stereotype threat fear that others are judging their performance according to a negative stereotype about their group (Steele and Aronson, 1995). The resulting anxiety interferes with task performance. Stereotype threat is created when the employee is performing a difficult task and a stereotype is salient and believed relevant for performance. When people encounter problems in task accomplishment, the stereotype is likely to come to mind as a reason for their difficulty. In many organizations, women and people of color are likely to experience stereotype threat in managerial and professional jobs, as stereotypes about members of these groups are often seen to be relevant for task and role performance (Roberson et al., 2003). In addition, the salience of stereotypes is increased when members of the stereotyped group are in token positions (Inzlicht and Ben Zeev, 2003). Stereotype threat can limit advancement in several ways. Because of its negative effect on task performance, decision-makers may be unaware of an employee's true potential. Stereotype threat is also related to discounting performance feedback from superiors (Roberson et al., 2003). When employees believe that decision-maker judgments are affected by stereotypes, they suspect that organizational feedback does not reflect their true performance. If employees discount feedback, they may be less likely to use that information to improve their skills and performance (Roberson and Block, 2001). The employee's apparent disregard for supervisory feedback may also negatively impact the supervisor's perceptions of the employee's promotion potential.

Effective strategies for reducing stereotype threat and its impact on performance include coaching on task strategies, providing stereotype disconfirming role models, and focusing employee attention on self-improvement and development rather than on comparing one's performance and outcomes with others (Roberson and Kulik, 2007). To the extent that mentors engage in these activities, they may enhance a protégé's job outcomes by reducing stereotype threat. There is some evidence that effective mentors of people of color utilize some of these strategies (Thomas, 2001). However, these strategies may be more effectively implemented by the immediate supervisor, who has more frequent contact with employees and the opportunity to intervene on a daily basis.

Mentoring to enhance retention

Although studies typically find that mentoring is negatively related to intentions to quit (Wanberg, Welsh, and Hezlett, 2003), some aspects of formal mentoring programs may actually *increase* the likelihood of turnover. Unmet expectations have been found to be related to higher turnover (Hom and Griffeth, 1995), and participation in a formal mentoring program may raise protégé expectations for enhanced outcomes beyond what is realistic (Blake-Beard, 2001). Eby and Lockwood (2005) found that protégés' unmet expectations were among the most common problems in formal mentoring programs, mentioned by 20% of participants in their study.

Further, mentors may have less impact on turnover than other people in the work environment. New hires typically have high turnover rates (Hom and Griffeth, 1995) and a lack of adequate socialization has been posited as one of the causes. Mentors might facilitate new employee socialization, and aid adaptation to the new organization and work role (Wanberg *et al.*, 2003). However, Louis, Posner, and Powell (1983) found that new hires rated mentors as less available and less helpful in their socialization and adjustment than senior coworkers, peers, and the immediate supervisor. Further, the perceived helpfulness of mentors was unrelated to intentions to quit. In contrast, the perceived helpfulness of peers and the supervisor was more strongly related to turnover intentions. Raabe and Beehr (2003) reported similar findings. Among employees in a mentoring program, relationships with peers and the immediate supervisor predicted intentions to leave – but mentoring relationships were not related to these intentions. These two studies highlight the role of peer relationships in determining turnover.

Exclusion from informal communication networks is frequently cited as another barrier to advancement for women and minorities (Kilian *et al.*, 2005). These networks aid career development, providing information, resources, and support (Noe *et al.*, 2002). People's social networks are generally characterized by homophily – interactions with similar others (Rogers and Kincaid, 1981). However, developing homophilous relationships can be difficult for women, members of racial minority groups, gay and lesbian employees, and other individuals who differ from the majority in their work group or organization. Members of minority demographic groups have a much smaller set of similar others with whom they can develop professional relationships (Ibarra, 1993). To compensate for a lack of homophily, members of minority groups tend to form distinctly different friendship and instrumental networks, with friendship networks characterized by homophily and instrumental networks characterized by heterophily (Ibarra, 1992). Unfortunately, this means that their instrumental networks also tend to be characterized by weaker ties, because instrumental relationships in the organization are not reinforced by the social support contained in friendship relationships (Friedman, 1996). The inability to form strong-tie relationships with similar others can have a negative effect on people's experience in the workplace, leading to social isolation and a lack of identification with the organization (Ibarra, 1995; Tsui and O'Reilly, 1989). In the absence of strong attachments to coworkers, employees may be less embedded in their jobs and be more likely to leave the organization (Lee *et al.*, 2004; Mitchell *et al.*, 2001).

Group mentoring programs are likely to increase the overall number and strength of participant network ties. Participation in these programs is usually based on experience level (Noe, 1999) rather than demography. Therefore, in an organizational context where White men constitute the largest proportion of the overall workforce, group mentoring is more likely to increase heterophilous ties than homophilous ones for women and people of color. In contrast, employee network groups are intended to directly increase homophilous ties because they are organized around an identity group characteristic (e.g., race, gender, sexual orientation). Network groups are usually initiated by employees, but are formally recognized by the organization and may even receive some financial support (Friedman, 1996; Friedman and Holtom, 2002). SHRM's Workplace Diversity Practices Survey Report found that 29% of HR professionals surveyed reported that their organization supported such groups (Esen, 2005). Corporate policies on employee network groups vary, but they usually require network groups to state their purpose, have some type of charter and leadership structure, and be open to anyone in the company (Friedman and Holtom, 2002). In practice, however, few people join who do not have the central demographic characteristic on which the group is based (Friedman, Kane and Cornfield, 1998).

Employee network groups facilitate homophilous networking by helping minority employees become better connected to one another and thus gain greater access to information, social support, and mentoring (Friedman and Holtom, 2002). Occasionally, these groups do play an advocacy role in the organization. For example, some gay and lesbian groups have advocated for partner benefits in organizations (Friedman and Craig, 2004). However, the dominant purpose of employee network groups is to address career concerns and build a sense of community. Members get together for social gatherings, discussions about what is going on in the company, or fundraising for minority scholarships (Friedman and Holtom, 2002).

Unfortunately, there has been little research directly examining either the antecedents or consequences of employee network groups in organizations. Friedman and Craig (2004) found that membership in employee network groups was predicted by employee perceptions of the potential gains of joining and the strength of group identity, but not by employee dissatisfaction with the organization. Friedman *et al.* (1998) surveyed members of the Black MBA Association and found that members who worked at organizations with network groups were more optimistic about their careers and reported stronger relationships with other Black employees and more access to mentoring. Friedman and Holtom (2002) surveyed employees from one company with 20 different network groups and found that managerial employees who joined the groups were less likely to report an intention to turn over. In this study, groups were especially beneficial in reducing turnover intentions when the group membership included some high-ranking minority managers.

What organizations can (and cannot) expect from formal mentoring programs

Formal mentoring programs can result in a high-quality mentoring relationship, and, particularly for group mentoring, expand participants' network ties. These programs thus have some potential for increasing advancement and decreasing turnover of women and minorities. However, theory and research also point to the relationship with the immediate supervisor as a primary influence on advancement and retention (Kilian *et al.*, 2005). Research comparing the relative influences of mentors and supervisors tends to indicate a greater impact of the supervisor on job satisfaction and turnover intentions. These results suggest that organizational efforts should also be directed toward programs to improve the relationship of women and people of color with their immediate supervisors. Such programs should train supervisors in providing mentoring functions (Kilian *et al.*, 2005) and address other advancement barriers such as the need for visible challenging job assignments and stereotypes.

Theory and research also point to the importance of peer relationships in determining turnover among women and people of color. Employee network groups are likely to be effective in addressing this, because they promote the development of relationships among same-race employees (Friedman *et al.*, 1998). These ties create opportunities for same-race mentoring (Friedman *et al.*, 1998) and reduce turnover intention (Friedman and Holtom, 2002). Unfortunately, we were unable to find any research that replicated these findings for other demographic groups (e.g., women or gay and lesbian employees).

Thus, employee network groups may be an effective, low-cost tactic for organizations trying to retain non-traditional employees because they can provide both networking and mentoring. It may be difficult for an organization to take proactive steps in developing or promoting employee network groups – by definition, these groups are grassroots-grown and employee-organized. However, if these groups spontaneously emerge, organizations can actively support them, and encourage managerial participation. In groups that include high-ranking managers, the social support provided by homophilous ties is more likely to be accompanied by instrumental career support (Friedman and Holtom, 2002). Many of the concerns managers might have about network groups (e.g., that they will aggressively advocate diversity policies or take on union-like characteristics) appear to be unfounded (Friedman and Craig, 2004).

Research on formal mentoring has increased in recent years. However, the outcome variables examined generally have been limited to employee attitudes (e.g., job satisfaction, satisfaction with mentor). Studies that examine pay, promotion, and retention rates are needed. Although many formal mentoring programs are intended to influence these outcomes for women and people of color, in general, studies have not examined effects separately for members of these demographic groups. This makes it impossible to draw conclusions about the ability of mentoring programs to meet its intended diversity goals. In addition, research on the mechanisms through which mentoring programs are expected to influence outcomes is needed. For example, we have suggested that effective mentoring for women and people of color may decrease perceptions of stereotype threat. In educational settings, mentoring programs specifically designed to reduce stereotype threat have shown some promise in increasing retention and achievement (Good, Aronson, and Inzlicht, 2003). Similar programs might be developed in organizations as training programs for mentors and supervisors of diverse employees.

Mentoring researchers have moved from an exclusive focus on the traditional dyadic relationship to a broader consideration of the full constellation of developmental relationships that provide mentoring functions to employees (Higgins and Kram, 2001; Molloy, 2005). For diversity researchers as well, a broadening of perspective would be valuable. The research reviewed here suggested that relationships with peers and supervisors may be more important to outcomes than a traditional mentoring relationship. While research on the ability of formal mentoring programs to achieve diversity goals is needed, research should also examine how the broader set of workplace relationships influences outcomes.

Pulling it together: What diversity initiatives can do

Our review demonstrates that the three diversity initiatives (diversity recruitment, diversity training, and formal mentoring programs) affect different outcomes of interest to organizations. As shown in Figure 8.1, each initiative affects a particular diversity outcome (employee attraction, skill development, or advancement and retention), but simultaneously creates new challenges for the organization. These three initiatives can work together to create an integrated diversity strategy.

Diversity recruiting efforts, especially the way diversity is promoted in recruitment advertising, do affect how attractive the organization is likely to be perceived by diverse job applicants. These effects are consistent with signaling theory (Spence, 1973) and social identity theory (Tajfel, 1982). However, the available research stops short of demonstrating whether diverse job applicants will "vote with their feet" and be more likely to accept jobs as a function of diversity recruitment. Further, diversity recruitment must accurately reflect organizational reality. If

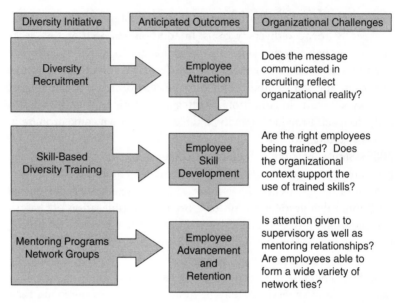

Figure 8.1 Diversity initiatives, anticipated outcomes, and organizational challenges

the organization is misrepresenting the organizational context in which diverse hires will work, the costs of this may outweigh the attraction advantages (Avery and McKay, 2006; McKay and Avery, 2005).

Once diverse job applicants get through the organizational door, the problem becomes one of creating an organizational context in which diverse employees can work together. Organizations have focused on diversity training as a major way to accomplish this. On a positive note, our review of diversity training suggests that, given appropriate attention to needs assessment and transfer issues, skill-based training can change employee behavior. On a more negative note, our review revealed little research-based guidance about the particular skills that organizations should focus on in diversity training. Conflict management and communication skills are often mentioned as components of diversity competence (Holvino *et al.*, 2004; Kochan *et al.*, 2003). Yet we have seen no studies that assess behavioral change, intergroup attitudes, or the quality of intergroup interactions resulting from training on these skills. Recent work designed to identify the behavioral competencies involved in effective diversity management (Chrobot-Mason, 2004) is addressing an important gap by specifying which skills should be the focus of training. In the training literature, task or competency analysis is a crucial part of the needs assessment phase, used to identify *what* needs to be trained (Salas *et al.*, 1999). Diversity training research seems to have ignored this critical step. Even with effective skill training, there are challenges for the organization. The organization has to ensure that those who need the training receive it – this may mean sponsoring a mandatory training program rather than a voluntary one (Kulik *et al.*, 2007). And the organization has to ensure that the skills acquired through training receive ongoing support on the job (Mager and Pipe, 1984; Roberson *et al.*, in press; Rouiller and Goldstein, 1993).

Finally, being able to interact effectively with colleagues may not be enough to retain diversity in the organization. Employees need access to advancement and promotion opportunities (Hom and Griffeth, 1995). Diverse employees also need to become part of an extended network that embeds them within the organizational social context (Lee *et al.*, 2004; Mitchell *et al.*, 2001). These networks should include both similar and dissimilar others, because these different types of ties are differentially effective in providing socioemotional support and instrumental career outcomes (Ibarra, 1992; Thomas and Gabarro, 1999). For women and people of color, employee network groups seem an effective way for strengthening ties with similar others, while mentoring programs are more likely to increase dissimilar ties. Challenges here include developing a mentoring program that will create a satisfying relationship among the parties, and will deliver in terms of advancement and promotion. Research to date is helpful only in specifying how to achieve the first objective, as there is little research on hard outcomes of formal mentoring for women and people of color.

The supervisor as diversity manager

Our review highlights the critical role of the front-line supervisor in ensuring that organizational goals for diversity initiatives are achieved. Kramar (1998) explains that diversity management initiatives operate at three distinct levels: The strategic level encompasses the culture of the organization and the managerial level includes the specific organizational policies and programs that are developed. The operational level is the level at which those policies are implemented, and most barriers to diversity management are found here. A supervisor's diversity missteps can potentially lead to discrimination, inconsistency, or abuse of the diversity policies introduced by top management or the human resources department (Bond and Wise, 2003; Earnshaw, Marchington, and Goodman, 2000; Renwick, 2003). The newly-hired job applicant's expectations about the value of diversity will be tested in the organizational context (McKay and Avery, 2005), and particularly in the relationship with the immediate superior. The supervisor plays a critical role in recognizing and rewarding employee diversity skills when they are displayed on the job (Roberson *et al.*, in press). The supervisor is one of the most likely sources of on-the-job mentoring, development, and sponsorship (Ragins and McFarlin, 1990; Scandura and Williams, 2004; Thomas and Gabarro, 1999). All of these factors emphasize the need for diversity initiatives to be particularly sensitive to the supervisor's role in developing and retaining a diverse workforce. Not every supervisor is prepared to effectively manage a diverse work-group. Supervisors may need extra attention or training to develop the skills they need to nurture and support diversity in their day-to-day management (Thomas and Gabarro, 1999). They need to understand that diversity is an important, non-discretionary part of their role (Giscombe and Mattis, 2002; Kilian *et al.*, 2005).

One way to help supervisors take greater responsibility for diversity outcomes might be to link diversity outcomes to their compensation or bonuses (Giscombe and Mattis, 2002). Merrill Lynch, for example, recently began basing part of its branch managers' compensation directly on their success in hiring and developing female and minority brokers (Juan, 2006). Companies are starting to use measurement tools such as 360-degree feedback, peer reviews, and employee attitude surveys to assess how well supervisors and managers are enacting diversity strategies (Giscombe and Mattis, 2002). However, this practice is still in its infancy – only 12% of human resource professionals report that their organizations use this practice (Esen, 2005). And because no academic research has assessed their impact, the academic literature can offer little advice to organizations about the types of accountability practices that might be most beneficial to a diversity initiative.

Organizational influences on diversity initiative choices

Figure 8.1 suggests that organizations may not tackle all three diversity initiatives simultaneously. Instead, organizations may identify the particular diversity problems they are facing and select a diversity initiative that specifically targets those problems. The front-and-center diversity problems an organization is experiencing, and the tactics the organization chooses to address these, may both derive from the organization's perspective on workforce diversity: the normative beliefs and expectations about cultural diversity and its role in the organization (Ely and Thomas, 2001; Thomas and Gabarro, 1999).

Thomas and Ely (1996) identified three distinct diversity perspectives. The discrimination-and-fairness perspective focuses an organization's attention on providing equal opportunities in hiring and promotion, suppressing prejudicial attitudes, and eliminating discrimination in its practices. It is associated with "policing" or "advocacy" behaviors, where the organization consciously dismantles hurdles that might be constraining its ability to attract a diverse workforce. Once in the organization, however, diverse hires are expected to assimilate into the dominant organizational culture. An access-and-legitimacy perspective is based on an organization's recognition that its markets and customers are diverse. Therefore, it is beneficial for the organization to match that diversity with diversity in its workforce. Organizations adopting this perspective increase diversity, but only at the margins, where diverse employees have contact with the corresponding customer markets. The integration-and-learning perspective suggests that the insights, skills, and experiences employees acquire due to their group identity membership are valuable resources that the organization can use to rethink its primary tasks and redefine its business practices in ways that will advance its mission. However, in order for these changes to take place, diversity cannot be confined to a single product or market; there has to be opportunity for diverse employees to influence one another and impact the organization as a whole.

Ely and Thomas (2001) demonstrated that organizations adopting these different perspectives tend to experience different types of diversity-related challenges. The discrimination-and-fairness organization they studied attracted diverse employees but was unable to provide the kind of quality experience that would retain them. The access-and-legitimacy organization had essentially created a two-tiered, segregated system in which some units (reflecting the dominant culture) received better treatment and higher status than others (reflecting the non-dominant culture). This organization experienced ongoing resentment and competition among the units. The learning-and-effectiveness organization experienced frequent conflict resulting from the different points of view brought by members of different identity groups. The organization saw these conflicts as inevitable, recognizing that diversity would periodically challenge members to effectively use their own and others' cross-cultural knowledge to work together effectively.

Any of these diversity problem sets can motivate an organization to take action, but the specific tactics that an organization chooses to address its diversity challenges will also reflect its diversity perspective. For example, Thomas and Gabarro (1999) described the diversity strategy adopted by an organization with assimilation goals characteristic of the discrimination-and-fairness paradigm. In this organization, the diversity initiative began with a focus on hiring and affirmative action. Later activities included diversity education programs, active mentoring of minority managers by executives, and the use of monitoring systems to track the organization's progress in promoting minorities. However, homogeneous employee network groups were antithetical to the organization's "color blind" perspective, and this type of program never became part of the organization's overall diversity agenda. In contrast, in an organization characterized by a more pluralistic perspective that valued differences and multiple identities, employee network groups based on identity group membership emerged as an important component of their diversity initiative.

Therefore, an organization's diversity perspective predicts the kinds of diversity challenges it is likely to experience – and the activities it initially adopts to address them. What distinguishes the *long-run* success of an organization's diversity initiative is the organization's ability to expand its repertoire of diversity programs beyond those immediately suggested by its underlying diversity perspective. Thomas and Gabarro (1999) found that, regardless of their underlying diversity perspective and their entry-point diversity strategies, all of the organizations they studied were eventually successful in increasing organizational diversity and maintaining organizational performance. Over time, each organization moved from an initially narrow focus on diversity at organizational entry (e.g., affirmative action and other targeted recruitment strategies) to a broader focus on diversity education and employee development. Similarly, our developing model in Figure 8.1 emphasizes that any one of these diversity initiatives needs to be supported and complemented by the other two. An organization that focuses only on employee attraction may find itself caught in a continuous cycle of diversity hiring. An organization that emphasizes diversity training but not recruitment or development risks having employees question its real commitment to diversity. However, an organization that focuses on cyclical efforts associated with employee attraction, skill development, and advancement and retention will eventually be able to reduce its diversity recruitment efforts as the organization acquires a diversity-sensitive reputation in the marketplace.

Sustaining diversity change through prejudice reduction

One of the biggest challenges for an organization is establishing that self-sustaining diversity cycle, where the diversity management skills of individual employees are sufficiently high that their aggregated daily behavior creates a supportive diversity culture that simultaneously retains existing diversity and attracts diverse job applicants. In this chapter, we focused primarily on the formal organizational initiatives (diversity recruitment, diversity training, formal mentoring) that can contribute to this cycle. However, an assumption guiding many diversity efforts seems to be that a diversity initiative will be more effective, and its results more sustainable, if it is accompanied by a reduction in employees' prejudicial attitudes and their use of stereotypes. The diversity literature places a heavy emphasis on reducing the use of stereotypes, yet our review does not indicate that reduction in stereotype use will be an immediate outcome of any of the three diversity strategies.

The primary vehicle for reduction in stereotype use in organizations has been diversity awareness training (e.g., Bendick *et al.*, 2001), but as we reviewed earlier, there is little theoretical or empirical evidence that such training reduces stereotype usage. In the social psychology literature, research has shown that people who are motivated to avoid prejudice can be successful in monitoring and controlling their use of stereotypes. People with goals to avoid prejudice experience guilt and negative affect when they find themselves reacting to others on the basis of stereotypes, as such behavior is inconsistent with their goals (Monteith, 1993). This research suggests that if people regularly practice detecting and rejecting stereotypes, eventually they will no longer activate and use stereotypes automatically (Monteith, Sherman, and Devine, 1998; Moskowitz, 2005).

Because people who are motivated to avoid prejudice are already aware of their stereotypes, training to increase awareness of bias is not necessary and not likely to be beneficial. These individuals might benefit from self-regulation training instead (Brief and Barsky, 2000). Self-regulation training is designed to improve skills in monitoring and controlling stereotype use. This kind of training would not involve imparting knowledge of cognitive processing biases, as is typically done in awareness training. Instead, it would refine the skills associated with self-observation, administration of self-rewards, anticipation of difficulties in behavior change, and development of strategies for over-coming difficulties. Overall, self-regulation training is designed to increase the trainee's self-efficacy and skill for successfully controlling stereotypes (Brief and Barsky, 2000).

If individuals are not internally motivated to avoid prejudice and the use of stereotypes, interventions could be designed to increase their motivation. Motivation to avoid prejudice can result from external sources such as social disapproval (Crosby, Bromley, and Saxe, 1980; Lowery, Hardin, and Sinclair, 2001). In organizational contexts, norms and accountability systems can also increase the motivation to avoid prejudice (Kunda and Spencer, 2003; Perry, Davis-Blake, and Kulik, 1994). Accordingly, Brief and Barsky (2000) recommended that for employees not internally motivated to avoid prejudice, pro-grams to reduce the use of stereotypes should define bias unambigu-ously, create strong organizational norms against bias, and establish clear rules for avoiding bias in human resource policies and proce-dures. These tactics should be supported by an accountability system that systematically rewards unbiased behavior and punishes bias. Many diversity strategies do include such features (Esen, 2005; GAO, 2005).

A different approach to changing attitudes and reducing stereotype use comes from the contact hypothesis (Allport, 1954), which specifies that intergroup contact reduces prejudice and stereotype use when four conditions are met: members of different groups have equal status; they share common goals; they are encouraged to cooperate rather than compete; and intergroup interaction is supported by higher authorities. Some scholars have argued that the typical organizational context rarely delivers these conditions (Brief and Barsky, 2000; Devine and Vasquez, 1998). For example, demographic group membership is often disproportionately distributed across the organizational hierarchy (so equal status is not achieved) and organizational settings frequently require employees to compete for scarce resources (so intergroup cooperation is neither encouraged nor rewarded). However, recent work suggests that these four conditions, while facilitating prejudice reduction, need not be strictly met for intergroup contact to have positive effects (Pettigrew and Tropp, 2005). Research has also proposed underlying mechanisms through which contact results in attitude change (Dovidio, Gaertner, and Kawakami, 2003). The common ingroup identity model (Gaertner and Dovidio, 2000) states that cooperative intergroup contact changes attitudes by facilitating recategorization, so that members of different groups come to view themselves as members of a single more inclusive group. Then, all members benefit from being categorized as part of the ingroup. Pettigrew and Tropp (2005) suggests that emotion is a key mediator of the effect of intergroup contact on attitudes. Cooperative intergroup contact changes attitudes because it increases positive affect toward different others and decreases negative affect and anxiety (Dovidio *et al.*, 2003).

One way to assess the potential effectiveness of diversity programs is to ask how likely they are to reduce employees' stereotype use and change employee attitudes. The psychological research on prejudice reduction suggests that diversity activities and programs that encourage cooperative intergroup contact should be most successful in reducing prejudice and stereotypes. From this perspective, diversity awareness training would not be expected to be effective; training groups are typically assembled for only a brief period and may not involve trainee interaction toward a common goal. Our review bears out this prediction: Awareness training is largely ineffective in reducing stereotypes and changing behavior (e.g., Sanchez and Medkik, 2004). The source of the problem may not be awareness training per se, but unrealistic expectations about what training can accomplish. Chrobot-Mason and Quinones (2001) proposed a progressive multi-stage model of diversity competence based on the multicultural literature. In this model, employee awareness precedes the learning of diversity skill behavior. According to this theoretical perspective, a more immediate and realistic objective of awareness training efforts might be employee readiness for skills training. Unfortunately, diversity training is rarely delivered as a multi-step progression. More than ten years ago, Rynes and Rosen (1995: 257) found that the "vast majority" of diversity training programs lasted a day or less, and today's trainers continue to express concern about what can be delivered in a stand-alone half-day workshop (Blyth, 2006).

Group mentoring programs may be better candidates for reducing stereotype use than awareness training because these programs create more ongoing opportunities for cooperation among members of diverse groups. Diversity councils (diverse employee groups that continuously monitor an organization's diversity challenges and climate and recommend corrective actions) may serve a similar purpose. Because council members have to cooperate to diffuse and support diversity initiatives throughout the organization (GAO, 2005; Jayne and Dipboye, 2004), diversity councils may encourage diverse individuals to recategorize themselves as members of the same team/council, reducing stereotype use.

The emerging research agenda

In our review of research relevant to diversity recruitment, diversity training, and mentoring programs, we have identified a number of "gaps" where research fails to address the most pressing questions associated with diversity initiatives. At this point in the chapter, we present a "wish list" to diversity researchers and hope that these gaps will soon be filled by academic researchers interested in diversity issues.

We need research that examines the impact of different recruiting practices (e.g., pictures of diverse employees or explicit diversity statements in recruiting materials) on the long-term behavior of actual job applicants. The experimental methods and student samples used in the recruiting literature suggest that recruiting variations impact organizational attractiveness, but we have yet to see evidence that these recruiting variations result in a greater "yield" of diverse applicants. In particular, we advocate research that demonstrates the utility of presenting diversity messages in attracting qualified diverse applicants relative to other types of messages (e.g., messages that communicate financial rewards or training opportunities) typically contained in recruiting materials. We also advocate research that goes beyond simple demographics as predictors of applicant reactions to diversity recruiting. Each applicant is a member of multiple identity groups simultaneously, and each applicant may be described using objective demographic categories and more subjectively-experienced individual differences (e.g., ethnic identity, social dominance orientation). We know little about how these individual differences interact with one another to impact an applicant's reactions to an organization's recruiting effort.

We need research that directly examines the effectiveness of skill-based diversity training using rigorous designs that make use of random assignment to training conditions and non-trained control groups. Ideally, this research would examine not only the impact of providing skill-based training, but would compare-and-contrast the effectiveness of training programs based on different academic theories (e.g., self-efficacy models, the theory of planned behavior). In particular, this research needs to go beyond immediate learning as an indicator of training success and begin to examine transfer of training to on-the-job behavior. Research should also explore interventions based on the psychological literature on prejudice reduction as alternatives to diversity awareness training. These alternative interventions may not involve training at all, focusing instead on efforts that restructure organizational networks to put members of different identity groups together for a common cooperative purpose (e.g., diversity councils, group mentoring programs). Diversity interventions that involve inter-group contact warrant greater research attention. As a result of changes in prejudice, group mentoring programs and diversity councils should diminish the homophily commonly seen in workplace relationship networks. Indeed, a measure of relationship diversity (tie heterophily) might be more informative as an indicator of diversity program success than the typical focus on the numbers of women and minorities moving in and out of an organization.

We need research that examines the outcomes of mentoring programs for members of different identity groups. This research needs to link mentoring program participation with "hard" outcomes including pay, promotion, and retention rates. Research should also compare the impact of mentors with the impact of other developmental relationships (including participation in network groups, informal peer relationships, and the relationship with the immediate supervisor).

Finally, we need organizational-level research that examines the where, when, and why behind organizational diversity efforts. We need more evidence about organizational decision making as managers develop diversity priorities and allocate budgets to diversity programs. We need to understand how organizational culture and diversity perspective affect an organization's choice of interventions and the success of those interventions. And, eventually, we need to see how these diversity initiatives unfold over time to result in a broadening or a narrowing of the organization's diversity agenda, with concomitant effects on outcomes.

Full circle: Back to the business case

We opened this chapter with a discussion of the "business case" for diversity (Cox and Blake, 1991; Johnston and Packer, 1987; Robinson and Dechant, 1997) and it is fitting that we return to it at the chapter's end. The business case promised managers that a diverse workforce would deliver a wide range of outcomes that ultimately benefited the organization's bottom line. Diversity researchers have been issued a challenge to deliver information on the best way to manage organizational diversity to achieve those outcomes.

Is diversity research meeting that challenge? Our review of the academic literature on three common diversity initiatives suggests that they can deliver several mid-range outcomes: applicant attraction, employee skill development, and employee advancement and retention. Our research is yielding information on how best to use these initiatives to achieve these focused outcomes. But this research does not address the basic question underlying the business case: what diversity management strategies will best leverage diversity to achieve bottom-line benefits on organizational productivity and effectiveness? Although we argue above for more specific research on each initiative – recruiting, training, and mentoring – research efforts focused on individual programs *alone* are unlikely to answer the broader question associated with the business case. The diversity research literature is becoming increasingly "siloed" with some researchers studying diversity recruitment, some researchers studying diversity training, and still others studying mentoring or network groups. While this specialized approach yields detailed information on each initiative, in practice, organizations tend to "bundle" these initiatives into a larger diversity strategy. Research on HR systems suggests that consistency among a strategy's component programs is critical (Becker *et al.*, 1997) – a diversity strategy may overall convey a stronger, weaker, or just plain different message than that communicated by the individual components. And the organizational context may have additional, but untested, effects on the diversity message (Johns, 2006). Ely and Thomas (2001) argue that only the learning-and-effectiveness diversity perspective achieves the long-term benefits of diversity, but Thomas and Gabarro (1999) have argued for equifinality, believing that it is the alignment of diversity initiatives with organizational culture and values that determines the strategy's overall success and sustainability.

Diversity research to date says little about the effects of diversity initiatives in combination or in context, but it is the study of these effects – in combination *and* in context – that will address the business case challenge.

References

Adler, N. (1986). *International Dimensions of Organizational Behavior*. Boston: Kent.

Allen, T.D., Eby, L.T., and Lentz, E. (2006). The relationship between formal mentoring program characteristics and perceived program effectiveness. *Personnel Psychology, 39*, 125–153.

Allport, G.W. (1954). *The Nature of Prejudice*. Cambridge: Addison-Wesley.

Anonymous (2004). Wanted: More and better HR metrics and benchmarks. *HR Focus, 81*(4), 8.

Arredondo, P. (1996). *Successful Diversity Management Initiatives: A Blueprint for Planning and Implementation*. Thousand Oaks: Sage.

Avery, D.R. (2003). Reactions to diversity in recruitment advertising: Are differences Black and White? *Journal of Applied Psychology, 88*, 672–679.

Avery, D.R., Hernandez, M., and Hebl, M.R. (2004). Who's watching the race? Racial salience in recruitment advertising. *Journal of Applied Social Psychology, 34*, 146–161.

Avery, D.R., and McKay, P.F. (2006). Target practice: An organizational impression management approach to attracting minority and female job applicants. *Personnel Psychology, 59*, 157–187.

Azjen, I. (1991). The theory of planned behavior. *Organizational Behavior and Human Decision Processes, 50*, 179–211.

Babcock, P. (2006). Detecting hidden bias. *HR Magazine, 51*(2), 50–55.

Backhaus, K.B., Stone, B.A., and Heiner, K. (2002). Exploring the relationship between corporate social performance and employer attractiveness. *Business and Society, 41*, 292–318.

Becker, B.E., Huselid, M.A., Pickus, P.S., and Spratt, M.F. (1997). HR as a source of shareholder value: Research and recommendations. *Human Resource Management, 36*, 39–48.

Bendick, M., Egan, M.L., and Lofhjelm, S.M. (2001). Workforce diversity training: From anti-discrimination compliance to organizational development. *Human Resource Planning, 24*, 10–25.

Blake-Beard, S.D. (2001). Taking a hard look at formal mentoring programs: A consideration of potential challenges facing women. *Journal of Management Development, 20*, 331–345.

Blyth, A. (2006). Compassion or compliance? *Personnel Today*, January 17, 20–22.

Bobo, L. (1998). Race, interests, and beliefs about affirmative action: Unanswered questions and new directions. *American Behavioral Scientist*, *41*, 985–1003.

Bobo, L., and Kluegel, J. R. (1993). Opposition to race-targeting: Self-interest, stratification ideology, or racial attitudes? *American Sociological Review*, *58*, 443–464.

Bond, S., and Wise, S. (2003). Family leave policies and devolution to the line. *Personnel Review*, *32*(1), 58–72.

Bowen, W. G., and Bok, D. (1998). *The Shape of the River: Long-term Consequences of Considering Race in College and University Admissions*. Princeton: Princeton University Press.

Brief, A. P., and Barsky, A. (2000). Establishing a climate for diversity: The inhibition of prejudiced reactions in the workplace. *Research in Personnel and Human Resource Management*, *19*, 91–129.

Carter, S. L. (1991). *Reflections of an Affirmative Action Baby*. New York: Basic Books.

Chao, G. T., Walz, P.M., and Gardner, P.D. (1992). Formal and informal mentorships: A comparison on mentoring functions and contrast with nonmentored counterparts. *Personnel Psychology*, *45*, 619–636.

Chen, C. C., and DiTomaso, N. (1996). Performance appraisal and demographic diversity: Issues regarding appraisals, appraisers, and appraising. In E. E. Kossek and S. A. Lobel (eds.), *Managing Diversity: Human Resource Strategies for Transforming the Workplace* (pp. 137–163). Cambridge, MA: Blackwell.

Chrobot-Mason, D. (2004). Managing racial differences: The role of majority managers' ethnic identity development on minority employee perceptions of support. *Group and Organization Management*, *29*, 5–31.

Chrobot-Mason, D., and Quinones, M. A. (2001). Training for a diverse workplace. In K. Kraiger (ed.), *Creating, Implementing, and Managing Effective Training and Development* (pp. 117–159). San Francisco: Jossey-Bass.

Colquitt, J. A., LePine, J. A., and Noe, R. A. (2000). Toward an integrative theory of training motivation: A meta-analytic path analysis of 20 years of research. *Journal of Applied Psychology*, *85*, 678–707.

Combs, G. M. (2002). Meeting the leadership challenge of a diverse and pluralistic workplace: Implications of self efficacy for diversity training. *Journal of Leadership and Organizational Studies*, *8*, 1–16.

Cox, T. H. Jr. (1994). *Cultural Diversity in Organizations: Theory, Research, and Practice*. San Francisco: Berrett-Kohler.

Cox, T. H. Jr., and Beale, R.L. (1997). *Developing Competency to Manage Diversity: Readings, Cases, and Activities*. San Francisco: Berrett-Kohler.

Cox, T. H. Jr., and Blake, S. (1991). Managing cultural diversity: Implications for organizational competitiveness. *Academy of Management Executive*, 5(3), 45–56.

Cropanzano, R., Slaughter, J. E., and Bachiochi, P. D. (2005). Organizational justice and Black applicants' reactions to affirmative action. *Journal of Applied Psychology*, 90, 1168–1184.

Crosby, F. J. (2004). *Affirmative Action Is Dead; Long Live Affirmative Action*. New Haven, CT: Yale University Press.

Crosby, F. J., Bromley, S., and Saxe, L. (1980). Recent unobtrusive studies of Black and White discrimination and prejudice: A literature review. *Psychological Bulletin*, 87, 546–563.

Crosby, F. J., Iyer, A., and Sincharoen, S. (2006). Understanding affirmative action. *Annual Review of Psychology*, 57, 585–611.

Devine, P. G., Monteith, M. J., Zuwerink, J. R., and Elliot, A. J. (1991). Prejudice with and without compunction. *Journal of Personality and Social Psychology*, 60, 817–830.

Devine, P. G., and Vasquez, K. A. (1998). The rocky road to positive intergroup relations. In J. L. Eberhardt and S. T. Fiske (eds.), *Confronting Racism: The Problem and the Response* (pp. 234–262). Thousand Oaks: Sage.

Diamante, T., Reid, C. L., and Giglio, L. (1995). Make the right training move. *HR Magazine*, 40(3), 60–65.

Douglas, C. A., and McCauley, C. D. (1999). Formal developmental relationships: A survey of organizational practices. *Human Resource Development Quarterly*, 10, 203–224.

Dovidio, J. F., Gaertner, S. L., and Kawakami, K. (2003). Intergroup contact: The past, present, and the future. *Group Processes and Intergroup Relations*, 6, 5–21.

Dovidio, J. F., and Hebl, M. R. (2005). Discrimination at the level of the individual: Cognitive and affective factors. In R. L. Dipboye and A. Colella (eds.), *Discrimination at Work: The Psychological and Organizational Bases* (pp. 11–36). Mahwah: Erlbaum Associates.

Dreher, G. F., and Cox, T. H. (1996). Race, gender, and opportunity: A study of compensation attainment and the establishment of mentoring relationships. *Journal of Applied Psychology*, 81, 297–308.

Dunham, K. J. (2003). The Jungle. *Wall Street Journal*, November 25, B8.

Earnshaw, J., Marchington, M., and Goodman, J. (2000). Unfair to whom? Discipline and dismissal in small establishments. *Industrial Relations Journal*, 31(1), 62–73.

Eby, L. T., and Lockwood, A. (2005). Proteges' and mentors' reactions to participating in formal mentoring programs: A qualitative investigation. *Journal of Vocational Behavior, 67,* 441–458.

Egodigwe, L. (2005). Back to class. *Wall Street Journal,* November 14, R4.

Ehrhart, K. H., and Ziegert, J. C. (2005). Why are individuals attracted to organizations? *Journal of Management, 31,* 901–919.

Ellis, C., and Sonnenfeld, J. A. (1994). Diverse approaches to managing diversity. *Human Resource Management, 33,* 79–109.

Ely, R. J., and Thomas, D. A. (2001). Cultural diversity at work: The effects of diversity perspectives on work group processes and outcomes. *Administrative Science Quarterly, 46,* 229–273.

Esen, E. (2005). *2005 Workplace Diversity Practices Survey Report.* Alexandria, VA: Society for Human Resource Management.

Fagenson-Eland, E. A., Marks, M. A., and Amendola, K. L. (1997). Perceptions of mentoring relationships. *Journal of Vocational Behavior, 51,* 29–42.

Feldman, D. C. (1989). Socialization, re-socialization, and training: Framing the research agenda. In I. L. Goldstein *et al.* (eds.), *Training and Development in Organizations* (pp. 376–416). San Francisco: Jossey-Bass.

Fiske, S. T. (2002). What we know now about bias and intergroup conflict, the problem of the century. *Current Directions in Psychological Science, 11,* 123–128.

Ford, J. K., and Fisher, S. (1996). The role of training in a changing workplace and workforce: New perspectives and approaches. In E. E. Kossek and S. A. Lobel (eds.), *Managing Diversity: Human Resource Strategies for Transforming the Workplace* (pp. 164–193). Cambridge: Blackwell.

Freeman, C. (2003). Recruiting for diversity. *Women in Management Review, 18,* 68–76.

Friedman, R. A. (1996). Defining the scope and logic of minority and female network groups: Can separation enhance integration? *Research in Personnel and Human Resources Management, 14,* 307–349.

Friedman, R. A., and Craig, K. M. (2004). Predicting joining and participating in minority employee network groups. *Industrial Relations, 43,* 793–816.

Friedman, R. A., and Holtom, B. (2002). The effects of network groups on minority employee turnover intentions. *Human Resource Management, 41,* 405–421.

Friedman, R. A., Kane, M., and Cornfield, D. B. (1998). Social support and career optimism: Examining the effectiveness of network groups among Black managers. *Human Relations, 51,* 1155–1177.

Gaertner, S. L., and Dovidio, J. F. (2000). *Reducing Intergroup Bias: The Common Ingroup Identity Model.* Philadelphia: Taylor & Francis.

Gentile, M. C. (1996). Managerial effectiveness and diversity: Organizational choices. In M. C. Gentile (ed.), *Managerial Excellence through Diversity* (pp. 225–256). Chicago: Irwin.

Giscombe, K., and Mattis, M. C. (2002). Leveling the playing field for women of color in corporate management: Is the business case enough? *Journal of Business Ethics, 37*, 103–119.

Gochman, I. R. (1989). Two ways to cope with tomorrow's diversity. *The Personnel Administrator, 34*(11), 120–121.

Goldberg, C. B. (2003). Applicant reactions to the employment interview: A look at demographic similarity and social identity theory. *Journal of Business Research, 56*, 561–571.

Good, C., Aronson, J., and Inzlicht, M. (2003). Improving adolescents' standardized test performance: An intervention to reduce the effects of stereotype threat. *Journal of Applied Developmental Psychology, 24*, 645–662.

Government Accountability Office (2005). *Diversity Management: Expert Identified Leading Principles and Agency Examples*. Washington, DC: US Government Accountability Office.

Grossman, R. J. (2000). Is diversity working? *HR Magazine, 45*(3), 46–50.

Hanover, J. M., and Cellar, D. F. (1998). Environmental factors and the effectiveness of workforce diversity training. *Human Resource Development Quarterly, 9*, 105–124.

Hansen, F. (2003). Diversity's business case: Doesn't add up. *Workforce, 82*(4): 28–32.

Hayes, E. (1999). Winning at diversity. *Executive Excellence, 16*(5), 9.

Hegstad, C. D., and Wentling, R. M. (2004). The development and maintenance of exemplary formal mentoring programs in Fortune 500 companies. *Human Resource Development Quarterly, 15*, 421–448.

Heilman, M. E., Block, C. J., and Lucas, J. A. (1992). Presumed incompetent? Stigmatization and affirmative action efforts. *Journal of Applied Psychology, 77*, 536–544.

Heilman, M. E., Block, C. J., and Stathatos, P. (1997). The affirmative action stigma of incompetence: Effects of performance information. *Academy of Management Journal, 40*, 603–625.

Helms, J. E. (1990). *Black and White Racial Identity*. New York: Greenwood.

Higgins, M. C., and Kram, K. E. (2001). Reconceptualizing mentoring at work: A developmental network perspective. *Academy of Management Review, 26*, 264–288.

Highhouse, S., Stierwalt, S. L., Bachiochi, P., Elder, A. E., and Fisher, G. (1999). Effects of advertised human resource management practices on attraction of African American applicants. *Personnel Psychology, 52*, 425–442.

Holvino, E., Ferdman, B. M., and Merrill-Sands, D. (2004). Creating and sustaining diversity and inclusion in organizations: Strategies and approaches. In M. S. Stockdale and F. J. Crosby (eds.), *The Psychology and Management of Workplace Diversity* (pp. 245–276). Malden, MA: Blackwell.

Hom, P. W., and Griffeth, R. W. (1995). *Employee Turnover.* Cincinnati: South-Western.

Hom, P. W., Griffeth, R. W., Palich, L. E., and Bracker, J. S. (1998). An exploratory investigation into theoretical mechanisms underlying realistic job previews. *Personnel Psychology, 51,* 421–451.

Hom, P. W., Roberson, L., and Ellis, A. (In press). Challenging conventional wisdom about who quits. *Journal of Applied Psychology.*

Hoobler, J. M. (2005). Lip service to multiculturalism: Docile bodies of the modern organization. *Journal of Management Inquiry, 14,* 49–56.

Ibarra, H. (1992). Homophily and differential returns: Sex differences in network structure and access in an advertising firm. *Administrative Science Quarterly, 37,* 422–447.

Ibarra, H. (1993). Personal networks of women and minorities in management: A conceptual framework. *Academy of Management Review, 18,* 56–87.

Ibarra, H. (1995). Race, opportunity, and diversity of social circles in managerial networks. *Academy of Management Journal, 18,* 673–703.

Inzlicht, M., and Ben Zeev, T. (2003). Do high-achieving female students underperform in private? The implications of threatening environments on intellectual processing. *Journal of Educational Psychology, 95,* 796–805.

Jackson, S. E., Brett, J. F., Sessa, V. I., Cooper, D. M., Julin, J. A., and Peyronnin, K. (1991). Some differences make a difference: Individual dissimilarity and group heterogeneity as correlates of recruitment, promotions, and turnover. *Journal of Applied Psychology, 76,* 675–689.

Jayne, M. E. A., and Dipboye, R. L. (2004). Leveraging diversity to improve business performance: Research findings and recommendations for organizations. *Human Resource Management, 43,* 409–424.

Jehn, K. A., Northcraft, G. B., and Neale, M. A. (1999). Why differences make a difference: A field study of diversity, conflict, and performance in workgroups. *Administrative Science Quarterly, 44,* 741–763.

Johns, G. (2006). The essential impact of context on organizational behavior. *Academy of Management Journal, 31,* 386–408.

Johnston, W., and Packer, A. (1987). *Workforce 2000: Work and Workers for the Twenty-first Century.* Indianapolis: Hudson Institute.

Juan, E. (2006). Merrill to include office diversity in criteria to base managers' pay. *Wall Street Journal,* February 15, 1.

Kidder, D. L., Lankau, M. J., Chrobot-Mason, D., Mollica, K. A., and Friedman, R. A. (2004). Backlash toward diversity initiatives: Examining the impact of diversity program justification, personal and group outcomes. *International Journal of Conflict Management, 15,* 77–102.

Kilian, C. M., Hukai, D., and McCarty, C. E. (2005). Building diversity in the pipeline to corporate leadership. *Journal of Management Development,* 24(2), 155–168.

Kim, S. S., and Gelfand, M. J. (2003). The influence of ethnic identity on perceptions of organizational recruitment. *Journal of Vocational Behavior, 63,* 396–416.

Kirnan, J. P., Farley, J. A., and Geisinger, K. F. (1989). The relationship between recruiting source, applicant quality, and hire performance: An analysis by sex, ethnicity, and age. *Personnel Psychology, 42,* 293–308.

Kochan, T., Bezrukova, K., Ely, R., Jackson, S., Joshi, A., Jehn, K., Leonard, J., Levine, D., and Thomas, D. (2003). The effects of diversity on business performance: Report of the Diversity Research Network. *Human Resource Management, 42,* 3–21.

Konrad, A. M. (2003). Defining the domain of workplace diversity scholarship. *Group and Organization Management, 28,* 4–17.

Konrad, A. M., and Linnehan, F. (1995). Formalized HRM structures: Coordinating equal employment opportunity or concealing organizational practices? *Academy of Management Journal, 38,* 787–820.

Koonce, R. (2001). Redefining diversity. *T + D, 55*(12), 22–33.

Kramar, R. (1998). Managing diversity: Beyond affirmative action in Australia. *Women in Management Review, 13*(4), 133–142.

Kravitz, D. A. (1995). Attitudes toward affirmative action plans directed at Blacks: Effects of plan and individual differences. *Journal of Applied Social Psychology, 24,* 2192–2220.

Kravitz, D. A., and Platania, J. (1993). Attitudes and beliefs about affirmative action: Effects of target and of respondent sex and ethnicity. *Journal of Applied Psychology, 78,* 928–938.

Kristof, A. L. (1996). Person-organization fit: An integrative review of its conceptualizations, measurement, and implications. *Personnel Psychology, 49,* 1–49.

Kulik, C. T. (2004). *Human Resources for the non-HR manager.* Mahwah: Erlbaum Associates.

Kulik, C. T., Pepper, M. B., Roberson, L., and Parker, S. (2007). The rich get richer: Predicting participation in voluntary diversity training. *Journal of Organizational Behavior, 28,* 753–769.

Kunda, Z., and Spencer, S. J. (2003). When do stereotypes come to mind and when do they color judgment? A goal-based theoretical framework for stereotype activation and application. *Psychological Bulletin, 129,* 522–544.

Langevoort, D. C. (2004). Overcoming resistance to diversity in the executive suite: Grease, grit, and the corporate promotion tournament. *Washington and Lee Law Review, 61,* 1615–1643.

Lankau, M. J., Riordan, C. M., and Thomas, C. H. (2005). The effects of similarity and liking in formal relationships between mentors and protégés. *Journal of Vocational Behavior, 67,* 252–265.

Larkin Ford, R. (2004). Needs assessment helps ensure effective diversity training. *Public Relations Tactics, 11*(7), 6.

Lee, T. W., Mitchell, T. R., Sablynski, C. J., Burton, J. P., and Holtom, B. C. (2004). The effects of job embeddedness on organizational citizenship, job performance, volitional absences, and voluntary turnover. *Academy of Management Journal, 47,* 711–722.

Louis, M. R., Posner, B. Z., and Powell, G. N. (1983). The availability and helpfulness of socialization practices. *Personnel Psychology, 36,* 857–866.

Lowery, B. S., Hardin, C. D., and Sinclair, S. (2001). Social influence effects on automatic racial prejudice. *Journal of Personality and Social Psychology, 81,* 842–855.

Lynch, F. R. (1997). *The Diversity Machine: The Drive to Change the "White Male Workplace."* New York: Free Press.

Lyons, B. D., and Oppler, E. S. (2004). The effects of structural attributes and demographic characteristics on protégé satisfaction in mentoring programs. *Journal of Career Development, 30,* 215–229.

Mager, R. F., and Pipe, P. (1984). *Analyzing Performance Problems: Or You Really Oughta Wanna.* 2nd edn. Belmont: Pittman Learning.

McKay, P. F., and Avery, D. R. (2005). Warning! Diversity recruitment could backfire. *Journal of Management Inquiry, 14,* 330–337.

McNab, S. M., and Johnston, L. (2002). The impact of equal employment opportunity statements in job advertisements on applicants' perceptions of organizations. *Australian Journal of Psychology, 54*(2), 105–109.

Mitchell, T. R., Holtom, B. C., Lee, T. W., Sablynski, C. J., and Erez, M. (2001). Why people stay: Using job embeddedness to predict voluntary turnover. *Academy of Management Journal, 44,* 1102–1121.

Molloy, J. C. (2005). Development networks: Literature review and future research. *Career Development International, 10,* 536–547.

Monteith, M. J. (1993). Self-regulation of prejudiced responses: Implications for progress in prejudice reduction efforts. *Journal of Personality and Social Psychology, 65,* 469–485.

Monteith, M. J., Sherman, J. W., and Devine, P. G. (1998). Suppression as a stereotype control strategy. *Personality and Social Psychology Review, 2,* 63–82.

Moskowitz, G. B. (2005). *Social Cognition: Understanding Self and Others.* New York: Guilford Press.

Nemetz, P. L., and Christensen, S. L. (1996). The challenge of cultural diversity: Harnessing a diversity of views to understand multiculturalism. *Academy of Management Review, 21,* 434–462.

Noe, R. A. (1986). Trainees' attributes and attitudes: Neglected influences on training effectiveness. *Academy of Management Review, 11,* 736–749.

Noe, R. A. (1999). *Employee Training and Development.* Boston: Irwin-McGrawHill.

Noe, R. A., Greenberger, D. B., and Wang, S. (2002). Mentoring: What we know and where we might go. *Research in Personnel and Human Resources Management, 21,* 129–173.

O'Reilly, C. A., Williams, K. Y., and Barsade, S. G. (1998). Group demography and innovation: Does diversity help? In D. Gruenfeld, B. Mannix, and M. Neale (eds.), *Research on Managing Groups and Teams* (pp. 183–207). Stanford: JAI Press.

Perkins, L. A., Thomas, K. M., and Taylor, G. A. (2000). Advertising and recruitment: Marketing to minorities. *Psychology and Marketing, 17,* 235–255.

Perry, E. L., Davis-Blake, A., and Kulik, C. T. (1994). Explaining gender-based selection decisions: A synthesis of contextual and cognitive approaches. *Academy of Management Review, 19,* 786–820.

Pettigrew, T. F., and Tropp, L. R. (2005). Allport's intergroup contact hypothesis: Its history and influence. In J. F. Dovidio, P. Glick, and L. A. Rudman (eds.), *On the Nature of Prejudice: Fifty Years after Allport* (pp. 262–277). Malden: Blackwell.

Pfeffer, J., and Sutton, R. I. (2006). *Hard Facts, Dangerous Half-truths and Total Nonsense: Profiting from Evidence-based Management.* Boston: Harvard Business School Press.

Phillips, J. M. (1998). Effects of realistic job previews on multiple organizational outcomes: A meta-analysis. *Academy of Management Journal, 41,* 673–690.

Phinney, J. S. (1996). Understanding ethnic diversity: The role of ethnic identity. *American Behavioral Scientist, 40*(2), 143–152.

Raabe, B., and Beehr, T. A. (2003). Formal mentoring versus supervisor and coworker relationships: Differences in perceptions and impact. *Journal of Organizational Behavior, 24,* 271–293.

Ragins, B. R. (1997). Diversified mentoring relationships in organizations: A power perspective. *Academy of Management Review, 22,* 482–521.

Ragins, B. R., and Cotton, J. L. (1999). Mentor functions and outcomes: A comparison of men and women in formal and informal mentoring relationships. *Journal of Applied Psychology, 84,* 529–550.

Ragins, B. R., Cotton, J. L., and Miller, J. S. (2000). Marginal mentoring: The effects of type of mentor, quality of relationship, and program design on work and career attitudes. *Academy of Management Journal, 43*, 1177–1194.

Ragins, B. R., and McFarlin, D. B. (1990). Perceptions of mentor roles in cross-gender mentor relationships. *Journal of Vocational Behavior, 37*, 321–340.

Rau, B. L., and Adams, G. A. (2005). Attracting retirees to apply: Desired organizational characteristics of bridge employment. *Journal of Organizational Behavior, 26*, 649–660.

Rau, B. L., and Hyland, M. M. (2003). Corporate teamwork and diversity statements in college recruitment brochures: Effects on attraction. *Journal of Applied Social Psychology, 33*, 2465–2492.

Renwick, D. (2003). Line manager involvement in HRM: An inside view. *Employee Relations, 25*(3), 262–280.

Reskin, B. F., McBrier, D. B., and Kmec, J. A. (1999). The determinants and consequences of workplace sex and race composition. *Annual Review of Sociology, 25*, 335–361.

Roberson, L. (2004). On the relationship between race and turnover. In R. Griffeth and P. Hom (eds.), *Innovative Theory and Empirical Research on Employee Turnover* (pp. 211–229). Greenwich, CT: Information Age Publishing.

Roberson, L., and Block, C. J. (2001). Racioethnicity and job performance: A review and critique of theoretical perspectives on the causes of group differences. *Research in Organizational Behavior, 23*, 247–325.

Roberson, L., Deitch, E., Brief, A. P., and Block, C. J. (2003). Stereotype threat and feedback seeking in the workplace. *Journal of Vocational Behavior, 62*, 176–188.

Roberson, L., and Kulik, C. T. (2007). Stereotype threat at work. *Academy of Management Perspective, 21*, 24–40.

Roberson, L., Kulik, C. T., and Pepper, M. (2001). Designing effective diversity training: Influence of group composition and trainee experience. *Journal of Organizational Behavior, 22*, 871–885.

Roberson, L., Kulik, C. T., and Pepper, M. B. (2003). Using needs assessment to resolve controversies in diversity training design. *Group and Organization Management, 28*, 148–174.

Roberson, l., Kulik, C. T., and Pepper, M. B. (in press). Individual and environmental factors influencing the use of transfer strategies after diversity training. *Group and Organization Management*.

Robinson, G., and Dechant, K. (1997). Building a business case for diversity. *Academy of Management Executive, 11*(3), 21–31.

Rogers, E. M., and Kincaid, D. L. (1981). *Communication Networks.* New York: Free Press.

Rouiller, J. Z., and Goldstein, I. L. (1993). The relationship between organizational transfer climate and positive transfer of training. *Human Resource Development Quarterly, 4,* 377–390.

Rousseau, D. M. (1995). *Psychological Contracts in Organizations: Understanding Written and Unwritten Agreements.* Thousand Oaks: Sage Publications.

Rynes, S. L., and Barber, A. E. (1990). Applicant attraction strategies: An organizational perspective. *Academy of Management Review, 15,* 286–310.

Rynes, S., and Rosen, B. (1995). A field survey of factors affecting the adoption and perceived success of diversity training. *Personnel Psychology, 48,* 247–270.

Salas, E., Cannon-Bowers, J. A., Rhodenizer, L., and Bowers, C. A. (1999). Training in organizations: Myths, misconceptions, and mistaken assumptions. *Research in Personnel and Human Resources Management, 17,* 123–161.

Sanchez, J. I., and Medkik, N. (2004). The effects of diversity awareness training on differential treatment. *Group and Organization Management, 29,* 517–536.

Scandura, T. A., and Williams, E. A. (2004). Mentoring and transformational leadership: The role of supervisory career mentoring. *Journal of Vocational Behavior, 65,* 448–468.

Schmidt, P. (2004). An approach to diversity training in Canada. *Industrial and Commercial Training, 36*(4), 148–152.

Slaughter, J. E., Sinar, E. F., and Bachiochi, P. D. (2002). Black applicants' reactions to affirmative action plans: Effects of plan content and previous experience with discrimination. *Journal of Applied Psychology, 87,* 333–344.

Son Hing, L. S., Bobocel, D. R., and Zanna, M. P. (2002). Meritocracy and opposition to affirmative action: Making concessions in the face of discrimination. *Journal of Personality and Social Psychology, 83,* 493–509.

Spence, M. (1973). Job market signaling. *Quarterly Journal of Economics, 87,* 355–374.

Steele, C. M., and Aronson, J. (1995). Stereotype threat and the intellectual test performance of African Americans. *Journal of Personality and Social Psychology, 85,* 440–452.

Sturm, S. (2001). Second generation employment discrimination: A structural approach. *Columbia Law Review, 101,* 458–568.

Tajfel, H. (1982). Instrumentality, identity, and social comparisons. In J. Tajfel (ed.), *Social Identity and Intergroup Relations* (pp. 483–507). Cambridge: Cambridge University Press.

Taylor, M. S., and Bergmann, T. J. (1987). Organizational recruitment activities and applicants' reactions at different stages of the recruitment process. *Personnel Psychology, 40,* 261–285.

Thomas, D. A. (2001). The truth about mentoring minorities: Race matters. *Harvard Business Review, 79*(4), 98–107.

Thomas, D. A., and Ely, R. J. (1996). Making differences matter: A new paradigm for managing diversity. *Harvard Business Review,* September–October, 79–90.

Thomas, D. A., and Gabarro, J. J. (1999). *Breaking Through: The Making of Minority Executives in Corporate America.* Boston: Harvard Business School Press.

Thomas, K. M., and Wise, P. G. (1999). Organizational attractiveness and individual differences: Are diverse applicants attracted by different factors? *Journal of Business and Psychology, 13,* 375–390.

Tsui, A. S., Egan, T. D., and O'Reilly, C. A. III (1992). Being different: Relational demography and organizational attachment. *Administrative Science Quarterly, 37,* 549–579.

Tsui, A. S., and O'Reilly, C. A. III (1989). Beyond simple demographic effects: The importance of relational demography in superior-subordinate dyads. *Academy of Management Journal, 32,* 402–423.

Turban, D. B., and Dougherty, T. W. (1992). Influence of campus recruiting on applicant attraction to firms. *Academy of Management Journal, 35,* 739–765.

Umphress, E. E., Smith-Crowe, K., Brief, A. P., Dietz, J., and Baskerville, M. (2007). Do birds of a feather flock together or do opposites attract? Organizational diversity, social dominance orientation and organizational attractiveness. *Journal of Applied Psychology, 92,* 396–409.

Wanberg, C. R., Welsh, E. T., and Hezlett, S. A. (2003). Mentoring research: A review and dynamic process model. *Research in Personnel and Human Resources Management, 22,* 39–124.

Wentling, R. M., and Palma-Rivas, N. (2000). Current status of diversity initiatives in selected multinational corporations. *Human Resource Development Quarterly, 11,* 35–60.

Wiethoff, C. (2004). Motivation to learn and diversity training: Application of the theory of planned behavior. *Human Resource Development Quarterly, 15,* 263–278.

Williams, M. L., and Bauer, T. N. (1994). The effect of a managing diversity policy on organizational attractiveness. *Group and Organization Management, 19,* 295–308.

Williams, R. (2004). Management fashions and fads: Understanding the role of consultants and managers in the evolution of ideas. *Management Decision, 42,* 769–780.

Wyse, R. E. (1972). Attitudes of selected Black and White college business administration seniors toward recruiters and the recruitment process. *Dissertation Abstracts International, 33,* 1269–1270.

Young, I. P., Place, A. W., Rinehart, J. S., Jury, J. C., and Baits, D. F. (1997). Teacher recruitment: A test of the similarity-attraction hypothesis for race and sex. *Educational Administration Quarterly, 33,* 86–106.

Zenger, T. R., and Lawrence, B. S. (1989). Organizational demography: The differential effects of age and tenure distributions on technical communication. *Academy of Management Journal, 32,* 353–376.

9 | 1964 was not that long ago: A story of gateways and pathways

DOLLY CHUGH AND ARTHUR P. BRIEF

How long ago was 1964? A long time ago, some would say. The Beatles had just arrived in America, the World Trade Center design was underway, and Nelson Mandela was sentenced to his eventual 27-year imprisonment. The world of 1964 seems very distant from the world of today.

In that year, Title VII of the Civil Rights Act became law in the United States, outlawing discrimination in employment in any business on the basis of race, color, religion, sex, or national origin. Black or white, male or female, the gateway to opportunity opened.

Yet, stunning levels of segregation still exist in the workplace (Tomaskovic-Devey *et al.*, 2006). In the United States, male–female and black–white segregation lessened between 1966 and 1980, but after 1980, only male–female segregation continued to significantly decline. Black–white segregation has essentially remained the same since 1980, and may have worsened in some sectors since 1995.

In fact, in order for sex-neutral employment distribution (i.e., true desegregation) to exist, more than half of all workers would have to switch jobs; for race-neutral (black–white) employment distribution to exist, more than half of all African-Americans would need to switch jobs (Tomaskovic-Devey *et al.*, 2006). Both race and gender segregation remains significant, more than 30 years after the passage of the 1964 Civil Rights Act.

This puzzling state of affairs can be explained, we propose, by distinguishing between the *gateway* to opportunity and diversity in the workplace, and the *pathway* to success and effectiveness in the workplace. From the individual perspective, the gateway is about things like getting hired, getting appointed, and getting admitted; it is about getting in the door. The pathway is about getting heard, getting credit, and getting second chances; it is about getting a fair shot once in the door. From an organizational perspective, the gateway is about hiring processes while the pathway is about the formal and informal

318

forms of recognition and advancement, about moving up and being groomed to do so, within an organization.

The focus of the first generation of legislation, enforcement, and research was largely, and logically, on the gateway. A clear, but inaccessible pathway is useless, after all. The focus of the second generation, in which we are currently immersed, has shifted to the pathway, as the disconnect between ensuring equal access and ensuring equal opportunity for success has become salient.

The Equal Employment Opportunities Commission (EEOC), which is charged with enforcing the Civil Rights Act, notes this shift in their 2004 report to the public: "In EEOC's early days, the agency dealt primarily with issues that were related to race and hiring, gender and hiring – getting a foot in the door. Later, the glass ceiling was at the forefront – that invisible barrier that seemed to prevent women and people of color from rising through the ranks. While these issues have not gone away, no longer are they the sole focus of our mission" ("Performance and Accountability Report FY 2004," 2005). The report goes on to discuss forms of harassment once in the employer's door, both overt and subtle, as a newly emerging focus of the organization, illustrating the growing importance of the pathway.

This shift to an emphasis on the pathway is also reflected clearly in this volume, in which all of the chapters focus exclusively or largely on the pathway, and none focus exclusively on the gateway. Two chapters in this volume examine the state of the pathway from a mostly individual, cognitive orientation. Fiske and Lee use social psychological insights about the "tripartite foundation of intergroup relations" of stereotypes, prejudice, and discrimination to illuminate "what happens after the recruitment," that is, after the gateway and on the pathway (Fiske and Lee, this volume). Ellemers and Barreto point to the difficulties faced by targets of bias in assessing whether they are, or are not, being treated fairly, highlighting the challenges of targets who wonder if their pathways have been blocked (Ellemers and Barreto, this volume).

Three chapters assess the pathway from a dyadic or group perspective, focusing on the interpersonal processes that contribute or detract from a smooth, level, open pathway. Ely and Roberts reframed the prevailing "difference paradigm" as a "relational paradigm," arguing that relationships flourish across diverse group members so long as the members submit to outward-focused goals (Ely and Roberts, this volume). Jehn, Greer, and Rupert delve into what happens to performance after a diverse workforce has been created, and the specific role of conflict in that relationship between diversity and performance (Jehn, Greer, and Rupert, this volume). Polzer and Caruso explore how identity negotiation is affected by status differences in the workplace, emphasizing how group members establish a working consensus of "who is who" (Polzer and Caruso, this volume).

And, finally, two chapters call for a clearer message from social scientists to practitioners, whose actions to date are typically guided by legislation or litigation at the gateway, and by anecdote or trend along the pathway. Kulik and Roberson take a much-needed look at the effectiveness of diversity interventions, examining those influencing decisions at the gateway (recruitment, diversity training) and along the pathway (diversity training again, mentoring) (Kulik and Roberson, this volume).

Bielby argues that both context (social, institutional, and organizational) and psychological processes are implicated in workplace discrimination, illuminating the multiple levels of the gateway/pathway framework (Bielby, this volume). The placement and size of a gateway, and the incline and shape of a pathway, will be determined largely by the contextual factors studied by sociologists. At the same time, the decision-making at the gateway, and the micro-behaviors along the pathway, will be determined largely by the mental processes studied by psychologists. The questions to be asked, posits Bielby, are along the lines of "how will this policy facilitate or minimize stereotyping processes?" (Bielby, this volume).

"Gateway behaviors," such as interviewing, hiring, admitting, and appointing, are easily measured and generally non-spontaneous, and probably more egalitarian than they used to be. Once through the gateway, however, individuals still face the possibility of bias in the workplace along the pathway to success and further opportunity. In contrast to gateway behaviors, "pathway behaviors" are those that are generally more spontaneous and less measurable. Pathway behaviors include the many non-formalized, seemingly minor ways in which an individual's chances for success are improved or worsened. For example, is the employee interrupted during meetings? Do others ask the employee to lunch? How long does it take before others respond to the employee's emails? What attributions do others make when the employee arrives a few minutes late for a meeting? What sort of eye contact is given to the employees? Where do others sit relative to the employee in meetings?

All of these behaviors are subtle, and may, in fact, be unlikely to be recognized consciously by either party. But ample evidence exists that these subtle behaviors are surprisingly influential (Word, Zanna, and Cooper, 1974). Despite the decrease in blatant bias at the gateway, it is possible that pathway bias remains strong, and poses a contemporary obstacle to an effective and diverse workforce. The study of pathway behaviors may clarify why dramatic improvements in opportunity have not led to dramatic improvements in equality. We offer the gateway and pathway framework as a useful way of conceptualizing how, when, and where diversity is successfully achieved in the workplace. Next, we use this framework as a means of articulating research questions still unanswered, and requiring answers, if a diverse workplace is to be achieved.

A research agenda for the coming decade

In this section, we outline our proposed research priorities for the coming decade. How did we determine that these three topics require more urgent and more focused attention than many of the other useful topics of study? We used two simple criteria:

- *Heat to light*: To what extent will insights on this topic resolve fundamental intellectual debates that currently have the potential to advance (i.e., light) rather than polarize (e.g., heat) the field?
- *Journals to organizations*: To what extent will insights on this topic fundamentally influence the decisions of practitioners?

With these criteria in mind, we propose the following three directions:

(1) Behavioral consequences of implicit bias
(2) Role of context
(3) Strategies and solutions

The remainder of this section will elaborate on each of these three directions, briefly summarizing current work on the topic and offering ideas on specific course of study.

Behavioral consequences of implicit bias

Do milliseconds matter? (Chugh, 2004)

Each chapter in this volume notes the demise of blatant biases and the rise of subtle, ambiguous forms of bias (Bielby; Kulik and Roberson; Jehn, Greer, and Rupert; Ely and Roberts; Polzer and Caruso; Fiske and Lee, this volume). We begin with an overview of the theoretical and methodological underpinnings of research on implicit bias. Then, we turn to the specific topic of behavioral consequences, outlining work done and to be done.

Subtle bias has been conceptualized in a variety of forms (e.g., modern racism [McConahay, 1983], aversive racism [Gaertner and Dovidio, 1986], everyday discrimination [Brief *et al.*, 2000], implicit bias [Greenwald and Banaji, 1995]). For our purposes here, all of these conceptualizations and methods are relevant to understanding a form of bias that is not intentional, blatant, controllable, and/or reportable: We will use the concept "implicit bias" (Banaji and Greenwald, 1995) as an umbrella term.

Tackling implicit biases has been made more possible due to major methodological advances in the past decade. Today, the Implicit Association Test (IAT; Greenwald, McGhee, and Schwartz, 1998) is a dominant (but not the only) method in use (for an excellent overview, see Kihlstrom, 2004). The original IAT paper by Greenwald, McGhee, and Schwartz (1998) has been cited at least 541 times in published works since its publication a decade ago. The IAT is, of course, only a measure of the construct of implicit bias, and while our focus is on implicit bias, not the IAT, we will take a moment to summarize the basic features of the measure, given its current prevalence in the field.

The IAT is a response latency measure, often administered by computer. Subjects categorize words or pictures as quickly as they can into one of four categories. Two of the categories require a keyboard response from the right hand and two of the categories require a keyboard response from the left hand. The challenge is to remember which categories are which, while still performing each categorization in less than a second. For example, in the "race IAT" (a measure of implicit race attitudes), the categories are black, white, good, and bad. Subjects categorize stimuli (e.g., black faces, white faces, good words such as love, and bad words such as war) into one of these four categories. The task is presented in two different versions: (1) white paired with good and black paired with bad, and (2) white paired with bad and black paired with good. The difference in the test-taker's average response time for the two versions (sometimes described as the congruent and incongruent versions, respectively) represents a measure of implicit race bias. The majority of white American subjects who take the race IAT are faster in the congruent version of the task than the incongruent version, implying that they hold an implicit race attitude favoring whites over blacks.

An educational website (http://implicit.harvard.edu) was established in 1998, allowing the general public to take self-administered IATs on a wide range of topics in less than ten minutes followed by an individualized score. To date, 4.5 million tests have been taken (Nosek *et al.*, 2006).

The psychometric properties of the IAT have been the subject of intense scrutiny and the source of growing confidence among psychologists (for an ongoing list of many associated papers, see http://faculty. washington.edu/agg/iat_validity.htm). The most recurring and charged psychometric debate among psychologists is regarding *what* the IAT measures, and whether it is more a measure of the person or of the culture surrounding the person. The perspective that the IAT is a measure of the culture has been articulated by Karpinski and Hilton (2001), Olson and Fazio (2004), and Arkes and Tetlock (2004), and challenged by Nosek and Hansen (2004) and Banaji, Nosek, and Greenwald (2004).

If implicit bias exists, and if it can be measured, then the time has come to assess its implications. To what extent does implicit bias influence workplace behaviors? Under what conditions? With what consequence? For whom? Are the behavioral implications of implicit bias pervasive and problematic, or largely undetectable and irrelevant?

How does implicit bias affect diversity at the gateway, versus along the pathway? If one assumes gateway behaviors to be mostly deliberative and pathway behaviors to be mostly spontaneous, do the potential roles of explicit (or blatant) and implicit bias start to diverge? Explicit bias, with its intentionality and awareness, would seem to have a starring role in many gateway behaviors because those behaviors seem to rest on conscious choices (e.g., hiring). Implicit bias, with its automaticity and immediacy, would seem to have a starring role in many pathway behaviors because of their seemingly spontaneous and

uncalculated nature. Can this framework help us understand the progress made, and the struggles remaining, in the workplace?

In fact, the connection between spontaneous behaviors and implicit
bias is becomingly increasingly clear. A meta-analysis of 103 studies
(Greenwald *et al.*, 2007) revealed that the IAT was especially predictive
in socially sensitive domains (like those involving social categories) and
behaviors which are difficult to control (like non-verbal behaviors),
behaviors that we would describe as pathway behaviors. Importantly
for this discussion, the IAT was more predictive than self-report measures of stereotyping and prejudice. And, the importance of non-verbal
behaviors, however subtle, is significant (Deitch *et al.*, 2003). A self-
fulfilling prophecy can occur when a target decodes subtly negative
non-verbal cues from a bias holder, and subsequently, behaves subop-
timally (Word *et al.*, 1974).

For an example of the impact of implicit bias on pathway behaviors,
consider the work of McConnell and Leibold (2001). They found that
the race IAT predicted white subjects' smiling, speaking time, extem-
poraneous social comments, and general friendliness, as well as speech
errors and speech hesitation, towards a white experimenter (as compared to a black experimenter). That is, higher levels of implicit bias
predicted less favorable treatment of the black experimenter.

In another study (Hugenberg and Bodenhausen, 2003), white participants saw faces morph from one facial expression to another (e.g.,
from unambiguous hostility to unambiguous happiness). Some faces
were black and some faces were white. Participants indicated when
they noticed the onset of a hostile expression during the morphing
process, and also completed the race IAT and an explicit measure of
race attitudes. The IAT was correlated with participants' perceptions of
hostility on black faces, meaning that higher levels of bias were associated with hostile expressions on a black being perceived sooner and
lingering longer than on a white face. The IAT did not predict performance on white faces, however, nor did the explicit measure predict
performance on either face.

Pathway behaviors obviously need not be non-verbal. They include
the many informal channels of information and influence within an
organization. To illustrate, consider the following thought experiment
involving two identical individuals, named W and B, equal in all ways
except race. If W is in the loop, sought out as an expert, and taken
seriously when arguing a point, while B is not, will W and B experience

dramatically different performance and satisfaction outcomes? Presumably, they will. That is, the sharing of information, the seeking of expertise, and the treatment of advice are all pathway behaviors which have consequences for both job satisfaction and job performance.

The relationship between implicit bias and gateway behaviors, what Ziegert and Hanges (2005) refer to as "macrolevel behavior," is likely more complex than between these biases and pathway behaviors. They note that "although research has documented that implicit measures correlate with other attitudes and predict microlevel behavior, there is currently little evidence indicating that such implicit attitudes are useful for predicting more macrolevel behavior, such as discriminatory hiring decisions" (Ziegert and Hanges, 2005). For example, an interaction between corporate climate and implicit bias may be required for discriminatory gateway behavior to occur, as they found, and motivation to control prejudice may moderate the relationship between explicit and implicit attitudes.

Another important category of behaviors to study are those with practical consequence for the bias holder, both gateway and pathway. Stereotypes likely offer both benefits and costs to the holder. Stereotypes are often described as cognitively efficient mental processes (Axelrod and Hamilton, 1981). Additional benefits may exist beyond the individual's need for efficiency. For example, Watkins *et al.* (2006) ask "Does it Pay to Be a Sexist?" In this field study, they find modern sexists (Swim *et al.*, 1995) were more likely to seek advice from men, and also, more likely to be promoted, than non-modern sexists. These effects were true for both male and female modern sexists, suggesting that women who acted in ways contrary to their group's long-term interests received better individual outcomes. Are there strategies that promote *both* the self and the group that we can recommend to targets?

But, what are the costs of stereotypes to the holder? When are mistakes made and with what consequence? This "stereotype tax" (Chugh, 2004) represents the potential dark side of cognitive efficiency. By more fully understanding the benefits and costs of stereotypes, we potentially provide individuals with pragmatic motivation to debias their own behavior, in addition to the obvious moral motivation. We are not envisioning the impossible task of "computing" whether stereotypes are a net-benefit or net-cost, nor are we imagining any sort of abdication, even were it possible, of cognitively efficient mental processes.

However, we believe that more can be understood and taught about the types of mistakes that can be made, and the costs associated with them. Bias has a price. When and how much? Consider the elegant and persuasive work of Richeson and Shelton (2003) as one example. White study participants took an IAT, and then interacted with either a white or black confederate in what they believed was a second experiment. Then, they completed yet another seemingly unrelated executive function task, the color naming Stroop task, where subjects are asked to name the color in which a word is printed, a seemingly easy task (Stroop, 1935a). However, the task is made more difficult by the fact that the word in print is the name of a color. So, for example, the word "red" may appear in green font, and the subject is expected to say "green" when naming the color of the font. To perform this task, subjects must employ executive function, the mental processes associated with handling two competing responses (e.g., green and red) and allowing the "correct" response to dominate.

Returning to the Richeson and Shelton (2003) design, subjects were either interacting with a black confederate or a white confederate, and then were asked to perform this test of executive function. The hypothesis was that IAT scores would predict Stroop (Stroop, 1935a, 1935b) task performance (more bias, lower performance) for subjects whose executive function resources had been depleted; that is, subjects in the black confederate condition. This is exactly what occurred. Participants whose implicit biases were activated by the black confederate interaction depleted their executive function resources prior to the Stroop task, and thus, performed worse on the task, with their performance predicted by their IAT scores. For subjects who interacted with a white confederate, their performance on the Stroop task was not related to their IAT score.

Implicit bias was predictive (beyond an explicit bias measure) of executive function after interracial interactions, but not after same-race interactions. The implication is that biased individuals working in a diverse work environment will experience worse cognitive performance. This implication is worth repeating, so as to avoid confusion. The implication is not that all individuals working in a diverse work environment will experience worse performance, only that the bias of the individuals will correlate to the performance. An unbiased person in a diverse workplace would presumably have the same performance as a random person in a non-diverse workplace. This stereotype tax is a real liability for biased individuals, as workplaces are simultaneously increasingly diverse and increasingly demanding of executive function.

Assessing advice may entail another possible stereotype tax (Chugh, 2006). One would expect the recipient of advice to be motivated to avoid bad advice and take good advice, as mistakes in either direction might be costly. Yet, when given advice of equal quality by white males, black males, Hispanic males, or white females, advice-takers showed a preference for white male advice over advice from other sources (Chugh, 2006). In a related study in which the advisors were white males or white females, advice-takers placed greater weight on male advice than on female advice (Chugh, 2006). Because the advice-takers had been given an incentive to answer the questions correctly, and because all of the advice was actually correct, participants who were randomly assigned female advisors earned 69 cents for every dollar earned by participants who were randomly assigned male advisors. In both studies, participants denied that race or gender played a role in their decision making. What remains unanswered in these preliminary studies is the role of implicit bias in this behavior. Thus, there is clear evidence suggesting it is worthwhile to pursue research on the stereotype tax. Research should address not only when it is levied in the workplace, but also the ways it may be paid in forms other than poor performance and advice ignoring.

Context matters

It is time (to) look outside the organizations . . . to understand better what is happening inside them. (Brief *et al.*, 2005)

Scott observed that "employees come to the organization with heavy cultural and social baggage obtained from interactions in other social contexts" (Scott, 1995). Building on this point, Brief, Butz, and Dietch (2004) remarked that, "it would be naïve to assume that even if this baggage could be unloaded in the workplace that it would not be repacked the same way at home." "Organizations," they argue, "[are] reflections of their environments."

Specifically, the racial composition of organizations is influenced by the organization's environment in ways that are not well-reflected in the psychological literature. They discuss four specific environmental influences worthy of, but lacking sufficient, study: (1) the social structure surrounding an organization; (2) the black population share of the community in which the organization is located; (3) the customer base of an organization; and (4) the legal environment of an organization. Here, we first reiterate this essential point – that context matters – through more detail on these four specific examples, and then, seek to broaden the scope of what is meant by context to include one additional dimension: (5) individual psychological context of an organization's employees.

Social structure

People tend to infer stereotypes from social structure, from the roles they see members of groups performing in society (Eagly, 1987). By acting on those stereotypes, organizational decision makers may create a vicious cycle contributing to the reproduction of the existing occupational structure. Evidence speaking directly to the possibility that such a cycle exists is needed. For example, is it, in fact, the case that a nurse administrator who observes few black nurses and many black nursing aides, infers a negative stereotype of blacks to explain those observations (e.g., blacks lack the intelligence or motivation to become nurses), and perhaps unconsciously, makes hiring decisions influenced by that stereotype?

Black population share

Attitudes about race and gender do vary between individuals, and are not evenly distributed across communities. Taylor's (1998) review of the evidence suggested that as the proportion of the black population increases in a community, the level of prejudice among whites in the community increases. This finding suggests an ironic possibility: as the percentage of blacks in a community rises, one might forecast an increase in the hiring of blacks by organizations in that community, but at the same time, an increase in prejudicial attitudes within an organization, thus, potentially dampening the projected diversification. Or, under these circumstances, gateway problems especially may be minimized and pathway problems exacerbated.

   Moreover, realistic group conflict theory predicts that competition between groups for limited resources leads to conflict. With this basis, Brief *et al.* (2005) hypothesized that "'baggage' develops for employees when they are living in diverse communities in which tensions arise from competition over scarce resources" (page 831). Accordingly, they found that the closer whites lived to blacks, the more negative the relationship between diversity and the quality of work relationships in their organizations. They also found that interethnic conflict in participants' communities (between Latinos and Anglos) predicted prospective, white job applicants' reactions to a diverse organization. Do Brief *et al.*'s findings hold for other outgroups (e.g., religious minorities)? Can other theoretical approaches (e.g., social identity theory [Tajfel, 1981]) provide a richer explanation? However approached, the impact of communities on organizational processes and diverse outcomes warrant further attention.

Customer base

A commonly-expressed "business case for diversification" rests on a logic of race matching which posits that because the demographics in the customer population are changing, the demographics of the workforce should reflect this change to maximize organizational effectiveness. Modern racists tend to view blacks as "pushing too hard, too fast and into places they are not wanted" (McConahay, 1986), but do not necessarily discriminate against blacks under all conditions. Indeed, Brief *et al.* (2000) found that modern racists (McConahay, 1986) did not discriminate, unless they were provided with a business justification to do so.

The implications of this logic are worthy of additional study, as evidence suggests that this same logic for diversification might be used as a rationale for excluding minorities and women. For example, would race matching (and gender matching) be applied when the customer base is comprised of affluent blacks (e.g., wealthy African-Americans, such as Oprah Winfrey), and the related employment opportunity (e.g., high net worth financial advisor at a leading bank) is extremely scarce and high-status; will the business case to match prevail or would some rationale supporting a rich black customer and white financial advisor win out?

The legal environment of an organization

The 1964 Civil Rights Act, and the enforcement of the legislation by the Equal Employment Opportunities Commission, has led a wide range of formal policies and procedures within many organizations. The degree of efficacy of these structures remains a question of study. Because organizations "take substantive action or merely comply symbolically" (Bielby, 2000), further research is required to determine the consequences of symbolism. That is, can and if so when can, symbolic organizational actions suffice for substantive ones, or is it always the case that substance trumps symbolism?

Individual psychological context of the organization's employees

Maintaining our emphasis on implicit bias, we highlight the need to understand how exposure to stimuli outside of the workplace affects attitudes brought into the workplace. As a starting point, we consider two important forces in many employees' home life: popular media and marriage.

Popular media: Imagine this scenario. Manager X leads a work team and makes decisions regarding his team members' task assignments, performance levels, and work relationships. On a typical day, he leaves work fairly stressed, and after a quick check of the traffic report on the radio, he drives home listening to a popular radio station. At home, he and his wife catch up and prepare dinner while the kids enjoy a popular DVD in the kitchen. After dinner, he and his wife clean up and put the kids to bed. Then, they watch a popular television program. Finally, they get ready for bed, catching the headlines of the 11:00 local news as they drift to sleep. The next morning, Manager X gets up early to head to work, where he has his usual array of personnel issues to resolve.

Based on this recap of Manager X's time away from work, there is little to suggest that his home life would have much impact on his decision-making at work. But, consider whether the same might be said when more detail is provided.

Manager X leads a diverse work team and makes daily decisions regarding his black, white, and Hispanic team members' task assignments, performance levels, and work relationships. On a typical day, he leaves work fairly stressed, and after a quick check of the traffic report on the radio, he drives home listening to a popular radio station, which features "gangsta rap" as part of its regular rotation. At home, he and his wife catch up and prepare dinner while the kids enjoy a popular Disney DVD in the kitchen, featuring light-skinned beauties as the good guys and dark-skinned uglies as the bad guys. After dinner, he and his wife clean up and put the kids to bed. Then, they watch a popular television program, *Law and Order*, which opens with a close-up of a bloodied victim of a random, and violent crime. Finally, they get ready for bed, catching the headlines of the 11:00 local news as they drift to sleep, most of which features alleged criminals who are black.[1] The next morning, Manager X gets up early to head to work, where he has his usual array of personnel issues to resolve, including a conflict between a white and black salesperson over fair allocation of a commission.

What are the organizational implications of this hypothetical, but hardly unusual, home life? In the time that Manager X was not at work, he was privy to a slew of racially-charged images. But as soon as he arrived at work, he committed himself to maintaining his egalitarian values as he made decisions in a deadline environment, based on minimal information and ambiguous anecdotes. To what extent will the negative stereotype-tinged images embedded in his home life leak into his work life? Rained on by these images on a regular basis, is it psychologically plausible to expect no impact on his subsequent biases and perhaps, even his behavior? Are his implicit attitudes fixed or malleable in this context? While these questions require additional study, what we know so far about implicit mental processes suggests that malleability is likely (for an excellent meta-analysis, see Blair [2002]) and leakage into behavior is possible (again, for an excellent meta-analysis, see Poehlman [2004]).

The question for organizational researchers is whether well-meaning egalitarians in managerial positions unintentionally take on burdens outside of work that significantly lower their odds of behaving in a truly egalitarian way. As researchers, we can contribute to society's, and Manager X's, understanding of how heavy (or light) a burden this truly is.

---

[1] For example, Gilliam and Iyengar (2000) argue that local television news relies on a "script" with two consistent themes: (1) crime is violent and (2) perpetrators of crime are non-white males. They assess the impact of this crime script on viewers' attitudes, both blacks and whites. White viewers exposed to the racial element of the crime script were supportive of punitive responses to crime and expressed more negative attitudes about African-Americans; black viewers did not show this effect.

Marriage: Many people have chosen to live in a household characterized by traditional marriage roles, in which the wife is the primary
caregiver, household manager, and community liaison and the husband is the primary breadwinner. This division of labor may coexist
even if both the husband and wife work outside the home. In some
cases, these roles are not the result of an explicit negotiation between
husband and wife, but tend to emerge organically. The result is a
division of labor in which the woman performs the domestic duties,
which ease the household burdens placed on the husband at home, and
the husband performs the status-defining duties outside the home. She
washes his laundry, makes his dinner, and he asks her to follow up on
various clerical issues on his behalf, including a mistake on his cell
phone bill and a missing shirt from the dry cleaners. Her efforts ensure
the smooth running of the home, and enable him to focus on his
responsibilities and ambitions at work. In organizational language,
she is in a staff role and he is in a line role. Neither minds nor questions
this division of labor. It just evolved this way and it seems to work.

We wonder whether a domestic traditionalist can also be an organizational egalitarian? How do the assumptions about division of labor
and roles at home influence the assumptions about division of labor
and roles at work? Work by Cejka and Eagly (1999) demonstrates that,
to the extent that occupations are female dominated, feminine personality or physical attributes were thought more essential for success; to
the extent that occupations were male dominated, masculine personality or physical attributes were thought more essential. In other words,
the gender distribution within the job seemed to define the gender
stereotypes associated with the job. If the assumption is that being
female qualifies one for a staff role at home, and being male qualifies
one for a line role at home, to what extent are these assumptions similar
or different in the workplace? What are the organizational implications
of a traditional marriage?[2]

---

[2] We certainly believe that the choices made within a marriage are first and
foremost, the business of those within the marriage, and additionally, rarely so
unidimensional so as to be fully grasped by those outside the marriage. So, to be
absolutely clear, we are not proposing an agenda for the marriages of others. We
are, however, reasoning that gender-based choices in the home may have
implications for how gender is perceived in the workplace.

Solutions and strategies

At best, 'best practices' are best guesses. (Kalev, Dobbin, and Kelly, 2005)

Both academics and practitioners face a sizable challenge in recommending and implementing organizational approaches to diversity as lay views, trendy notions, and legal defensiveness dominate the planning of diversity approaches. Kulik and Roberson used keywords such as "diversity" and "employee" in performing a literature search, and came up with more than 2,000 hits (Kulik and Roberson, chapter 8 in this volume). However, only 20% of the hits related to peer-reviewed research, highlighting the dearth of empiricism in the diversity field. Their chapter compiles "needle in the haystack" academic findings in an attempt to bring rigor and empiricism to bear on organizational diversity initiatives. Because so little clarity exists on this topic, we begin with a brief summary of their findings, and then also review another important contribution in this area by Kalev, Dobbin, and Kelly (2005). On the surface, it appears that the two papers offer contradictory prescription, so we will also attempt to reconcile this possible contradiction. Finally, we will argue that this area of diversity research is in dire need of additional attention, and suggest some possible future directions.

Kulik and Roberson state that success "hinges on the organization's ability to implement the right diversity initiative to address the right problem at the right time" and on implementing an overall diversity strategy (Kulik and Roberson, this volume). Specifically, they examine three common diversity initiatives: diversity recruitment, diversity training, and formal mentoring programs. Diversity recruitment is best suited at addressing attraction issues; skill-based diversity training is best suited for addressing a lack of support for diversity within the organization; formal mentoring programs are best for addressing retention problems. Also of note, they find little support for awareness-building diversity training programs, but do find evidence supporting skill-building diversity training programs, particularly those designed to help employees respond to displays of prejudice. The implication of this contingency-based recommendation is that the diagnosis of the organization's situation is a necessary, first step.

Kalev, Dobbin, and Kelly (2005) also undertake the much-needed task assessing the success of commonly used approaches to promoting diversity. Using data provided by medium to full-sized private sector companies to the EEOC, they find three general approaches to promoting diversity in management (beginning at first-level supervisor ranks): (1) establishing organizational responsibility (which includes, but is not limited to, Kulik and Roberson's recruitment initiatives); (2) moderating managerial bias (which includes all forms of training, as opposed to delineations made in chapter 8); and (3) reducing social isolation of women and blacks (which sounds similar to Kulik and Roberson's mentoring initiatives). They reach a less contingent conclusion than Kulik and Roberson, recommending that while managerial bias and social isolation are likely important causes of the problem, organizational responsibility – through affirmative action plans, diversity staff, and diversity committees – is the most effective solution to the problem (Kulik and Roberson, this volume).

While it appears that a contradiction may exist between the Kulik and Roberson and Kalev *et al.* findings, we see important common ground. First, Kulik and Roberson stress the importance of an integrated diversity strategy, and Kalev *et al.* stress the value of ensuring clear organizational responsibility for diversity issues. Both of these findings emphasize organizational-level approaches, simply differing in the emphasis placed on integrated strategic thinking (design) versus accountability (implementation).

We also see useful connections between these recommendations and the gateway/pathway framework we proposed earlier in this chapter. The Kalev *et al.* conclusion seems most focused on the gateway, and we wonder if the importance of efforts directed at the pathway might be lost in the measures captured by EEOC data. Perhaps awareness training and isolation reduction have more impact on the types of micro-behaviors displayed, but are not easily measured on the pathway.

Attempts to reduce the isolation of minorities and to facilitate networking take into account the role targets of discrimination (potential and actual) can play in facilitating a diverse workplace. What can targets do to help or harm themselves? What is the impact on the self of these strategies?

Ellemers and Barreto take this perspective in their chapter, identifying psychological mechanisms that are harmful to targets (Ellemers and Barreto, this volume). For example, stereotype threat (Steele and Aronson, 1995) occurs when members of negatively stereotyped groups internalize and even confirm the stereotype of their group. The necessary conditions for stereotype threat include a situation where there is a negative group stereotype concerning their performance in a domain, self-relevance of the domain, awareness of the negative group stereotype (note that belief in the stereotype is not necessary – mere knowledge of the stereotype is sufficient), and belief that the task undertaken reveals ability in the domain (Steele, 1997, 1998). These conditions can easily be imagined in organizational, including interview, settings. And, the subtlety of these conditions captures the elusive ways in which the pathway can prove uphill for negatively stereotyped individuals in organizations. Shockingly, little organizational work on stereotype threat exists, to our knowledge (Roberson *et al.*, 2003). Understanding how women and blacks are affected by stereotype threat, and developing strategies for them to overcome that threat, is an area of high potential for research.

Another rich area for research on strategies and solution comes with the rise of implicit bias. Implicit bias creates a detection challenge for targets in accurately perceiving discriminatory behaviors. Remember, behaviors driven by implicit biases tend to be subtle rather than overt in nature. And, potential misunderstandings can occur between those who detect and those who do not detect discriminatory behaviors, cultures, or policies, leading to the accusation that so-and-so "just doesn't get it." This asymmetry relates back to our discussion about the behavioral implications of implicit bias. For example, in a study by Dovidio, Kawakami, and Gaertner (2002) whites' implicit bias (not measured with the IAT) predicted non-verbal behavior towards blacks (pathway), while their self-reported racial attitudes predicted their more controlled behaviors (gateway). However, the whites' self-reported attitudes also predicted how they assessed their own friendliness, but their implicit attitudes predicted how blacks and independent observers perceived the whites' friendliness levels.

Such asymmetry in perspective may contribute tremendously to conflicts and misunderstandings in organizations, where interdependent parties may both be well-intended but deeply divided regarding their perception of the organizational climate for minorities. What should minorities do in these situations? Is accurate detection an asset or a liability? What tools can we offer minorities facing this perceptual asymmetry? Chapter 7 discusses all of these questions, and considers the impact of an individual discrimination target's behaviors on the group as a whole (Ellemers and Barreto, this volume).

Unspoken in the chapter is the assumption that the individual target has some responsibility to the group as a whole. Tennis champion and civil rights activist Arthur Ashe wrote, "Living with AIDS is not the greatest burden I've had in my life. Being black is" (Ashe and Rampersad, 1993). The week before he died of AIDS, Ashe said, "AIDS killed my body, but racism is harder to bear. It kills the soul." Ashe goes on to talk about the obligation he felt to his group, and the burden such an obligation sometimes posed. This burden is significant and stressful (Deitch *et al.*, 2003). What tools and strategies can be recommended for coping with, or deciding whether to cope with, this burden?

Conclusion

Perhaps 1964 was not that long ago.

"Can't Buy Me Love" (which topped the charts that year) still comes on the radio, and we still sing along. "Rudolph, the Red-Nosed Reindeer" (which premiered that year) still appears every Christmas season on television. Shea Stadium (which opened that year) is still home to the Mets and their perpetually heartbroken fans.

Until 1964, the unfathomable was legal *and* commonplace in America. It was legal to advertise "white men only" when hiring. It was typical to read articles in women's magazines explaining that "a good wife always knows her place." Until 1964, all things being unequal, many jobs were unapologetically unavailable for a stunning majority of Americans. To get to the professional workplace, one needed access to a gateway of opportunity, and that gateway was only open if you were a white, Christian male. Thus, "good jobs" were not options if you happened to be black or female.

Have things changed? Economists Marianne Bertrand and Sendhil Mullainathan (2005) were interested in whether employers discriminated based on race when simply evaluating a resumé, and to study this, they submitted experimentally designed, but presumably real, resumés in response to real help-wanted ads for service and clerical positions in Boston and Chicago. In this highly-controlled field experiment, the researchers randomly assigned either "black-sounding" (e.g., Lakisha, Tyrone) or "white-sounding" (e.g., Emily, Greg) names to equivalent resumés. They were prepared for a null effect or perhaps a reverse discrimination effect, or perhaps a discrimination effect, but in any case, they did not expect the effect to be huge, and thus, they submitted 5,000 resumés to ensure statistical power.

They were wrong; the effect was huge. Applicants with white-sounding names were 50% more likely to be called for interviews than those with black-sounding names. Interviews were requested for 10.1% of applicants with white-sounding names and only 6.7% of those with black-sounding names. There was no null effect and there was no reverse discrimination. Instead, whites stood a far better chance of employment than blacks, not unlike 1964.

How do we make sense of this robust effect? Is this explicit gateway discrimination, plain and simple, or something more complicated? Is this a finding we would have expected in 1965 or 2005? Would our explanation for the finding vary based on when it occurred? Has the story changed?

Perhaps, the story today is of biases implicit more than explicit, of business justifications more than hostile prejudice, and of gateways only partially open and pathways only partially clear. The story, and our work, is not done.

References

Arkes, H. R., and Tetlock, P. E. (2004). Attributions of implicit prejudice, or "Would Jesse Jackson 'fail' the Implicit Association Test?" *Psychological Inquiry*, 15(4), 257–278.

Ashe, A., and Rampersad, A. (1993). *Days of Grace*. New York: Random House.

Axelrod, R., and Hamilton, W. D. (1981). The evolution of cooperation. *Science*, 211(4489), 1390–1396.

Banaji, M. R., and Greenwald, A. G. (1995). Implicit gender stereotyping in judgments of fame. *Journal of Personality and Social Psychology*, 68(2), 181–198.

Banaji, M. R., Nosek, B. A., and Greenwald, A. G. (2004). No place for nostalgia in science: A response to Arkes and Tetlock. *Psychological Inquiry*, 15(4), 279–310.

Bertrand, M., and Mullainathan, S. (2005). Do People Mean What They Say? Implications for Subjective Survey Data. *The American Economic Review*, 91(2), 67–72.

Bielby, W. T. (2000). Minimizing workplace gender and racial bias. *Contemporary Sociology*, 29(1), 120–129.

Blair, I. V. (2002). The malleability of automatic stereotypes and prejudice. *Personality and Social Psychology Review*, 6(3), 242–261.

Brief, A. P., Butz, R. M., and Deitch, E. A. (2004). Organizations as reflections of their environments: The case of race composition. In R. L. Dipboye and A. Colella (eds.), *Discrimination at work* (pp. 119–148). San Franciso: Jossey Boss.

Brief, A. P., Dietz, J., Cohen, R. R., Pugh, S., and Vaslow, J. B. (2000). Just doing business: Modern racism and obedience to authority as explanations for employment discrimination. *Organizational Behavior and Human Decision Processes*, 81(1), 72–97.

Brief, A. P., Umphress, E. E., Dietz, J., Burrows, J. W., Butz, R. M., and Scholten, L. (2005). Community matters: Realistic group conflict theory and the impact of diversity. *Academy of Management Journal*, 48(5), 830–844.

Cejka, M. A., and Eagly, A. H. (1999). Gender-stereotypic images of occupations correspond to the sex segregation of employment. *Personality and Social Psychology Bulletin*, 25(4), 413–423.

Chugh, D. (2004). Why milliseconds matter: Societal and managerial implications of implicit social cognition. *Social Justice Research*, 17(2), 203–222.

Chugh, D. (2006). *Whose Advice Is It Anyway? An Exploration of Bias and Implicit Social Cognition in the Use of Advice*. Doctoral Dissertation, Harvard University, 2006. *Dissertation Abstracts International* (UMI 3217701).

Deitch, E. A., Barsky, A., Butz, R. M., Chan, S., Brief, A. P., and Bradley, J. (2003). Subtle yet significant: The existence and impact of everyday racial discrimination in the workplace. *Social Relations*, 56(11), 1299–1324.

Dovidio, J. F., Kawakami, K., and Gaertner, S. L. (2002). Implicit and explicit prejudice and interracial interaction. *Journal of Personality and Social Psychology*, 82(1), 62–68.

Eagly, A. H. (1987). *Sex Differences in Social Behavior: A Social-role Interpretation*. Mahwah: Lawrence Erlbaum Associates.

Gaertner, S. L., and Dovidio, J. F. (1986). The aversive form of racism. In J. F. Dovidio and S. L. Gaertner (eds.), *Prejudice, Discrimination, and Racism* (pp. 61–89). Orlando: Academic Press.

Gilliam, F. D., and Iyengar, S. (2000). The influence of local television news on the viewing public. *American Journal of Political Science*, 44(3), 560–573.

Greenwald, A. G., and Banaji, M. R. (1995). Implicit social cognition: Attitudes, self-esteem, and stereotypes. *Psychological Review*, 102(1), 4–27.

Greenwald, A. G., McGhee, D. E., and Schwartz, J. L. K. (1998). Measuring individual differences in implicit cognition: The Implicit Association Test. *Journal of Personality and Social Psychology*, 74(6), 1464–1480.

Greenwald, A. G., Poehlman, T. A., Uhlmann, E., and Banaji, M. R. (2007). Understanding and Using the Implicit Association Test: III. Meta-analysis of Predictive Validity: (manuscript under review).

Hugenberg, K., and Bodenhausen, G. V. (2003). Facing prejudice: Implicit prejudice and the perception of facial threat. *Psychological Science*, 14(6), 640–643.

Kalev, A., Dobbin, F., and Kelly, E. A. (2005). *Best Practices or Best Guesses? Diversity Management and the Remediation of Inequality.* Working Paper. Department of Sociology, Harvard University.

Karpinski, A., and Hilton, J. L. (2001). Attitudes and the Implicit Association Test. *Journal of Personality and Social Psychology*, 81(5), 774–788.

Kihlstrom, J. F. (2004). Implicit methods in social psychology. In C. Sansone, C. C. Morf, and A. T. Panter (eds.), *The SAGE Handbook of Methods in Social Psychology*. Thousand Oaks: Sage Publications.

McConahay, J. B. (1983). Modern racism and modern discrimination: The effects of race, racial attitudes, and context on simulated hiring decisions. *Personality and Social Psychology Bulletin*, 9(4), 551–558.

McConahay, J. B. (1986). Modern racism, ambivalence, and the Modern Racism Scale. In J. F. Dovidio and S. L. Gaertner (eds.), *Prejudice, Discrimination, and Racism* (pp. 91–125). San Diego: Academic Press.

McConnell, A. R., and Leibold, J. M. (2001). Relations among the Implicit Association Test, discriminatory behavior, and explicit measures of racial attitudes. *Journal of Experimental Social Psychology*, 37(5), 435–442.

Nosek, B. A., and Hansen, J. (in press). The associations in our heads belong to us: Measuring the multifaceted attitude construct in implicit social cognition. *Cognition and Emotion*.

Nosek, B. A., Smyth, F. L., Hansen, J. J., Devos, T., Lindner, N. M., Ranganath, K. A., *et al.* (2006). Pervasiveness and Correlates of Implicit Attitudes and Stereotypes. Unpublished manuscript.

Olson, M. A., and Fazio, R. H. (2004). Reducing the influence of extrapersonal associations on the Implicit Association Test: Personalizing the IAT. *Journal of Personality and Social Psychology*, 86(5), 653–667.

Performance and Accountability Report FY 2004 (2005). *Management's Discussion and Analysis*.

Richeson, J. A., and Shelton, J. (2003). When prejudice does not pay: Effects of interracial contact on executive function. *Psychological Science*, 14(3), 287–290.

Roberson, L., Deitch, E. A., Brief, A. P., and Block, C. J. (2003). Stereotype threat and feedback seeking in the workplace. *Journal of Vocational Behaviour*, 62(1), 176–188.

Scott, W. R. (1995). *Institutions and Organizations*. London: Sage Publications.

Steele, C. M. (1998). Stereotyping and its threat are real. *American Psychologist*, 53(6), 680–681.

Steele, C. M., and Aronson, J. (1995). Stereotype threat and the intellectual test performance of African Americans. *Journal of Personality and Social Psychology*, 69(5), 797–811.

Stroop, J. R. (1935a). Studies of interference in serial verbal reactions: George Peabody College for Teachers.

Stroop, J. R. (1935b). Studies of interference in serial verbal reactions: George Peabody College for Teachers.

Swim, J. K., Aikin, K. J., Hall, W. S., and Hunter, B. A. (1995). Sexism and racism: Old-fashioned and modern prejudices. *Journal of Personality and Social Psychology*, 68(2), 199–214.

Tajfel, H. (1981). *Human Groups and Social Categories: Studies in Social Psychology*. Cambridge: Cambridge University Press.

Taylor, M. C. (1998). How white attitudes vary with the racial composition of local populations: Numbers count. *American Sociological Review*, 63, 512–535.

Tomaskovic-Devey, D., Zimmer, C., Stainback, K., Robinson, C., Taylor, T., and McTague, T. (2006). Documenting desegregation: Segregation in American workplaces by race, ethnicity, and sex, 1966–2003. *American Sociological Review*, 71, 565–588.

Watkins, M. B., Kaplan, S., Brief, A. P., Shull, A., Dietz, J., Mansfield, M. T., and Cohen, R. (2006). Does it pay to be a sexist? The relationship between modern sexism and career outcomes. *Journal of Vocational Behavior*, 69, 524–537.

Word, C. O., Zanna, M. P., and Cooper, J. (1974). The nonverbal mediation of self-fulfilling prophecies in interracial interaction. *Journal of Experimental Social Psychology*, 10(2), 109–120.

Ziegert, J. C., and Hanges, P. J. (2005). Employment discrimination: The role of implicit attitudes, motivation, and a climate for racial bias. *Journal of Applied Psychology*, 90(3), 553–562.

Index